THE LIFE AND DEATH OF

Chopin

by *CASIMIR WIERZYNSKI*

Translated by Norbert Guterman
with a Foreword by
Artur Rubinstein

D0125252

A Touchstone Book
Published by Simon and Schuster

A Touchstone Book
Published by Simon and Schuster
Rockefeller Center, 630 Fifth Avenue
New York, New York 10020

First paperback printing 1971
SBN 671–20910–8 Touchstone paperback edition
Manufactured in the United States of America

To My Wife

FOREWORD

By Artur Rubinstein

Books about Chopin are my favorite reading. I always derive great pleasure from them, yet most of them thus far have left me unsatisfied. In all the works on Chopin that I have read, I have been annoyed by a certain lack of proportion—so much so that I have often been tempted to leave my keyboard for my desk and to write his story myself. I find myself particularly protesting against the inclination of most biographers to slur over the significance of his childhood and youth.

Chopin was a case of remarkable early development. He was completely mature spiritually before he reached the age of twenty. The rest of his life was a quest for artistic perfection. The point I wish to make is evidenced not only by the fact that by twenty he had composed his two concertos, his first études, and the outlines of his first scherzo and first ballade. Chopin's entire personality was formed in the years of his youth, and all of his work drew upon his early years in Poland. The spirit of Poland remained the living source of his inspiration, the touchstone of his being, to the end of his life.

Every lover of Chopin feels frustrated by the meagerness of the information supplied by most biographers in relation to his formative years, and by their haste to enter upon that phase of his life which began with his departure from his home in Warsaw. For instance, Guy de Pourtalès' otherwise excellent biography devotes less than twenty pages to those crucial years of youth. I am not surprised that conscientious students have been as much dissatisfied as I was over this neglect, and that Arthur Hedley, the latest English biographer of Chopin, learned to speak Polish and actually went to Poland in order to study the composer's native environment at first hand. But even Mr. Hedley was at a disadvantage in this regard, for he was not a native Pole.

It is a matter of profound gratification, therefore, to all students and devotees of Chopin, that the present book constitutes a notable departure. Casimir Wierzynski, himself a voice of the spirit of Poland as one of its greatest living poets, has given us a story of the composer's life that includes an authentic, detailed, and colorful record of the years of his youth and of that emotional dynamic of his early manhood which will always vibrate in Chopin's melodies. His family, his friends, his school, the Polish countryside—all this is here for the first time spread before the American reader, like a fresh and living landscape. I was so absorbed by this book that I confess to having lost the sense of time while accompanying the author on this reliving of Chopin's days, on this tragically brief but stirring journey of sorrows, struggles, and rare moments of happiness.

In the appreciation of the public at large Chopin is usually misinterpreted in both the human and the artistic aspect. Chopin the man is seen as weakness personified; Chopin the artist is seen as an unrestrained romantic. All in all, it has become customary to conceive of him as an effeminate though charming figure, as a frail recluse who carried his soul-sadness from salon to salon, as a sickly artist given over to changeable moods and a morbid sensitivity—a slave to overintense emotional preoccupations. Nothing could be more false than such an image.

Mr. Wierzynski's biography gives the reader a true portrait of Chopin's personality, in which passion was combined with lucidity, temperament with discretion, and forcefulness with self-control. *L'ami angélique,* as Delacroix called Chopin, was a full-blooded male; for all his feminine delicacy and perceptiveness, which exposed him to facile suspicion of effeminacy, his was a character endowed with astounding strength and endurance. It is to be hoped that as a result of the portrait drawn in this book, the image of Chopin as a prince of the romantic realms of the mysterious, the idol of sentimental

Foreword

young women, the wraith writing nocturnes with a pen dipped in moonlight, will be relegated to the limbo of spurious legends.

Speaking of Chopin's music is for me like confessing my greatest love. I am moved, stirred to the depths, happy. But as with the man, so with the music—my love has most often been tricked out in the garb of romanticism, has been made to appear completely unlike itself, and I must protest.

In his human relations, Chopin counted many romantics among his friends. But in his art he held himself free of them. He was irritated by their exhibitionism, their self-pity, their tendency to give a literary content to music. To all this he opposed a scrupulous self-discipline, a purely musical content, and classical norms. Of his twenty-four preludes, twenty-four études, four ballades, and four scherzos, not one has a literary designation, and when his English publishers added artful titles to his compositions, he was beside himself with anger.

Schumann's literary bent seemed to him ridiculous, he was repelled by Berlioz's noisy tumultuousness, and he held Liszt in slight esteem as a composer. Even Beethoven, the progenitor of romanticism, remained for him a genius whom he admired from a distance, who filled him with respect but also with uneasiness.

On the other hand, he loved Mozart ardently and unreservedly. Throughout his life he worshiped Mozart's *clarté*, his poise, his perfection of form, his art in expressing feelings without resort to extraneous means. Bach inspired him with an almost religious reverence. Chopin played Bach as one recites prayers, and it was a wish dream of his that his own works might have been judged by Bach.

These preferences and aversions suffice to show that Chopin cannot be labeled a romantic in the accepted sense of the term. His true place in music is in fact defined by the instrument whose essence he revealed to the world and in which he revealed a world. Chopin revolutionized traditional piano music and created a new art of the keyboard. In place of the old rules he introduced principles of his own, and his iconoclastic romanticism was at the same time an original classicism.

Even before this the piano had a magnificent history written in the pages of Beethoven, Schubert, and Weber, but it was Chopin who discovered its soul and gave form to its unique poetry. In the period of *Klavierauszüge*, when the piano was often used to play works that had been conceived in the spirit of orchestral or vocal compositions, or of chamber music, Chopin created an authentic piano music. His compositions are born of the piano and intended for the piano. All attempts to adapt them to other instruments end in failure or result in distortion.

Chopin was the Prospero of the piano; he cast his spell on it and transformed it. He touched the keys of what had been till then merely a percussion instrument, and worked miracles. How did this come about? The answer to this question contains the entire secret of Chopin.

First of all, he made the piano sing. This idea was not an abstract invention, nor was it born in him by accident. From his childhood he had had a passion for opera, especially Italian opera; he had made himself an expert in vocal music, and he could have become a distinguished vocal teacher. He understood instinctively that a melody, if it is not to sound mechanical, must breathe like a human voice, and he commanded the piano to breathe. Thus was born his famous *tempo rubato*. He used it sensing in an uncanny way where this breath was needed, without losing sight of the basic framework of the composition and without overstepping its boundaries. He left behind the teaching that *tempo rubato* can be applied properly on one condition: namely, that the player must have an unerring sense in the use of it.

Chopin also possessed the secret of the pedal, and with this knowledge he opened a great unexplored world of new sounds and vibrations. He mixed sounds as paints are mixed on a palette, and produced colors that had not even been imagined before, and this in an ever more delicate variation. He developed his own alchemy of tones; he ventured unexpected combinations, created harmonies with extraordinary freshness, and opened up new horizons of musical poetry. This enabled his successors to make further discoveries; Debussy above all others excelled in such discoveries, although he

Foreword

exploited them for their magic rather than for their potentialities of musical content.

Chopin was a genius who lived for the sake of music and who acted through music. Simply by force of his compositions and without verbal statement, without expounding of theories, he overthrew the piano scholasticism of the established schools, according to which technical fluency was secured by means of a specific method of using one's hands, fingers, elbows, etc. He emancipated the pianist from servitude to pedantic canons and hastened the development of individual freedom in the realm of piano playing. Today no one finds it surprising that the performance of a given masterpiece is not limited to any one way of using the hands and fingers.

Nevertheless, Chopin's compositions present great difficulties for the performer. In the course of my world-wide travels I have met many promising pianists. As a rule they give adequate performances of Bach fugues; their playing of Scarlatti sonatas is almost always perfect; their interpretations of Mozart and Beethoven sound correct and are held to a good style; but when they come to Chopin, I am for the most part disappointed. Even if my young friends have mastered the technical requirements, they lack the key to Chopin's magic.

It seems to me proper to stress here that even the most difficult figurations of Chopin belong to creative music. Liszt cultivated technical preciosity; the difficulties he contrived were a camouflage, and he exploited them for greater effect. Chopin was interested only in the musical idea, and the difficulties of his works are logically inherent in his thought. This requires a completely different attitude on the part of the performer. I can play a pyrotechnical Liszt sonata, requiring forty minutes for its performance, and get up from the piano without feeling tired, while even the shortest étude of Chopin compels me to an intense expenditure of effort. I never cease to marvel that such lofty heights of artistic invention were attained by a sickly, fragile man, and I am always filled with admiration for the strength of his mind, his creative will, and the purity of his musical intentions.

After a hundred years the works of Chopin have lost nothing of

xi

their vitality. How many great names have been forgotten, how many famous works have fallen into oblivion, while Chopin's piano music is still heard throughout the world. What has become of the renown of Kalkbrenner, Thalberg, Moscheles, Field, and so many other contemporaries of Chopin, while his name shines with increasing splendor as the years go by.

It is extraordinary to observe how the most diverse audiences are conquered by the music of Chopin. I have met with lack of understanding for Bach in some places, with slight enthusiasm for Mozart in Italy, with a curious antipathy to Brahms in Latin countries, with distaste for Tchaikovsky in France—but Chopin has a hold on the hearts of men everywhere. This most national of composers is also the most cosmopolitan. I have always been struck by this fact when I played mazurkas in China, polonaises in Japan, and ballades in Australia or South Africa.

What accounts for this immediate understanding and indubitable love for Chopin among all peoples? I think that this is another of Chopin's secrets: the appeal lies in his directness, in the fact that he has a language of his own that is at the same time universal, in the boundless wealth of his musical ideas, which, in the view of Finck, a brilliant student of Chopin, would suffice for a half dozen average composers of symphonies and operas.

Chopin's secret was rediscovered by Debussy and Ravel. He has had many imitators, and two of the most felicitous of these were Scriabin and Szymanowski. Unfortunately, the later masters were unfaithful to Chopin's pianistic art. Schönberg, Stravinsky, Bartok, Milhaud, Honegger, Prokofieff, Shostakovich have written beautiful and great works, but they have lost contact with the soul of the piano. For them it has once again become a mere percussion instrument or not much more than that.

A return to the full potentialities of the piano can take place only through a return to Chopin's secret. But Chopin himself will remain unique.

Whence his genius came, how it was formed, is another of his many secrets. From the outset his music came from within himself, and even in the first works of his youth, as in his variations on a theme

Foreword

from *Don Giovanni,* one feels his incomparable individuality. He remained faithful to his beloved piano and did not yield to the friends who urged him to write operas, although in this pre-eminently operatic period such a temptation was insistent and difficult to surmount. He perfected his art by working with unremitting application, never revealing the source of his inspirations. The world in which he lived with his work remained like a charmed circle.

When I am questioned as to how one may find the way into this charmed circle, how one is to play Chopin—whether in the romantic spirit or in the manner of the school that holds the piano to be solely a percussion instrument—I seek for an answer in Chopin himself. His meticulous precision and his economy of means are inseparable from his moving warmth and deep feeling. On the one hand heroism, with its absolute rejection of compromise, on the other, supreme delicacy and sensitivity—his world in all its richness revolves between these two poles.

How this unusual combination of traits shaped the life of Chopin is told in this book, which I commend to those who would enlarge their understanding of the music and of the man.

CONTENTS

Contents

From portraits by Miroszewski

NICOLAS AND JUSTYNA CHOPIN, THE COMPOSER'S PARENTS
See especially Chapters 1 and 2.

CHOPIN'S BIRTHPLACE

The little house on the Skarbek estate at Zelazowa Wola where Nicolas
Chopin and his bride Justyna made their first home. See page 15.

Always deeply devoted to his family, Chopin remained in close contact with Ludwika throughout his
life. Emilia, the "intellectual" of
the family, died early. Izabela
married his former tutor, Barciń-
ski. See especially pages 21 ff., and
and 403 ff.

THE THREE SISTERS OF CHOPIN: LUDWIKA, IZABELA, AND EMILIA

WOJCIECH ŻYWNY

[C]hopin's eccentric and lovable [fir]st formal teacher of the piano [w]ho quickly recognized that he [ha]d taught his gifted pupil all [th]at he could and sent him on. [Se]e pages 26 ff.

[BELOW]
DRAWING ROOM
OF THE CHOPIN HOME
IN WARSAW

[A] sketch made by Antoni Kol[b]erg, a schoolmate of Chopin's.

Portrait by Miroszewski

JOZEF ELSNER

who, as Chopin's composition teacher, had the foresight and insight to encourage the young genius to develop in his own way, regardless of conventional requirements. So appreciative was Chopin of his teacher's wisdom that Elsner continued to exercise a strong influence long after Chopin's Conservatory days (1826-1829). See pages 63 ff., 153 ff.

SOME OF CHOPIN'S COMPETITORS

A contemporary lithograph of "Famous Pianists, Young School" comprising some of the foremost keyboard virtuosos of the mid-nineteenth century. Standing: Jacob Rosenhain, Edward Wolff, Frederic Chopin, Theodor Döhler, Adolf Henselt. Seated: Alexander Dreyschock, Sigismond Thalberg, Franz Liszt. See especially pages 84, 136, and 222 ff.

MARIA WODZINSKA

Chopin's childhood playmate and the heroine of his romantic fantasy of love and marriage, which ended in frustration. See pages 201 ff.

Drawing by Delaroche

Armee Museum Collection   *Culver Service*

Delphine Potocka

Three studies of the highly gifted and somewhat promiscuous Polish beauty who was Chopin's first mistress and remained his friend and confidante to the day he died. See especially pages 171 ff.

DELACROIX'S PORTRAIT OF GEORGE SAND

The great French romantic painter was a close friend of George Sand's, and it was at her home that he met Chopin. See pages 289, 312.

à la Dante ?

DELACROIX'S SKETCH FOR A PORTRAIT OF CHOPIN

Though Chopin had no great admiration for Delacroix's type of romanticism, the composer and painter remained great friends. This sketch was probably made at Nohant, the country estate of George Sand. See page 39.

CHOPIN, FROM A DRAWING BY GEORGE SAND

So well established and recognized was Chopin's relationship with his most famous mistress that after the composer's sister Ludwika had visited the lovers *en famille* at Mme. Sand's country estate, this drawing was sent to Ludwika in Poland as a memento. See page 319.

CHOPIN'S LAST WISH

On his deathbed, in shaky French and a shakier handwriting, the composer expressed his fear of being buried alive. Various other interpretations have been given this pathetic scrawl. See page 413.

Reproduced in Nauka i Sztuka, May-June, 1946

FRAGMENTS OF A LETTER FROM
CHOPIN TO DELPHINE POTOCKA

From the sensational correspondence that remained hidden for a hundred years. For some quotations from this correspondence, see pages 176 ff., and 292; for an account of its discovery, see pages 419 ff.

RELIC OF A PHANTOM LOVE

The envelope of letters from Maria Wodzinska and her mother found in Chopin's desk after he died. The inscription in Polish, in the composer's hand, means "My Misery." See pages 237, 415.

Deveria

Jane Wilhelmina Stirling

The Scottish devotee and patroness of the final years, whom Jane Carlyle called "Chopin's widow." See pages 371 ff.

FREDERIC CHOPIN

Now proven as a photograph

The composer in the last year of his life.

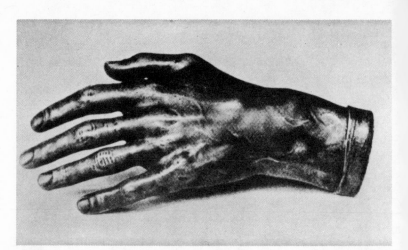

Prince Czartoryski Museum, Crakow

CAST OF CHOPIN'S HAND

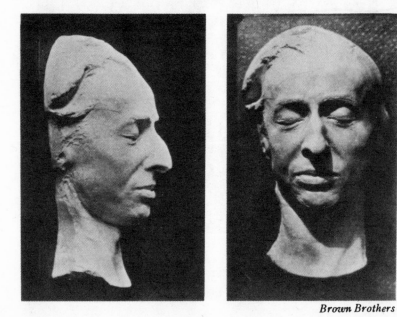

Brown Brothers

DEATH MASK OF CHOPIN

Newcomer from Lorraine

NICOLAS CHOPIN was on his way to Zelazowa Wola, where he was to take up the duties of a tutor in the manor house of Count Kasper Skarbek. The Skarbek estate was situated about thirty miles from Warsaw, near the main highway running from the Polish capital to the west. The road led through an open plain bordered by dark-blue streaks of forest on the distant horizon. To the right and left lay harvested fields, warmed by the slanting rays of the autumn sun, and divided by boundary strips on which grew wild pear and apple trees. Wherever this expanse, endless as the sea, peaceful, somewhat monotonous and somewhat melancholy, was broken by a large island of trees, one could be sure that a manor was to be found under their shadow.

The traveler was familiar with this landscape. He was acquainted of old with the Polish countryside; he knew the stormy history of this land and had taken active part in its vicissitudes, although not a drop of Polish blood flowed in his veins.

Nicolas Chopin was born in the village of Marainville, in Lorraine, on April 15, 1771. He was the son of a wheelwright and vinegrower; at the age of seventeen, on his graduation from the secondary school, he had left France for Poland.

The two countries were associated by a peculiar whim of history. For some time Lorraine had been ruled by Stanislas Leszczynski, King of Poland, who owed his throne to his son-in-law,

Louis XV, King of France. *Le bon roi Stanislas* had become famous in the French province for his skill in government. He founded schools, introduced legislative reforms, concerned himself with the welfare of the people, and never forgot Poland. Possibly the fame of this ruler, who died before Nicolas was born, or the influence of the large Polish colony in Lorraine, accounts for the fact that the young Frenchman set out to seek his future in a distant land buffeted by incessant storms.

Nicolas Chopin arrived in Warsaw in the latter half of 1787. All his luggage consisted of a few volumes of Voltaire, a violin, a flute, and vague hopes. He took up the uninspiring job of bookkeeper in a small factory owned by another Frenchman, a manufacturer of snuff, then a fashionable stimulant. He spent his days over columns of figures, and only at night was he able to see the Polish capital.

Warsaw was a city of a hundred thousand inhabitants; this made it a major urban center for that day. It had many beautiful old churches, theaters, and schools. Through the main thoroughfares—Miodowa, Krakowskie Przedmiescie, and Dluga—whirled the gilt-ornamented carriages of the magnates, escorted by retinues of young noblemen in honorary service to their lords. Tall cabriolets, called *whiskies,* were drawn by two, three, or even four pairs of horses. The carriages would stop before the residences of the nobles, magnificent, huge palaces, usually set back from the street, and surrounded by large courtyards or gardens. Their style had shifted from Italian baroque to Saxonian rococo, but their environment remained the same as before, without any style whatsoever. The palaces rose impassively amidst dilapidated old houses and wretched hovels.

Fantastic tales were told about the fabulous wealth of the magnates. No one could keep track of the fortune of Prince Karol Radziwill, who owned close to six hundred villages. Princess Elizabeth Lubomirska was said to possess gold in as many millions as the number of her years, and she seemed to be destined to live as long as Methuselah. The owners of the great Czartoryski palace at Pulawy spent a hundred and fifty thousand zlotys a

year for the kitchen alone. A bookkeeper in a small snuff factory
might well become giddy at the mirage of such figures.

Life was more peaceful and quiet on the right bank of the
Vistula, in the town of Praga. The Vistula was crossed by ferry,
for the last remaining bridge had been carried away by ice floes
and had long since become merely a legend. In the eyes of the
inhabitants of Warsaw, the other bank of the Vistula was the
beginning of the countryside, and a favorite site for excursions
and picnics. Nicolas grew fond of this spot, where many Polish
and foreign painters used to go to paint pictures of Warsaw.
From Praga, the capital appeared as though transfigured, red and
silver on a high hill, dominated by the great royal castle whose
façade descended in terraces to the river.

The castle was inhabited by Stanislas August Poniatowski, a
handsome king in a white wig, an artist and patron of the arts,
but a man of weak character. It also harbored the Diet chamber,
where the fate of the realm was decided. At free moments Nicolas
went to the Diet and from the crowded second-floor gallery listened to the debates. Here he had the best opportunity for ac-
quainting himself with the spirit and true picture of Poland,
which probably remained a riddle to him for a long time. "How
has it come about," he must have wondered, "that this nation has
fallen from the heights to the very brink of ruin?" Europe regarded Poland as a land of chaos, a people at the mercy of foreign
powers. Yet it was impossible to forget its recent glory. The
name of Jan Sobieski, the great Polish king—patriots often wrote
it on the walls of Warsaw—still had an electrifying ring, and his
victory over the Turks, which the world had once hailed as the
salvation of Christendom, could not have vanished without a
trace in the memory of a people reputed for its pride. By August,
1772, only eighty-nine years after that victory, the nation was
reduced to such helplessness that the rulers of Russia, Austria,
and Prussia were in position to agree on the first partition of
Poland, in a document opening with the words: "In the name of
the Most Holy Trinity . . ."

Nicolas Chopin would doubtless have been unable to say what

historical factor played the largest part in the decline of Poland —the selfishness of the magnates and the gentry, the corrupt rule of the last Saxonian kings, or the intrigues of aggressive neighbors. But he could not help seeing that the Poles were intent upon eradicating the blight that was dragging their country down to ruin. The Diet, whose sessions he could witness, brought together the noblest patriots, who publicly discussed the evils besetting Poland. After three years of debate and political conflict, they succeeded in evolving a new constitution that won the support of the King.

One evening in the spring Nicolas, having come out for his usual walk after working hours, noticed a crowd assembled in front of the castle. The populace had apparently begun to gather from the early hours on, and it was clear that they had not merely come to enjoy the fine warm weather. Familiar, now, with the local ways for several years, he realized that something unusual was about to take place. The people were animated, talking excitedly with one another, and they kept their eyes on the windows of the Diet chamber. Soon he learned that the Diet was about to enact the long-awaited new constitution that was to do away with the sins of the past and pave the way for a better future. The final debates lasted from early morning to sundown. At the end the King pledged himself to uphold the new constitution and summoned the deputies to attend a thanksgiving service in the cathedral.

Dusk was falling when the monarch, together with the speaker and the members of the Diet, appeared at the gate of the castle. The crowd surged toward them and lifted their ruler and their representatives on their shoulders. Someone shouted, "The King with the nation, the nation with the King!" The cry was echoed a thousandfold in the square. This was on May 3, 1791, soon after Easter, and it seemed that this Easter had come to symbolize the resurrection of Poland.

The King and the court, the ministers, the clergy in scarlet robes, and the men of the guilds set out in a great procession for St. John's Cathedral. Companies of troops lined the road and presented arms to the august cortege. Thirty thousand people were gathered for the occasion. Windows were illumined; the whole city was aglow.

Returning home, Chopin could feel that together with all Warsaw he had lived through the first day of the reborn state. He realized the significance of the new constitution. It abolished the absurd *liberum veto,* which empowered any deputy to abrogate any law adopted during a session of the Diet merely by exclaiming, "Veto!" It also abolished another Polish institution that had contributed to the paralysis of the country—the election of the king, which was free in theory but in practice was always determined by foreign influences. The new constitution granted extensive rights to the middle class and emancipated the serfs. Several other of its provisions were in the spirit of the most progressive ideas of the time and in keeping with the highest earlier tradition of Poland, when as a great and powerful nation it boasted a combination of strength with freedom and stood as a refuge of liberty and tolerance in Europe.

The young Nicolas, who had a French propensity for politics, saluted the new constitution as the best possible step in the existing circumstances. This was the opinion of all enlightened Poles and of many prominent personalities of Western Europe. Edmund Burke compared the new Polish constitution to the achievement of the French Revolution, emphasizing the fact that in Poland the change had been effected without bloodshed. King Stanislas was thus accurate in saying that while other kings paid for reforms with their heads, he lost only his hat—it fell from his head while he was being borne by the crowd.

Unfortunately, the years that followed saw the end of Polish freedom, and the constitution remained only as a testament to the future. The Prussian King and the Russian Tsarina refused to recognize the peaceful revolution of the Poles. Catherine resented the fact that King Stanislas, her former lover and political confidant, and now an insolvent debtor, had made common cause with the audacious reformers. Together with all Poland, Chopin heard the earth rumble under the heels of the troops marching to crush the "Polish Jacobins." Tadeusz Kosciuszko and Prince Jozef Poniatowski, the King's nephew, struggled in vain to resist the onrush of the vastly superior forces of the Russians. On January 23, 1793, Poland was partitioned for the second time.

A difficult period followed. Poland, reduced in area, was dying. People deserted the cities, industry declined, banks suspended payments. The snuff factory was shut down, and its bookkeeper roamed about aimlessly in the deserted streets of Warsaw. It appeared that after six years in Poland, his only recourse was to return to France. Deeply shaken by his experiences, dejected by his personal frustration, and depressed by the tragedy of Poland, he made up his mind to leave. The journey ahead was a long one; it would take fourteen days to reach Paris. He had a seat reserved in the stagecoach when he suddenly fell ill. He had never enjoyed the best of health, and now he was suffering from fevers and asthma. When he finally rose from his sickbed, new developments had taken place, in view of which he was moved to change his plans for departure.

Poland did not accept the new partition and rose against the foreign aggressors. The air was full of the great ideas of freedom: the revolutionary Polish spring of 1794 was approaching. Kosciuszko assumed leadership of the movement. Warsaw revived; the conspiracy had reached down to the slums and hovels. By word of mouth the news was carried that Kosciuszko, in peasant garb, had sworn in the market square of Cracow that he "would fight not for the nobility alone but for the freedom of the entire nation." At Raclawice, he led three hundred and twenty peasants, armed with scythes, against the Russian batteries, and won the day against two Russian generals.

Two weeks after this victory, news of which spread through the capital with lightning speed, Chopin was awakened by the sound of firing in the streets. The people of Warsaw, led by a cobbler, Kilinski, a butcher, Sierakowski, and a priest, Majer, rose up in arms. After thirty-six hours of fighting, the Russians were driven out. Warsaw was free. Easter was approaching, and once again it seemed to symbolize the resurrection of Poland.

Newcomer from Lorraine

Nicolas could hear the bells ringing in all the churches; he could see the enthusiastic crowds surging through the streets. This was the victory of a foreign but just cause. He was carried away by the general intoxication. Instead of going to France, he threw in his lot with Poland. He stood in line at the enlistment bureau and left it as a soldier of the insurrection.

For six months, until the end of the uprising, he served in the Warsaw militia. Like his brothers-in-arms, he waited for the news from the battlefield with anguished impatience. He won an officer's commission, and he identified himself ever more closely with Poland. The foreign cause became his own. He was ready to sacrifice his life for it.

At one point he came close to this extremity. It was when the insurrection had begun to ebb. General Suvorov was marching on Warsaw, advancing along the right bank of the Vistula, and making ready to take Praga by storm. Nicolas Chopin was stationed with his unit in one of the fortifications of Praga. The outcome of the battle was a foregone conclusion.

During the night, however, Chopin was ordered to take up position with a neighboring unit, withdrawing his company to the left bank. Thus he and his men were in Warsaw on November 4, when Suvorov captured Praga and massacred the survivors. More than ten thousand men, women, and children were killed that day.

In the following year, 1795, Poland was partitioned for the third time. The King abdicated, Poland ceased to exist as an independent state, and Warsaw fell under German occupation. Once again Chopin decided to return to France, but once again his plans were thwarted by illness. When he recovered, he gave up his idea of leaving, having made up his mind that Providence wanted him to remain in Poland.

He did remain. He supported himself by teaching French, struggling against poverty and hardship. He began to gain recognition; he received invitations to the countryside. The former bookkeeper and erstwhile army officer now was seeking his fortune as a tutor. Having spent his youth in a country of turmoil and misfortune, he acquired something that gave him strength and endurance. This Frenchman had been given a taste of Polish unhappiness, had known the bitterness of a just but hopeless struggle. Men nurtured on such food are stubborn; once they have embraced an idea, they cling to it through thick and thin, and the more defeats they suffer, the stronger their devotion to it. The former commander of a militia unit that had faced the armies of Suvorov no doubt became infected with this arch-Polish philosophy, and this probably accounts for the phenomenon of his assimilation. He was never to return to or revisit France. He even lost contact with his family. When his son, Frederic Chopin, came to Paris, the young man was not aware that he had two aunts living in a provincial town in France.

The Manor Under the Chestnut Trees

T HE estate of Zelazowa Wola was administered by the Countess Skarbek. In household matters she was assisted by Justyna Krzyzanowska, an orphan and a distant relative of the Skarbeks. The Count, a rake and spendthrift, preferred living abroad, away from debts, creditors, work, and other inconveniences.

The life of Countess Ludwika Skarbek, née Fenger, was anything but easy, because in addition to her administrative duties she had to oversee her five children. The eldest, Frederic Florian, had reached the age of ten and needed a teacher. Countess Skarbek did not wish to entrust her son's education to an ordinary tutor. She insisted upon a Frenchman, because the Poles regarded France as a second homeland; besides, the profession of tutor had become something like a French monopoly.

There were many Frenchmen available. After the storming of the Bastille, all Europe was overrun with French refugees—persons who were not certain that they could keep their heads on their necks in the revolutionary capital. A number of them reached Poland, where the Comte de Provence, who was to style himself Louis XVIII, had taken refuge in his flight from the terror. Many of these involuntary travelers remained in Poland, exploiting their only marketable possession, namely, their knowledge of the French language. In the seigneurial manors, the

The Life and Death of Chopin

French tutors were most often priests, but occasionally even counts and princes tried their luck in this profession. These pedagogues were not always equal to their tasks; Countess Skarbek was quite likely to hear rather adverse opinions about them.

The emigrees brought with them the persisting horror of their recent experiences—frightening visions of terror, such as recollections of heads impaled on pikes and of distinguished court ladies dragged to the guillotine. What was worse, they were unable to forget their lost wealth and the erstwhile elegant life of France; and their complaints about Poland were all the more heartfelt because they were faced with the misfortune of having to earn their daily bread. Their pupils thus were inculcated both with a misplaced admiration for the virtues of fallen France and with contempt for their native land. Countess Skarbek had no use for such an upbringing, and it was not among such emigrees that she looked for a tutor for her son Frederic.

She had been favorably impressed by a young Frenchman she had met in the house of a friend, Madame Laczynska of Czerniejew. He was then the tutor of the two sons and two daughters of the house, and their mother was fully satisfied with him. Thus young Frederic Skarbek had met his future mentor in Czerniejew, which he visited at every opportunity, attracted there by the first rapture of his ten-year-old heart, which he was offering to the younger of the girls, Maria, already famous for her extraordinary beauty. Following the normal course of such youthful infatuations, their romance was as unhappy as possible, and passed with lightning speed. Maria Laczynska soon after became Madame Walewska, and under that name achieved a niche in history as the mistress of Napoleon and the mother of his son, Alexander Walewski.

Nicolas Chopin thus was not a complete stranger in Zelazowa Wola, where he arrived in the fall of 1802. He soon felt at home in his new surroundings and at once sensed his importance in this family, in which the eldest male was only ten years of age. Madame Skarbek could congratulate herself on her choice. The tutor commanded respect by his natural authority, and he was not afflicted with any mannerisms and ridiculous traits that would have made him a butt of criticism in as merciless an observatory of human defects as a world of five children can be. The slender, self-possessed gentleman with black eyes and black hair was simple and easy in his demeanor; his conversation was always interesting, and like any newcomer he was able to find novel aspects in the most familiar things. Thanks to him the children probably discovered many previously unsuspected marvels in the great park with its elm-lined avenues, in the old mill on the Utrata River, and in the parish church at Brochow, a beautiful two-hundred-year-old edifice that had once served also as a fortress.

The manor itself was a small, one-story structure, with a shingled roof and whitewashed walls. It was surrounded by old chestnuts and lindens; in front of its unassuming façade spread a lawn with flower beds, and next to it stood the outbuildings.

Madame Skarbek placed Nicolas on her right at table; opposite him sat Justyna Krzyzanowska. She was referred to as "the housekeeper," or facetiously as "the court housekeeper"; she was entrusted with the key to the medicine cabinet, which symbolized the fact that she had the house under her care. Her main task, however, was to attend to the children, and to some extent Nicolas could look upon her as his colleague, although this carefree twenty-year-old girl was still very much a child herself.

Frederic Skarbek's younger brothers and sisters worshiped Justyna, and her charm made itself felt with everybody else as well. In keeping with the requirements of a Polish manor, she was distinguished by modesty, which in her was an innate trait rather than a laboriously acquired virtue. Her abundant blond hair, tied in a high knot, illumined her head with a pale-yellow light, and its warm luster was also reflected in her delicate, thin face, with its small features and beautiful, proudly arched nose. Her eyes were very blue, lively, and quick to smile.

The Life and Death of Chopin

Nicolas did not avoid the eyes of the girl sitting opposite him, nor was he excessively absorbed in them. But what could have greater power to attract him amid the monotony of country life? Autumn was spreading a blanket of cobwebs on the fields of stubble, the trees were taking on a bronze luster like old gold, and the weather was so warm that some of the chestnuts were blossoming for a second time. When winter came, the wind swept the level plains, swirled the snow into spinning funnels in the fields, and whistled in the chimneys. The family sat by the fireside, while neighbors dropped in bringing the latest news. The tutor was always invited to join the company.

The fireside chats in the manors of the nobility had lost the principal topic that had enlivened them in former times—news of the King and the court. All recollections of the former had been exhausted; all anecdotes of the latter had grown stale. Stanislas Augustus had died in St. Petersburg after living only a short time on the Tsarina's charity, and the melancholy fate of the monarch who had lost his kingdom was not a subject for enjoyable conversation. Lacking themes of royalty, the company had to content itself with gossip concerning the local aristocrats. From the fireside chats Nicolas could learn, for instance, of the existence of a certain Madame Chrzanowska, about whom reports came from Pulawy, the splendid seat of the Czartoryskis. It was rumored that this eccentric lady had fallen in love with a sheep, which she took into her bed and her carriage. The rustic influence of the Trianon similarly affected another capricious lady, Madame Oledzka, who became enamored of a goose, which she took on walks, leading it on a bright-colored ribbon. But the peak of eccentricity was attained by a certain Uniatycki, a most hygienic squire, who, fearing infection from the excessive amount of carbon dioxide exhaled by the congregation during services, sat in church under an enormous glass hood.

Nicolas could not add much to such conversations; he knew no gossip and did not venture his opinion concerning public affairs. He was relieved when after dinner the company moved to the drawing room and listened to music. Here the new resident of Zelazowa Wola had a more important part to play. His luggage included two precious cases, one containing a violin and the other a flute; for in addition to being at home in French, German, and calligraphy, he was an expert performer on these two instruments. No one knew that his secret passion was poetry: he wrote verse in French and even in Polish, which he spoke fluently, although with a foreign accent.

In the course of time it was discovered that this serious-minded gentleman had one weakness. He resented being considered a dilettante in music; on the contrary, he looked upon himself as a virtuoso in this art, at least a local one. However, except from the organist of the Brochow church, he had no one to vie with; and the competition he found in the manor was neither unpleasant nor unsympathetic—it was embodied in Justyna, who played the piano and had a lovely soprano voice. The concerts usually began with a violin or flute piece with piano accompaniment; then came Polish and French songs. The love story told in the song *Laura and Filon*, written by the famous poet Karpinski, with music by the no less famous composer Kurpinski, could be sure of a favorable audience in every Polish manor, on every Sunday evening, not only at that time but also for generations to come. Rousseau's *Consolations des misères de ma vie* similarly conquered all hearts, if not by its poetic mood, then at least by the infallible magic of fashion.

In the spring the plains around Warsaw exhaled the breath of warm winds, and the manor stood steeped in the odors of freshly plowed earth. The trees suddenly turned green, sometimes overnight. First to bloom were the willows; branches of these trees were blessed in church on Palm Sunday and carried home and hung behind the images of the saints. The lilacs and jasmine symbolized more secular joys; but these shrubs dedicated to love had so far flowered in vain at Zelazowa Wola.

Thus years went by—one year, two, three. Madame Skarbek periodically opened her secretary of ashwood, entering figures in her ledger, until she learned that Monsieur Nicolas could perform this task more speedily and easily, with the expertness of a professional bookkeeper. Justyna, often summoned to minister to the sick in the village, searched for remedies in her closet, not too sure of her therapeutic science, until it was recalled that Nicolas had had an opportunity to study these matters during the war years, and was more reliable as a makeshift physician. He became indispensable, and as the years passed he gradually came to share in every aspect of the family life. He accompanied Justyna to the village huts, which, thanks to the interest of the intelligent and progressive Countess, were less miserable than similar dwellings elsewhere. The ex-soldier of the Kosciuszko insurrection was familiar with the hard lot of the Polish peasants, with their disappointed hopes, and their importance to the country. He was interested in political developments, and eagerly studied such occurrences, wondering whether they would turn out to Poland's advantage. For a veritable avalanche of events was approaching from distant lands; it made the earth tremble, and its echoes reverberated against the walls of every house in Poland. Napoleon had begun to shake Europe.

During the peaceful village evenings, electrifying rumors were repeated. Poles were fighting under the banners of Napoleon. Twenty-five thousand were serving in the Polish legions in Italy; their armbands bore the inscription *"Gli uomini liberi sono fratelli"*—"Free men are brothers." Old hopes were reviving throughout Poland, which expected the god of war to bring back its freedom. But Nicolas Chopin had a different view of these developments. He did not trust Napoleon, who was signing peace treaty after peace treaty, repeatedly making promises to the Poles but never touching on the fate of their country. In 1802 five thousand Polish legionnaires who had survived his European campaigns were sent overseas to San Domingo, to quell the revolutionary uprising of the Negroes and to die of malaria. The noble motto on the armbands remained only a phrase.

The young admirer of Voltaire who had become a rural tutor in Poland was characterized by soberness, which did not, however, lessen the warmth of his feelings. This became clear after four years spent under the same roof with Justyna Krzyzanowska. The common life, the evening concerts, and similarity of tastes had brought the two young people so close to each other that Madame Skarbek had betimes prepared her answer to the formal proposal she expected from Nicolas. She had not looked forward to finding any better husband for Justyna; besides, any other choice would have run counter to her charge's feelings. The Krzyzanowskis were only distant relatives of the Skarbeks, and there was no need to take family considerations into account. True, Chopin was of modest origin, and to associate him, even remotely, with a house that boasted a count's coronet was not in accord with usage, but Madame Skarbek was above such caste prejudice. She herself was a descendant of German bankers, and her mother, who lived in Torun, could scarcely speak Polish. Moreover, Nicolas was noble-minded, cultivated, intelligent, and trustworthy. What more could she ask for?

On June 2, 1806, the Reverend Duchnowski recorded in the Brochow parish register that Nicolas Chopin, aged thirty-five, and Justyna Krzyzanowska, aged twenty-four, had entered upon matrimony.

The young couple moved to one of the smaller buildings on the estate. They were given three rooms, small and less than modestly furnished. A corridor divided the house into two parts; the Chopins occupied one part. The rooms, with their whitewashed walls, were light, although the crude timbered roof hung very low. The first room belonged to Nicolas, who furnished it with objects he had accumulated during his wanderings and put his French volumes on the shelves. The second was arranged as a drawing room, and Madame Justyna contrived to create an atmosphere of warmth and coziness with the help of a few miniatures and other souvenirs of her family. The third was the bedroom, which offered a view of the alder-lined banks of the Utrata.

The other part of the building housed the kitchen and the bakery that served the manor. Although the apartment had occasionally to be aired of the odors of meats and soups, the smell of freshly baked bread was always welcome, as though this transformation of the fruit of the earth into human food were an invigorating symbol.

The marriage of Justyna and Nicolas did not bring about any

important changes in the daily routine of the manor. Justyna surrendered the key of the medicine closet to the eldest of the Skarbek daughters, who now assumed the leading position in the household, but the new Madame Chopin continued to assist the Countess. The eldest son, Frederic, went to Warsaw to take his examinations at the lyceum, the headmaster of which, Samuel Bogumil Linde, had joined the circle of the Countess's friends, often visiting Zelazowa Wola, bringing the latest news from the capital, and enjoying the drawing-room concerts. As of old, Nicolas played the violin and the flute, and his wife accompanied him on the piano and sang Polish and French songs in her pleasant voice.

These concerts were soon drowned out by other, more resounding music. The broad Warsaw highway, which ran not far from the manor, rumbled with the tread of marching armies. After the victories of Austerlitz and Jena, Napoleon headed his battalions toward the Polish capital. Tsar Alexander and King Friedrich Wilhelm were fleeing by way of side roads. Polish units had fought under French banners for Grudziadz, Kolobrzeg, Danzig. Poland believed that all this heralded the restoration of its independence, and gave Napoleon new contingents of tens of thousands of soldiers.

In the little home in the outbuilding in Zelazowa Wola, the old distrust of the French leader was increasing. Nicolas Chopin was entitled to find a mournful satisfaction in not having been mistaken in his premonitions. Poland regained freedom, but it was a freedom as crippled as a war invalid. In 1807, Zelazowa Wola became part not of a restored republic but of the Duchy of Warsaw. This name for the miniature state was devised at Tilsit by Napoleon, who did not wish to annoy Tsar Alexander with a revival of the name of Poland. The map of the new duchy comprised only one-fifth of the area encompassed within the former borders of Poland.

Simultaneously with these great historical developments in the larger world, important events were taking place in the small personal world of the Chopins. Madame Justyna was expecting a child in the spring. On April 6, 1807, she gave birth to a daughter, dark-eyed and dark-haired like her father. The parents named her Ludwika, thus expressing their gratitude to Countess Skarbek. The child was pretty and healthy. The increase of the population of Zelazowa Wola by this little person coincided with a general intensification of life on the estate. The manor was not so far from Warsaw, which was again becoming a bustling capital, and Chopin began to look toward the city. Linde, the headmaster of the lyceum, had often talked to him about his school. The younger Skarbek children were growing up, and plans were being made for sending them away to school. The eldest, Frederic, was to go to France after his graduation.

Two years after the birth of Ludwika, Madame Justyna informed her husband that the dark-eyed girl was not to remain their only child. This strengthened Nicolas's conviction that he must move to Warsaw and try to increase his earnings in view of his growing needs. Linde sympathetically encouraged him in these plans, and Madame Skarbek too promised to help him. But it was decided that they would await the birth of the new child in Zelazowa Wola.

This event took place in the winter, which in this year, 1810, was particularly cold and snowy. The severe weather, however, did not prevent either the rich or the poor from indulging in a boisterous carnival. Merrymakers drove in sleighs from manor to manor for entertainment and dancing. It was also customary for peasant bands to play under the landowners' windows to make it known that a wedding was taking place in the village. One night, musicians drove up to Zelazowa Wola to make such an announcement; they played with gusto, stamping their feet on the ground to fight off the cold. The Countess could not give much attention to them; she was busy elsewhere. In the outbuildings all the windows were lighted. Here there was intense activity, and before the peasant fiddles and viols had finished playing, the second child of Nicolas and Justyna had come into the world. It was a boy.

Even if, as some writers maintain, it was only a *post factum* legend that brought a village band to celebrate the birth of Frede-

March

ric Chopin, the other recorded details of the event can be documented. The boy was born on Thursday, February 22, 1810, at six o'clock in the evening. At the baptism, performed by the Reverend Ignace Marjanski, curate priest of the Brochow parish, he received the name of Frederic Francis. The godparents were Anna Skarbek and, by proxy, Frederic Skarbek, who had gone to Paris and who was represented by Francis Grebecki. The boy was called Frederic in honor of his godfather and Francis in honor of the deputy. The document officially registering the birth was drawn up by the Reverend Jan Duchnowski, parish priest of Brochow, on April 23, 1810, in the presence of the father and two witnesses, Jozef Wyrzykowski and Frederic Geszt.

The new member of the family had blond hair and brown eyes, and was of delicate build. His features resembled his mother's. Six months after the birth of the infant, his father's plan for leaving Zelazowa Wola became a reality. The instructor in French in the lower grades of the lyceum fell ill, and it did not seem likely that he would be able to continue his classes in the coming school year. Linde asked Nicolas Chopin to substitute for the sick teacher. Soon after he entered upon this arrangement, the position became a permanent one.

Thus in the fall of 1810 the little household bade farewell to the pleasant rural seat that had been its first home. Eight years before, Nicolas had come to Zelazowa Wola as a tutor; now he was departing as a member of the family.

CHAPTER

3

A Ghost in the House

THE Saxon Palace in Warsaw stood as a relic of the dynasty of the worst kings that had ever reigned on Polish or non-Polish soil. Several large buildings in horseshoe formation flanked an immense courtyard, which later became the largest square in the capital. For the past hundred years these buildings had served various purposes, until eventually the lyceum was housed in them. It was there that Nicolas Chopin moved with his family, occupying an apartment in a wing reserved for teachers.

He began his classes immediately, and soon realized that his new position would not pay him enough to support his family. His salary was modest, and, worse yet, was paid irregularly. But the teachers were allowed to take pupils as boarders, and Chopin at once applied for permission to engage in this subsidiary but profitable occupation. Linde backed his protégé. The first boarders of the Chopins were the two younger Skarbek boys, their cousins from Zelazowa Wola.

Nicolas Chopin was a practical-minded Frenchman and liked to quote the proverb *Garder une poire pour la soif* ("Keep a pear handy against thirst"). Especially in his present situation, when he could not have too many pears, he bent all his energies toward keeping his boarding establishment on a high level. He accepted only boys of the best families and personally assisted them in their lessons. No one could have enjoyed greater trust as a guardian of youth, and his wife contributed domestic warmth. While the lyceum treasury might be late in paying the instructor's modest salary, the well-to-do landowners whose sons boarded with the Chopins proved themselves generous. Chopin's house soon began to enjoy a high reputation in Warsaw.

The new teacher's efforts to make both ends meet completely absorbed him during the first years of his residence in Warsaw. On July 9, 1811, he became the father of a third child, the fair-haired Izabela, and Monsieur Nicolas realized that the ingenious financial structure he had contrived was tottering on its very foundations. Thanks to his energy he again succeeded in balancing his budget, adding two new items to his income—the salaries he received as teacher of French in the military preparatory school and in the school of artillery and engineering. In 1813, when the Chopins were blessed with a fourth child, a girl who was named Emilia, Chopin was promoted to teaching in the higher grades. His new salary provided him with a solid foundation. The family did not increase beyond these four children, and the former book-keeper was able to keep his accounts clear of deficit.

Nicolas could consider himself fortunate, all the more so because during the years in which he succeeded in achieving economic security, Poland was ravaged by a new hurricane. Napoleon declared war on Russia, marched on Moscow at the head of an army "of twenty tongues," which included eighty thousand Poles, and after his defeat hurried back to Paris on a sleigh. All hopes for Polish freedom were buried under the snows of Russia or scattered to the winds with the ashes of the dying campfires. After the Congress of Vienna consigned Poland, splintered into three parts, to the rule of its dominant neighbors, Warsaw became the capital of the so-called Kingdom of Poland, and Tsar Alexander was crowned King of Poland.

This whimsical liberal on the throne of ancient despots seemed, to the minds of many, favorably inclined toward the Poles; he allowed them to keep their own army, schools, and administration. In actuality, even his first actions did not augur a happy co-operation of the two nations. Contrary to expectations, the Tsar did not appoint as his viceroy the wise and influential Adam Czartoryski, who had served as Russian Minister of Foreign Affairs; instead he named General Zajaczek, an opportunist as unstable as a weathercock. Instead of appointing Kosciuszko as supreme commander of the army, he gave the post to his brother, Grand Duke Constantine, and this was an even greater disappointment to the Poles. Nevertheless, the country began to rise from its ruins, and Warsaw prospered with a new life.

Having steered his family to safety through these stormy years, Nicolas Chopin could allow himself an occasional interlude of well-deserved relaxation in his private life. Every Thursday he received at home; he would take out a bottle of French wine from the cupboard and begin a game of whist or a political discussion. When young people gathered, the receptions had a different, more vivacious program: Madame Justyna would sit at the piano, and the boys and girls would dance.

In this home, the idea of the family was considered sacred. Two patriarchal traditions, the Polish and French, contributed to this attitude. It is not surprising, therefore, that to Justyna and Nicolas their children became the core of life. The children throve, although the younger girls were anemic and susceptible to colds, while Frederic, always frail, refused to eat and had to be coaxed at every meal. Two physicians, Roemer and Malcz, made frequent visits; Madame Justyna added many new herbs and potions to her medicine chest, and the maid often had to take on the function of a nurse.

The younger generation of Chopins fell naturally into two branches: the elder comprised Ludwika and Frederic, the younger Izabela and Emilia. Ludwika was the leader. The very appearance of the robust girl inspired respect in her younger sisters and her brother, who were of more delicate physique. Soon this bold and resolute little person became conscious of her dominance over the other children. At an early age she learned to play the piano and to read Polish and French. She was the very embodiment of wisdom and solicitude. From her earliest years she made herself useful to her parents in every way, and showed particular tenderness toward Frederic. She taught him to read and write in the two languages she knew, and her pupil proved so apt that her lessons were a kind of game. Frederic's favorite place, however, was not at the nursery table, as a docile pupil to his sister, but under the clavichord. He usually stole into this retreat when his mother was playing and singing; there he would listen with amazement to the waves of sound surging in the mysterious box. He also liked to touch the keyboard and to pound on it until he was removed from the piano stool.

This was all the more strange because in infancy Frycek, as he was called, had reacted to music quite differently. Whenever he heard the sound of playing he would begin to cry, and it was difficult to pacify him. His parents did not understand the meaning of this violent reaction, and they were glad when, as he grew older, he shifted from crying to laughter and was irresistibly attracted to the magical instrument.

The wise Ludwika displayed initiative in this matter too, and decided to teach him to play the piano. These lessons likewise soon developed into a game. Frederic grasped the mechanics of playing at once; he learned the positions of the hand with amazing speed and was able to play every tune he heard. The knowledge possessed by the seven-year-old teacher soon proved insufficient. Before a year had elapsed Ludwika was forced to ask her mother to help her; after two years, the two teachers were increasingly baffled by the demands of their exacting pupil.

This patriarchal family observed its own festive days, the most important of which were the father's and mother's name days. The children would present their parents with gifts, with congratulations memorized in advance, and with verses of their own composition, copied in elaborate characters. Three such samples of little Frycek's calligraphy have by some miracle been preserved to this day.

Most solemnly celebrated of all holidays was Christmas, which in Poland marked the culmination of the year, as it were. The extant chronicles do not mention the manner in which it was celebrated by the Chopins, but judging from the fact that Frederic remembered his childhood Christmas Days all his life, and often referred to them in his letters, Christmas in the Chopin household must have been observed in the Polish and the Catholic tradition, and must have been particularly impressive.

Several days before the great holiday, the tree was set up in the house, and the organist of the Bernardine church brought the traditional brightly colored holy wafers. The day before Christmas began with the visits of strangers—poor students and schoolboys appeared at the door, and from a small book called the "Little Gospel" they would recite a passage from Luke: "And she brought forth her firstborn son, and wrapped him in swaddling clothes, and laid him in a manger, because there was no room for him in the inn . . ." The visitors were given a few coppers and sometimes a snack.

The Christmas table was spread with hay and covered with a cloth. Sheaves of unthreshed grain stood in the corners of the dining room. A star and a cradle—both molded from the colored wafers—each with a lighted candle in it, hung from the ceiling. There was an atmosphere of fairyland in the house. At sunset everyone watched for the appearance of the first stars in the sky: this was the signal for the beginning of the celebration. Everyone was dressed in his Sunday best. The mother would enter carrying a plate, on which were two wafers held together with honey. First she and the father would break the wafer, then she would approach the children. "May we a year from now again break the wafer together" were the ritual words, uttered in deeply moved tones, amidst embraces, kisses, and unconcealed tears. After this exchange of wishes, the whole family would go to the kitchen to break the wafer with the servants.

When they were seated at the table, they were permitted to look under the cloth, where each found a gift. The Christmas Eve menu consisted traditionally of almond soup, a pike, cabbage stuffed with rice and mushrooms, noodles with poppyseed, and fritters. After dinner, the father would lead the procession to the drawing room. The mother would intone, "He lies in the manger; who will hasten to sing carols to the Little One?" or "Sleep, Baby

Jesus," and thus this most memorable of all evenings would proceed to the accompaniment of naïve ancient melodies, in an atmosphere of mystical enchantment. Usually there was the interruption of a knock at the door; there stood an aged man in a rosy mask, with a long white beard reaching to his waist. "Kriss Kringle!" the children would greet him with joyous exclamations.

The character of Kriss Kringle had been imported to Poland from Germany only a few years before, together with the Christmas tree. The Catholics had quickly adopted these two customs from the Protestants. The role of Kriss Kringle was usually played by a friend of the family, who was unrecognizable in his disguise, and who gave the children moral admonitions, for which they kissed his hand.

The great day had its epilogue at midnight, when the whole family went to Mass. Such occasions must have left ineradicable impressions on the children; for Frederic, these were his first sleepless nights. The Chopins usually went to the Church of the Visitation, which was close to their house.

The baroque church was brightly illumined. The priest, surrounded by a throng of altar boys and attendants, began the solemn service. The bells rang out, frankincense was wafted from the altar, and the sound of carols came from the choir. When the chorus intoned, "The starling will call in a tenor voice, and the pigeon will coo in a bass," the audience could actually hear the voices of birds and beasts, and it was as though the enchanted scene about the manger in Bethlehem was being re-enacted. Some of the choristers imitated blackbirds, others thrushes. One could hear the mooing of cows and the bleating of sheep. In the words of the old carol, "God was being born, every creature was greeting him." Heaven and earth were reconciled.

After the Mass, a manger beside the side altar was unveiled. The little Jesus was lying there, and the Mother of God, crowned with a golden halo, knelt at his side. The chant of the choir was taken up by the congregation below. This was indeed a sacred night.

Such spectacles must have had a particularly vivid effect on the

A Ghost in the House

imagination of Frederic, although he never composed sacred music. There can be no doubt that the atmosphere of the home during the Christmas holidays, the marvels of all these days, the excitement and tenderness of all the family, were among the strongest of the influences that shaped the boy's imagination and emotional susceptibility.

His aroused sensitivity began to seek its own expression. According to a plausible family tradition, the maid burst into the parents' bedroom one cold and stormy night, crying, "God Almighty, there are ghosts in the drawing room!"

There was a great commotion. The parents, followed by the girls, jumped from their beds and dashed through the cold rooms. The ghost they found in the drawing room was no strange intruder. At the piano sat Frederic, drumming the melodies that he had heard his mother play for her dancing guests. He played them accurately, and, what was even more extraordinary, added embellishments of his own. He was clad only in his nightshirt, and his bare legs dangled pathetically from the high stool. He merely smiled at his parents, declaring that he wished to replace his mother the next time they had dancers. There was a great deal of bustle that night before the ghost quieted down and returned to bed.

It is possible that this trivial incident gave the Chopins much food for thought and that it was responsible for their decision that their son should have a professional teacher. Frycek was then six years old.

Child Prodigy

T HE appearance of the piano teacher, Wojciech Zywny, in the house of the Chopins must have marked an occasion. In the first place, it meant that the amateurish home instruction was at an end and that little Frycek would now begin to study seriously. In the second place, Zywny himself was something of a character.

He was sixty years of age, but moved about with youthful energy. Tall, somewhat stooping, he presented a picture of romantic negligence. He wore a long frock coat, usually green; an immense red-checked handkerchief protruded from his pocket, and from his yellow velvet vest there stuck out a huge square pencil that could serve as a baton or, if need be, as a terrifying instrument of punishment. He constantly fingered his loose white silk cravat, twisting and turning it as though trying in vain to conceal the past recorded on it in indelible spots. Hessian boots reaching up to his knees gave him a solid pediment, while a tight-fitting yellow wig, combed from the back to the front and parted in the middle, crowned this incarnation of a comic-opera professor. His lively little eyes darted busily back and forth in his oblong face, which was adorned with a goatee; but they were vastly overshadowed by his imposing nose, of suspicious color, long and saturnine like the beak of a pelican. Even from a distance he exhaled a smell of snuff, which he took from an enormous box. His cravat, vest, and coat were covered with tobacco stains.

Child Prodigy

Zywny was certainly not the best available piano teacher in Warsaw, where such famous masters as Krogulski, Weinert, Wieman, Zawadzki—not to speak of Würfel, the Viennese—were then active; but he was a popular figure. He supported himself by giving lessons, and his daily tour began at an early hour each morning. He charged three or four zlotys per hour, which was a fair fee. Rumor had it that he had even saved up a tidy sum for rainy days, for his needs were small. His only vice was rather frequent indulgence in a stiff drink of vodka. He concealed this weakness as well as he could, but his red nose betrayed him.

Zywny had had his romantic years, but poverty had soon clipped his wings and harnessed him to strenuous work. A native of Bohemia, he had studied music under a teacher who had inculcated in him a lasting admiration for Johann Sebastian Bach. He played the violin and the clavichord, had tried his hand at composition, and had conducted a few times, but he ended up as a teacher. Prince Sapieha had brought him to Poland and appointed him court pianist and music teacher at his family seat; but the promise of a brilliant career came to naught when he lost his position in the aftermath of the partition of Poland. It was then that he moved to Warsaw and began his daily rounds, summer and winter, protected from frost and thaw by his eternal high boots.

Untidy, garrulous, with a tendency to sponging and stinginess, Zywny had nevertheless preserved an undimmed respect for true art. He admired perfect expression and knew that the instrument on which his pupils banged their fingers, and which he himself bespattered with snuff, could speak with the eloquence of angels. He kept his faith to himself because he had no one to whom he could communicate it; but he had not held on to it in vain.

Frederic was a revelation to him. Contact with this boy reawakened in him the artistic instinct smoldering under the ashes of time and failure. His high aspirations and his love for music, which his uncouth exterior concealed from the less sensitive observers, now found an outlet in his paternal solicitude for his pupil. He corrected Frederic's inaccuracies, showed him the best models to follow, taught him to love Bach, and introduced him to the genius of Mozart. Frederic could not help feeling this. He developed a real affection for his teacher and listened to his counsels with confidence. He revealed to his new friend his most important childish secrets—his ideas for original compositions. He played polonaises and marches, which his teacher often recorded with his huge square pencil.

The lessons were irregular; that is to say, Zywny devoted all his free time to Frederic. He became a steady visitor in the Chopin house, dropping in there after his daily tours for a game of cards. It turned out that he was a living chronicle of olden times and an eager collector of current news items. He recounted these in a strange language of his own concoction, in which the German, Czech, and Polish words often were less expressive than his enthusiasm and gestures. In addition to friendship, he found at the Chopins' a new occupation: he began to give lessons to the girls and the boarders.

At about that time the lyceum was transferred from the Saxon Palace to the Casimir Palace on the Krakowskie Przedmiescie. The removal had been ordered by Grand Duke Constantine, who organized military reviews in the immense courtyard of the Saxon Palace and assigned all the surrounding buildings to the army.

The change turned out to be advantageous for the Chopins. Their new apartment was more spacious, and they set up their household quite comfortably in the second story of an annex to the palace. The boarding establishment was enlarged; Monsieur Nicolas hired a tutor, Antoni Barcinski, for the boys, and Madame Justyna got a housekeeper. All their neighbors were friends. The first story of the building was occupied by Linde, and the ground floor by the poet Casimir Brodzinski and by Professor Juliusz Kolberg and his three sons, who were friends of Frederic's.

The Casimir Palace was separated from the street by a high railing and constituted a self-contained little community, with a population of several hundred. The houses stood amidst trees and bushes; lilacs and jasmine blossomed in the spring, and lindens and beeches rustled in the summer. At the back of the lyceum rugged slopes, only partly cultivated, fell sharply toward the Vistula. From there one could see Praga and the vast expanses beyond the river, blue in fine weather, silvery on misty days, but always entrancing. The children came to this spot to play, the younger students to study, and the older to dream and love.

Frederic was now seven years of age. He was growing normally amid the normal pleasures and duties of family life. He studied at home, sometimes complained about a toothache, and as always was unwilling to eat. He was witty, charming, and whimsical, like many other children of his age. Only his relation to music distinguished him from his playmates: in this respect, there was no common ground between him and them. He spent long hours at the piano, practicing with enthusiasm or improvising in pursuit of a goal he alone knew. He absorbed his teacher's instruction with extraordinary ease, grasping Zywny's ideas instantaneously, often anticipating them, and displaying an astonishing inventiveness. His phenomenal memory enabled him to repeat his improvisations or unrecorded compositions. More and more often Zywny drew his enormous snuffbox and his huge pencil from his pockets, to scatter tobacco on the keyboard and to write down his pupil's melodies.

The old gossip soon spread the story of the extraordinarily gifted boy all over Warsaw. Everywhere he went, he exhibited the dances and variations that he had written down at his pupil's direction. Madame Skarbek, who had remained a close friend of the family, did not conceal her sincere admiration for the boy. The neighbors of the Chopins' also talked about him, and less than a year after he began his lessons with Zywny, Frederic was well known in Warsaw. He was invited to the houses of the most prominent families, and his performances were marveled at in the salons. The sensational reports reached Grand Duke Constantine, who expressed the wish to meet Frederic. One day the Bruhl palace, where the Tsar's viceroy had his official residence, resounded with the strains of a new march. The morose duke ordered the player to repeat his piece. It raised his spirits considerably—he marched around the drawing room as if he were taking part in a military review.

The Life and Death of Chopin

Madame Justyna was happy but a little frightened. Her house-keeping duties, her concern with her family, the boardinghouse, the visitors, and even the daily Mass at the Church of the Visitation could not crowd out her constant awareness that Frederic was an exceptional child.

Soon she had more tangible proof of this fact. One day Zywny informed the Chopins that one of Frederic's polonaises was to be published, thanks to the efforts of the Reverend Cybulski, rector of Our Lady's Church, who had a printing shop in his parish and who wept with Zywny whenever he listened to the little boy's playing. A short time later the teacher handed to Justyna a white sheet with her son's composition engraved on it. She took it with a trembling hand. And how moved she must have been when she read a notice published in the Warsaw *Review* of January, 1818, under the heading "List of Polish Works Published in 1817," as follows:

Composers usually are not included among writers (despite the fact that they too are authors). Yet we cannot pass over in silence the following composition, engraved and circulated by friendly hands: *Polonaise pour le pianoforte dédiée à son Excellence Mademoiselle la Comtesse Victoire Skarbek par Frédéric Chopin âgé de 8 ans*. The composer of this Polish dance, eight years of age, is a real musical genius. He is the son of Nicolas Chopin, professor of French language and literature at the Warsaw lyceum. He not only performs the most difficult pieces on the piano with the greatest ease and extraordinary taste, but is also the composer of several dances and variations that fill experts with amazement, particularly in view of the author's youth. If this boy had been born in Germany or France, his fame would probably by now have spread to all nations. May the present notice remind the reader that geniuses are born in our country also, and that they are not widely known only because of the lack of public notice.

This was the first printed comment on Frederic Chopin. So it had come—Frederic was now officially acknowledged a child prodigy. Prince Czartoryski, Count Potocki, Prince Sapieha,

Child Prodigy

Prince Czetwertynski, Viceroy Zajaczek, Prince Lubecki—the cream of Warsaw's nobility—opened their doors to the schoolteacher's son. Prince Radziwill of Poznan, viceroy of the Prussian-annexed part of Poland, also became interested in Frederic and heard him play whenever he visited Warsaw. These illustrious names meant but little to the small boy. In his eyes these people were strangers; he did not understand their snobbery, and his ingenuousness protected him against their flatteries. Yet he had many experiences that might have turned the head of an eight-year-old child.

In the palace of Madame Grabowski, renowned for her brilliant salon, he was called the heir of Mozart. The march that Grand Duke Constantine had enjoyed in his palace was also published, although anonymously. More important, it was played by military bands during the reviews so dear to the heart of the Grand Duke: Frederic often heard his composition performed in an orchestral arrangement, and saw companies, battalions, and regiments marching to its measures.

He was also asked to give a public performance—his first concert. The élite of Warsaw society supported this project, which was organized for the benefit of the local charitable society. Countess Zamoyska, sister of Prince Adam Czartoryski, was the chief sponsor. Julian Ursyn Niemcewicz, the Nestor of Polish writers, personally asked the family to permit Frederic to participate in the event. This renowned poet, who had been Kosciuszko's aide-de-camp during his American sojourn, had a keen mind and a biting tongue. Having observed how the Warsaw ladies went about exploiting the young virtuoso, he wrote a sarcastic comedy in which he ridiculed the zealous philanthropic ladies and their craving for the sensational. In one scene they are shown vying with each other in reducing the age of "the little Chopin," and finally adopting a resolution to announce in the program that the child prodigy would be carried on stage by his nurse.

The concert took place on February 24, 1818, two days after Frederic's eighth birthday. The whole family was in a state of tremendous excitement. The young pianist was dressed in a dark velvet jacket, with a broad white collar, short trousers, and white stockings. His mother stayed at home because of illness.

The foremost scions of Polish aristocracy and wealth were assembled in the auditorium when the diminutive performer walked to the stage with childish gait. His curly hair, the color of burnt straw, fell about his neck. His beautiful arched nose was sharply outlined against his pale face. His limpid brown eyes scanned the audience.

Frederic played a piano concerto by Adalbert Gyrowetz of Vienna, and his technical skill stirred the admiration of his audience. The boy's virtuosity was enhanced by the legend that had been built up about him, and his success was immense, undimmed by any other performance in the varied program. The child prodigy had lived up to the greatest expectations of him.

His mother awaited her son's return with impatience. Nicolas Chopin and Zywny, who had witnessed his triumph, had to describe the entire concert to her from beginning to end. They sat at the table with a bottle of wine, reciting the great names among the audience, and telling over and over again how Frederic looked, how he played, and how he was applauded. Madame Justyna gazed tenderly at her son's small figure, at his pale face, still transfigured with intense excitement, and asked him what the audience had liked best. The answer was unexpected. "The white collar you gave me," he said.

The Chopin household now entered upon a period of prosperity. The boardinghouse had six, sometimes eight boarders. On Thursdays and Sundays there were many guests, with music, whist, and political discussion. Zywny had become a part of the family. He introduced Frederic to the leading musicians of Warsaw. Würfel, famous pianist and teacher, Elsner and Kurpinski, the composers, Jawurek, the conductor, and Soliva, the singing teacher, meant more than the élite of the Warsaw aristocracy to the Chopins. These gentlemen often quarreled among themselves; they were driven by various ambitions and gossiped maliciously about one another. But all of them were under the spell of Frederic's boyish charm, and all their angry jealousies were silenced by the recognition of his phenomenal gift. Würfel often sat with him at the piano, Elsner discussed composition with him, and the others offered various suggestions.

Frederic remained unspoiled by adulation, although he continued to be a focus of public attention. When Maria Feodorovna, the Tsar's mother, came to the Polish capital, the boy was presented to her as the city's famous young prodigy. This was done with the consent, and perhaps on the initiative, of his father. Although Frederic studied at home, he found himself, during the period of the Tsarina's visit to the lyceum, transplanted to Monsieur Nicolas' classroom, where he recited a French poem in tribute to the occasion and offered the imperial guest two polonaises that he had composed.

Frederic attended concerts, plays, and operas, in which he heard such eminent singers as Madame Elsner and Madame Meier. Now commonly referred to as the "new Mozart," the boy was introduced to every visiting celebrity; among these was Maria Szymanowska. a famed pianist and composer, a friend of Goethe, and a frequent visitor to Warsaw. Angelica Catalani, one of the greatest singers of the time, also wanted to hear him play. Frederic played before her, and it so happens that out of all his recitals of that period, this one remained in his memory for all time. The renowned soprano did not conceal her enthusiasm for the youthful virtuoso, and she bestowed upon him a souvenir that made Frederic happy as only a child can be. It was a gold watch, and the inscription on its case read: *Madame Catalani à Frédéric Chopin âgé de dix ans.* à Varsovie le 3 Janvier 1820,

But his staunchest devotee was Grand Duke Constantine. On a day in May, 1820, the Tsar's brother drove through the principal streets of Warsaw in an open carriage, with his young and dazzlingly beautiful bride beside him. After this tour of display, the carriage turned toward Warsaw's outskirts, to the little Belvedere palace, a remodeled former factory building. The populace gazed at the newly wed couple with mixed emotions of fear, sympathy, and admiration. Constantine was well known by reason of his endless military reviews and, worse, his violent, unpredictable outbursts of temper. Any trifle could send him into an uncontrollable rage, and then he would toss about him like a madman and belabor his subordinates. His very appearance was repulsive. People were frightened by his wolflike face, with its sunken nose between enormous cheekbones, and his high, open nostrils; his faded eyes moving restlessly under bristling white eyebrows gave him a demonic expression. These brutish eyes had fallen one day upon a twenty-year-old girl of Warsaw, one of the three step-daughters of the superintendent of the royal castle. He chanced to meet the Grudzinski sisters in the castle courtyard. At sight of the golden-haired Joanna, a delicate creature with blue eyes and long eyelashes, the Grand Duke forgot the demons that tormented him and his wild heart was filled with emotions that no one would have suspected in him.

Constantine was living in separation from his wife Juliana, Princess of Coburg, and in a liaison with Josephine Friedrichs, a Frenchwoman, by whom he had a son, Paul. It is difficult to imagine how he managed to win over Joanna, and even more difficult to believe that his love was not unrequited. He parted with his French mistress and married her off honorably, but kept his son. It must have taken great effort to reconcile the court and his brother—the relations between the two being strained—to his new marriage. The Tsar finally assented to a divorce, to a marriage with a Polish woman, and conferred upon Joanna the title of Princess of Lowicz.

When the door of the Belvedere closed behind the Duke and his bride, no one would have ventured to predict what course the married life of this ill-matched couple would take. Various tales about it circulated in Warsaw. Apparently the savage-minded Duke shortly forgot his love, for mysterious signals came from the silent house from time to time. They were calls for help, and this help was sought in the most unexpected place. A messenger would dash at great speed from Belvedere to the Krakowskie Przedmiescie. A cabriolet drawn by four horses, each bearing a Cossack rider, would stop in front of the lyceum annex. An aide-de-camp of the Grand Duke—Lieutenant Kicki, or Count de Moriolles, Paul's tutor, or General Kuruta, Constantine's closest confidant —would knock at the Chopins' door. These visits did not exactly fill Frederic's parents with enthusiasm, but it was difficult to avert them. The messengers came from the Duchess, and everybody knew why: the Grand Duke was in a fit of temper and could not be placated. Frederic then would go to the Belvedere, sit at the piano, and play. Music affected the Tsar's brother as it affects a snake. This poisonous man would grow calm and humble, charmed by the child's magic. Often, when he heard Frederic playing, he would interrupt whatever he was doing, enter the drawing room, and become oblivious of the rest of the world. Sometimes he sat for long hours next to the player, intoxicated with the music, and completely unlike his usual self.

"Why are you looking upward? Do you read your music on the ceiling?" he once asked Frederic with a smile. A smile was the rarest phenomenon in the Belvedere.

When the Grand Duke's violent mood was allayed, and Frederic had finished his Orphean role, he would return from the other-worldly realms of music to the earth, and play in the park with two children of his age, Paul and the little Countess Alexandrine de Moriolles. This girl was the only attractive being in this uncanny house, where the Grand Duke spread his terror while the Duchess endured its ravages. Paul was tormented by childhood complexes, the tutor was under suspicion of depravity, and the General had the soul of a slave. Frederic liked Alexandrine's company; he played four-handed pieces with her, and befriended her more than anyone else in this sinister circle of power, perversity, and misfortune.

The young virtuoso felt most at ease, however, at his own pine-wood piano, made in the Bucholz factory in Warsaw; the lion of the salons, the boy with the broad white collar, had his real world in the parental home. He continued to practice diligently, never bored with this tiring occupation; he now wrote down his compositions himself, and found his greatest satisfaction in improvisations. These experiments probably represented his first contacts with the creative spirit, and his first excursions into the depths of his being.

At this time he also suffered his first physical ordeal for art's sake. He knew that in order to advance his technique he must be able to stretch a tenth on the keyboard, and he made up his mind to exercise his hands for this purpose. Unable at his age to attain such a great span, he tried to increase the spread of his hand by mechanical means. Every night he fastened wooden wedges between his fingers and went to bed suffering from this painful contrivance. These attempts ended harmlessly in failure. He released his fingers from their self-inflicted torture and saved them from the deformation that Schumann did not avoid in a similar attempt.

The years went by. Frederic's progress amazed everyone, Zywny most of all. The teacher, familiar with every detail of the boy's work, more and more often stood helpless before the enigma confronting him. He rejoiced that he had succeeded in initiating his pupil into the supernatural transparency of Bach. He shared Frederic's enthusiasm for Mozart. They were also agreed about the operas of Rossini and Weber. But there were things before which he was silent, overwhelmed by admiration and awe. This was particularly true in regard to Frederic's improvisations—his inventiveness in creating new themes and the poetic imagination with which he developed them. Zywny listened to them pensively, both proud and sad, and perhaps murmured to himself, "I am no longer of any use here."

During one such lesson, which was more disturbing to Zywny than to the boy, the teacher found on the piano rack a music sheet with a beautifully penned inscription: *Polonaise pour le Pianoforte composée et dédiée à Monsieur A. Zywny par son élève Frédéric Chopin à Varsovie ce 23 Avril 1821.**

The date was significant—it was the feast of St. Wojciech, Zywny's name day. The polonaise itself came as a surprise, but it also, in a sense, symbolized a farewell. The following year it

* The German equivalent for the Polish "Wojciech" is "Adalbert," as often used by Zywny himself; hence the initial "A."

became obvious that the teacher no longer had anything to teach. In the course of six years Frederic had surpassed Zywny as a pianist, and his musical knowledge and skill had outstripped the lifetime experience of the Czech master. The lessons came to an end. But Zywny remained a member of the family. He had his place at the table and was a regular participant in the games of piquet or whist. No family celebration took place without him, and his yellow wig and velvet vest were always conspicuously to be seen in the first row of chairs at the plays and pantomimes that became the children's passion.

The year 1823 brought important developments. Madame Skarbek invited the Chopins to Zelazowa Wola for the summer, and in September Frederic was to go to school.

As far as is known, this was his first vacation in the country. Returned to his birthplace, he probably looked with curiosity upon the manor, the park, the mill, and the Utrata River, so familiar to his parents. The piano that brought back memories of his mother's songs and his father's music-making now became the instrument of their virtuoso son. At Madame Skarbek's behest, it was carried outdoors in the evening and placed under the chestnut trees. The manor residents and their visitors gathered around. Frederic played in the open air, his eyes, as always, turned upward, toward the star-studded ceiling of the world. The fame of these private recitals long remained vivid in the region, and later re-echoed in legends of Chopin.

CHAPTER

5

Discovering Poland

FROM home to school was a matter of only a few steps for Frederic, but this daily walk meant a great change in his life. He wore the regulation student cap and uniform—a spencer jacket reaching almost to his knees, buttoned high at the neck, and belted at the waist. He passed the entrance examination without difficulty and was admitted to the fourth form of the lyceum. He attended this school for three years, from 1823 to 1826, and left it as graduate at the age of sixteen.

What he acquired during these three years was to influence all of his later life. The school and his father's boarding establishment formed one world, in which he found his first friends. His vacations spent away from the city enabled him to become truly intimate with nature and with the Polish countryside. Finally, it was during this period that he felt for the first time what might be called the spirit of the nation.

From that time on, intimate relationships with friends were a deep need of his life. In the country he discovered sources of emotional stimulus that were later reflected in his music, and the fate of his nation became a constant inspiration for his art. Chopin's temperament was formed extremely early, as was the general rule at that time. For romanticism granted adolescence the privileges of mature age. The goal was not to grow up but to remain young. Exaltation was more important than reason, enthu-

38

siasm was valued above experience, passion was elevated above all virtues, and genius manifested itself long before wisdom began to develop. A man's fame came sooner than the first down on his cheeks.

This paradoxical chronology is strikingly reflected in the records of the romantic Muse. Goethe began publishing at the age of sixteen, Byron and Poe at eighteen; de Musset and Pushkin patiently put off to their early twenties their claim to recognition as geniuses. Schiller produced *The Robbers* at twenty-two; Dickens was only twenty-four when he wrote *The Posthumous Papers of the Pickwick Club*. Mendelssohn had several operas and chamber music pieces behind him when, at the age of fourteen, he wrote a symphony; at the age of sixteen he composed his overture to *A Midsummer Night's Dream*. Schumann had founded a musical review and was a renowned critic at the age of twenty-four. Delacroix's first picture made him the standard-bearer of romanticism and the target of attacks from academic painters. Similarly, Mickiewicz, Slowacki, and Krasinski in Poland were young and great simultaneously, and Krasinski wrote one dramatic poem of genius at the age of nineteen and a second at twenty.

At school Frederic found the same warm atmosphere that he had at home and that was always indispensable to him. His classmates did not point him out, for everyone knew him. The lyceum was proud to see its uniform on the boy who was so much sought after in the great city, and who was featured in the newspapers. Although he was thus singled out, this schoolboy hero was free of any tendency to show off, for he was not given to conceit. He had his defects, and no one indulged more readily in boyish pranks. Some of his schoolmates became his lifelong friends. The Kolbergs were his neighbors; music drew him close to Fontana, Woyciechowski, and Matuszynski. Marylski became his echo, and Bialoblocki his first bosom friend.

A diligent student of Polish literature and history, he was bored by mathematics, and his mind wandered in the clouds during the classes in natural science, Greek, and Latin. But even his favorite subjects could not entirely engross his exuberant imagination.

The Life and Death of Chopin

When his teacher discussed the reign of King Ladislas the Dwarf, the student drew a picture of a tiny manikin; and when he reached the chapter dealing with Longinus, the figure of the learned chronicler appeared in his copybook, elongated over a whole page. In the evenings at home, the same subjects stimulated his imagination in an entirely different way: he would open the piano and offer his classmates musical illustrations of the history of Poland. The deaths of young King Ladislas at Varna and of the aged Zolkiewski, commander at Cecora, were rendered so movingly that the boyish group would grow solemn and forget their pranks.

People and their peculiarities stimulated Frederic's wit to an ever greater extent. He was as good at drawing cartoons as he was at imitating the voices, postures, and gestures of his chosen victim. He mimicked his teachers and schoolmates with so much humor that his class often rewarded him with applause. Headmaster Linde became the special target of the young cartoonist. This famous author of the *Polish Dictionary* was of diminutive size; his tiny face pointed like the snout of an anteater, and he looked as if he had been dried and preserved between the pages of the bulky volumes of his work. One day Linde discovered a caricature of himself in Frederic's copybook. He immediately confiscated it, and Frederic felt downcast, expecting a reprimand in school and a scolding at home. To his surprise and joy, however, the headmaster a few days later gave the copybook back to him with a friendly smile. Under the portrait was the annotation, "Well drawn."

About this time a new tutor made his appearance in Nicolas Chopin's boardinghouse. His name was Feliks Zochowski, and it was his task to help the boarding pupils and Frederic with their homework. Frederic's studies with Zochowski, like his earlier studies with his sister Ludwika, were like a game. He was a brilliant pupil, and it soon was conceded that the first prankster in the class was also one of the top students.

Within the family Frederic gained new authority because of his school uniform. Although Ludwika clung to her privileges of seniority, and as of old fell easily into a commanding tone, her superiority was now merely nominal. She played the piano willingly and charmingly, and also composed waltzes and mazurkas; but there was no doubt as to who held supremacy in this field. She surpassed Frederic only in verse writing; her brother decidedly preferred chords to rhymes.

Ludwika's rival in literature was little Emilia, who wrote short poems with extraordinary facility, and was constantly devouring Polish and French books. She was more inventive than her brother and her sisters in staging their children's plays, and she could have supplied all of Warsaw with ideas for *tableaux vivants*. More than that, the ten-year-old girl displayed such intelligence and exquisite taste in everything she did that she, too, was considered an extraordinary child. She was frail, all nerves and feeling; a miniature by a mediocre and unknown painter, which Madame Justyna must have forgotten to throw away, has failed to preserve for posterity anything of this little person's charm. She was prone to illness and often had to be kept in bed, but she always filled the sickroom with merriment and fun. Emilia and Frederic together organized a club called the Literary Entertainment Society, which met in the evenings and was devoted to reciting their own works. When the program ran short of these, the society relegated literature and indulged in childish antics. Frederic was president, Emilia was secretary; the remaining membership consisted of the boarders.

This group of boys and girls soon became a community of close friends. Barcinski, the tutor, wanted to be counted in the student-group intimates rather than among the elders, particularly because his heart was conquered by Frederic's sister Izabela. After classes, the young people often gathered in the Chopins' drawing room, where they played games, while Frederic readily performed for them on the piano. But the audience was not always eager to hear the "new Mozart," preferring the prankster. The musician would then close his piano and metamorphose himself into an actor. By general request, he stretched himself to the giant size of Woyciechowski, shrank to that of Linde the anteater, and thus went through the whole repertory of his classroom mimicry.

When the girls were absent, the boys were so carried away by their high spirits that they could not be controlled. One day, when Monsieur Nicolas was out and the fun grew tumultuous, Barcinski implored Frederic, "For heaven's sake, do something. I am at the end of my rope!"

Frederic sat down at the piano and began a hurriedly improvised tale about robbers, illustrating their breath-taking adventures with music. There was a raid, an escape, and a division of the loot in the woods, until at last night came and time to sleep. The lullaby with which the improviser put the robbers to bed was so effective that his listeners' eyes began to close and their heads dropped one by one. After a while the magician could contemplate his work in triumph. All of them were sound asleep, including the tutor.

The end of the school term was approaching, and Frederic's parents began planning to send him to the country for the summer. They were worried by his emaciated appearance; although he was under constant medical care, he continued to be frail, especially now that he was growing rapidly. They chose from among many invitations the village of Szafarnia, which belonged to the Dziewanowskis, the parents of Dominik, a classmate of Frederic's who boarded with the Chopins. Dziewanowski's name had been made famous throughout Poland by Dominik's uncle, a captain in Napoleon's army, who died during the storming of Somo-Sierra by his company of lancers. The Dziewanowskis were a musical family; the lady of the house and her daughters worshiped the piano, and Frederic looked forward with joy to his vacation in their house.

The lyceum graduation exercises were attended by the representatives of the government. The place of honor was occupied by Bishop Kaliski, and His Excellency the Minister of Religion and Public Education in person read the roll of the pupils who had earned commendations and prizes. Frederic heard the names of classmates cited for honors—Dominik Dziewanowski, Julian Fontana, Wilhelm Kolberg. Then His Excellency named those who had been awarded prizes—Frederic Chopin, Jan Matuszynski.

These prizes brought more honor than pleasure. Frederic's

prize was a book that could easily kill any enthusiasm for study in its new owner by its very title: *Outline of Statistics for the Use of County and District Schools.* On the flyleaf it bore an inscription: *Moribus et diligentiae Frederici Chopin in examine publico Licei Varsoviensi die 24 Julii 1824.*

The next day Frederic was on his way to Szafarnia, which lay northwest of Warsaw. In the manor house he found cordial hosts and a constant solicitude about himself. The regimen for which Madame Justyna had sent along instructions was applied at once. He took the pills he had brought with him to help him to gain weight, drank half a decanter of linden infusion every day, together with six glasses of roasted acorn coffee, as recommended by his doctor, and ate only white rolls baked especially for him. The day began at seven in the morning and was arranged on the principle of as much air and as much exercise as possible. Such were his orders from home, and Madame Dziewanowska observed them scrupulously.

After the customary evening walk, Frederic would sit down at the piano with his hostess and her daughter, whose name was Ludwika, and who emulated his sister in constantly watching over him. His repertory now included a difficult concerto by Kalkbrenner, and to his own compositions he had added a new mazurka dedicated to Wilhelm Kolberg, and another in A minor, named the "Little Jew" mazurka because of a motif representing a dance at an inn. This was the prototype of the later Mazurka in A minor, Opus 17, No. 4.

When he mounted a horse for the first time, he boasted of it in a letter to his parents, writing facetiously: "I am riding on the gray participle of the French verb *connaître.*" (This is an untranslatable pun. The French participle *connu* sounds like the Polish word for horse, *koniu*.) He roamed on horseback over the fields in the vicinity, but he felt safer on his own legs. He walked where his eyes led him, guided by a sense that he had only recently developed—a feeling of closeness to nature and earth.

The harvest began, a period of most intense activity in the village. The reapers, men and women, moved in even lines, bending low, cutting the wheat and oats with their scythes, and sweeping aside the fallen rows in rhythmic movements. At noon food and water were brought to them in earthen pots, and after a short respite they were herded back to work, lest they be overtaken by rain, which was always to be feared. Sometimes a song surged forth from the toilers, as though they were seeking relaxation or incentive in the sound. Frederic absorbed this music thirstily.

"I walk in the woods," he wrote from Szafarnia to Wilhelm Kolberg, and refrained from going into details in order "not to bother you with my concerns." Indeed, he had a concern in the woods. The sun beat down on glades like mysterious graveyards, suffused with the smell of freshly felled trees. Each had a different fragrance—the hazelnut trees had a bitter aroma, the willows had the smell of moldy wood, and the pines that of sour bread, which he was not allowed to eat.

The earth irresistibly attracted him, and he yielded to its fascination all the more easily because the village life was monotonous. The arrival of guests (on one occasion Nicolas Chopin was among them) always caused a great commotion. Everyone rushed out to welcome them on the porch; refreshments were served under the lindens in front of the house. The family liked to visit neighbors, and on such occasions Frederic was honored by being given the best seat in the carriage. These houses enshrined Polish tradition: sabers and family portraits hung on the walls; mahogany furniture glittered with gilded Empire ornament. Here was preserved the style of life of an old nobility, the outward expression of the Polish spirit, full of ostentatious gestures and pride, impulsive but sociable, hospitable to strangers but infatuated with its own land.

Frederic was everywhere cordially received; hence he traveled often and felt at home throughout the whole region. At Obrow, encountering a party of Jewish merchants who had come to the manor to buy grain, he treated them to such a traditional *maiufes* dance that they tucked up their caftans and danced, and finally invited the young player to a Jewish wedding. At Golub, he and Dominik improvised a stage performance in a Protestant church just then under construction. Frederic climbed up on the pulpit and delivered a sermon imitating the broken Polish of the German pastors, while Dominik, standing behind him with his arms in Frederic's sleeves, supplied the gesticulation. The effect was highly comical and greatly enjoyed by the audience, which consisted of the visitors from Szafarnia and the local masons.

Frederic's sense of humor never failed him, and he had an inexhaustible store of jokes. Instead of letters to his mother and sisters, he sent them issues of a pseudo-newspaper, written in his own hand, which he called the *Szafarnia Courier*. His editorial nom de plume was "Pichon." Of this journalistic product, four complete and two incomplete issues have been preserved. The first issue was dated August 16, 1824. The newspaper consisted of a single sheet and contained two columns, one headed "Local News" (covering Szafarnia), the other "Foreign News" (covering the neighborhood). For the sake of historical accuracy, it must be said that the contents of the paper dealt mostly with trifling matters. Nicolas Chopin's visit is recorded in an item stating that "every day he eats four rolls, *nota bene,* in addition to a mighty dinner and a three-course supper."

More interesting are the editor's journalistic indiscretions concerning musical matters. It seems that in Szafarnia Frederic met a good pianist, Madame Lagowska, and a few local piano teachers. One of them, a certain Herr Better from Berlin, as we read, "plays with such feeling that almost each of the sounds he makes seems to issue not from his heart but from his mighty belly." As for Pichon's own successes, the *Szafarnia Courier* appreciates them variously. It reports that he performed "at a musicale attended by a score of persons and half-persons, and played the Kalkbrenner concerto, which, however, impressed the listeners, especially the small ones, less than the 'Little Jew.' " Apparently this latter composition was always popular. When its author played it on another occasion, the *Courier* reports, Dziewanowski called the local innkeeper, a Jew, who declared upon hearing it that "if Mr. Pichon would agree to play at a Jewish wedding, he would earn at least ten thalers."

The Life and Death of Chopin

At the end of August, the *Courier* carried the following story:

On the 29th inst. Mr. Pichon, passing through Nieszawa, heard a Catalani, as she sat on a fence, singing at the top of her lungs. He became so absorbed that although he heard the aria and the voice, he was not satisfied, but tried also to hear the lines. He passed by the fence twice, but in vain, for he could not understand one word. Finally, unable to get the better of his curiosity, he took three pennies out of his pocket and offered the sum to the singer if she would repeat the ditty. For a long while she fidgeted, made faces, and refused, but encouraged by the prospect of the three pennies, she finally consented and began to sing the little mazurka, from which the editor, with permission of the authorities and the censor, quotes only one stanza as a sample:

Look there beyond the hills, how the wolf is dancing!
Alas, he has no wife—that's why he is so downcast. . . .

We also learn from the newspaper that Frederic took part in a local ceremonial called *okrezne*. It was held at Obrow, in the home of Ramocki. Carrying out an old custom, the reapers after the harvest presented their master with wreaths made of grain stalks, as a symbol of the gathered crops. The master in return entertained them with a copious meal. On that day, landowner and servitor met on an equal footing, in a common festival. The whole village gathered in front of the manor, and after the traditional rituals and songs, the peasant band summoned all present to the dance. On the tables set up in the courtyard stood steaming bowls of food; jugs of vodka and apple and plum cordials passed from hand to hand. At first the farmhands were too shy to ask a girl from the manor for a dance, while the young masters did not hesitate to snatch up the prettiest village girls. But in the end everyone was swept up by the excitement, and long-trained silken gowns and starched peasant petticoats whirled all together.

Frederic, who had danced in the salons of counts and princes, was not the worst dancer on the village lawn. But dance was not his element; it tired him fairly soon, and he stood panting on the sidelines. He was, however, under another kind of spell, as intoxicating as spirits. It came upon him from the very air, which rang with the sounds of the peasant band, the choruses, and the solo refrains. Dance upon dance swelled from the violins and bagpipes, the dance leader calling now for a mazurka and now for a *kuja-wiak*. A singer would begin a ditty with laughter and then fall into wailing and sadness. This chaos of melodies that Frederic had never heard before, these intertwining and overlapping rhythms, the false notes of the drunken musicians, and the exuberance of the revelers merged into one vast chord, one great wave of sound.

This peasant ball in the manor courtyard, the feast of the Ceres of the Vistula, continued for many hours, and in the torch light it must have seemed something unreal. The night after such a spectacle, the night of the Polish countryside, when, half asleep, one hears the fruit falling in the orchard with a mysterious thud, and when the smell of the wallflowers comes through the open windows, certainly could not pass without reveries and poetic dreams. It is permissible to assume that one who yields to this magic in his youth will always remain under its spell.

The vacation was at an end. A month and a half in the country had made Frederic taller and stronger, and brought him close to his native soil, which he was never again to forget.

The Patriot

FREDERIC, now in the fifth form, began his new school year in the middle of September, 1824. The boarding establishment was filled to capacity, and the Chopin home bustled with activity as never before. The Literary Entertainment Society entered upon a new stage of development. While literature was somewhat neglected, its entertainments acquired new splendor. The youngsters were seized with a mania for the theater. Frederic and Emilia composed French and Polish charades about their friends, and the audience guessed at the hidden names with curiosity and varying success. The *tableaux vivants* fascinated even the older people, who after a performance were asked to stay for a game of cards. Ludwika looked very touching in the role of the legendary Princess Wanda, who drowned herself in the Vistula rather than marry a German. She was also beautiful as Barbara Radziwill, whom King Sigismund Augustus (played by Frederic) took to wife, although she was not of royal blood.

The latter performance was memorable because it ended with unexpected drama, through the fault of the impersonator of the King. He appeared in a costume that the spectators—to their horror—recognized as Monsieur Nicolas's Freemason garb. Like Elsner, Brodzinski, and Kolberg, Nicolas Chopin belonged to one of the three Masonic lodges in Warsaw, and together with his friends he practiced the forbidden rites. He naturally kept his membership in the organization secret, though he did not consider it reprehensible.

Madame Justyna, who was a very pious Catholic, took a different view of the matter. What the parents said to each other in their closed room that night remained between them. Nevertheless, discipline in the boardinghouse became more rigorous after this incident. The boys marched to church in double file, and Frederic hid away the Bible in which in a frivolous moment he had inscribed his name as "Chochochochochopin." He now played the organ as a well-conducted youth, and together with Jas Matuszynski, a master of the flute, aroused the admiration of the devout. Apparently the trowel and the hammer was not all-powerful with the men who wore this sign, since Elsner too attended church and even directed the lyceum choir during the services.

The incident of the purloined robes had no other consequences of import, and when St. Nicholas' Day came, the professor could celebrate it in keeping with the proudest family traditions. The drawing room was transformed into an auditorium, with chairs and armchairs set up in rows. The numerous guests were tremendously excited when they heard that an entirely new attraction figured on the program of the soiree. The Chopin home theater was presenting a comedy written by Frederic and Emilia Pichon —as we know, Pichon was the nom de plume of the editor of the *Szafarnia Courier*. The play was entitled *The Mistake, or the Pretended Rogue*. The script has unfortunately not come down to us, but on that evening it was a great success, particularly because the authors were also leading members of the cast. The slender Frederic played the paunchy mayor, and Emilia his ethereal daughter. After the performance, when the audience was discussing the play, Emilia emphasized the fact that the comedy was written in verse, and moreover had been turned out by the two authors in a single creative session.

Few Warsaw salons could boast gatherings like those that adorned the salon of the Chopins. Among the visitors were scientists, musicians, poets, actors, all with distinguished names. Elsner and Linde were old friends; Frederic Skarbek, erstwhile pupil of Monsieur Nicolas, a university professor at the age of twenty-six, and author of several important works on law and economics, was almost a member of the family. A frequent visitor at the Chopins' was Casimir Brodzinski, former soldier of Napoleon and then also a professor at the university; he was a champion of romanticism and was now publicizing the poems of a young poet from Wilno, Adam Mickiewicz, who had recently been arrested by the Russians. Frederic was particularly fond of Jacob Frederic Hofman; this friend was in his seventies, but his heart was a half century younger, and he made it a point to associate with youth. Frederic Chopin often dropped in at the professor's apartment in an adjacent building, admired the curios collected there, and played the piano with Madame Hofman or her son, Alexander. The elder Hofman had an exuberant vitality and extraordinary ingenuity, and he suffered from a secret mania for inventions. A passionate naturalist, he founded a mineralogical museum at the university, and through his efforts the vacant lots behind the Casimir Palace were transformed into a botanical garden. His special hobby was to mold plant forms in wax, and he acquired such skill in this pursuit that his artificial ferns and tuberoses were almost indistinguishable from real ones. He invented a device that enabled nonswimmers to traverse a hundred and twenty yards of water in one minute. Unfortunately, in spite of its unique qualities, this invention fell into oblivion. Hofman was more successful with improvements in the musical field. He invented a new instrument, the aeolomelodicon or choraleon, which he asked Brunner, a manufacturer of musical instruments, to construct, and with which he expected to revolutionize music.

Several of these friends of the Chopins' were first-generation Poles, by choice. Linde had a brother in Danzig who was a sincere German. In the home of the professor of geodesy, Julius Kolberg, born in Mecklenburg, German was not spoken; his six children grew up as Poles, and one of his sons, Oscar, devoted his life to collecting Polish songs and folk legends. Hofman, who had come to Warsaw as a young physician, worked in the hospitals during the Kosciuszko insurrection and won the praise of the leader.

The Patriot

Frederic was completely at ease in the circle of his father's friends; he respected their attainments and liked their picturesque characters. From their reminiscences the boy painted for himself a picture of the recent past of Poland; and the endless sufferings of his country, to which these made constant allusion, became deeply engraved in his memory.

Like all of Poland, and like Europe, Warsaw at that time was in ferment with ideas of freedom. Count Novosiltsov, special Russian commissioner in Warsaw, was regarded as a symbol of despotism. He was an exponent of police rule: his spies tried to discover what the people were thinking, and his censors tried to prescribe their thinking. In spite of his sixty-three years, he was unable to control his vices—drinking and debauchery. The nightly adventures of this imperial plenipotentiary, who used to elude his bodyguards when he was drunk and was often found in the morning near the walls of a brothel, with his clothes in tatters, were notorious. Grand Duke Constantine contributed to the growing aversion for the Russian rule. Mounted on a white steed, he would indulge in his favorite pastime, military reviews; but one loose button on a soldier's uniform would suffice to make him behave like an enraged corporal. He occasionally slapped his subordinates in the face, and several of his officers committed suicide after such public humiliation. Novosiltsov and Constantine ignored treaty obligations; the Polish Diet had not been convened for years, and the liberal constitution was gathering dust in the files of the chancellery.

While Tsar Alexander liked to call himself "the liberator of Poland," his rule only fanned the spirit of opposition and revolt. A net of underground organizations—reflecting the revolutionary currents then stirring in many parts of the world—spread ideas of freedom and printed officially suppressed literature. When the police tracked down such secret societies, the conspirators were sent to prison, but their places were soon filled by new conspirators.

The echoes of such incidents reached the Chopins. The lyceum and the university were important centers of the underground movement. The professor's family was deeply affected when the Russian police discovered the patriotic society that had been founded and directed by Major Walerian Lukasinski of the popular Fourth Infantry Regiment. Charged with high treason, imprisoned and tortured for two years, the Major did not reveal the names of his associates and was sentenced by a court-martial to ten years of confinement in a fortress. Two of his companions were sentenced to six years of imprisonment each. By order of Constantine, the three convicted officers, in full dress uniform, were publicly degraded. An executioner clad in black tore off their epaulets and medals and broke their swords. Their heads were shaved, chains were put on their legs, and they were forced to push wheelbarrows filled with stones before the lines of the military. Lukasinski walked this gauntlet with raised head, proud and pale, looking directly into the eyes of the soldiers. The crowd assembled behind the troops wept.

A year after this gruesome ceremony, the Russian authorities made a gesture of conciliation, announcing that the Tsar would come to Warsaw and open a session of the Diet. Some years were still to elapse before the Poles attempted to throw off their yoke in an open revolt. In 1825, the spirit of Lukasinski had not yet swept the whole of Poland. The upper classes—the aristocrats and the wealthy—favored a moderate policy. But among the lower and middle classes, and no less among the youth, a spirit of opposition prevailed. The two contradictory currents found expression on the second floor of the annex of the Casimir Palace. There boys of the upper forms of the lyceum discussed in secret the affair of Lukasinski, while Monsieur Nicolas mourned the mounting wave of arrests but was skeptical of the prospect of foreign help, which was indispensable if Poland was to be liberated.

By the end of April, 1825, when the Tsar arrived in Warsaw, the opposition camp had to admit its defeat. The opening of the Diet attracted many visitors to the capital. The mood of dejection suddenly yielded to a spirit of carnival. Military bands played in the public squares; the houses were brightly lighted. Numerous concerts were announced, the theaters were preparing gala performances, and the palaces of the aristocracy were dressed for gorgeous balls. Prince Radziwill came from Poznan, and the presence of the Prussian king's viceroy in Warsaw during the session of the Diet added fuel to the political debates in the cafés. Then word came from the Belvedere, through the Duchess's ladies-in-waiting, that Tsar Alexander was favorably disposed toward Poland. And true enough, this time the Tsar behaved otherwise than on his two previous visits: he did not avoid contact with Poles, but granted them audiences, and received their petitions.

Brunner, the manufacturer of musical instruments, inquired at the chancellery whether His Majesty would not graciously consent to attend a musical performance featuring Hofman's aeolomelodicon. The Tsar consented, and Brunner and Hofman hastened to the home of the "foremost pianist in town," as Frederic was called. It did not take long to convince Monsieur Nicolas, who always liked to show off his son and had a weakness for courtly performances; but Frederic was not too eager, while his lyceum friends were openly opposed to the whole idea. However, resistance was hopeless; in the patriarchal home of the Chopins it was inconceivable that the son should disobey his father. Moreover, Frederic would have needed a heart of stone to refuse the prayers of Hofman, a frequently disappointed inventor and a cherished friend. The instrument was transported to the Protestant church, where Brunner and Hofman, as Protestants, had some influence, and where the recital was to take place.

The aeolomelodicon was as complicated as its name. It resembled a harmonium, but had a deeper and fuller tone, enhanced by copper tubes. Frederic's hand easily manipulated the mechanism, and with the help of the numerous pedals regulated the volume and resonance of the notes. The young pianist, whom Würfel personally had taught to play the organ in the Church of the Visitation, won the Tsar's favor for the invention, and attracted the monarch's attention to himself. Brunner and Chopin were each rewarded with a diamond ring.

Although the performance in the Protestant church received wide publicity, it had no musical consequences—a fact that obviously could not be mentioned in the presence of Hofman. Worse yet, the aeolomelodicon was soon overshadowed by a more successful rival invention. Dlugosz, a Warsaw cabinetmaker, a friend of the Chopins', contrived a new instrument similar to Hofman's and gave it the no less complicated name of aeolopantalon. Warsaw was introduced to this instrument in a concert at the Conservatory on May 27, 1825. Needless to say, Frederic was the performer. This concert was so successful that on June 10th it was repeated before an audience of a hundred and seventy, who, according to the newspapers, "spent a pleasant evening." Frederic played the allegro movement of Moscheles' G minor concerto, together with some improvisations. The Warsaw correspondent of the Leipzig *Allgemeine Musikalische Zeitung* (perhaps it was Elsner) reported that the concert had "made a great impression," and that "Chopin proved to be a master of the instrument and distinguished himself in his free variations by a wealth of musical ideas."

Dlugosz was overjoyed by his success and had great hopes for the future. He manufactured and sold many aeolopantalons, tried to introduce them abroad, and looked for a market in Paris, but in the end his invention shared the fate of the aeolomelodicon; that is to say, it fell into oblivion.

Warsaw remained faithful to its favorite instrument, the pianoforte. While elsewhere in Poland it was part of a good upbringing to play the Spanish or English guitar, the flute, or the clarinet, the capital was in love with the keyboard. Warsaw had a considerable musical industry. There were thirty factories devoted to musical instruments, of which four produced pantalons and pianofortes. This may not have been as excessive as it seems in view of the fact that there were sixty music teachers, that printed music was sold by nine bookstores, and that there were five concert halls. Be that as it may, Warsaw gave its preference to the pianoforte, and Chopin's fame was later to exalt it to the status of a national instrument.

The daily Warsaw *Courier*, in its issue of June 2, 1825, carried the following advertisement: "A new rondo for the pianoforte,

The Patriot

composed by Frederic Chopin and dedicated to Madame Linde, has been published by A. Brzezina, lithographers. Price, 3 zlotys."

The publication of the Rondo in C minor by the most important music dealer in Warsaw made Frederic a full-fledged composer. He was introduced to the public at large; he was no longer sponsored merely by friends but by a publisher. Dreams no longer counted; from now on work was all that mattered. The rondo was marked Opus 1. In it, the fifteen-year-old composer spoke in his own voice, and this was considered the most important fact. True, critics discovered traces of Weber and Hummel in this work, but what composer has ever concealed his masters and favorites in his first opus?

At about the same time, Chopin's Mazurka in G major and the Mazurka in B-flat major appeared in a more modest edition, without mention of the publisher and without opus number. The bravura of these youthful pieces, which reflected an individual interpretation of the songs and dance tunes that Frederic had heard at Szafarnia, won him a first compliment from the rigid Warsaw musical experts. They reproached the daring young man with offending their ears by violating "all the rules of musical grammar."

Frederic waited with impatience for the end of the school term. He had experienced a great deal during this period; the classes bored him somewhat, and he yearned to be alone and to enjoy the charms of summer in the country. His recent concerts and compositions had made it clear that he should devote himself entirely to music. Elsner insisted that he must do so, and Skarbek went even further, trying to convince Monsieur Nicolas that he should send Frederic abroad at once. But the young student would not have any of this. "I am going to the country," was his answer to all suggestions, and he exchanged smiles with Dziewanowski. The magnet of the earth attracted him to familiar haunts.

The three-day graduation exercises were held with even greater solemnity than they had been the year before. Among the fifth-form students who received commendations were Chopin, Fontana, and Magnuszewski. This time there were no book prizes, no *Out-*

line of Statistics, a circumstance that Frederic could not help mentioning with some sarcasm.

At long last he found himself at Szafarnia, amidst rolling country and sun-baked fields. In the morning he was awakened by the whistling of blackbirds, and a day of laziness began. He said that he was living in clover and fattening like a pig on acorns. He rode more often and with greater skill than in the summer before; he was promoted to the rank of an adult, and together with Dominik was included in hunting parties. He wrote to his friend Matuszynski, who had gone to Pulawy and was also engaged in hunting, that he had left the field with one rabbit and four partridges strapped to his belt.

He was resting. He played and dreamed. Only a small waltz has been preserved from that period; this he intended to send to his sisters, but he had no time to copy it. He was just leaving for Danzig—this was one of the many journeys of that summer.

"Today at Plock, tomorrow at Rosciszew, the day after at Kikol, a few days at Turzno, a few days at Kozlow," he wrote his family, outlining the itinerary of this longer than usual rambling expedition. In all these places he would be welcomed to manor houses situated amid ponds, linden rows, and orchards; he would find cupboards filled with the fragrance of coffee and apples, people full of jollity and vigor, customs peculiar to each family, and the spirit of the Polish squires that was common to them all.

He made his longest stop in Torun, which at that time belonged to Prussia; it was a city of red-brick houses, granaries, Gothic churches, world-renowned for its ginger cakes and its association with Copernicus. Frederic visited the great astronomer's homestead, but felt far from edified when he found it to be now the residence of a German, whom he described in a letter to his friend Bialoblocki:

Imagine, dear Jas, in a corner of the room where the famous astronomer came into the world, there stands the bed of some German who no doubt, after he has stuffed himself with potatoes, sprawls himself there and vents some zephyrs. These are the very bricks of which one was sent to Pulawy with great ceremony; the rest here are crawling with bedbugs.

After his return to Poland he stayed only a short time in Sza-farnia, absorbing as much of its charm as he could. He came back to Warsaw invigorated and full of energy. The sixth form of the lyceum would require more diligent work than the terms that had gone before; at the end of it he would receive his bachelor's diploma, the dream and the nightmare of all students. At home, he was given the usual exuberant welcome. Ludwika played him a mazurka of her own composition, of which he said, "It's excellent. It's a long time since Warsaw has danced to such a tune!"

Emilia initiated him into her great theatrical projects for the fall and winter seasons, and they proceeded to carry out these plans at once. The young pianist, composer, and draughtsman rose to the apogee of his stage career. It goes without saying, he played only leading parts and excelled in comedy. Piasecki, a local actor who assisted the young people in staging their plays, urged Frederic to leave everything and go on the stage. Hervé, a member of the French company playing in Warsaw (for Warsaw could not do without a permanent French stage), witnessed a truly bold undertaking when the young Chopins gave their own version of a play that the French theater was then producing. Frederic was cast in the role of a *nouveau riche* merchant who was trying to imitate the manners of a nobleman; it was the very part played in the French theater by Hervé, who at this performance sat as a spectator between Monsieur Nicolas and Madame Justyna. This risky feat came off unexpectedly well. The Frenchman con-gratulated Frederic on his talent and especially admired his hilarious mimicry of a tailor's motions at his work.

On December 1, 1825, Alexander I, Tsar of Russia and King of Poland, died in distant Taganrog. Rumor had it that he had suc-cumbed to cholera. A period of official mourning began. Some citizens wore black; others received the news of the Emperor's death without regret. In the underground it served as a spur to renewed struggle against the Russian oppressor. The Christmas holidays, which the Chopins this year spent at Zelazowa Wola, brought still more exciting news. In St. Petersburg, a group of Russian officers had launched the Decembrist revolt. It was said that the Russians who had become familiar with life in the West during the invasions of Germany and France in the final phases of Napoleon's retreat had returned infected with European ideas of freedom. But the uprising was quickly crushed, the leaders were sentenced to death, and the most powerful police in the world soon unearthed the lists of conspirators who lived far from St. Petersburg. It became clear that the Polish hatred of oppression and violence could be shared by Russians.

The Chopins returned to Warsaw worried and depressed. The discovery of new Polish plots unleashed the frenzied zeal of Novosiltsov's spies. When the dungeons of the Carmelite monastery proved insufficient to hold the patriots arrested in the dark of the night, the cellars of the city hall and of the Bruhl palace were transformed into prisons. The difficult year of 1826 began: January and February brought an uninterrupted sequence of dates of despair, there were so many arrests, so many acts of violence and despotism. In the lyceum and the university the excitement could hardly be suppressed; the populace openly manifested its feelings. Memorial masses were held for the victims of Suvorov's massacre in Praga. The funeral of Staszyc, the great patriot who bequeathed his lands to the peasants, served as the occasion for a national demonstration. Twenty thousand people took part in it. The pall covering the coffin was torn to shreds by the mourners who carried off the pieces as relics. One such memento was preserved by Frederic.

It was only after the six-week period of official mourning ended that black clothes were seen conspicuously throughout Warsaw. Madame Justyna and Ludwika also wore black. This was the Polish mourning. The students manifested their sympathy with the patriots by wearing a white piping on their uniforms.

The Patriot

Frederic was busy leafing through piles of music; as he said, he was buried in hundreds of Hummels, Rieses, and Kalkbrenners. But all this did not make him forget what was going on. Poland's martyrdom was one of his first experiences; it became an inseparable part of his view of the world. He reacted to the events with the sensitivity of an artist, and locked his experiences within himself like intimate secrets. This secrecy later became part of his psychological make-up—he protected his emotions with a veil of discretion. He engaged in everyday pursuits all the more readily because this helped him to conceal his inner state. Every Sunday he played the organ in the Church of the Visitation; he jokingly referred to himself as the "lyceum organist." He took up skating, and shortly suffered an accident, cutting his head in a fall. He also tried dancing during the carnival season, and the result was illness, swollen glands, and treatment with leeches applied to the throat.

When summer came he realized with relief that the final examination was at hand. He set to work diligently. It was fashionable for students to study in the botanical garden, while walking with an open book along the acacia-lined avenues, set out in English style. However, Frederic was seen there not only with a book, and not always alone. He had frequent trysts there with a girl; concerning her, the betrayer of this secret, Eugene Skrodzki, says only in his memoirs that she was the young student's first love—a distinction that had seemed to belong to Alexandrine de Moriolles, whom Frederic's classmates regarded as the object of his fancy. According to Skrodzki, Monsieur Nicolas one day came to the park to see his son. Perhaps he would have found him in the acacia avenue had it not been for Skrodzki, who, desiring to shield the supposed lovers, declared to Monsieur Nicolas that he had not seen his son.

However that may be, the dutiful student presented himself for the examination well prepared and was graduated with honors from the sixth form and the lyceum. He did not apply for admission to the university because it had been decided that he was to continue his studies at the Conservatory. The Warsaw *Courier* of

August 6, 1826, in a belated account of the exercises, mentions that Frederic received a book prize. The title of this book remained unknown—and it scarcely arouses curiosity, in view of the nature of the previous award in this category. It seems more important to state that on July 27th Frederic discarded the uniform of the Warsaw lyceum, the only one he ever wore. It still had its white piping.

Pupil and Master

FREDERIC spent his first evening in mufti with Wilhelm Kolberg, attending a performance of Rossini's *La Gazza ladra* at the National Theater. Kolberg was enthusiastic about it. On the following day Frederic left with his mother, Ludwika, and Emilia for the Silesian spa of Reinerz. Doctor Malcz had ordered the trip. Frederic had again grown thin, and Emilia was pitifully emaciated. Izabela stayed at home with her father, to look after the household. Madame Justyna was going with the children to take care of them, with Ludwika as her helpmate.

On the day of departure, July 28, 1826, Frederic handed Wilhelm a sheet of music on which the ink had hardly dried. It was entitled "Good-by!" and based on an aria from Rossini's opera, *La Gazza ladra*. It was a new polonaise, a farewell to his friend.

The trip through Kalisz and Wroclaw took seven days. Two weeks after his arrival in Reinerz, Frederic described in a long letter the splendors and miseries of a resort visitor's life. It began at six in the morning with drinking the water of the Laubrunn spring. Until eight o'clock the patient walked in the main *allée* of the resort. Breakfast was followed by another walk, then came lunch served at noon. After lunch there was another trip to the spring, then again a walk, consuming the time until nightfall. This was the fixed pattern of day after day. A mediocre brass band, hounding the ears of the guests from morning to night, provided the only diversion in this spiritless ritual. Confined to such a quarantine of boredom, Frederic vented his spleen on the other inhabitants of the place. "The bassoonist," he wrote, "might be a scarecrow for frightening ladies who are afraid of horses, and the promenading guests are carnival masks." He was not permitted any escape from all this. He was forbidden to make excursions into the mountains, whose wonders he had heard of, and whenever he ventured even on a much less strenuous expedition, he returned exhausted. He suffered because no good piano was available, as he complained in a letter to Elsner. But he comforted himself with the thought that he was recovering strength, and in the same letter reported that he was "quite different" as compared with his state in Warsaw.

This Silesian trip would be of no importance were it not for the fact that Frederic gave two public concerts in Reinerz. These were his first recitals beyond the borders of Poland.

The project was arranged on Frederic's own initiative, with the help of his mother and Ludwika. According to an unverified but plausible account, Frederic had become interested in a pretty Czech girl, Libusha, who waited on the guests at the spring, where he met her daily. Her father worked in a foundry, and the girl took the place of her dead mother in their household. One day Frederic did not find her at the spring, and learned that her father had been killed by an iron roller that had crushed his lungs. Libusha had not even enough money to pay for the funeral, and the concert was undertaken as a benefit for her and her brothers and sisters. The spa auditorium was filled to capacity, the concert had to be repeated, and its purpose was achieved.

How Frederic succeeded in this enterprise, with only a nondescript piano at his disposal, remains a mystery. Perhaps he did not take his recital too seriously; at all events, he did not mention it in a letter to Kolberg written two days later.

The cure lasted over five weeks. On September 11th, when the family started for home, the wearied patient was beside himself with joy. In Wroclaw he presented Elsner's letters of introduction to two local celebrities, Schnabel and Berner, and for several days enjoyed a friendly association with them.

Upon his return to Warsaw, he registered for the courses in harmony, counterpoint, and composition at the Conservatory. The curriculum provided for seven hours a week of these studies; the class in theory, held in the university building, was limited to one hour; the practical exercises, held in the Conservatory building, occupied six hours.

When Frederic came to the opening class, he found there, of all his old friends, only Fontana. Tytus Woyciechowski had registered in the law faculty, and Jas Matuszynski was taking up medicine. But Frederic did not feel ill at ease in the great university auditorium. The short plump gentleman whose serene countenance looked down on him from the rostrum was an old friend. Elsner was not his teacher in the same sense as Zywny had been. He was much more. After six years of piano lessons and the three years at the lyceum, during which he studied music alone, Chopin now passed under the tutelage of a man who was to introduce him into the very heart of music. Even then he was more interested in composition than in the art of piano playing, and all his knowledge of composition was to come from Elsner.

Chopin realized that actually Elsner epitomized the Conservatory. He had even heard that Elsner was the most complete expression of all of contemporary Polish music. Indeed, his status was unique. He was revered as a great composer; the opera at the National Theater lived by him; the entire country played and danced his mazurkas. His compositions included every possible form—opera, melodrama, ballet, symphony, sonata, Mass, oratorio, passion, cantata, chamber music. His works were strictly in the style of the period; they were born of the spirit of Simon Mayer and Ferdinand Paër.

When Chopin entered the Conservatory, Jozef Ksawery Elsner was fifty-seven years old, and had lived thirty-four years in Poland. He was born in Grodkow, Silesia, of a family regarded as German. He himself thought otherwise. Somewhat in the style of the *Ursprung der musikalisch-Bachischen Familie*, the genealogy

of Johann Sebastian Bach, the thirty-second of thirty-eight Bachs
who were musicians, Elsner wrote a genealogy of the Elsners. He
claimed that his family had originated in Sweden, and that he was
a descendant of the royal Vasas. According to his account, his
Swedish ancestor had come to Poland in 1699, married a Polish
girl, and become the progenitor of a family that eventually became widely ramified with branches in Poland, Ruthenia, and
Prussia. He stressed his royal origin by using a seal representing
a knight leaning on two shields: on one was engraved a bull's
head surmounted by a plume and a five-pointed coronet; on the
other was the monogram "J.E."

Jozef's father, a manufacturer of musical instruments, wanted
his son to become a clergyman, and he was enrolled as a student
of theology in Wroclaw. The curriculum required him to learn
Polish, the language spoken by the natives of this ancient Polish
province then belonging to Prussia. From Elsner's memoirs we
learn that this linguistic problem led to many complications in
his life. The young theology student refused to learn Polish and
shifted to medicine; at the same time he began to study harmony
with Foerster, a popular Wroclaw musician. This whole the-
ologico-medical experiment came to an end abruptly when he
went to Vienna and discovered that he was a musician. For one
year he served as first violinist in the orchestra of the theater of
Brno, Moravia. At the age of twenty-three he was appointed conductor of the opera of Lwów, and there the subsequent course
of his life was decided. In this city of beautiful parks and beautiful women, the blood of his ancestors and a feeling for the language
he had so passionately refused to learn awakened in him. What
theology could not achieve was achieved by Clara Abt, afterward Madame Elsner. During his seven years' stay in Lwów he
wrote five of his twenty-seven operas, all of them using Polish
librettos. He came to Warsaw to assume the direction of the opera,
and the many years of his comprehensive work won him the title
of creator of Polish music.

Frederic did not exploit his friendship with Elsner, although
he naturally could count on it. He was late in beginning his course,

but no one recorded, then or afterward, how many hours he did not attend. His classmates sensed his superiority; they were not jealous when Elsner showed him exceptional favors. As an intelligent teacher, the Conservatory professor was no slave of routine; he applied a special method in Frederic's case and tolerated his pupil's innovations. He did not, however, renounce his personal tastes; like the other students, Frederic was required to write classical sonatas—his master's favorite genre—and countless Masses with choral and orchestral scores. He submitted only reluctantly to exercises in orchestration; they left no room for the sweeping, colorful harmonies that spoke spontaneously to his innovating spirit at the keyboard. In routine work he even lagged behind his classmates, who deluded themselves with the belief that quick assimilation of ready-made formulas means development.

He was, however, unsurpassed in the practical expression of his own inspirations. On neatly and beautifully written sheets he brought Elsner mazurkas, polonaises, and waltzes. These gave rise to a peculiar kind of lessons—hours of intimate discussion and suggestion, discussion between youth and experience, between inspiration and science. Chopin thus obtained the kind of help that is most important for a creative artist—certainty as to things that were uncertain to him, and the ability to judge for himself.

Jozef Elsner was liked by all his students. Each year the Conservatory celebrated St. Joseph's Day in its own special fashion. One of the students would write a poem in honor of the teacher, another would set it to music, and the whole group would sing it as a choral tribute in front of the director's office or at his home. Frederic was not among the name-day composers; he preferred to appear as a chorister.

The director's house was full of music and friends. His second wife was a star of the Warsaw opera, and their daughter Emilia, who had begun to study singing, was already a fairly good pianist. The students of the Conservatory had no musical secrets from these two ladies, who were usually the first to hear their compositions, and the Elsners' piano was in constant use. It was played by Frederic and the very talented Nidecki brothers; Antoni Orlowski played the violin, and Ignacy Dobrzynski would come to present his new compositions. These informal tests and practical exercises were a prime source of pleasure to both the hosts and their guests. Elsner was pleased that the young people came to him, and would welcome each one with a kiss on both cheeks.

Aside from his studies at the Conservatory, Frederic attended the lectures of Brodzinski and Bentkowski at the university, choosing subjects connected with music. To the languages he knew—Polish, French, and German—he added Italian, by means of lessons with a private tutor. His love for theater and opera was as vital as it had always been; he would not miss one new work. Mozart, Rossini, and Weber made their appearance on the playbills at that time. However, these predilections could not be indulged without some sacrifice. The old building of the National Theater was cold and drafty, the lamps dropped oil on the heads of the audience, and the stage was darker than the auditorium. In the autumn sleet storms, the return home was like an ocean crossing in almost complete darkness. Some aid was provided by night guides—these were most often old Napoleonic veterans. Lantern in hand, they steered their charges homeward through the pools of water, often carrying them on their backs. Frederic must have been one of their lightest loads. In those days his health was not of the best; he had again lost weight, and, as he himself said, the air of Warsaw did not agree with him. Doctor Malcz again threatened him with exile abroad and a Silesian spa.

"Wouldn't it be better for me to go to Paris?" he wrote wistfully in his letters. "When shall I finally get there? In how many years? Fifty?"

At home he was kept on a strict diet. He was made to consume emetic waters and oatmeal, which he hated. He caught cold so easily that his mother kept him indoors in bad weather.

The great solemnities of Christmas were observed as usual in a happy mood, but shortly afterward ominous clouds gathered over the Chopin home. In the middle of February, 1827, Emilia fell gravely ill. Frederic wrote to Bialoblocki: "She had a cough, then began to spit blood, and Mother became frightened. Malcz ordered bloodletting. She was bled once, twice; they applied countless leeches, vesicatories, sinapisms, wolfsbane; it's trouble no end. Throughout this time she has not eaten anything; she has grown so emaciated that she is not recognizable, and only now she is beginning somewhat to be herself. You can imagine what was going on in our home. Do imagine it, because I cannot describe it to you."

This letter announcing an improvement was written in March, 1827. As is evident from the remedies that were applied, treatment of tuberculosis at that time served only to accelerate the end. Less than a month later Emilia was dead. Her tombstone in the Powazki cemetery bears the following inscription:

Emilia Chopin,
passed away in the fourteenth spring of her life,
like a flower blossoming
with the hope of a beautiful fruit.
April 10, 1827

The family was inconsolable. The sisters again donned their somber mourning attire, and Madame Justyna from that time on never wore anything but black. When the Chopins had to give up their apartment because it was needed by the university, they left it with no regrets. They moved to new quarters in the Krasinski palace, situated almost opposite the university and the lyceum. Frederic waited impatiently for the end of his classes, when he could leave Warsaw. He passed his examinations in the middle of July. Elsner wrote in his annual report on "the lessons in composition and counterpoint" that Frederic was distinguished by "special ability."

He left the city with relief. This time he went to the village of Strzyzewo, in Poznan province, where he had been invited by his godmother, Anna Skarbek, now Madame Wiesiolowska. There, physically exhausted, dejected by his first intimate experience of death, he could once more roam the fields and breathe the country air. A welcome diversion were his trips, the longest of which took him for a second time to Danzig, where he stayed for a short time with Linde's brother.

He had a great deal of music during this vacation. Prince Radziwill was spending the summer near Strzyzewo on his estate Antonin, where Chopin visited him with the Wiesiolowskis. There he met the Princess, who was of German birth, a niece of King Frederick II; there were also two Radziwill daughters, Eliza and Wanda, both very musical. The Prince, a dilettante in the best sense of the word, played the cello, sang tenor, and composed music to Goethe's *Faust*. For many years he was sincerely and deeply interested in Frederic's development. Some writers maintain that Radziwill paid the cost of Frederic's studies and supported him financially, but this is a legend without foundation. It is possible that the child prodigy's recitals in aristocratic salons were rewarded with more than applause, and that Madame Catalani's gold watch was not the only expensive memento he received. It is also possible that the princely lover of music, who was particularly fond of Frederic's delicate art, displayed greater munificence than others in remunerating his performance. But there is no valid reason for attributing to Antoni Radziwill the role that was the paternal prerogative of Nicolas Chopin.

Frederic began his second year in the Conservatory in October, 1827. He quickly set to work, but, as in his first year, he was averse to following the classical rules, and once again met with difficulties in the domains of orchestration and vocal music. In these genres he was hampered by technical routine; he did not go beyond the accepted style, and felt that he did not have much to say in this language. He confided his anxieties to Elsner, but even the director of the Conservatory was unable to dispel his doubts or to encourage him. At times Elsner rated Frederic as less able than Dobrzynski and Nidecki; then again he was dazzled by the young pianist's inventiveness and looked with complaisance on his compositions, in which he found grave sins against the commandments of harmony. In some respects, however, he was unyielding. He was stubborn when it came to vocal music, and considered opera the peak of the composer's craftsmanship. His pupil, though he worshiped musical spectacles, turned a deaf ear to these suggestions. To those who criticized Frederic's independence, Elsner always answered, "Let him alone. True, he does not follow the usual path, but then his talent is not usual either. You say he does not stick to the routine methods, but he has his own, and unless I am mistaken, he will be judged by his originality."

From the vast universe of music that Frederic's studies opened before him, the piano began to emerge as a world apart. He was conditioned in this respect also by his compositions, which linked him ever more closely with his favorite instrument. Among these was his set of variations on a German song entitled *Schweizerbub'*, which he is said to have written without effort, in less than a hour, during a visit to the home of General Sowinski. Chopin liked the latter's company, often visited him, and played four-handed compositions with the aged General's wife. Sowinski, a hero haloed with legend, gray-haired, with a noble face, would hasten to welcome him; he walked tapping the floors with his wooden leg, a memento of Napoleon's expedition to Moscow.

In addition to these somewhat schoolboyish variations, he wrote the much more original Rondo in F major à la Mazur (Opus 5), dedicated to Countess Alexandrine de Moriolles, whom he called the "little devil." In the same period he wrote also his two salon waltzes, in A-flat major and E-flat major, which were later inscribed in the album of Elsner's daughter. In his Polonaise in D minor (published posthumously as Opus 71, No. 1) he gave expression to a mood of his own, although he did not avoid some influence of Weber. The beautiful Mazurka in A minor (Opus 68, No. 2) is unmistakably individual in character.

In this year also Frederic tried his hand for the first time at composing a nocturne; up until then this form had been the exclusive domain of John Field, an Irish-born composer. But his Nocturne in E minor did not satisfy him and was published only posthumously (Opus 72, No. 1).

At the end of 1827, probably in response to Elsner's urgings that he venture beyond the keyboard, Frederic wrote his Variations in B-flat major for piano and orchestra (Opus 2) based on the duet "Là ci darem la mano" from Mozart's *Don Giovanni*. He also worked, under his teacher's affectionate eye, on his Sonata in C minor (Opus 4). Both these works suggest that he was wrestling with himself and asking his muse whither to go and whom to obey—the professional canons or his own still indistinct inspirations. The variations that he wrote to demonstrate his virtuosity proved most beautiful in their poetic passages, where the poet forgot about the virtuoso. But the orchestral accompaniment betrayed to the whole world what Chopin whispered to Elsner, namely, that such work was not to his taste. The sonata even more clearly reveals Chopin's youthful uncertainty.

In February, Brzezina published the Rondo dedicated to Countess de Moriolles. Frederic worked indefatigably. He began to compose his Trio in G minor for violin, cello, and piano (Opus 8), dedicated to Prince Radziwill. He also sketched the Rondo in C major for two pianos (Opus 73), and spent a great deal of effort on it. He was so absorbed in his work that only the arrival of Hummel, the well-known pianist, wrested him away from his manuscripts. Needless to say, he did not miss even one of the concerts given by this pupil of Mozart and Haydn, who was also a colleague of Beethoven. Frederic met Hummel personally, and saw him several times at receptions.

Even before the end of the school year he left for the country, going this time to Sanniki, an estate of his friends named Pruszak. When Elsner was citing Frederic's "special ability" in his annual report, the young musician was visiting unfamiliar villages, listening to peasant songs, and revising his Rondo for two pianos.

Meanwhile the variations on a theme from *Don Giovanni* and the sonata had been sent abroad, to a Viennese publisher, Haslinger, who promised to print them. Frederic dedicated these two works to close friends—the sonata to Elsner and the variations to his beloved Tytus Woyciechowski. Upon his return from Sanniki, he wrote to Tytus about it in tender words: "Such was the wish of my heart, friendship did not object, and you do not take it amiss."

This period of exuberant creative work was suddenly interrupted. A friend of Nicolas Chopin, Feliks Jarocki, professor of natural history at the University of Warsaw, was invited to an international congress of naturalists in Berlin, which was held under the patronage of King Friedrich Wilhelm III. The chairman was Alexander von Humboldt, famous traveler and explorer, whose thirty-volume work describing his scientific discoveries in Central and South America had contributed a great deal of material to science, from botany to astronomy. Nicolas immediately thought of his son, on whom the family's entire solicitude had been centered since Emilia's death. Frederic's career required as much effort and concern as his health. His practical-minded parents realized that in Poland a musician without international reputation had little chance of success. The time was ripe for establishing contacts with the outside world. A trip to Berlin, it seemed to the Chopins, would provide an excellent opportunity. They counted on Prince Radziwill's help in making the proper connections.

Thus, soon after his return from Sanniki, Frederic began to prepare for a journey abroad. In Berlin he hoped to meet Spontini, Mendelssohn, and Zelter, and to hear Paganini; he also looked forward to seeing Radziwill, and expected to attend several plays.

Accompanied by Jarocki, he left on September 9, 1828. The journey by mail coach took five days—a severe endurance test for Frederic, which, however, was passed successfully. The two travelers from Warsaw put up at the Kronprinz Inn. But the composer of the Rondo in F major and the author of the treatise on *Spinning Spiders* were denizens of two different planets. When Frederic craved opera, the professor took him to a meeting of the congress; and on the day of a recital by a nine-year-old violinist, Birnbach, Frederic had to be satisfied with a banquet of elderly scholars. He was saved from dejection by his sense of humor. Without respect for the dignity of the botanists and the merits of the zoologists, he drew caricatures of these eminent personages, amassing a whole portfolio of such souvenirs. He had a keen eye for comical traits, and even Alexander von Humboldt in his uniform of a royal privy councilor seemed to him the figure of a valet. However, Jarocki did not impose the congress on his youthful companion for all of the time, and Chopin succeeded in escaping most of the official functions, for, as he said, he never liked to be in a place that was not his own.

He attended five operas—Spontini's *Cortez*, Cimarosa's *Il matrimonio segreto*, Onslow's *Colporteur*, Weber's *Freischütz*, and Winter's *Das unterbrochene Opferfest*. His impression of the singers was not altogether favorable, and many of the ladies reminded him of the Warsaw "screech owls." He was most enthusiastic about Handel's *Ode for St. Cecilia's Day*, which, he wrote, "comes close to the ideal I have formed of great music."

He was disappointed in his hopes of new musical acquaintances. "I saw Spontini, Zelter, and Mendelssohn," he wrote, "but I did not speak with any of them, because I was too timid to introduce myself." Prince Radziwill did not come to Berlin, nor did Paganini. In the way of musical contacts, all Frederic did was to visit two piano factories and the Schlesinger bookstore, where he glanced through musical publications unavailable in Warsaw. He also visited the university library, where he met Falkenstein, biographer of Kosciuszko, giving him some help in deciphering and translating one of the Polish hero's letters. He spent a good deal of time wandering in the city, which seemed to him big enough to contain twice its actual number of inhabitants. All told, his two weeks in Berlin fell far short of his father's expectations, but Frederic enjoyed his stay and did not feel frustrated.

Jarocki and Chopin set out for Warsaw via Poznan. In the diligence they had as companions three Germans, who so tired them with their political discussions and the smoke from their pipes that they could not sleep at night. Frederic moved to an outside seat of the coach, and soon was joined by the professor. Beyond Frankfurt an der Oder they stopped at the post station of Sulechow to change horses. But it turned out that they would have to wait some time for the fresh horses. This distressed Frederic, who was anxious to get back to Warsaw, and who still had to stop in Poznan to pay visits to Prince Radziwill and Archbishop Wolicki. With Jarocki he went to see the town, but they found nothing interesting either in the streets or on the old battlefield. When on returning to the station they saw that the horses had not yet come, they resignedly entered the adjoining inn and to their surprise discovered a piano there. It was a battered old instrument, probably a veteran of many dancing parties held by the postmaster-innkeeper's family. The diligence passenger tried the keys; and the old instrument sounded far better than it looked. Frederic sat at the keyboard, and the wayside inn resounded with a music never before heard within its walls. What he played was probably the germ of his future Grand Fantasy on Polish Airs. Guests of the inn, one old resident of the town, and fellow-passengers filed into the room, followed by the astonished postmaster, his wife, and his two daughters. The concert continued; the old piano played everything that the young hands commanded. The audience was enraptured, when suddenly the postilion burst in, shouting, "The horses are ready!"

Frederic stopped and rose from his seat, but his audience insisted that he go on playing. In vain did he explain that he was in a hurry, that he was expected in Poznan. The postmaster embraced him and reassured him: "You won't be late. I'll see to it that you get a special coach."

The postmaster's wife joined in the entreaties, and finally the two daughters came up to him. "They are pretty," he thought, and sat down at the piano, once again extracting ineffable magic from the sturdy old box. The concert lasted for a long time. Finally the postmaster's wife bethought herself of hospitality; her daughters brought wine and cakes, and the postmaster drank Frederic's health. It is reported that the elderly native, who turned out to be the local organist, came to him and said, "I am old now, but I know what good music is. If Mozart had heard you, he would have pressed your hand and shouted, 'Bravo!' It would not be proper for me to do so."

Frederic was exhausted; the performance had lasted for more than two hours. He played another mazurka and rose to take leave. The girls loaded him with sweets, and the postmaster carried him to the coach. The people at the inn waved their hands in a long salute after the diligence carrying the magician away in the autumn mist.

In Poznan the two travelers visited Prince Radziwill, with whom Frederic played chamber-music pieces for cello and piano. He also played duets with Klingohr, the piano teacher of the princesses, and concluded with improvisations. They dined with Wolicki, archbishop of Gniezno, a relative of the Skarbeks, and after a two-day visit hurried posthaste to Warsaw, where they arrived on October 6th.

Frederic probably lost no time in resuming his studies; Elsner had begun his course at the end of September. This third and last year at the Conservatory (1828-1829) was merely a formality. Chopin had outgrown the school. His practical exercises always ended with a rambling off into his own compositions, and the lessons in theory wound up in intimate conversations with Elsner. The director had given the student everything he had to bestow on him. He had not broadened the range of Chopin's interest; on the other hand he had confirmed the young composer in his originality and made him feel sure of his own bold ideas. Elsner realized that he was dealing with a strongly marked individuality, one that would never submit to classical rules and that would seek its own mode of expression. In the end the teacher only helped Chopin to become Chopin. He was probably thinking of himself and Frederic when he repeated his favorite saying: "It is a bad master who is not surpassed by his pupil."

Triumph in Vienna

IN THE fall of 1828, Frederic's parents arranged a studio for him in the attic of their house. Now he was living the independent life of a young man of eighteen. He was passionately interested in the theater, and attended opening-night performances of plays of Corneille, Racine, Shakespeare, Molière, and Schiller. He also frequented the cafés. At Madame Brzezicka's—which had a colorful atmosphere because of its waitresses in Cracow folk costumes—he read foreign periodicals; at the Little Hole he met with a coterie of romanticists, iconoclasts, and revolutionaries whose leading spirit was Maurycy Mochnacki, a young critic and pianist. Nor did he neglect the salons; when Madame Pruszak staged a performance of the French comedy *Les projets de mariage* in her home, she invited the well-known amateur actor Frederic Chopin to play the lead. In the household of Count Wodzinski he was the idol of the three boys of the family, whom he had befriended in his father's boardinghouse. Ostensibly he came to give lessons to their younger sister Maria, a pretty little girl with dark eyes; actually the time was spent chiefly in the pranks of mimicry and caricature that he called "Punch and Judy shows." The young people played like children, with Frederic chasing little Maria through the rooms, shouting that he was in love with her.

Meanwhile, in the Chopin home, in the room just below Frederic's attic, a bizarre literary venture of Frederic's sisters had come to a head: they had finished a novel begun earlier in the year. Strictly speaking, its author was Izabela, the quiet, silent, unobtrusive Izabela. Ludwika had merely helped her. The novel was entitled *Ludwika and Emilka, a Moral Tale for Young Readers*. As is apparent from the names of the chief characters, the work was based on recollections of family life. But the belletristic ambition of the two girls was satisfied only partially: the novel was published anonymously.

Frederic, up in his attic, looked with indulgence on his sisters' efforts; he soared far above the naïve pride of the novelists. He worked a great deal. In his studio he had a piano, a desk, and privacy. From his windows in the upper story, above the tree-tops, he could see a great open expanse—a silvery gray sky, the glittering Vistula, and the dark-blue shadows of the Grochow alder trees on the boundless plain. He had known this landscape ever since his schoolboy days. Under the spell of this Mazovian landscape, he played and replayed the countless folk songs and dance tunes that had been sung under this sky and danced on this river bank, in the end to transform and sublimate them in his Grand Fantasy on Polish Airs (Opus 13). He labored over the Trio in G minor (Opus 8), composed the Polonaise in B-flat major (Opus 71, No. 2), and the Rondo à la Krakowiak (Opus 14), which has the most carefully elaborated orchestration of all of his six works for piano and orchestra. His projects grew increasingly bolder, and it was at this stage that he conceived the idea of his Concerto in F minor.

The spring of 1829 brought new revolutionary ferments in the Polish capital. In the cafés of the romantics, Mochnacki gave vent to his impatience, heedless of Novosiltsov's spies. Chopin, usually so pale of countenance, listened to these tirades with flushed cheeks. Tsar Nicholas I, who had succeeded Alexander, was expected to make a visit to Warsaw, where he was to be crowned King of Poland. Elsner was composing a new Mass for this solemn occasion, but the young people who were looking forward to revolution ignored the official preparations. Frederic rejoiced at the announcement that Paganini was to visit Warsaw, and attended concerts arranged at the Conservatory by Soliva, Elsner's rival. One of these soirées, held April 21, 1829, remained forever in his memory. He listened to a program that featured Haydn, Handel, and Cherubini, with orchestra, choirs, and soloists. Madame Meier of the opera received the loudest applause, but Frederic was even more particularly enraptured by another soloist, a beautiful girl with blond hair, dark blue eyes, and a graceful figure. Her full soprano voice resounded without any sign of nervousness, and although Frederic's expert ear caught some imperfections in her singing, he could not take his eyes off her. She must have had many friends among the audience, for she was warmly received and applauded; Frederic joined in with them wholeheartedly.

That night an unknown feeling was added to his attic inspirations. A few days later he read in a review of the concert published in the *Polish Gazette*: "The beautiful performance of the orchestra, composed of more than one hundred players, and the outstanding talents of the pupils of this school, as well as of the artists of the Polish opera, deserve honorable mention. The solos of Madame Meier and of Mesdemoiselles Wolkow and Gladkowska were particularly appreciated."

So her name was Gladkowska—Konstancja Gladkowska. He did not share his particular secret about her with anyone, nor did he seek an opportunity to meet her. He was content with seeing her at church services or at the theater. There were many occasions for such meetings, because the presence of the Tsar in the city was celebrated by a number of new spectacles and entertainments. Representatives of foreign courts arrived from abroad and Warsaw was crowded with other notable visitors. Among the distinguished guests was also Prince Radziwill, who paid the Chopins a visit during his stay. But at the solemn service in the cathedral on the day of the coronation, May 24, 1829, when Elsner took his place before a choir of three hundred singers, Frederic may well have thought with malicious pleasure that the Tsar had a redoubtable rival in Warsaw. For the king of violinists had given a concert in Warsaw the night before.

77

Paganini, Nicolò Paganini—the name eclipsed the splendor of thrones and dazzled all Europe. As he went from city to city he left 'in his wake whispers of admiration and hatred, echoes of ecstasy and slander, a chronicle of art and of scandal. It was rumored that this Italian master had a pact with the devil, and that it was only thanks to this pact that he could extract from his Guarnerius such sounds as had never been heard before his time. An extraordinary occurrence during one of his concerts was being widely discussed. One string of his violin had broken; he had not interrupted his performance, but finished the piece he was performing by playing on the three remaining strings. Since that time, it was said, his strings had acquired a strange habit of breaking more and more often; yet Paganini always continued his magic— and, according to some, charlatanic—playing. As though he had found the number of strings on his violin excessive, he wrote a composition for two strings, and later even a piece for one string, the military sonata entitled *Napoleon*; when he performed it, he basked in a prestidigitator's success. In Vienna his fantastic career touched new heights. He became the favorite of the Austrian capital, and both the aristocracy and the commonalty made an idol of him. Everything in fashion was à la Paganini—hats, shoes, gloves, perfumes, dishes. He came to Poland in a nimbus of glory and adulation, after a tour of Austria, Bohemia, and Saxony.

Paganini gave a series of ten concerts, all of them in the National Theater, the largest auditorium in the city, crowded to its full capacity—about a thousand persons. Warsaw succumbed to the magnetism of the virtuoso no less completely than had Vienna; public excitement was additionally fanned by the arrival at the same time of Karol Lipinski, a Polish violinist who considered himself to be a rival of Paganini. Twenty years earlier he had met Paganini in Milan, played with him at his home, and even appeared jointly with him in two concerts. But the friendship of the two violinists changed to jealous rivalry, and now Lipinski had come to Warsaw to challenge Paganini to an artistic duel that would decide the question of which of them was the superior artist—an issue that, for Lipinski, was still unsettled.

Triumph in Vienna

The kind-hearted Elsner, who had an old score to settle with Lipinski, forgave him everything, tried to reconcile the former friends, and even arranged a great dinner to celebrate the anticipated reconciliation. But neither the duel nor the dinner took place. Lipinski played to empty halls, although many of his admirers placed him above Paganini. He felt that Warsaw had offended him, and left.

Chopin was dazzled by Paganini. To be sure, he disliked the histrionics of this man, with his cadaverous figure (he was said to subsist exclusively on chocolate and camomile), his Mephistophelean face framed in tousled black hair, and his burning black eyes, but behind all this the young Polish virtuoso felt the indubitable presence of genius. Paganini would casually take double stops in harmonics—something previously held to be impossible. He not only ignored but deliberately created technical difficulties for himself, and his brilliance of tone magnetized his listeners. As compared with the classicist Lipinski, he seemed to Chopin an innovator and a revolutionary, a creator in a category to which he himself wanted to belong. Under the spell of this experience, the grateful listener wrote the variations entitled *Souvenir de Paganini*, a composition of somewhat conventional style, but bearing the mark of Chopin's individuality. More significant is the fact that at about this time Chopin wrote his first étude in that style which was to become the unique musical speech of all his work. Perhaps the older artist's bold self-display lured the young experimenter to his first assertion of his own temperament.

After a visit of two months Paganini left Warsaw. On the day following his departure Chopin passed his final examinations at the Conservatory. In his report of July 20, 1829, Elsner wrote: "Frederic Chopin, special ability, musical genius, etc." This "etc." may have expressed the teacher's supreme faith or a possible doubt as to his competence to judge the capacities of his pupil, or it may have been a capsule expression of inexpressible thoughts.

The young graduate of the Conservatory courses in harmony and counterpoint was ready to confront the broader world. His goal was Vienna, the former capital of music, which now reluctantly was yielding its primacy to Paris. Frederic's father had long been preparing this trip and had even applied for a government subsidy for his son; but the Commission for Internal Affairs ruled that "public funds cannot be used for the support of this class of artists." In this dictum the word "used" appeared where the original wording "wasted" was crossed out.

Chopin had to make his sortie on his own funds. Elsner, Zywny, Skarbek, and Monsieur Nicolas hoped that the results that had not been achieved in the hastily contrived trip to Berlin would be achieved in Vienna—namely, establishment of contacts, publication of Chopin's works, and perhaps even a concert. In Vienna they could count on help from Würfel, an old friend of the Chopins', and from Thomas Nidecki, a pupil of Elsner's. Frederic packed up his compositions, and with them a few letters of introduction, and set out on his journey.

He traveled with four classmates—Hube, Celinski, Maciejowski, and Brandt. Their first stop was in Cracow, where they stayed a week—hardly long enough to see the historic treasures of this ancient capital of Poland. Frederic must have been quite absorbed by this visit, for he wrote that he "had little time to think of home." From Cracow the friends made an excursion to Ojcow and its picturesque surroundings, where they had an adventure that Frederic described at length in his letters, but that actually amounted to little more than losing their way and wandering through the night. They continued their journey in a private chaise through the beautiful Beskid mountains, and after two days found themselves, on July 31, 1829, in Vienna.

Frederic at once called on Würfel and Nidecki, who received him cordially. They showed him the streets and the houses that had become shrines to Schubert, a native of Vienna, and those adopted sons of Vienna, Gluck, Haydn, Mozart, and Beethoven; the latter had died two years before. These demigods of music had left behind so many mementos that for Chopin each trip was like a journey into the past. Haydn as an eight-year-old boy had sung in the cathedral choir under the Gothic spires of St. Stephen's; Mozart as a six-year-old prodigy had given a recital before an august audience in the imperial palace; and in the Hamberger Haus, Beethoven had taken his first lessons in counterpoint from Haydn, paying eight *groschen* an hour. Frederic attended the Vienna opera, where he heard Méhul's *Joseph*, Rossini's *La Cenerentola*, Boïeldieu's *La Dame blanche*, and Meyerbeer's *Il Crociato in Egitto*.

The people he met bore famous names and were extremely kind to him. Ignaz Schuppanzigh, conductor of the imperial opera, a cheerful fat man whom Beethoven had nicknamed "Lord Falstaff," took such a liking to Frederic that he wanted to give a special concert to enable the guest from Warsaw to hear his quartet. The aged Adalbert Gyrowetz, upon hearing that Frederic had played his concerto at his debut as an eight-year-old pianist, embraced his young visitor with emotion. Through Würfel, who was one of the conductors at the Kaerntnerthor theater, he met Count Gallenberg, director of this theater, composer of ballets, and husband of Giulietta Guicciardi, Beethoven's "immortal beloved," to whom the *Moonlight* Sonata was dedicated. Würfel's colleagues Lachner, Seyfried, and Kreutzer, plied the young man with questions about his playing and composing. They had been greatly impressed by what they had heard about him.

Everyone urged Frederic to give a concert. Haslinger, the publisher, who promised to hasten the printing of the Variations, which were to appear in the Odeon series, insisted that nothing could do as much to further the young author's popularity as a public appearance. Frederic played with Marie-Leopoldine, the eighteen-year-old daughter of Blahetka, a journalist and music critic. Blahetka, upon hearing him, became enthusiastic about the idea of a concert, predicting that Chopin would be a sensation and would take rank beside such masters as Moscheles, Herz, and Kalkbrenner. Gallenberg at once offered his theater, but Frederic politely refused.

The ability to make quick decisions was not one of Chopin's qualities. He was timid by nature; for two weeks he had not played, and he was associating with great celebrities; this made him more than ever diffident in the face of plans for concerts.

But Würfel kept urging him, his traveling companions left him no peace, and finally he remembered his father's and Skarbek's injunctions. Thus passed the young man's first week in Vienna— seven beautiful and happy days, clouded only by the thought that in the end he would have to give a concert after all.

Suddenly the spirit of decision descended upon him. He wrote about it at length in a letter to his family. On Saturday, August 8th, he was standing in front of the Kaerntnerthor theater, when Gallenberg came up to him and said, "I suggest Tuesday. Will you play?"

"Yes," said Frederic.

Now everything went with lightning speed. Würfel took care of the formalities. The programs appeared the next day; Frederic put one copy into his portmanteau to show to his parents. He renounced all remuneration, a gesture that pleased the Count, who was notorious for his stinginess. Two piano manufacturers offered him instruments for practicing at home, but he availed himself of none of these. For the concert he chose a Graff piano, at the risk of offending Stein; he had met both of these piano makers, and both had been extremely kind to him. The program arranged by Gallenberg featured Beethoven's *Prometheus* over- ture, Chopin's Variations (*Là ci darem*), arias by Rossini and Vaccai (sung by Charlotte Veltheim of the Saxon court opera), Chopin's Rondo à la Krakowiak, another vocal performance, and a short ballet.

On Tuesday morning, August 11th, the rehearsal with orchestra took place. Several of Chopin's new friends attended. The Varia- tions went off smoothly, but the Rondo caused complications. The fault lay with the author. He had always been an accurate calligrapher of his own works, but in the orchestral score of the Rondo he marked each rest twice, and although he had directed the players to follow one set of signs, they became confused. In addi- tion, some of them resented the fact that Würfel, who was un- popular with them, wanted to conduct that morning. Frederic was in despair and was ready to cancel the concert by pretending sudden illness, when Démar, the aged stage director, came to his

rescue. He suggested that Chopin replace the Rondo with improvisations, and Frederic, irritated as he was, agreed without a
moment's hesitation. After the rehearsal Nidecki, who had not left
Chopin for a moment, made some corrections in the orchestral
score of the Variations, and everything was ready for the evening.

The hall at the concert hour was not full, a fact that, as Chopin
himself states, actually encouraged him. It could hardly have been
otherwise in the summer, at a concert by an unknown pianist.
The kindhearted Démar would run out to look over the audience,
returning each time to announce the presence of some notable—
Lichnowsky, Schwarzenberg, Wrbna. "Count Dietrichstein of the
imperial court," he called out. "It could not be better."

Frederic's traveling companions undertook to serve as under-
cover reporters. They dispersed themselves about the auditorium
ready to observe the audience and to listen to opinions and criticisms. They were enjoined not to start the applause.   *commanded*

While the orchestra played the Beethoven overture, Würfel
was pressing Chopin's hand in the green room; Nidecki, although
stricken with stage fright, tried also to hearten his friend. A
Polish member of the ballet brought lemonade and purveyed jokes.
Finally, Chopin's turn came.

Greeted by the surging sound of applause, he found himself
alone on the stage of the great theater. The orchestra was in the
pit, as for an opera performance. By Chopin's side sat a rouged
gentleman to turn the pages, who whispered to him that he had
rendered the same service to Moscheles, Hummel, and Herz.

"I played with desperation," Chopin wrote about his first test
at the keyboard before the "great world." The phrase probably
was meant to express the determination and passion of a naturally
shy man who even in this trial by fire remained faithful to his
principle: he would play softly, with his characteristic delicacy,
according to his own style. He did not have to wait long for
applause. After the very first variation, the hand clapping was
so loud that he could not hear the orchestra's tutti.

The second part of the concert, the so-called *Freie Fantasie*,
that is, the solo improvisations that replaced the Rondo, began

in a peculiar manner. The director appeared on the stage and in the name of the artist asked the public to choose a theme for improvisation. Somebody suggested a motif from Boïeldieu's *La Dame blanche*, an opera that Frederic had attended a few days before. This was the occasion for the display of an art very popular at that time but discarded later—composition *ex abrupto*, in which Chopin, according to his contemporaries, had no equal. When Chopin added to the Boïeldieu theme an improvisation on the Polish drinking song *Chmiel* ("Hops"), the audience went wild with enthusiasm. Shouts mingled with the bravos; even the rebellious orchestra surrendered to the virtuoso and showered him with applause.

The first to rush backstage were Frederic's traveling companions. "People were jumping on the benches," they said, embracing him.

Würfel was beside himself with joy. Gallenberg at once suggested a second concert. Démar added, "You still must play the Rondo."

All of them grew silent when someone suddenly said, "Count Dietrichstein is coming." The court dignitary was extremely amiable; he congratulated Frederic heartily and asked him to prolong his stay in Vienna. It may be conjectured that Count Dietrichstein did not come to the concert as a representative of the court; nor is it likely that he was solely motivated by his love of music. He was the father of Sigismond Thalberg, whose pianistic fame was then in the ascendant, and he doubtless wished to ascertain what sort of rival his son might have to reckon with in the young Polish virtuoso.

After the great evening came the time for comments and reflections. The reports of the scouts indicated that the audience was satisfied. The most decided criticism, overheard by Hube, came from a lady who observed: *"Schade um den Jungen dass er so wenig Tournure hat"* ("It's a pity that the boy is so badly turned out"). More serious was the verdict of some expert listeners— that he played too softly. Chopin had expected this reproach, but he did not fear it, and was even ready to argue it. He knew that contemporary taste required loud playing, but he deliberately opposed this fashion. Of Mademoiselle Blahetka, who had been praised by Beethoven, he wrote: "She pounds frightfully on the piano."

We may infer from his various remarks that he conceived of the keyboard as an instrument intended to express feelings but not to imitate natural sounds. He believed that its eloquence could be perfected and extended to include the boldest colorations, and he did this in his compositions. But he disliked exaggerated intensity of sound, which he compared to common noise. It even reminded him, he said, of the barking of a dog.

He did not have much time for developing his theories. The fame of his concert spread far and wide, and all sorts of people wanted to entertain him. He was a frequent visitor at the Blahetkas', where he played with Marie Leopoldine, defending his *piano* and criticizing her *fortissimo* until the amiable young lady, falling under the spell of her partner, in the end agreed with him. He was also invited to the home of Karl Czerny, well-known composer and brilliant instructor, a pupil of Beethoven and the teacher of Liszt. On these occasions Czerny and Chopin played compositions for two pianos.

Frederic was particularly popular with younger people. Haslinger's son played for him, and Stein's son followed him like a shadow. In an antique shop a stranger came up to him and congratulated him on his success. "You have really enchanted and thrilled me," he said.

Most of all Chopin enjoyed his visit at the Lichnowskys', who through Würfel invited him to their home. Count Moritz Lichnowsky had been one of Beethoven's most intimate friends, one of the few who succeeded in preserving friendship with this difficult personality to the end of his life. Moritz's brother Karl (honored by the Tsar with the title of prince), who was Beethoven's patron and protector for many years, had been less fortunate in this friendship. The Count's house was renowned for its spacious tradition and its musical culture, and its hospitality brought together the élite of Viennese society. There new congratulations were showered upon Frederic by the Count's family, as well as by Schuppanzigh, Gyrowetz, and other eminent new acquaintances. For his second concert Lichnowsky offered him a piano on which Beethoven had played. Referring to this offer, Frederic wrote: "He thought that the Graff was too weak in tone. But that was only my own way of playing."

He readily agreed to give a second concert. The date set was August 18th. This concert was in the nature of a farewell to Vienna; Frederic had reserved a seat in the stagecoach for August 19th. He again decided to play without fee. "That is to please the Count, whose pockets are empty," he wrote.

The program included the overture to Lindpaintner's opera *Bergkönig*, Chopin's Rondo à la Krakowiak, Mayseder's Polonaise for violin performed by the young violinist Joseph Khayl, the variations on *Là ci darem*, and a ballet.

This time the rehearsal of the Rondo was successful (Nidecki had corrected the manuscript). The orchestra had to exert itself only to catch the rhythm, and Frederic was much more self-assured than in the preliminaries of his first concert. His ardor was not diminished by the fact that the audience this time was larger. He played in his best style and triumphed both as pianist and as composer. After the Rondo there was a tremendous outburst of applause; the aged Gyrowetz not only clapped his hands but shouted, "Bravo!" at the top of his lungs, and Démar was radiant with joy. From Lachner, the conductor, to the piano tuner, everyone congratulated Frederic on his performance. This began all over again after the Variations, which particularly captivated Haslinger and Blahetka. "I am surprised only at one thing," said Blahetka. "How could you learn all this in Warsaw?"

Frederic, who often concealed his modesty and shyness under blunt language, answered, "Under Zywny and Elsner even the greatest ass would learn."

Next morning Chopin quickly packed his bags and took leave of his new friends. He made brief stops at the homes of some Polish friends, and at the café near the Kaerntnerthor theater he shook hands with Gyrowetz, Lachner, Kreutzer, and Seyfried.

Marie Leopoldine offered him as a souvenir her own composition, with a dedication, and Blahetka asked him to congratulate his parents on having such a son. Schuppanzigh urged him to return to Vienna as soon as possible. Würfel gave him five letters of introduction, urging him to give concerts in Prague and Dresden. His young friend Stein wept on saying farewell.

At the last moment Frederic wrote a letter to his parents, expressing regret that he was leaving before seeing the newspapers, and informing them that they would receive the reviews before his return: "You will read ahead of me the favorable or unfavorable criticisms of my concert."

Only three of the companions who had come with him to Vienna joined him in the stagecoach; the fourth, Hube, had left for Italy. Several loyal Poles saw him off at the station, among them the faithful Nidecki. It was nine o'clock in the evening when the express chaise set out for Prague.

Return with Laurels

A TWO-DAY stagecoach journey might have been an ordeal for a traveler who only a short time before had not been allowed outdoors in bad weather. But Chopin now was a different man. He arrived in Prague at noon on August 21st, had dinner at the hotel, and, showing no sign of fatigue, at once set out with his companions in search of Waclaw Hanka, whom they intended to enlist as their cicerone in the unfamiliar city. No one was more suited for this function than this friend of Frederic Skarbek, a distinguished Slavic scholar and linguist, collector of folk songs and librarian of the Czech National Museum. He took them to the cathedral to stand before the silver altar of St. John of Nepomuk, to the amethyst-studded St. Venceslas chapel, and to the castle hill, from which they could see the whole city spreading its gilded baroque treasures before them. The young men inscribed their names in the museum visitors' book; Maciejewski wrote in it four stanzas in Hanka's honor, and Frederic added the music of a mazurka that he composed on the spot.

In this city devoted to music and singing Chopin was naturally urged to give a concert, but he wanted his visit to be a vacation; moreover, he was somewhat afraid of Prague, where, as he wrote, even Paganini had been "torn to shreds." He confined himself to calling on Friedrich Wilhelm Pixis, opera conductor and conservatory professor, to whom he had letters from Blahetka and

Würfel. The visit went beyond the conventional exchange of courtesies. In the home of Pixis he met 'August Klengel, a Dresden celebrity, who was stopping in Prague on his way to Vienna and Italy. In a session of two hours, Klengel played before them his forty-eight fugues and canons, of which it was said that Bach himself could have composed them. "He plays well," Frederic wrote to his family. "But I should have liked to hear something better."

After three days in Prague, the travelers proceeded to Dresden. On their way they stopped at Teplitz, a famous resort. Invited to a reception by Prince Clary, owner of Teplitz, Frederic donned his tailcoat and white Viennese gloves and drove to the castle. Princess Clary, sister of Count Chotek, governor of Bohemia, had gathered together many distinguished guests that evening. Frederic moved with difficulty in this crowd of princes, counts, and generals. He felt more at ease near the beautiful Graff piano, and when he was asked to play he assented at once, improvising on a theme from Rossini's *Mosè in Egitto* suggested by his hearers.

'Next morning at five o'clock the favorite of princes, with his retinue, set out in a peasant cart (hired for two taler) for Dresden. The Saxonian capital was not another Vienna, but it had a claim on Frederic's heart. It was in Dresden that Karl Maria von Weber, who had died three years before, had written *Der Freischütz* and laid the foundation of German national opera. To emulate this achievement in Poland was the dream of Elsner and Kurpinski.

After eleven hours of bumping and jolting, Frederic got out of the cart and at once wrote his parents a letter that began: "I am safe and sound and cheerful." On the following day he visited the famous Dresden gallery, and saw Francesco Morlacchi, conductor of the royal orchestra and musical dictator of Dresden. He called on the master of ceremonies of the court and on several other persons, and finally went to see a performance of Goethe's *Faust*. The occasion was in celebration of the poet's eightieth birthday, and the crowd was so great that Chopin had to stand in line for an hour and a half before he got into the theater. The performance lasted from six to eleven. The famous German actor

Karl Devrient was in the leading role, and between the acts the orchestra played selections from Spohr's operatic adaptation of the play. "A terrible but great fantasy," Chopin wrote to his parents, referring to *Faust*.

He played before Morlacchi, who complimented him and called on him at his hotel, and introduced him to Dresden's best pianist, Antoinette Pechwell, about whose playing Chopin spoke with sincere appreciation. He also made a few excursions to the so-called Saxon Switzerland, so that his stay in Dresden, devoted to art, the salons, and such tours, gave him as many impressions as could be crowded into seven days. He lived in a state of elation, absorbing the world greedily, and his strength was seemingly inexhaustible.

After a few days in Wroclaw, he went to visit Madame Wiesiolowska in Strzyzewo and Prince Radziwill in Antonin. In the home of the former Anna Skarbek the conqueror of Vienna was again the little Frycek, and here he reported the great events of his trip in a facetious tone. At the Radziwills' the atmosphere was different; there his success in Vienna was regarded as marking the beginning of a brilliant career, for which further plans had to be laid. The Radziwills invited him to Berlin, offering him quarters in their own palace, and with great kindness suggested that he might give lessons to the princesses.

His next stop was in Kalisz, where Doctor Helbich, an old friend of the family, took him to the country for three days. He arrived in Warsaw only in the middle of September.

Frederic had been away for two months, and now on his return the family shut itself off from the rest of the world, while he recounted to his parents and sisters the details of his trip that he had not mentioned in his letters and showed them the program of his first concert, the piece composed by Blahetka's daughter, and the gifts he had brought them from Vienna, Prague, and Dresden. He found waiting for him the Vienna newspapers containing the reviews of his performance, which he undoubtedly read with eager interest.

"In Herr Chopin we have discovered one of the most excellent pianists, full of delicacy and deepest sentiment," he read in *Der Sammler*. "Composition, technique, interpretation—everything must be considered brilliant; and general success was the artist's reward," wrote the *Allgemeiner musikalischer Anzeiger*. *Die Zeitschrift für Kunst, Literatur, Theater und Mode* discussed each concert at length. The first was accorded only words of praise: "Chopin surmounts the greatest difficulties with accuracy and precision, and the purity of his passages is flawless. The success won by this skillful artist was very great. His composition for concert and orchestra was particularly liked." The second notice contained some reservations; while the critic recognized that the Rondo was rich in musical ideas, he thought that the work lacked variety. The same reviewer spoke in warmer terms of the Variations on *Là ci darem la mano*: "In conclusion Chopin played his variations on a Mozart theme, which he had performed with such facility and bravura in his first concert. The pleasant and restrained diversity of this composition as well as the beautiful execution again won the pianist loud acclaim. Connoisseurs and amateurs manifested their approval loudly and freely."

The *Wiener Theaterzeitung* devoted to Chopin two keen articles by Adolph Bäuerle, who because of his high standards and critical severity was known as the terror of the virtuosos. Frederic had met this writer in Vienna. The reviews began with the statement that Chopin had amazed everyone, that he was a musician of outstanding talent who possessed "certain traits of genius" and was distinguished by originality in performance and composition. The evaluation went on: "It would seem that this young man does not try to dazzle and astonish his listeners, although his execution conquers difficulties the overcoming of which cannot fail to be striking even here, in the homeland of pianoforte virtuosos."

Several of these remarks must have seemed convincing to Chopin. Bäuerle commented on the restraint and composure of his playing as well as on his unwillingness to obtrude himself on his audience:

His touch, though neat and assured, has little of that flashiness which our virtuosos display from the very first bars. He only suggests the tone, like someone speaking to a group of well-bred people, dispensing with the rhetorical flourishes that virtuosos have deemed to be indispensable.

The critic eloquently praised the compositions and improvisations:

As in his playing, he was like a young, beautifully and freely developed tree, full of fragrant blossoms and ripening fruit, so he showed equally noble qualities in his compositions, which revealed constantly new figures, new passages, new forms. Full of composure and ease, the young virtuoso was prevailed upon to conclude his concert by improvising before a public that had acclaimed only few improvisers aside from Beethoven and Hummel. Although this young man, by frequently changing themes, suggested that he considered such improvisations a diversion or pastime, it must be said that both the quiet fluency of his thought and his beautiful developments and combinations were sufficient proof of his ability in this rare art.

Bäuerle's second article was written much in the same adulatory tone, but the greatest praise was bestowed upon him by the Leipzig *Allgemeine musikalische Zeitung,* which incidentally had mentioned Chopin before. Its correspondent in Vienna reported that:

Herr Chopin, pianofortist from Warsaw, revealed himself at once as a master of the first rank. The marvelous delicacy of his touch, his indescribable technical dexterity, his shading, which reflects deepest feeling, the rare lucidity and transparency of his interpretations and his compositions, which bear the mark of genius, reveal in this generously endowed virtuoso an artist who without previous publicity appears on the musical horizon as a most brilliant new meteor.

If Chopin thereupon read the Warsaw papers, he must have been amazed by their parsimony of praise and what might seem even ill will. Some carried brief notices; the others were silent.

Still worse, some of the notices mistranslated Bäuerle's judgment to the effect that the young artist was more concerned with good music than with pleasing the audience, and made the critic appear to be saying exactly the opposite. Perhaps the mistranslation was deliberate, or perhaps it was only a manifestation of unconscious envy. However that may be, Warsaw reacted to the Vienna concert with an aloof <u>parochialism</u>.

Narrowness

Music and Love

THERE is a street in Warsaw that Chopin might have called the street of his youth. He had lived on it or close to it throughout all the years of his early life in Warsaw. It was to this street that the lyceum had been moved from the Saxon palace; here also stood the university. It was Krakowskie Przedmiescie. Frederic had traversed the long span of this street so many times that its appearance must have become thoroughly familiar to him. Yet it is certain that after his return from Vienna he could not scan its perspective with indifferent eyes. For at one end of Krakowskie Przedmiescie, opposite the royal castle, stood the Conservatory. 'And in the Conservatory lived the girl whom he loved but whom he did not know.

Since Konstancja Gladkowska held a scholarship at the Conservatory, she had the privilege of free living quarters in the school's boardinghouse for pupils. Chopin had ready access to the singing classes, where Konstancja often rehearsed. But he preferred not to approach in reality the person from whom he was never separated in his dreams. Apparently the need for love and the secret of love sufficed him. Although accustomed to the social contacts of the salon from his earliest youth, Chopin was shy; his delicacy required discretion and his feelings clung to secrecy.

The love that he hid from men he confided to music. The pianoforte in his attic studio had long been listening to such wordless

Music and Love

disclosures. The sheets of the Concerto in F Minor were spread on the rack. The part he wrote first was the adagio—a nineteen-year-old boy's romantic song of songs, a confession composed of sighs, a tapestry woven of mists.

To harbor a love that consisted in avoiding personal acquaintance with its object was a difficult and complicated matter. Only a few days after his return to Warsaw, Chopin began to plan a new trip. He spoke of Berlin, Vienna, Italy, France. When he had finished the adagio, having put into his music the whole content of his inner life, he suddenly became conscious of unbearable loneliness. It was then that he mentioned his love for the first time; he revealed his secret to Tytus Woyciechowski, his friend and former classmate, who was living on his farm in Poturzyn. On the morning of October 6, 1829, with the image of Konstancja in his mind, Frederic wrote a waltz; on the evening of the same day he realized that he could no longer keep his feelings to himself. He had just received a letter from Tytus, and he answered it at once, writing as follows:

You want to know what I intend to do with myself this winter? Well, I advise you that I won't stay in Warsaw, but I don't know where circumstances will take me. It is true that Prince Radziwill, or rather the Princess, who is very kind, has invited me to Berlin, even offering me lodgings in their own palace, but of what use will this be to me when I now should go where I made my debut. . . . You must realize yourself that it is necessary for me to return to Vienna, not for the sake of Miss Blahetka, about whom, I think, I have written to you (she is young, pretty, and a pianist), for I, perhaps unfortunately, have my own ideal. I have served her faithfully (although I have never spoken to her) for half a year; an ideal of which I dream, to which the adagio of my concerto belongs, and which this morning inspired the little waltz I am sending you. Note one place marked x. No one knows this, except you. How sweet it would be if I could play it to you, my dearest Tytus!

He had intended to let the matter go at that, but apparently he felt so relieved by this first confession that in the same letter he returned once more to the subject of his loneliness:

The Life and Death of Chopin

You can't believe how dreary Warsaw seems to me now; if it were not for my family cheering me up, I shouldn't be able to stay. And how hard it is not to have someone to go to in the morning, to share my grief and joy with him—how intolerable to have a burden on one's mind and no place to put it down. You know what I am referring to. I tell my piano what I would often have been telling you.

Indeed, music was his only comfort. He played the adagio to Elsner, who praised it. He worked at the rondo of his concerto, which still did not satisfy him; he finished the Trio in G minor (Opus 8), the Fantasy on Polish Airs (Opus 13), the Waltz in B minor (Opus 69, No. 2), Mazurkas in C major and F major (Opus 68, Nos. 1 and 3), the Funeral March in C minor (Opus 72), and wrote several études and songs. He often went to Brzezina's bookstore and looked through new musical publications, and he missed no opening night at the theater. Having attended a performance of Rossini's *La Cenerentola*, he conceived the idea of adapting some themes of this opera as a set of variations for the flute, probably having his friend Matuszynski in mind, but soon abandoned this plan. He also put away the waltz (Opus 70, No. 3) that he had mentioned in his letter to Tytus. Every Friday he played with Joseph Kessler, a German pianist who had recently come to reside in Warsaw, and who arranged concerts with impromptu programs in his home. The two liked each other; Kessler later dedicated twenty-four preludes to Chopin, and the latter reciprocated by inscribing to Kessler the German edition of his own twenty-four preludes. Among the works performed at Kessler's soirées were Spohr's *Ottetto*, Ries's Quartet in C-sharp minor, Hummel's Trio in E major, a quartet by Prince Ludwig Ferdinand of Prussia, Prince Radziwill's brother-in-law, and Beethoven's *Archduke* trio, of which Chopin wrote to Tytus: "I haven't heard anything so great for a long time; with this work Beethoven thumbs his nose at the whole world."

He escaped from Warsaw for a short visit to the Radziwills, who had come for an autumn vacation to Antonin. In connection

96

Compare his opinion of Beethoven's Sonata Op. 31, No. 3 "vulgar"

with this visit, Monsieur Nicolas had vague hopes that the Prince would proffer assistance to his son; these hopes were shared by the Wiesiolowskis, but Frederic himself had no illusion about it. "I have seen many a man disappointed in the favors of the mighty," he wrote to Tytus. This reference offers one of several proofs refuting the hypothesis that Radziwill supported Chopin.

Frederic turned out to be right; nevertheless, his stay at Antonin was as pleasant as possible. The castle in the woods looked dreary from the outside, but was splendidly appointed, and Chopin enjoyed its luxury. The week he spent there was filled with music. The evening concerts always wound up with improvisations by the young composer; his host liked to listen to these, with the lights out. From Princess Louise, Chopin learned many interesting details about her brother, an eccentric Prussian general and composer of the quartet he had heard played in Kessler's home. Prince Ludwig Ferdinand owned thirteen pianos, and was such a devotee of music that he invited virtuosos to army maneuvers and postponed military drills in favor of concert rehearsals. Prince Radziwill showed Chopin his music for *Faust*, played the cello with him, and altogether delighted his guest; this house was so greatly given over to the love of music that Frederic was moved to write his *Alla Pollacca* for cello and piano (Opus 3). He regarded this work rather lightly, calling it "a salon piece for ladies"; it contained, he said, "nothing but glitter," yet, partly for fun and partly in earnest, he wanted one of the princesses, Wanda, whom he was teaching, to learn to play the piano part. His battered heart, always sensitive to feminine charm, was having a respite after the passionate torments of the recent months in Warsaw, and probably beat with carefree joy at the side of this beautiful girl. "She is young—seventeen—pretty, and, forsooth, it's a real pleasure to guide her fingers."

The elder of the princesses, Eliza, who was equally fond of music and painting, conceived a special liking for the Polonaise in F minor (Opus 71, No. 3), and drew two excellent portraits of its author in her album. "I would have stayed there until I was driven out, but my other interests, particularly the concerto as

The Life and Death of Chopin

yet unfinished and waiting impatiently for the completion of its finale, hastened my departure from this paradise."

Before he left, the Radziwills reiterated their invitation to him to come to Berlin in May. On his return to Warsaw, he reverted to his old mood. Once again he yearned to go abroad; in December he planned to spend the winter in Vienna, and to proceed to Berlin in the spring. But these plans came to nothing.

On December 19th, he participated in a concert in the Merchants' Hall. The artists included Bielawski, a Conservatory professor and first violinist of the opera, and two singers—Copello, who was accompanied by Chopin, and Dorville, who was accompanied by Soliva. Chopin also performed as a soloist, improvising on themes from *The Peasant Millionaire*, a play then running in Warsaw. Strangely enough, this rather unimportant performance found a more vivid echo in the Polish press than had Chopin's Vienna concerts. On December 23rd, the Warsaw *Courier* published the following letter to the editor, over the initials St. Eg. K.:

Last Saturday's soirée in the Merchants' Hall was one of the most pleasant ever held in our capital. Mr. Chopin contributed a great deal to its brilliance. Our gifted fellow-countryman, who was enthusiastically received, had not until then been publicly heard in his homeland. Although modesty is the noblest virtue of talent, it seems less praiseworthy when we consider this fact. Is not Mr. Chopin's talent the property of his country? Is Poland unable to appreciate this talent? Mr. Chopin's works undeniably bear the mark of great genius; his latest compositions are said to include a concerto in F minor that deserves to be placed on a par with the works of the first musicians in Europe. Consequently we hope that Mr. Chopin, so many times acclaimed by us, will not longer endeavor, to the detriment of his own and his nation's fame, to stifle our pleasant conviction that Poland too produces great talents.

Chopin was thinking of giving a public recital at this time, but before carrying out this plan, he arranged two soirées at home, presenting his new works to a group of invited guests. Before the first gathering, he played his Concerto in F minor (Opus 21);

98

before the second, the concerto and the Grand Fantasy on Polish Airs. News of these private performances reached the press. An article (probably by Mochnacki) in the *Polish Gazette* reported that the concerto was a work "full of quite new ideas, and it can be counted among the most beautiful of new compositions." After the second soirée, the Warsaw *Courier* quoted it as universal opinion that "the young Chopin surpassed all pianists that we have heard before. He is the Paganini of the pianoforte, and his compositions are sublime, full of new ideas." Chopin now made up his mind to gratify the patriotic wish expressed in the letter to the editor of the Warsaw *Courier*.

He gave a first concert in the National Theater on March 17, 1830. The house was sold out three days before the performance. The program opened with the overture to Elsner's opera *King Leszek the White*. Then Chopin played the allegro of his Concerto in F minor, accompanied by the orchestra. Between the allegro and the other movements of the concerto, Görner played his Divertissement for French horn; Chopin's adagio and rondo concluded the first part of the program. After the intermission the orchestra played the overture to Kurpinski's opera *Cecylia Piaseczynska*, Madame Meier sang Paër's Variations, and as the final feature Chopin played his Grand Fantasy on Polish Airs. The conductor was Kurpinski.

This time the capricious press made a great hubbub. All the newspapers acclaimed the concert in lengthy articles full of magniloquent and sometimes extravagant phrases, although there were also some sober reviews. The *Correspondent's Gazette* said:

As a performer he surpassed even Hummel in tenderness of feeling and refinement of taste. If he did not equal Hummel in technique and evenness of tempo, he is unequaled by others in these qualities. As a composer he has assumed a distinguished place among the foremost music writers, and Hummel himself would not disown his adagio and rondo.

The critic of the *Official Bulletin* spoke of Chopin in terms reminiscent of the judgment of Bäuerle:

The Life and Death of Chopin

In overcoming the greatest technical difficulties, in the most brilliant passages, in the *cantabile* with its most tender and most evocative melodies, the pianist nowhere strove to shine at the expense of the total impression. . . . His playing seemed to say to the audience: "It is not I, it is the music!"

The *Polish Courier*, like the other papers, emphasized the characteristically Polish quality of Chopin's motifs, and commented:

Everyone was enchanted, particularly after the rondo of the concerto and the potpourri of national songs, in which many a listener caught the beautifully developed and felicitously echoed tune of his native village. . . . The spirit of the land that has given this artist life through its songs, and that has formed his musical temperament, often emerges in his compositions: many of his tone patterns seem like a spontaneous reflection of our native harmonies.

Of Chopin's friends, Kurpinski stressed the originality of the compositions, but Elsner regretted that the instrument was dull and that the bass passages could not be heard. Chopin himself, always sober, unassuming, and critical of himself and others, did not succumb to the general praise and reported to Tytus in a casual tone:

The first allegro, accessible only to the few, won acclaim, but I think only because the people were puzzled about it and had to pose as connoisseurs. The adagio and rondo produced the greatest effect; here the bravos were more spontaneous. But as for the medley of Polish themes, in my opinion it did not come off at all. The audience applauded to signify to me before leaving that they were not bored.

However that may have been, the demand for another concert was so fervent and insistent that five days later, on March 22nd, Frederic gave a second performance. The National Theater was again filled to capacity. In the first concert Chopin had played on his own piano; this time he used a different instrument of louder tone. The first part of the program included Jozef Nowakowski's symphony, the allegro of Chopin's concerto, de Bériot's Variations for violin, played by Bielawski, and the adagio and rondo of the concerto. The second part began with the Rondo à la Krakowiak; then Madame Meier sang the aria from Soliva's opera *Helena and Malwina*; and in conclusion Chopin improvised on the theme of the song, "There are strange customs in the town."

He was received even more warmly than before, with a spontaneous and unrestrained enthusiasm. After the Krakowiak he was called back to the stage four times, and after the improvisation the audience with wild applause shouted demands for a third concert. "At City Hall!" cried someone in the audience, thus calling for an even larger auditorium. The press, as though to make up for its attitude after the Vienna concerts, indulged in extraordinary panegyrics. Articles about him continued to appear for a month, and the *Official Bulletin* proclaimed that just as fate had presented the Germans with Mozart, so it had bestowed Chopin on the Poles. "Nonsense—it's very clearly nonsense," was Frederic's comment to Tytus on this pronouncement. Only Mochnacki, courageous and revolutionary as always, friendly toward Frederic but above all faithful to himself, managed to preserve his own judgment amid this chorus of enthusiasm, and in a critique in the *Polish Courier*, after expressing his admiration for the rondo and the medley of Polish airs, he wrote:

The improvisation did not and could not produce the same effect, because it was a true, not a pretended improvisation, and as such, what impression could it make beside compositions so felicitous in inspiration and so skillfully worked out? . . . Let Chopin leave this genre to wooden talents, to those creatures whose blood never pulsates with life—who function like inanimate mechanisms wound up by springs. The listener will perceive all of Chopin's compositions as improvisations: he does not chase after other people's ideas, but is always new, fresh—in a word, inspired.

An amusing if indirect effect of the concert was an outbreak of polemics between warring factions among the Warsaw music critics. One party praised Elsner as Chopin's teacher and taunted Kurpinski; the other defended Kurpinski and spoke deprecatingly of Elsner. It was as though, when Chopin had played his final note at the concert, the entire population of Warsaw fell into an uproar: the whole city was simply the pit, boxes, and the gallery of the National Theater. At home a magnificent bouquet of fresh flowers from an anonymous admirer awaited him. Countess de Moriolles sent him a wreath of laurel. The *Journal for the Fair Sex* published a poetic tribute, "Sonnet to Frederic Chopin Playing a Piano Concerto," by Leon Ulrich, who later won fame as the Polish translator of Shakespeare. Frederic had conquered Warsaw: his friends were enraptured and he had no enemies. Antoni Orlowski adapted several themes from the concerto as mazurkas, waltzes, and gallopades, and to Frederic's horror, and against his wishes, published them. Brzezina offered to print Frederic's portrait, but on this occasion the young composer succeeded in defending himself. "I don't wish to be used for wrapping butter," he said.

The income from the two concerts, after deduction of expenses, amounted to about five thousand zlotys. For the time being Chopin did not wish to give a third concert, either at City Hall or elsewhere. He planned to give one only before going abroad, and on that occasion to present his Concerto in E minor (Opus 11), on which he had begun to work. But he did not know when this would be. He had planned so many trips in vain, he had set and canceled so many dates of departure, that he no longer felt himself master of his decisions. Moreover, concerts ceased to appeal to him; the efforts connected with the arrangement of the last ones had exhausted him physically. "What misery the last three days before a concert!" he wrote to Tytus.

Although he had stopped reading press comments, and disliked listening to what people were saying about him, he continued to analyze his playing for himself. He was not fully satisfied with his performance, and he tried to exonerate his piano, which was possibly too dull for a large auditorium. And he must very often have evoked in memory his own picture of this auditorium of the National Theater, with its countless faces and eyes directed toward him. In the first row had been his mother, his father, and his sisters; next to them would be the smiling Elsner and the perennially yellow-haired Zywny, who was not ashamed of his tears in the presence of a thousand people. But had there been in that audience also someone whom he had "served faithfully" without ever having spoken to her, and of whom he dreamed? Had she been there? Had she heard him? What had she thought of him?

Konstancja and Tytus

IN APRIL, 1830, Frederic finally met Konstancja, and, judging from his correspondence, his youthful passion became the more intense. He was happier when he thought that she reciprocated his love, and he was more tormented when beset by doubts. Oversensitive, timid, and above all helpless and inexperienced, he was torn between contradictory feelings. In his love he followed the pattern of his time; he was unable to rise above romantic sentimentalism, worshiping a disembodied dream, mistaking his fantasies for real life. For half a year he had not disclosed to anyone that he had his "ideal" without knowing her personally; for another half year he contented himself with pouring out his feelings in his letters to Tytus. After meeting Konstancja he had only a final half year left for experiencing love beyond the realm of dreams and reveries. Then he left Poland and began a new life.

Konstancja Gladkowska, then twenty, and three months younger than Chopin, was the daughter of one of the superintendents of the royal castle. She had been studying voice at the Conservatory for four years and was considered one of Soliva's best pupils. She was also said to be one of the prettiest. Her regular, full face, framed in blond hair, was an epitome of youth, health, and vigor, and her beauty was conspicuous in the Conservatory chorus, for all that it boasted numbers of beautiful women. The young lady, conscious of her charms, was distinguished by ambition and diligence in her studies. She dreamed of becoming an operatic singer, of receiving tributes and acclaim, to which she had early become accustomed. Her conception of art thus differed considerably from Frederic's; but since he loved song and opera, it was easy for him to imagine that his "ideal" shared his artistic outlook.

There is little doubt that the unrealistic character of his love helped to stimulate his musical imagination and led him to seek in music the raptures that were inaccessible to him in real life. He worked intensively on the Concerto in E minor and he once more revised the Trio in G minor. In his Conservatory days he had not displayed particular interest or skill in composition for voice; but now he became enthusiastic about it and set poems of Mickiewicz and Witwicki to music. He inscribed eleven such songs in Mademoiselle Elsner's album, in addition to five mazurkas, three waltzes, and two *écossaises*. He would often drop in at the Conservatory, sit down at the piano, and accompany the singers—this most readily in the case of Gladkowska or Wolkow, another honor pupil of Soliva. In the evening after classes, he would improvise for them or play his compositions to them, performing with special feeling the adagio of the F minor concerto and the waltz that he had written one memorable October morning.

Soliva permitted his students to practice duets with outsiders. This custom, which Elsner severely criticized, was also distasteful to Frederic. He was annoyed by the fact that the pretty girl students attracted to the Conservatory certain local dandies who could be suspected of anything except devotion to art. What was worse, he learned that an extraordinary enthusiasm for music had also infected several members of the Grand Duke's retinue. The secret happiness he enjoyed when playing the adagio at the Conservatory was matched by his dejection over the visits of two young lieutenants, Bezobrazov and Pisarevsky, who had suddenly fallen in love with Gladkowska's soprano voice.

On such occasions he was seized with despair, set a new date for his departure, applied for his passport, and was ready to pack his things and leave. His family was baffled by his nervousness, even suspected that it was the result of some romantic attachment, but did not associate it with the person on whom it actually centered. From childhood on Frederic had not concealed his friendship for the little Countess de Moriolles, who was now very much devoted to him; and when he realized that his family mistook her for the cause of his depressed moods, he did everything to strengthen them in this conviction. He ostentatiously met the Countess in town and was happy that he had found such a plausible shield for his real love. Deeply hurt over the way in which Konstancja tolerated the company of the Russian officers, he ceased his visits to the Conservatory, sought distraction in parties and dancing, buried himself in his manuscripts, and spent long hours in cafés filled with tobacco smoke, which he hated. His favorite resort was the Little Hole, where he enjoyed the company of his poet friends—Witwicki, Magnuszewski, Odyniec, Goszczynski, and Bohdan Zaleski.

"I would gladly throw off the thoughts that poison my happiness, yet I delight in fondling them; I don't know myself what I want, and perhaps I'll feel relieved after writing this letter—you know how I enjoy writing to you," he confided to Tytus. Tormented, full of vague yearnings, exacerbating his wounds, he suddenly realized that his friend, who lived more than two hundred miles away, near Lublin, represented exactly what he needed most —a source of peace, confidence, and strength. He wrote to Tytus about everything, confiding to him matters unimportant and important, traveling plans, compositions, and his tormenting secret. This correspondence reflected a friendship all the more passionate because his feeling for Konstancja grew more and more harrowing. Frederic's fifteen letters to Tytus constitute a unique record of the development of two lines of feeling focused upon persons both so close to him that the two emotional strata overlapped like two photographic exposures on a single plate. Chopin's frustrated heart sought and discovered in friendship that which it had not found in love—spiritual closeness, understanding, the intimate exchange of ideas. He wanted to belong, to open himself to someone, and he found this refuge not in Krakowskie Przedmiescie but at Poturzyn. Frederic loved Konstancja, but he transferred the ardor of his emotion to Tytus.

He longed to see this friend as one longs to see one's beloved. "What a relief I feel in my unbearable dejection, the moment I receive a letter from you," he wrote. And again: "You know, I didn't think I could be as secretive as I am, since I haven't the courage to confide in you what torments me." He went to the house where Tytus Woyciechowski had lived, looked at the windows with their closed shutters, and reported this to him. One day, Celinski, who had been one of Chopin's companions on the trip to Vienna, and who was concerned about his friend's health, asked him to take a walk. Frederic wrote to Tytus: "I'll go with him—perhaps I'll see someone who will remind me of you, because I love only you." He always addressed his friend as "My dearest life," and his messages ended with vows like, "Believe me, I am almost always at your side, I never leave you, and so it will be till death."

In Chopin's affections Tytus even took precedence over Konstancja. "No one except you," Frederic wrote to him, "will have my portrait. Only one other person might have it—but never before you, because you are my dearest. No one except myself may read your letter. As always, I carry your letters with me. How blissful it will be, in May, when I go outside the city walls, thinking of my approaching departure, to take out your letter and to assure myself that you love me—or at least to cast a glance at the handwriting and letter of one whom only I know how to love."

When Tytus wrote him from Poturzyn that he must spare his health and avoid going out in the evening, Frederic at once refused several invitations in order to obey his friend's admonition. One of the reasons why he was planning to go abroad was that Tytus considered this indispensable for his career. Even in regard to music the judgment of Tytus was decisive: "A single glance from you after each concert would mean more to me than all the praise of the journalists, the Elsners, Kurpinskis, Solivas, etc.," wrote Chopin. When he composed the Concerto in E minor, he again thought of Tytus as his best audience and critic: "I don't know whether it is because I have learned to feel at your side, but whenever I compose something I should be happy to know whether you like it, and it seems to me that my second concerto will have no value until you hear it."

It is possible that Frederic saw in Tytus the paragon of all virtues, because Tytus was his exact opposite. Ever since their schooldays this tall and robust athlete had held the admiration of the pale and sickly dreamer. Tytus's large hands were as expert on the keyboard as they were skillful in fencing, and he could manipulate a medieval crossbow as easily as a pistol. Frederic's interminable hesitations left him cold and even irritated him. He did not split hairs, and had a highly developed sense of reality. He had to possess these qualities in order to manage his estate, and he remained rooted in his concerns about sowing and selling his wheat, about his mill and his distillery, his lambs and his wool, for all the aesthetic gibes he endured from the Warsaw Ariel.

Most important, however, was the fact that Tytus brought Frederic's ideal down to earth. He did not hurt his friend's feelings but moderated their extravagance by his sober attitude. Since romantic ecstasy was alien to him, he retained his critical sense in the face of Chopin's complaints, which seemed to him exaggerated rather than tragic. Frederic respected his friend's masculine dominance. Probably reproved more than once, he frankly confessed to him: "I don't know why, but I'm afraid of you. Heaven knows that you, and no one else, have power over me."

He dreamed of seeing Tytus again. He constantly urged him to come to Warsaw; he coaxed him in his letters like a lover. "Don't kiss me now, for I haven't washed yet," he wrote. "You? Even if I were to rub myself with Byzantine ointments, you would not kiss me if I did not force you to do so by magnetic methods. There is such a force in nature. Today you'll dream that you're kissing me!"

Such epistolary caresses probably made Tytus smile. But how could he help loving Frederic for so much affection? He admired his friend's talent and worshiped his compositions; the Variations on a theme from Mozart were always kept open on the rack of his piano. Moreover, Tytus too had his secrets and confided them to Frederic, who often assured him of his discretion and believed that he could be "as silent as an abyss." The secrets probably concerned Mademoiselle Poletyllo, his own "ideal," who later became his wife.

Tytus did not come to Warsaw, although the capital was the scene of many interesting events at that time. The whole town turned out to see the new Thorwaldsen monument to Copernicus, which was solemnly unveiled to the accompaniment of a cantata by Kurpinski. At the end of May, 1830, Tsar Nicholas came to attend the opening of the Diet, which again attracted many foreign visitors, among them Prince Radziwill. As was usual on such occasions, many concerts took place. There were recitals by two piano prodigies—the twelve-year-old Antoni Leskiewicz, and the sixteen-year-old Friedrich Woerlitzer, pianist to the King of Prussia. From France came Mademoiselle Belleville, whose repertory included Chopin's Variations. Mademoiselle Blahetka had also intended to come, but she was dissuaded, probably by Frederic. Chopin too was thinking of a concert; it was projected as a farewell appearance before his departure, but in the end he postponed his concert and his departure as well. Like his friend Mochnacki, he was opposed to the Tsar's visit. He manifested his hostility by neglecting his Russian friends and did not visit them at the Russian Easter. Only his relation with the music-loving General Diakov and his old friendship with Duchess Lowicz were saved from this patriotic ostracism.

Novosiltsov's spies probably got wind of Chopin's sentiments, and the programs for official receptions ignored him. Chopin was not even invited to the court concert arranged at the castle. "People were wondering why I was not there," he wrote to Tytus, "but I wasn't surprised a bit."

Just as the year earlier he had been more absorbed in the playing of Paganini than in the coronation of Tsar Nicholas, so now he was more interested in the arrival of Henrietta Sontag, to whom legend ascribed the greatest vocal talent in history, than in the Tsar's visit. The twenty-four-year-old soprano possessed a voice of crystalline brilliance, especially in the higher registers; famed since her debut as a child of six, she had been a favorite of Weber and Beethoven, and the toast of various German capitals, of Prague, Vienna, Paris, and London. She gave eight concerts before crowded audiences in the National Theater in May and June, 1830, conquering the city and sending Chopin into a whirl.

He was enchanted by everything about her—her singing, her appearance, her winning simplicity of manner, and her kindness. He attended all of her concerts; he implored Tytus to come to Warsaw to share his enthusiasm, and wrote about her: "Her diminuendi are *non plus ultra,* her portamenti are beautiful, her scales, particularly the ascending chromatic ones, are magnificent." Words failed him when he tried to describe the arias he had heard—one was sung "very, very, very beautifully," another "extra well," and a third "most marvelously." Even the unfavorable comparisons were held to an unusual tone:

Some of her embroideries are of a completely new kind. She creates an enormous impression with them, yet it is a different impression from that made by Paganini. Perhaps because the genre is inferior. It seems that she breathes some perfume of freshest flowers into the audience; she caresses voluptuously, she strokes, but she rarely moves one to tears.

Henrietta Sontag was also famous for her beauty; she had a slender figure and delicate features; her eyes were large and her hair had the color of a mellowed violin. Frederic decided that she was "not beautiful but pretty in the highest degree."

The "divine messenger," as he called her, was also amiable. She captivated him the moment he was introduced to her by Prince Radziwill. The latter sketched for her some variations based on a Ukrainian song, and asked Chopin to develop the composition; later he abandoned this idea, to the secret joy of both the composer and the singer. Frederic often visited the glamorous girl, and wrote of her to Tytus: "In morning attire she is a million

times prettier and more pleasant than in an evening gala dress."
He hastened to add that apart from conversing with her on the
sofa, he did not "engage in anything else."

One day he found Soliva and his two best pupils at Fräulein
Sontag's. Gladkowska and Wolkow sang a duet composed by their
teacher and received a rather severe judgment from the great diva.
According to Chopin's report to his friend,

Henrietta Sontag told them that their voices are strained, and
that their method is good, but that they should produce their tones
in a different way lest they lose their voices completely after two
years. In my presence she told Wolkow that she had much facility,
many beautiful devices, but *une voix trop aiguë*, and urged them to
come to see her more often, so she could show them her own methods
as far as possible. This is more than natural kindness.

Needless to say, the girls were not happy at this verdict.
Frederic suddenly became their most intimate confidant; they
spoke bitterly about Soliva, and Frederic comforted them as best
he could. After that he spent many evenings at the Conservatory.
In the eyes of the two aspiring novices, Sontag's friend had acquired new prestige; at the same time it became clear that Lieutenant Bezobrazov was interested in Mademoiselle Wolkow's
voice rather than in Gladkowska's, and Frederic's dejected mood
gave way before a new confidence. The girls were hard at work in
preparation for their public debut; Chopin accompanied them on
the piano, and entertained them with improvisations. He also was
working with concentration. He was now satisfied with the allegro
of his Concerto in E minor and won praise from his friends when
he played for them. About the adagio, he wrote to Tytus that it
was not supposed to be vigorous, but romantic, serene, and melancholy: "It should create the impression of a pleasant evocation of
a thousand agreeable memories. It is a kind of meditation in
beautiful spring moonlight."

At the same time he developed the third movement of the concerto, the rondo, and began his beautiful *Andante spianato*. This
was a song of happiness, serene in mood and yet suffused with a

somber sense of the transience of all things; it was like a song overheard in the gentle tones of old clocks or the sound of tranquil waters. Later it was linked most surprisingly with a splendid polonaise (Opus 22).

At the beginning of July, Chopin played in a concert given by Madame Meier, to whom he owed a great deal, and who had appeared in his two concerts. This performance, which took place in the National Theater, did not attract a large audience, for the summer holidays were at hand. Frederic played his Variations on a Mozart theme, and was rewarded by thunderous applause; he was called back to the stage three times.

Soon after this, he went to visit Tytus in Poturzyn. The two friends, who had been separated for a year, had a great many things to tell each other. They rode in the fields, now clad in opulent golden harvest, and once again Frederic listened to peasant songs and watched the dancing at the summer festivals.

The two young men were much at the piano. Tytus had a fine sense of music; his touch was delicate and soft—amazing in such powerful hands—in Frederic's own style. The urban visitor was treated to a bit of a physical ordeal when his friend made him handle an archaic crossbow. But for two serene and happy weeks Frederic was awakened every morning by the rustling branches of a beautiful birch that stood before the manor.

On July 21st he was back in Warsaw, living through a day of vicarious stage fright. In his seat in a box at the National Theater, he tried to look as unconcerned as possible. Konstancja Gladkowska was making her debut in the title role of Paër's opera *L'Agnese*. She looked lovely, but the first scene did not come off very well; later the young singer played with more assurance, and the performance ended with loud applause and curtain calls. Frederic, who after his stay in Poturzyn was somewhat more balanced in his relation to his ideal, praised Konstancja to Tytus without losing his critical sense:

Gladkowska has almost no defects. She makes a better impression on the stage than in the concert hall. I won't say anything of her excellent dramatic acting, for there is nothing to say; as for the singing, except for some of her F sharps and G's in the upper register, we could not wish for anything better. You would be delighted with her phrasing, and her inflections are perfect.

The press hailed her with equal friendliness, but the opera failed to win Warsaw's heart, and the general opinion was that Soliva would have done better if he had chosen *La Vestale* for Gladkowska's first appearance. Mademoiselle Wolkow made her debut in a less thankless role as Fiovilla in Rossini's *Il Turco in Italia,* and Chopin admitted that "she was liked better than Gladkowska." The gallant Tytus asked Frederic to convey his congratulations to both ladies, and Frederic complied with enthusiasm.

Konstancja was not so impartial in appraising the success of her friend and rival, but Frederic assured her that the second performance of *L'Agnese* was excellent. "She sang flawlessly, without a single doubtful note," he wrote to Tytus; being human, he could not refrain from adding, "While Mademoiselle Wolkow sang delightfully out of tune."

' He now had a great deal to talk about with Konstancja. They discussed the parts she was to play in Rossini's *La Gazza ladra* and in *La Vestale.* Frederic was thoroughly familiar with these operas and could give the fledgling prima donna a number of useful hints. Konstancja listened to him attentively and willingly, ever more willingly. His Variations on a theme from Mozart, published by Haslinger, had appeared on the shelves at Brzezina's bookshop; the name of the man who accompanied her at the Conservatory could be read on a beautiful foreign publication that was mentioned appreciatively in the newspapers. And how could she avoid guessing why her delicate and discreet friend so often, and with so much feeling, played for her his adagio and waltz?

Half in jest she asked him whether he would not compose an opera, and Frederic half seriously replied, "Why not?" When he considered this idea, the artist in him rebelled; but the man, happy for the first time after so much anguish, listened willingly to the whisper of temptation. If Elsner could write about King

Leszek the White, why should not he find some king too? This project perhaps associated itself with hopes that he did not confide even to Tytus; perhaps, falling asleep in his attic, he saw his opera produced with a cast he knew well from his repertory of dreams.

But he was sobered by one thought: he must go abroad. His father, Tytus, the Skarbeks, and common sense demanded that he go abroad. And was there anyone who would oppose it? He mentioned his plans for going away to Konstancja and no doubt waited for her reaction. But the young woman said nothing. On one occasion he asked her for a souvenir, something that he could cherish when he was far away. She gave such a trifle at once: it was a ribbon. He immediately wrote to Tytus: "I have a ribbon." And then again: "Your letters are next to my heart and to the ribbon."

Thus for him love and friendship were fused together like the two sides of a treasured medallion.

Farewell to Poland

E VERY evening the piano was rolled out on the lawn to a spot under the old chestnut trees. In an attentive circle around it sat family and friends—Monsieur Nicolas and Madame Justyna, Madame Skarbek and Frederic Skarbek; behind them were ranged the servants of the estate and peasants from near-by villages. All the neighborhood knew that the young master who had been born in the small house of Zelazowa Wola was about to go abroad for a long time, a year, perhaps two, and everyone wanted to see the fellow-countryman who had become famous in his own and foreign lands. He had come into the world amidst these peaceful fields and ancient trees above which his music was now soaring, under the same eternal stars. This was actually Chopin's last vacation before his departure, but no one suspected that it would be his last visit to Zelazowa Wola and his last vacation on Polish soil.

His short stay in the country was often interrupted by visits to neighbors, to the Brochow parish, and to Zaleski in Sochaczew; meanwhile he did not lose touch with his friends in the capital. By the end of August he was back in Warsaw, working on a polonaise for piano and cello and on a trio, and polishing the rondo of his concerto. He led an active social life, went often to the theater; on one occasion he saw a performance of *Hamlet*. He was troubled only by the thought of his imminent departure. Like most persons who find it difficult to make real decisions, he readily made plans and readily changed them. "Next month, on such a day, I'll leave," he would often state resolutely, or "I'll leave next week," but as often these were words thrown to the winds.

It is easy to guess what detained him in Warsaw. "I don't know the reason, but I feel happy," he wrote to Tytus. He lacked the strength to relinquish the figment of happiness he had won after so much torment, and frankly admitted it: "Perhaps only a few moments of joy are given to man in life. Why should he wrench himself away from such illusions, which in any event cannot last long?" His happiness was ephemeral, his certainty delusive; only his doubts were lasting. At the very moment when he thought that his love might be reciprocated, he realized that it had no future. Konstancja's career, his consecration to his own art, which made it imperative for him to go abroad—everything doomed their love.

He had probably anticipated this from the beginning. A year before, when he had for the first time confided to Tytus that he had his "own ideal," he had added, "perhaps unfortunately"; later he had written: "Against my own will something has entered my head through my eyes, and I like to toy with it, perhaps most foolishly." And now, when his departure was a certainty, he wrote: "I'll leave for the sake of my vocation, and to comply with reason, of which I must have very little, since it is not strong enough to destroy everything else in my head."

But he loved Konstancja, loved her despite everything. He mentioned her in every letter to Tytus, although he was aware of his friend's reservations; he did not part with the keepsake he had received from her, and one day when, at a friend's, he met a girl who resembled Konstancja, he could not take his eyes off her, and "could not find his fingers" while playing the piano part of Spohr's quintet. His feeling got the better of him, and he wrote to his friend about it in a disarming way:

When I reflect, I feel so sorry for myself that I often become completely distracted. When I am preoccupied in this way, I might be run over by horses, and I would not know it. The other day I almost suffered such an accident in the street. On Sunday, struck by an unexpected glance from someone in church—it happened to come at some moment of pleasant numbness—I ran out at once; for a quarter of an hour I did not know what was happening to me, and, running into Doctor Parys, I did not know how to explain my confusion to him. I finally pretended that a dog had run up against my feet and that I had stepped on it. Sometimes I act so like a madman that it's frightening.

Under such stress Frederic was moved to confide his love also to another friend—his former classmate Jas Matuszynski, who was now studying medicine. Jas had the advantage of being acquainted with the Gladkowski family; he often visited them and became the *postillon d'amour* between Frederic and Konstancja.

Aside from his love, there was another reason why Frederic looked forward to his departure with a heavy heart. He was to leave his parental home, and the close family group that was like a sacred circle in which he was fairly worshiped. It meant parting from the people who were dearest to him and always gave him the most tender care. Moreover, his father was aging—he was now close to sixty. Worst of all was his vague fear that he was going away not for a year or two, as everyone said, but forever. On one occasion, justifying his hesitations to Tytus, he mentioned his gloomy premonitions: "I haven't the strength to fix a date; it seems to me that I am leaving home never to return, that I am going away to die. How sad it must be to die far from the place where one has lived!"

The sudden wave of revolutionary unrest that swept Europe in the summer of 1830 delayed Frederic's departure once again. In France the absolutist regime of the Bourbons was overthrown. Louis Philippe, the new king, publicly embraced Lafayette, the hero of liberation on two continents, and began his reign with the avowed principle of serving the welfare of his people. The conflagration spread to Belgium, where the Dutch were driven out, and Italy and Austria seethed with unrest. At the end of September, in a letter sent to Tytus through an acquaintance (it was preferable not to mention certain things in letters sent by the post, on account of Novosiltsov's spies), Chopin reported:

It is true that Father did not want me to leave a few weeks ago because of the disturbances taking place throughout Germany. In addition to what happened in the Rhineland, in Saxony which has also got a new king, in Brunswick, Kassel, Darmstadt, etc., there were rumors that in Vienna too a couple of thousand people were growing restive on account of flour. I don't know what the flour had to do with it, but I do know that there was something.

He knew also that Warsaw was in a ferment, that there was an increasing number of arrests, and that everybody expected changes soon. He knew about everything, although the newspapers maintained an idyllic tone, and the censorship was so effective that not the slightest reference to political events was printed. Tsar Nicholas refused to grant recognition to Louis Philippe, "king of the grocers," and concentrated troops against him in Poland. One had to be blind and deaf to imagine that the Poles would go to war against France, from which they themselves expected help. In fact, the Poles were looking for means to make it difficult for the Tsar to attack the country that was held to be the homeland of freedom.

Frederic got his information from his friends at the Little Hole, from Countess de Moriolles, from her father, and from the Duchess of Lowicz. The Duchess had recently returned from Ems, bringing back the Grand Duke in a state of utter nervous collapse. The revolutionary mood of Warsaw caused greater anxiety and confusion in the Belvedere than ever before. Constantine vented his fury on his soldiers, forcing them to drill for twenty-four hours without interruption, and even on his horses, depriving them of fodder for a whole day. He had fits of panic, when he would order whole battalions to guard him, or would flee from his palace to sleep in a different place each night. His fears were not quite without cause. Every day his spies reported ominous incidents in the city, such as the discovery of an inscription on the walls of the barracks, saying, "Soldiers, be ready to defend your homeland," or the posting of a facetious sign on the walls of his own Belvedere: "Apartment for rent." Clandestine revolutionary literature was openly circulated among the population. At sunset one could hear shots from Praga and the district bordering on the Vistula.

Chopin shared the general excitement. He went every day to the cafés that served as headquarters of the young revolutionists. He was fascinated by the sharp, birdlike face of Mochnacki; and at nights in his attic he was inspired by a militant ardor. He worked tirelessly and was happy with his music. He was gratified when the *Allgemeiner musikalischer Anzeiger* in Vienna published the first review on his Variations (Opus 2); it was a flattering critique, although written in a somewhat complicated style (it consisted of one sentence of seventy-one words).

At Elsner's suggestion, Frederic rehearsed his E minor concerto with a string quartet, and on September 22nd he played it with full orchestra at a soirée in his home, before an audience of musicians representing various coteries and warring factions; because the composer stood above their petty quarrels, he had invited them all. Their opinion was that Frederic must not leave before giving a public farewell concert featuring his new work. Elsner admired the rhythm of the concerto, Kurpinski its originality, and Soliva said of the rondo: *"Il vous fait beaucoup d'honneur."*

Meanwhile, Frederic was preparing for his departure with heavy heart. He applied for a passport to Austria and Prussia. "My trunk for the trip is bought," he wrote to Tytus, "my outfit is ready, my scores are bound, my handkerchiefs hemmed, my trousers made. All that remains is to say good-by, and that's the worst."

The date of the farewell concert was set for October 11, 1830. In arranging the program he followed the dictates of his heart: he asked Konstancja—and Mademoiselle Wolkow, for the sake of appearances—to take part. He went to a great deal of trouble to obtain the necessary government authorization for the appearance of these singers. Soliva suggested a chorus; he promised to conduct, took the concerto score home, studied it diligently, and possibly made a few corrections. The sale of tickets proceeded successfully, first among friends, then at Brzezina's bookstore. On the day of the concert the National Theater was sold out. One of the boxes was occupied by the Duchess of Lowicz, pale and beautiful as a pastel, accompanied by a few ladies of the palace and some aides-de-camp. In the first row sat Nicolas and Justyna Chopin with their daughters, next to them Zywny, Elsner, Kurpinski, and Albert Grzymala.

The opening piece was a symphony by Görner, the soloist of Chopin's first concert in March. Then Chopin appeared to play the allegro of the E minor concerto. The word "determination" could hardly define his mood at this concert. This was not only the occasion of the *première* of his new work; it was also his farewell to Warsaw—and Konstancja was taking part in it. These personal accents could scarcely fail to affect him. "I played as I do when I am alone," he said later, and this directness of feeling no doubt was communicated to the audience.

He was followed by Mademoiselle Wolkow, who sang an aria by Soliva with the chorus. Chopin listened to her absent-mindedly, but noticed that she was dressed "in blue like an angel." Then he appeared again to play the adagio of his concerto and the rondo, a dreamlike dance, pure and delicate, simple and yet full of ornament.

During the intermission congratulating friends trooped backstage, and Frederic received first bulletins on opinions heard in the foyer and at the buffet. Mochnacki, it was reported, had said that Chopin had a sixth sense, a sense of the piano; and someone brought the news that an aide-de-camp had rushed from the Duchess of Lowicz's box to the Belvedere to report on the concert to the Grand Duke.

The second part of the program began with the overture to Rossini's *William Tell*. The rest of the evening belonged entirely to Konstancja and Frederic. His "ideal," dressed in white, with roses in her hair, held the audience spellbound from the moment she appeared. This time Frederic looked and listened attentively.

Farewell to Poland

She sang the cavatina with recitative from Rossini's *La Donna del lago*, and the words, *Oh quante lagrime per te versai*, probably had for both of them a meaning beyond their relation to the opera. Konstancja was showered with applause. Someone said that her low B was worth a thousand ducats. Frederic was radiant escorting her from the stage. Then he returned to play his Grand Fantasy on Polish Airs.

He was saying farewell to Warsaw with one of his most genuinely Polish works, the one that most literally renders the melodies and rhythms of the land that he loved so much and that he was now leaving. He disliked academic folklore and sought in popular music not ready-made themes but the breath of the earth rising clear of space and time; however, in this composition he was faithful as never afterward to the songs of the peasants and the tunes played in the manor houses. One of the themes of the Fantasy was taken from the popular song *Laura and Filon,* whose composer, Kurpinski, was now listening to it; and next to him sat Nicolas and Justyna, who had long ago been brought together by the same melody in the drawing room at Zelazowa Wola. The magnificent final mazurka swept the audience off its feet. The composer-pianist was called back to the stage four times; four times he had to bow—and he did it properly and elegantly, having rehearsed this point of the program before the performance. There were wreaths of flowers; the most beautiful of them was from Duchess of Lowicz, and the most moving one from the waitresses who wore Cracow costumes at Madame Brzezicka's.

The press once again proved unintelligent. The Warsaw *Courier* disposed of this concert—which was the most beautiful concert Chopin ever gave in Poland, and into which he had put all his heart—in a banal complimentary notice; the other papers paid it even less attention. Frederic hardly had time to think of it. He fixed the date of his departure for October 16th, then changed it to October 20th, and in the end bought his ticket for November 2nd.

He paid final visits to his friends, was embraced and kissed, col-

The Life and Death of Chopin

lected suggestions and advice. He cast a last glance about familiar salons, once again heard old General Sowinski tap across the floor on his wooden leg. In the cafés he breathed once more the spirit of revolt against tyranny, and his comrades exhorted him: "Go, play, make Poland's name famous, and we'll set things aright here."

In his album he carried away the following stanza, dated October 23, 1830, and signed "K.G.":

> You leave your dear friends and most cherished kin
> To clothe your fame in immortality;
> From foreigners much glory you may win;
> But never can they love you more than we.

Frederic thought differently: beside the last line he added, "They can!"

On November 1st he drove by hansom cab to pay his last calls, and everywhere he was late, everywhere he was detained beyond the allotted time. It was later reported by those who knew his secret that he met Konstancja in the Saxon Park in a quiet avenue about noon. The youngest Kolberg stood guard at the entrance to insure that no one should see them. They talked together only for a little while and exchanged rings. Frederic gave Konstancja an old-fashioned wedding ring with a diamond set in silver. They agreed that they would communicate through Jas Matuszynski. He pressed her hand for the last time. Kolberg escorted him to the cab.

On the eve of his departure his classmates and friends gave him a merry farewell party. There was a supper with drinks, songs, and laughter. The comrades presented Frederic with a silver cup filled with earth, which he was to carry with him as a souvenir of Poland. This unexpected gift touched him so deeply that his emotion was communicated to the others, and Zywny, covered with snuff and hidden behind bottles, was not the only one to shed tears. Then the happy mood was resumed. Frederic played on the piano and improvised music to a poem of Witwicki's entitled "Revelry." They sang it in chorus, constantly returning to it amid toasts, speeches, and a gay tumult that did not abate until late at night.

The next morning, behind the locked doors of the Chopin home, Frederic took leave of his family. It was All Souls' Day, a day of mourning devoted to the memory of the dead, and there is no doubt that the family said a prayer for Emilia.

The stagecoach left in the afternoon from the post depot on Castle Square. Frederic had a seat next to the window. The large coach had room for twelve passengers; the luggage was carried on the roof. The postilion, in a hooded coat with a broad shoulder cape and an oilskin top hat, blew his horn. The four horses started off; the heavy vehicle rattled over the cobblestones. Frederic was speeding away from everything that was dearest to him—his family, his home and his attic studio, his love and his friends, the street of his youth, and the city of the first twenty years of his life. All he was taking with him was a trunk behind the railing overhead, his bound musical scores, and something that belonged to the Muses. With this he was going into the future.

Reflecting on such an inventory, he might have fallen into gloom had it not been for Tytus. At the last moment he had decided to accompany Chopin as far as Vienna. The two friends would meet in Kalisz.

At the outskirts of Warsaw, beyond the toll gate of Wola, as the stagecoach was approaching the Kalisz highway, it suddenly stopped. A chorus of voices burst forth, a guitar resounded, and Frederic heard the first words of a song:

> Nurtured on the soil of Poland,
> May your fame ring through the world!

He leaned out of the window and stared in amazement. In front of a roadside inn stood Elsner conducting the Conservatory choir. They were singing a cantata composed by the director expressly as a valedictory to the departing pupil, in the last spot that was still Warsaw.

(Nov. 2, 1830 ?)

CHAPTER 13

Frustration in Vienna

A s HAD been agreed, Frederic met Tytus in Kalisz, and thence
they traveled on together. They followed a route that Chopin
recalled from his trip of the year before, and the journey thrilled
him. When they reached Wroclaw on the evening of November
6, 1830, there was no question of fatigue, and they did not hesitate
for a moment about what they were going to do. They put up at
the inn *Zur goldenen Gans* and went at once to hear a performance of Roser von Reiter's *Alpenkönig*, an opera based on a ro-
mantic-comic fairy tale by Ferdinand Raimund.

On the next day, which was Sunday, Chopin went to church.
There he saw Joseph Schnabel, *Kapellmeister* of the cathedral,
whom he had met four years before on his way back from the
Silesian spa. On Monday at noon, at Schnabel's request, he played
the adagio and rondo of his Concerto in E minor during a rehearsal of the orchestra. He wrote about it to his parents: "The Germans were amazed at my playing. '*Was für ein leichtes Spiel hat
er,*' they were saying, but nothing about the composition. Tytus
even heard one man remark that I could play but not compose."
But Schnabel recognized his worth, took him by the chin and
caressed his face, and urged him to appear again that same evening in a concert under his direction.

Thus the annals of the Wroclaw musical society would show
that on November 8, 1830, a gifted though little-known pianist

from Warsaw played in its clubhouse. He played the rondo of his Concerto in E minor and improvised on a theme from Auber's *La Muette de Portici*, amid great applause. Apart from this the concert was of no note, and at nine o'clock the dancing began. The pianist received numerous compliments, which he later reported to his parents. Schnabel was enthusiastic and once again took him by the chin and patted his face in a fatherly manner. It was the first time that Tytus had witnessed one of his friend's triumphs. Frederic merely remarked, "I'm glad that I have made the old man happy."

After four days in Wroclaw (where they also heard Auber's *Le Maçon* and Winter's *Das unterbrochene Opferfest*; Chopin spoke scathingly of both), they left for Dresden, where they arrived on November 12th. Chopin at once called on Antoinette Pechwell and that evening heard her play at a private concert in the home of Doctor Kreissig, a local patron of the arts. He went there in a sedan chair, which amused him. The music lovers among whom he found himself put him in an even gayer mood. At eight huge tables sat rows of bejeweled ladies knitting at top speed. They were surrounded by a group of elderly men, whose shiny bald heads and spectacles were the very hallmark of stodginess. The company conversed, drank tea, and clinked their spoons. As one of this audience he heard the overture to *Fra Diavolo*, a solo by the famous singer Palazzesi, and a good performance by Pechwell; then he slipped out for the rest of the evening to attend the opera.

Frederic and Tytus spent seven days in Dresden, leaving the hotel each morning and returning at night. The Italian opera company that performed *La Muette de Portici*—they heard it twice —and Rossini's *Tancredi* did not fill them with enthusiasm, but they were delighted by the famous picture gallery of the city, where Frederic showed Tytus some favorite paintings. "When I see these pictures," he is reported to have said, "it is as though I were hearing music."

Every day they were entertained by one or another of the many Polish compatriots residing permanently in the capital of the last Polish dynasty. In the home of Countess Komar, Frederic met the three beautiful and very musical daughters of the house. Delphine, the eldest, married to Count Mieczyslaw Potocki, whom she had left a short time before, was especially famous for her charm and seductive grace. In the course of this round of teas and dinners Chopin also visited Madame Dobrzycka, who was close to the court. He played in her home before a distinguished audience including the two princesses of Saxony and the heir to the throne, Prince Johann, a refined lover of the arts and translator of Dante. The royal family gave Chopin introductions to some of the reigning houses in Italy. But the person whose company he enjoyed most of all in Dresden was Klengel, whom he had met a year before in the home of Pixis in Prague. This court organist proved a charming and intelligent man, a connoisseur of music, critical in his judgment but capable of enthusiasm. Chopin played both of his concertos for him and felt that this musician's praise of the compositions and the performance was not an empty compliment. They engaged in long conversations, which Chopin said were instructive. Klengel urged him to give a concert and even took steps toward arrangements, but he was unsuccessful because no auditorium was available.

Shortly before their departure, Frederic and Tytus were in the home of a Polish lady, Madame Niesiolowska. At dinner Klengel raised his glass and drank to Frederic's success. The hostess added, "But you must call yourself Szopski, because the foreigners will take Chopin away from us."

They continued their journey through Prague, where they stopped only for one day, and on the morning of November 23rd, arrived in Vienna. They put up first at the hotel *Zur Stadt London,* then moved to *Goldenes Lamm,* and after a few days rented an apartment in the Kohlmarkt. Their landlady, Baroness Lachmanowicz, was an attractive and amiable woman; moreover, she had been in Poland and had heard about Chopin. Their elegantly furnished three-room suite in the third story cost fifty Rhenish gulden per month. The two friends shared expenses.

Both were in high spirits. Frederic, sure of himself and his future, planned concerts, publication of his works, resumption of contacts with the celebrities he had met before, and further travels. He cashed his draft for money remitted by his father to the bank, received a tender letter from home, enjoyed three operas he had not known before—works of Mozart, Auber, and Rossini—and was enthusiastic about the performances of the leading singers, Heinefetter and Wild. He naturally went to see his friends Nidecki and Würfel, who was afflicted with a serious pulmonary ailment. He avoided the salons, mainly because of a severe cold, or, to use his own words, a swollen nose. For the time being he confined himself to making acquaintance with Doctor Malfatti, physician-in-ordinary to the emperor, who was married to the Polish Countess Ostrowska, and who received him most cordially—"as though I were his cousin." He wrote a letter to Jas Matuszynski in which he confessed his nostalgia in veiled terms, and then asked bluntly: "Am I loved?" He began to practice immediately after his arrival, playing in the house of Graff, the piano maker, every afternoon. A short time later Graff sent a piano to add to the comforts of his beautiful Kohlmarkt apartment.

In brief, Chopin began his second sojourn in Vienna with pleasant occupations and great plans and expectations. He looked forward to a repetition of his successes of the year before, and hoped that after the Vienna sojourn, Italy, France, and other European countries would open before him. But things turned out otherwise. Unforeseen developments in the larger world led to a dramatic crisis in his life, upset all his plans, and abruptly summoned him from the self-absorption of youth to the challenge of maturity.

The beginning of these developments took place in Warsaw. On the evening of November 29, 1830, an old brewery near the Vistula burst into flames. It was not an ordinary fire; it was the signal for a rising against the Russians. This was the cue awaited by eighteen conspirators hidden in a park near the Belvedere Palace, who were assigned to kidnap or assassinate the Grand Duke Constantine. Simultaneously a unit of cadets attacked the barracks of the Russian troops stationed in Warsaw. The conspirators marching on the Belvedere divided into two groups: one struck at the palace from the courtyard at the front; the other set up an ambush at the other end of the park to intercept Constantine if he should try to escape by that route. The nine conspirators who stormed the main entrance forced open the door and searched offices and drawing room, shouting, "Death to the tyrant!"

Constantine was taking his after-dinner nap; when the shouts awakened him, the palace was in the hands of the insurgents. Clad only in his underclothing and helped by his servant, he reached his wife's apartments by a secret passage, and this saved him. The conspirators found his room empty, the bed still warm. Lubowidzki, Governor of Warsaw, tried to stop them from entering the bedroom of the Duchess and was felled by bayonets. But what the conspirators saw in Joanna's chambers checked their impetus. They confronted a group of terror-stricken ladies-in-waiting who were on their knees, loudly reciting prayers.

At that moment cries resounded: "The Grand Duke is dead!" The group hidden in the park was announcing that the objective of the attack had been achieved. It proved a false triumph. A Russian general named Gendre, trying to escape from the Belvedere, had run into the ambush and, mistaken for Constantine in the darkness, had been stabbed to death by bayonet thrusts.

The eighteen daredevils left the palace, joined with other groups, and marched through the streets shouting, "To arms, to arms!" But the townspeople, taken by surprise, closed their shutters, unaware of what was going on, and not foreseeing what was to happen.

Thus, on a misty November night, began the uprising that so many Poles had been vaguely thinking of for years, but for which nobody was adequately prepared. There ensued a night of chaotic fighting and confusion, and only a week later did the cadets' revolt flare into a general upheaval. Warsaw was free. Constantine left the city and withdrew his Russian troops, not forgetting to take with him the shackled Major Lukasinski.

Reports of these events spread abroad slowly; in Vienna, Count Sedlnitzky, chief of police, and Chancellor Metternich informed the Emperor about these occurrences only on December 5th.

Frustration in Vienna

Neither the absolutist government nor the people of Vienna received the news from Warsaw with sympathy—Austria was one of the powers that had shared in the partition of Poland. In their third-story apartment Frederic and Tytus felt as though they were on a desert island with hostile murmurings all about them. But this was a small matter compared to the great importance of the events, which struck them like a thunderbolt. The longed-for movement for liberation that had been spoken of in whispers for years in the lyceum and the university, in the boardinghouse and the smoked-filled cafés, had begun. Freedom, that mysterious and forbidden word, had become incarnate.

There is no doubt that Frederic took a special personal interest in the first reports. He well remembered the unfortunate Joanna, the ducal chambers, and the palace park where he had played with the little Countess de Moriolles. Constantine, who had escaped from the conspirators, was the same tall man with bristling eyebrows, wide nostrils, and unpleasant face for whom he had once played a march in the Bruhl palace, and whose demonic rages he had so many times appeased in the Belvedere. Chopin had never had any feeling toward him; he had never invited the Grand Duke to his concerts and had not paid him a farewell visit on his departure from Warsaw. Now he took from his papers a letter of introduction to the Russian ambassador, which he had obtained through the Duchess, and realized that he would never use it.

Chopin's heart was in Warsaw. He constantly discussed the events there with Tytus, and asked his parents what he should do. He wrote that he wanted to return to Poland. His father answered advising and imploring him to persevere in his plans and in his calling, by means of which he would be of greater service to Poland than with a gun in his hands.

Tytus was eager to return to Poland as soon as possible, to join the army and to fight. His departure was a new blow to Frederic. The two spent their last evening together in discussions that Frederic was to remember for years. He accompanied Tytus to the post depot and bade him farewell with a heavy heart. Everything he needed most—peace of mind, strength, courage—was being taken from him with his friend's departure. Upon his return to the apartment he became desperate. The idea of remaining alone was inconceivable to him. He snatched up a few necessities, rushed to the stagecoach station, hired an express chaise, and ordered the driver to race along the road by which Tytus had gone, hoping to overtake him at the next station. When he reached the place, it was deserted; the stagecoach had left long before. It was night and drizzling, and the road was dark; Tytus's coach was speeding away into space. Frederic returned to Vienna heartbroken.

The following days were an ordeal. Everything now weighed on him inescapably—his daily worries and his thoughts of home. He managed as best he could. Sometimes he was practical and successful; other times found him downcast, overcome by despair. He turned over his expensive apartment to some English people and moved to the floor above. He was visited by friends of the Polish colony in Vienna. Nidecki came to practice the E minor concerto under the eyes of its composer. Every day at nine in the morning his teacher of German appeared.

"Hummel and his son came to see me," Chopin wrote to his family. "He is finishing my portrait, which is so like me that one could not hope to have it better done. In it I am sitting on a music stool in my dressing gown, with an inspired face, I don't know why. He uses a pencil, or rather chalk. The size is quarto; I think it's an engraving. This old Hummel is extraordinarily polite."

Frederic now clung to people. He became especially attached to Joseph Slavik, first violinist of the imperial orchestra, whom he had met in Würfel's home, and whose playing had captivated him. "Excepting Paganini, I haven't heard anything like it. He plays ninety-six staccato notes in one stroke of the bow. It's unbelievable," he wrote. Slavik was four years older than Chopin; he was born in Bohemia and had studied with Pixis in Prague and with Pierre Baillot in Paris. In Vienna he had won extraordinary tributes; the critics actually compared him to Paganini and predicted a great career for him, but this hope was frustrated by his untimely death. Chopin became so fond of him that he decided to collaborate with him on variations on a theme from Beethoven, for violin and piano. They began work on this composition, but the times were not propitious for creative effort. This project, as well as a plan for a concerto for two pianos, which he intended to perform with Nidecki, eventuated in nothing more than preliminary drafts that were later used in the Allegro de Concert (Opus 46).

With Slavik he often visited Madame Bayer, whose friendly home became the scene of new tribulations for Frederic. The trouble was that Madame Bayer's first name was Konstancja, and this was enough. "I like to visit her because this evokes memories; all the music, handkerchiefs, napkins, are marked with *her* name," he wrote to Matuszynski. And referring to the uprising, he added, "My God, she and my sisters can make themselves useful at least by making bandages. But I?"

As he had arranged with Konstancja, he sent her news about himself through Matuszynski. It consisted of vows of fidelity and assurances of his attachment, against which everything conspired —distance, the revolution, and even current conventions. He did not relish the fact that he could communicate with her only through a go-between, but he felt that if he should attempt to write to a young lady without her parents' permission, he would expose her to unpleasantness or even to malicious gossip. He adjured Matuszynski in romantic language:

Tell her that as long as my strength endures, until death, and even after my death, my ashes will lie under her feet. But everything you could say would still not be enough. . . . I'll write myself! I would have written long ago, I would not have tormented myself so long, but for people. If by any chance my letter should fall into the hands of a stranger, it might harm her reputation, so it's better that you should be my spokesman. Speak for me, *et j'en conviendrai.* *invite* *incite*

In addition to his anxiety, he suffered from jealousy. "I tear out my hair when I think that I might be forgotten. Today I am an Othello."

Matuszynski wrote to him rarely, yet Chopin lived only for news from Poland. He would come away dejectedly from the post

remarval

depot window where he asked for his letters, sent *poste restante*, and hasten back to his piano, to brood over his disappointments and his misery. On one occasion, receiving an unexpected letter from Matuszynski, he read it at the post depot; he walked home reeling, and as soon as he was in his rooms, he burst into tears.

He went among people, smiled, and attended parties, concealing his inner wound. During the holiday season he was overcome by a flood of childhood memories. He spent Christmas Eve with Slavik at Madame Bayer's, trying to dispel his nostalgia with music. Then, he wrote to Jas:

At midnight I walked slowly all alone to St. Stephen's. When I entered, no one was there. Not to pray, but to look at the immense structure at this hour, I stood in the darkest corner, at the foot of a Gothic pillar. The splendor, the grandeur of these enormous vaults, is indescribable. It was quiet—only occasionally was my reverie broken by the footsteps of the sacristan lighting candles at the rear. A coffin behind me, a coffin beneath me . . . only above me there was no coffin. A mournful harmony was brewing in my head. . . . More than ever I felt my loneliness.

The stirrings of a mournful harmony did not vanish without a trace. They gave rise to the Scherzo in B minor (Opus 20), which was conceived and begun at that time. The composition reflects the main preoccupations of this spiritual recluse—the Polish patriotic uprising and his own homesickness, which is revealed in the touching *cantilena* based on the melody of the Polish carol, "Sleep, Baby Jesus."

He was continually obsessed by the thought of Poland, and was often made to realize how difficult it was to live as a Pole among strangers who were most of the time indifferent and sometimes directly hostile. Once in an Italian restaurant he overheard two Viennese discussing the uprising. "The Lord made one mistake—in creating the Poles," said one. The other answered: *"In Polen ist nichts zu holen* (There's nothing worth while in Poland)."

"What scoundrels!" Frederic exclaimed in one of his letters.

He was so irritated by the general hostility toward Poles that he ostentatiously emphasized his nationality on every occasion. He used cuff links engraved with a Polish eagle and carried handkerchiefs embroidered with a picture of a Polish insurrectionist holding a scythe.

His absorption in the tragedy of Poland went much deeper. He was tortured by remorse because he was not sharing the hard lot of those dearest to him—his family, friends, the whole nation. "Were it not for the fact that I might be a burden to my father, I would return at once. I curse the moment of my departure," he wrote to Matuszynski. Even in a letter to his parents, though he had concealed his depression from them, pretending that he was feeling very well, he could not refrain from confessing the truth: "Mother is glad that I am not there, but I am not glad. There's nothing to be done."

Matuszynski suggested to him that he should write a battle song for the insurgents, to the words of a poem which he should select. "If I could," he answered, referring to Sobieski's defense of Vienna, "I would move all the tones inspired by blind, furious, frenzied feeling, at least partly to recapture the songs that were sung by Jan's army, whose shattered echoes still haunt the banks of the Danube." However, he failed to choose a poem, and after some time he wrote to his friend: "I cannot send you any song."

He was unable to concentrate, unable to work, unable to think of anything except the threat to his dear ones. The reports he received from them were more and more distressing. All his friends had joined the army—Tytus, Wilhelm Kolberg, Fontana, Mochnacki, Zaleski. Then Jas wrote him that he too was donning a uniform and leaving for the front as an army surgeon. The last links with Konstancja were breaking; Jas could no longer serve as a liaison with his beloved.

Frederic now seemed at the end of his tether. He did not know what to do with himself, where to turn. He wanted to leave: but where should he go? "My parents tell me to do what I please— but I don't like this. Shall I go to Paris? My friends here advise me to wait a little longer. Shall I return home? Remain here? Kill myself?"

The Life and Death of Chopin

Indecision, despair, homesickness, depression brought him to the brink of nervous breakdown. His last letter to Matuszynski consists of nothing but short exclamations, as though it had been dictated by a heart torn to shreds:

I don't know what's the matter with me. I love you more than life. Write to me. You're in the army! Did you dig trenches? Our poor parents! What are my friends doing? I live with you. I would die for you, for all of you. Why am I now so deserted? Why should only you have the privilege of being together at this terrible moment? Your flute will have much to bewail, but first let the piano do its wailing. You write that you're about to march off. . . . Embrace me. You go to war. Come back as a colonel. Good luck to you. Why can't I at least beat the drum?

Night Hours in Stuttgart

IT SEEMED as though everything were conspiring against the exile stranded in Vienna. Even music was becoming a source of disappointment. Chopin had come to Vienna to give concerts, yet month after month passed and there was no talk of a public appearance. He had hoped that the proceeds from his concerts would enable him to undertake further trips; instead he had to count every kreutzer. The Viennese friends whose encouragement had been so precious to him during his first sojourn were no longer in the city. Würfel was confined to his bed, coughing blood; when he was finally allowed to get up, he felt like an invalid, drained of all strength and energy. The Blahetkas had left for Germany. Schuppanzigh, Beethoven's "Lord Falstaff," was dead. Count Gallenberg, former director of the Kaerntnerthor theater, had gone bankrupt and left Vienna, and Duport, the French ballet master who succeeded him, was unwilling to arrange a paid recital for an artist who had played twice without fee. Haslinger had proved as unreliable as he was amiable: he did not publish the Sonata or the *Schweizerbub'* Variations, nor had he paid one penny for the previously published Variations (Opus 2). And although Chopin maintained friendly relations with other publishers, he failed to come to an understanding with any of them.

Furthermore, Vienna was no longer the Vienna it had been only recently. Succeeding Haydn, Mozart, Schubert, and Beethoven

came Lanner and Strauss, fathers of the waltz, who inaugurated
a new era in musical taste. Conducting orchestras composed of
two hundred instrumentalists, they played at court balls, thrilled
audiences in restaurants, and, having conquered the Danube
capital, were preparing to invade other European cities. The
venerable Stadler, one of the few survivors of the old guard—he
was in his eighties—could only shake his head and observe mourn-
fully that this was "a different Vienna."

Chopin became friendly with Kandler, a musicologist, and
Merk, first cellist of the opera, with whom he played in the homes
of friends. He met Thalberg, the celebrated pianist of aristocratic
blood and manners, and wrote of him:

Thalberg's playing is impressive, but he is not a man to my liking.
He is younger than I, and the ladies favor him. He makes potpourris
of *La Muette de Portici*. He gets his piano effects by means of the
pedal instead of his hands, and he takes tenths as I take octaves. He
has diamond buttons on his shirts. He does not admire Moscheles. All
in all, it is not so surprising that he liked only the *tutti* of my
concerto.

He attended mediocre concerts and remained faithful to his
love for the opera; but his musical life did not go beyond this
point. Only occasionally could he boast a moment of personal
satisfaction—as when on a visit to the imperial library with
Kandler, he found in the catalogue the entry "Chopin": it referred
to his manuscript of the Variations, which had been deposited
there by Haslinger.

He was not exaggerating when he wrote to Elsner at the end
of January, 1831:

From the day I learned of the events of November 29th to this
moment, I have experienced nothing but anguish and longing; and
it is in vain that Malfatti tries to convince me that every artist is a
cosmopolitan. Even if that were so, I am still in my cradle as an
artist, while as a Pole I have entered upon my third decade. There-

fore I hope that, knowing me, you will not hold it against me if my older feelings get the upper hand, and if so far I have not given thought to arranging a recital.

Every day, in the café, he eagerly scanned the Vienna papers for news from Poland. The Diet had proclaimed the Tsar dethroned as King of Poland. The first battle had demonstrated the valor of the Polish soldiers. Nevertheless, the Russians had succeeded in reaching Praga and now confronted Warsaw. The Polish capital was experiencing an exceptionally severe winter. It was so cold that birds froze to death while flying. The Russian troops brought cholera in their train, and this dread disease spread panic among the population. Chopin read an account of the battle of Grochow, in which an alder grove became the object of fierce fighting and changed hands several times. Could he think of anything but the view from his attic? Was it not there, where the strip of blue shadow floated over the peaceful plain, that smoke now rose from the cannon that could undoubtedly be heard in Warsaw? Was it not on those very fields that seven thousand Poles had fallen, wounded or dead?

All these broodings affected his physical health. Doctor Malfatti noticed this and took him under his care. The one-time physician of Beethoven realized that his arguments about cosmopolitanism had no effect on this artist, and resorted to a medical regimen that did help. Moreover, Chopin's spirit was revived by more favorable news from Poland. Polish troops had crossed the Vistula one night on a bridge covered with straw, under the very noses of the Russians, and had attacked them near the village of Wielkie Dembe. A two-day battle left the Poles victorious and in possession of considerable booty, including guns, five flags, and nine thousand prisoners.

At about this time, after four months of inner discord and musical apathy, Chopin made a public appearance in a matinee given by the singer Madame Garcia-Vestris on April 4, 1831. Besides his performance, the program featured singing by the Wild brothers and the Heinefetter sisters, a horn duet by the Levy brothers, and a cello solo by Merk. Notwithstanding this array of popular artists, the hall was not filled, and the concert failed to arouse special attention. Chopin played his E minor concerto, received favorable press comment, and hastened to send the notices to his family.

By this time he had given up his hopes of Vienna and began to consider leaving for Paris—a visit to Italy was out of the question because of political disturbances there. He reasoned correctly that while he was unsuccessful in Vienna, where the Polish cause was unpopular, he might expect better luck in Paris, where enthusiasm was running high in support of Poland's fight for freedom. He had realized this when he wrote to Elsner: "Everything that has happened in Warsaw, and that has been of disservice to me here, may turn out an advantage to me in Paris." He only had to draw the logical conclusion from this reasoning and to act; but this was beyond the power of his morbidly irresolute mind. Seeking as always for someone to lean upon, he found a Polish friend named Norbert Kumelski who was ready to leave Vienna, and he began to plan for the trip together with this companion.

There were many difficulties to overcome. Chopin was short of funds and refused to borrow from friends, although one of them, Czapski, begged him to accept a loan. With a heavy heart he turned to his parents, asking them to sell the diamond ring received from Tsar Alexander, which had now become particularly repulsive to him. Then Kumelski fell ill, the preparations for the journey bogged down, and Frederic again fell into apathy.

Deprived of friends, dependent on letters from home that came more and more rarely, and that, as he said, "were stabbed" in the black chambers of the censor, he began to keep a kind of diary of his thoughts. An entry of May 1, 1831, runs as follows:

I feel strange, sad, I don't know where to turn—why am I alone? Today it was lovely on the Prater—crowds of people—to whom I was completely indifferent—I admired the verdure—the spring odor—this innocence of nature brought back to me my childhood feelings—a storm was in the offing—I went home—there was no storm, only I was sad—why? I don't even care for music today—it's late at night, yet I don't feel sleepy—I don't know what is wrong with me—and I have begun my third decade.

Nowhere could he see the slightest ray of hope. He could not open his heart to his parents because he did not want to worry them—he had caused them enough disappointment by staying in Vienna without purpose or profit. "I am fine and I am having a wonderful time," he lied to them. He learned that his parents had gone to Zelazowa Wola and the Gladkowski family to Radom, and this news seemed to him comforting in view of the increasingly tragic reports on the uprising. After another Polish victory at Iganie, and the capture of more flags and thousands of prisoners, there followed a series of defeats. Bad leadership and bad government had squandered the fruits of the previous military successes. Frederic felt that the end was near.

Indeed, the situation was desperate. The forces concentrated by the Tsar in Poland had been intended for an attack against France. Thus France had been saved by the Polish uprising, but on the other hand did not intend to come to the aid of the fighting Poles, even though Lafayette advocated such a course and supported the Polish mission to the King of France. Louis Philippe did not go beyond some vague promises, and the English did not give even that much.

Frederic had now come to regard departure from Vienna as his only means of personal salvation. But the Vienna police and the Russian embassy were not in a hurry to grant him a passport. At the end of June he wrote to his parents:

You know how irresolute I am, and I encounter obstacles at every step here. Every day they promise me a passport, and every day I drag myself from Ananias to Caiphas, to recover what I have deposited with the police. Today I learned something new again, namely, that my passport has been lost somewhere. In addition to the fact that they won't find it, I must apply for a new one. All of us meet with strange vicissitudes nowadays; although I am ready to

leave, I cannot. I am taking Bayer's advice; I'll obtain a passport
to England, but I'll go to Paris. Malfatti is giving me a letter of
introduction to Paër, his good friend. Kandler has written about me
for the Leipzig musical paper.

These friends were his only refuge from unbearable thoughts.
Malfatti in particular gave him so much kindness and solicitude
that Frederic always found great pleasure in visiting him. The
Doctor had moved to his summer residence, which had a beautiful
view of Vienna in one direction and overlooked picturesque mountain villages and cloisters on the other side. Chopin used to go
there with Hummel. On St. John's Day, the Doctor's name day,
he came with several musicians and singers, brought by the publisher Mechetti. Of this occasion Chopin wrote:

We gave him a good deal of music. A large crowd of strangers
listened to the concert on the terrace. There was magnificent moonlight, the fountains played, a wonderful fragrance from the hothouse
filled the air. In brief, it was a splendid night. The place is absolutely
delightful.

He mentioned also that one of the invited singers sang *Oh
quante lagrime per te versai*. What were his feelings when the
familiar aria resounded in this carefree company, suddenly reminding him of his loved ones, their flight from Warsaw in the
perils of war and epidemic, their still uncertain fate? His secretive heart must have throbbed with a surge of emotion, but in
his letter he confined himself to these words: "Gladkowska sang
much better at my farewell concert in Warsaw."

One day during this period, in which the news from Poland was
increasingly bad, Chopin went with Kumelski and Czapski on an
excursion to Kahlenberg. It was on this hill near Vienna, almost
one hundred and fifty years earlier, that King Jan Sobieski had
camped with his troops, attending Mass in the Camaldolite church
before giving battle to the Turk. Here, on this height, he had
dubbed his son a knight; here he had ordered his mailed hussars
to charge the infidels. A thousand Polish knights had fallen on

this battlefield—one fourth of the Christian army—to insure the victory of the cross over the crescent. Recalling these events in talking with his friends, Frederic must have meditated on the destiny of his country. Perhaps he evoked in spirit that long-ago pageant—the flowing banners of the hussars, the clatter of their charging horses, the echoes of glory and victory. In these days of Polish defeat, when hope of liberation was dying, the unfathomable processes of imagination perhaps stirred in him those visions of greatness and decline, power and impotence, happiness and grief, that later became the theme of so much of his musical creation. He plucked a leaf from a tree on the Kahlenberg and sent it to his sister Izabela.

At this time he added to his manuscripts a complete draft of his Scherzo in B minor (Opus 20) and some new études. These fragments reflected the sorrow, anger, and despair that were consuming him. He knew what his fellow-countrymen were expecting of him, and he was deeply moved when he read a letter from Witwicki, author of "The Revelry" and other poems which Chopin was setting to music. "You absolutely must become the creator of Polish opera," wrote Witwicki. "It is my deep conviction that you can achieve this, and that as a Polish national composer you will open for your talent an immensely rich field, in which you will win extraordinary fame. But you must always remember: your motif must be nationality, nationality, and again nationality."

He was slowly preparing for his departure, waiting for the passport and for money. The lost document was finally found at the police bureau and stamped *Passant par Paris à Londres*. The Tsarist embassy considered his application for two days and finally granted him permission to go only to Munich. This was merely a chicanery. What mattered was that he had the signature of the French ambassador.

In the meantime he obtained the health certificate that was required because of the prevalence of cholera. As the day of his departure approached, his spirits rose somewhat. He heard Rossini's opera *Le Siège de Corinthe*, which he praised greatly, and submitted to Mechetti the manuscript of his Polonaise for cello (Opus 3), which he dedicated to Merk. He assured his parents in cheerful and amusing letters that he was in good spirits. He informed them that he was growing side whiskers, which throve especially well on the right cheek, and added, "They aren't needed on the left, because only the right side faces the public." He resumed his old pranks, and in the houses of his friends he mimicked Austrian generals. With seven friends—among whom was Würfel, practically resurrected from the dead—he went to Luna Park, and enjoyed himself so much that he even tried the scenic railway, called the *Rutsch*. He mentioned it in a letter, scolding himself and execrating the others. "From a passionate deprecator of this stupid Viennese amusement, I developed into its zealous champion, until reason returned to my head, and with it the realization that the contraption serves to amuse sound, strong bodies and befuddle capable minds—and this at a time when all mankind needs these for its defense. Devil take it all!"

It is quite possible that he left Vienna with these same words. After eight months of adversity and unhappiness, he left on July 20, 1831. He had received no money from home and he asked his father to send it to Munich. With Kumelski he traveled through the lovely Danube valley, with its ancient castles crowning wooded hills, its charming little towns, its vineyards, and its abbeys. They passed through Linz and then Salzburg, with its memories of Mozart and its cathedral towers.

In Munich, Chopin immediately became a part of the world of musicians. He met Berg, a composer, Stunz, a conductor, and many singers. He became friendly with Peter von Lindpaintner, composer of the opera *Bergkönig*, who was considered the foremost master of the baton in Germany. On the initiative of these musicians, he gave a concert in the hall of the Munich Philharmonic Society on August 28th. He was assisted by several vocalists—Bayer, Lenz, Harm, and Pellegrini—and by two clarinet virtuosos, Bärman and Schubert; Stunz was the conductor. Chopin played his E minor concerto and the Grand Fantasy on Polish Airs, and was received most cordially. Only one review of this concert appeared, but it was intelligent and favorable, stressing the pianist's superior technique and delicacy of touch, the effectiveness of the concerto, and the charm of the Fantasy.

But it was not music that preoccupied him. On August 26th he made the following entry in his notebook:

The papers and posters have already announced my concert, which I am to give in two days, but it is as though it were never to take place, it concerns me so little. I don't listen to compliments, which seem to me more and more stupid. I wish I were dead. I'd like to see my parents again. Her image is before my eyes—it seems to me that I don't love her, but I cannot get her out of my head. Everything I have seen abroad so far seems to me old, unbearable, and only makes me long for home, for those blessed hours that I didn't know how to appreciate. What once seemed to me great today seems common, and what was once common is today incomparable —extraordinary—too great—too high. The people here are not my people; they are kind, but kind by habit. They do everything in an orderly, flat, mediocre way, and this kills me. I shouldn't ever want to feel mediocre.

A few days after the concert, having received the long-expected remittance from his father, he left for Stuttgart. Lindpaintner had informed his friends of Chopin's coming, and they received him with curiosity and cordiality. The most amiable of them was Johann Peter Pixis, pianist and composer, a younger brother of the director of the Prague Conservatory, whose guest Frederic had been in 1829.

Chopin intended to stay only a short time in Stuttgart. He unpacked only a few things, but among these were his manuscripts and notebook. He spent most of his time on these papers. The news from Warsaw was tragic. After a nine months' struggle against the Russian colossus, Poland was vanquished. Chopin sat at night with his notebook before him, envisioning in death the only escape from human misfortune:

Stuttgart. A strange thing! This bed to which I am going perhaps has served more than one dying man, and yet today it does not repulse me! Perhaps many corpses have lain on it, and for a long time. And why is a corpse a worse thing than I am? A corpse likewise knows nothing about father, mother, sisters, Tytus. Nor has a corpse a beloved. It can't speak its own language with those around it. Such a corpse is as pale as I am. It is as cold as now I am cold to everything. It has ceased to live, and I too have had my fill of living. My fill? Has the corpse had its fill of life? If it had had satiety, it would look well, and yet it looks so wretched—could it be that life affects one's features, one's facial expression, the human appearance, to such an extent? Why do we live such a miserable life, consuming us and serving only to change us into corpses?

The tower clocks of Stuttgart strike the night hours. Ah, how many corpses are being made in the world in this minute! Children have lost their mothers, mothers their children. How many plans have gone to waste, how much grief over the dead at this moment—and how much glee, how many dishonest guardians! How many oppressed creatures have become corpses! A vile corpse and a good corpse! Virtue and crime are one, they are sisters when they are corpses. So it's obvious that death is man's best action—and if so, what's his worst? Birth—since it is the exact opposite to the best action. So I'm right in being angry that I came into the world! Why wasn't I allowed to remain part of the nonliving world?

The memory of Konstancja paled before such thoughts; Frederic was no longer irritated by his uncertainty about her feelings. He moved away from her, resigned:

She was only pretending. Or she is pretending now. Ah, it's a nut that can't be cracked. Yes, no, yes, no, finger by finger—it has slipped! She loves me? She loves me surely? Let her do as she likes.

He found relief in tears:

It's a long time since they have flowed. Where do they come from? Haven't I been wrapped in a dry sorrow for a long time? Ah, I couldn't cry for a long time. How well I feel . . . full of longing! Full of longing, and well. What kind of feeling is this? Well, and longing. If you're longing, you don't feel well, and yet it's sweet! It's a curious state.

Night Hours in Stuttgart

In the outer world events took their course, and now his fatherland suffered the *coup de grâce*. On September 5, 1831, General Paskevich's Russian armies reached the fortifications of Warsaw; on the following day the assault began. The main defense line ran through Powazki, where Emilia was buried, and through Wola, the familiar Wola through which Frederic had so often passed on his way to the Skarbek estate, and where Elsner had bidden him farewell with his cantata. The Wola trenches were defended by General Sowinski, in whose home Frederic had written the *Schweizerbub'* variations. The old soldier had defended his positions to the bitter end. After the Russians had taken all the strongholds, he with a score of soldiers barricaded himself in a little church, and when the enemy broke in, he kept on firing until he was stabbed to death by Russian bayonets. He was found leaning against a gun set in the opening of a wall, his wooden leg still holding his body erect. There he stood, a gray ghost, bespattered with blood. The Russian soldiers told awed tales about the aged hero's valiant last fight: there was even a rumor that he had not died but had been taken prisoner.

On September 8th Warsaw capitulated. Chopin wrote in his notebook:

Stuttgart. I wrote the preceding pages knowing nothing—not even that the enemy was within the gates! The suburbs have been destroyed, burned down. Jas! Wilus! [Wilhelm Kolberg] probably died on the ramparts. Sowinski, that beloved man, in the hands of these scoundrels! O God, you exist! You exist and yet you don't avenge! Have you not had your fill of Moscow's crimes, or are you yourself a Muscovite? My poor father! That dearest man—perhaps starving, without a penny to buy bread for Mother! My sisters— perhaps they have fallen to the fury of the unleashed Muscovite beasts! Paskevich—that cur from Mohilev—conquering the seat of the first monarchs of Europe! A Muscovite ruling the world! O Father, such are your pleasures in your old age! Mother, suffering, tender Mother, you have survived your daughter only to live to see the Muscovite trample her bones as he came to oppress you. Ah, Powazki! Have they respected her grave? Trampled—a thousand other corpses heaped over the grave. The city burned! Ah, why couldn't I kill at least one Muscovite! O Tytus, Tytus!

When he had recovered from his first shock, Chopin returned in his thoughts to Konstancja, and wrote:

Stuttgart. What has happened to her? Where is she? Poor girl! Perhaps she is in the hands of the Muscovites! A Muscovite snatching, strangling, murdering, killing her! Oh, my life, I am alone here! Come to me, I'll wipe away your tears. I'll heal the wounds of the present, recalling the past to you. . . .

He wrote all this for himself alone, on broad album sheets, in words that were not always well chosen but that were the immediate speech of his emotions.

It is not known which of his musical manuscripts he had with him during these tragic nights. There are reasons for assuming that he revised his Scherzo in B minor (Opus 20), that he wrote down the bars of his Preludes in A minor (Opus 28, No. 2) and D minor (Opus 28, No. 24), and also composed the first outline of his Ballade in G minor (Opus 23). But it was most probably then that he wrote his Etude in C minor (Opus 10, No. 12), called the "Revolutionary" Etude. How he was able to extract such a clear, virile, and heroic voice from the dark chaos of feelings recorded in his notebook remains an element of the mystery of music.

The tower clocks of Stuttgart struck the night hours. They marked the hour at which the old world died. Freedom, that mysterious and forbidden word, had not become incarnate.

Frederic packed his manuscripts and notebook, and with this luggage he set out on his way, reaching Paris by the middle of September, there to wonder, "What next?"

15

Paris

CHOPIN would go out on his balcony to gaze at the boulevards, the crowds passing by, the silver and amethyst evening sky, and, at night, the millions of lights. All of Paris, from Montmartre to the Panthéon, lay before him as on the palm of his hand, immense and unknown, mysterious and alluring. He was very fond of his first apartment in Paris, a small room with lovely mahogany furniture, a wrought-iron balcony, and a dazzling view. It was high up, in the fourth story, at No. 27 Boulevard Poissonière.

He had only to descend the stairs to find himself in one of the busiest streets of the city. All about were throngs of people with an animation of glance and gesture that offered a striking contrast to the stolid ways of Germany. Only a year before these people had left their barricades after achieving an easy triumph in a revolution that in fact had not satisfied anyone. Paris continued to live in a state of suppressed excitement, and everyone was engrossed in politics. Day after day Chopin witnessed street demonstrations; he saw gatherings dispersed by the police. He seized upon newspapers sparkling with lampoons and caricatures —such of them as escaped confiscation.

Political opinions were reflected even in the way people dressed, and waistcoats were as significant as banners. The Carlists, partisans of the overthrown Bourbons, wore green ones; the republicans wore red ones. The Saint-Simonians, whom Chopin

a convert to religion

described as "new Christians who have created a religion of their own, who have a large number of proselytes, and who are also for equality," wore blue. The champions of the proletariat dressed in long redingotes reaching to their ankles, and the adherents of the *Jeune France* movement tied their cravats in a special way and wore goatees. Chopin met women in the garb of sutlers or pages, and listened to the tirades of ragged beggars who defied Louis Philippe, the new king, ignoring passing police patrols. He was baffled and somewhat embarrassed by the ingenuity of street peddlers who loudly called out the titles of the pamphlets they sold at one sou apiece: *L'art de faire des amants et de les conserver ensuite* ("How to get lovers and keep them"), *Les amours des prêtres* ("Gallant adventures of priests"), and so on.

There was plenty of material to whet his keen powers of observation and his passion for spying out human obliquities. After only a few days in Paris, on September 18, 1831, he ventured the following general estimate in a letter to Kumelski:

It is the greatest splendor, the greatest vileness, the greatest virtue, the greatest vice. At every step there are posters about venereal sickness; here is more noise, clamor, clatter, and mud than can be imagined. One gets lost in this paradise, and lost comfortably, because nobody asks how anyone lives. One can walk in the street in rags and frequent the best company. One day you eat an abundant dinner for thirty-two sous in a restaurant with mirrors, gold, and bright gas illumination, and the next day you may lunch at a place where they serve you portions fit for a bird and charge three times as much.

On another occasion he wrote to Tytus: "Paris is everything your heart desires—you may divert yourself, laugh, weep, do anything you please, and no one will pay any attention, for there are thousands doing the same thing as you—and each in his own way." Conquered by the charm of the capital, he gazed at it from his high observation post, often dazzled by the sight, but feeling isolated among strangers, uncertain of his future, cut off from Poland, his purse depleted by his journey.

Paris

Such then were his first feelings in the city upon which Louis Philippe was trying to impose the ideals of bourgeois mediocrity, while in the eyes of Europe it was the birthplace of a new art and a new thought. The Romantic movement contradicted everything that was advocated by the "bourgeois monarchy." And as though in defiance of the King, who always carried an umbrella, Romanticism fell on France like a fresh downpour of rain. The revolution that had failed to achieve its goals in street fighting rolled onward in men's minds. Tradition and its rules were being discarded, and enthusiasm for nature, life, and freedom was destroying every form of scholasticism and obsolete taboo.

No less important was the fact that in this era of planned mediocrity, Paris became the gathering point of the least mediocre men. The new arrival could easily feel timidity at the thought of joining the world of Paris artists, which boasted an extraordinary roster of genius. As he stood on his balcony he no doubt realized with emotion that in the city spread before him lived Chateaubriand, Hugo, Balzac, de Vigny, Sainte-Beuve, Lamartine, Lamennais, Delacroix, Rossini, Cherubini, Kalkbrenner, Lesueur, Auber, Meyerbeer, and many other luminaries of the arts. How fascinating this milieu must have seemed to him! How eager he must have been to meet these men!

He met them sooner than he expected. He took Malfatti's letter from his mahogany desk, and, with some apprehension over the memory of his Vienna experience, went to see Paër. He stood before the sixty-year-old author of forty operas that left an indelible mark on Elsner; in one of them, *L'Agnese,* Konstancja had made her debut. Ferdinand Paër, then court conductor, old and crotchety, unfriendly to people and not too popular, succumbed to the young visitor's charm. Less than a week later, Chopin had met Rossini, Cherubini, Baillot, and Kalkbrenner.

He felt that his good star was again in the ascendant. The news from home was that all his family was safe. He also heard from Tytus, about whom he had received disquieting reports after the uprising. What his parents had written about his friend was not quite clear, and he had feared the worst. Now it turned out that Tytus had suffered only a slight contusion, and had soon recovered. This was a great comfort. He missed Tytus as of old; no one could replace him, yet Chopin could not live without a kindred soul close to him. He tried to fill this gap as well as he could. He roamed about Paris in the company of Antoni Wodzinski and Antoni Orlowski, whom he had forgiven for writing waltzes and gallopades on the themes of his F minor concerto. In Walenty Radziwill he found a fanatical theatergoer like himself, and together with him he visited the three opera houses in Paris. The grand opera, known as the Académie Royale de Musique, offered a famous tenor, Adolphe Nourrit. The Opéra Comique had a splendid orchestra under Feydeau. And the Théâtre des Italiens, directed by Rossini, was considered the best in the world, because of such singers as Rubini, Lablache, Pasta, Malibran, and Schröder-Devrient. Chopin had intimate talks about music with Ludwik Norblin of Warsaw, first violinist of the royal opera, and was happy to discover in this subtle and sensitive artist a nature attuned to his own.

He met many other Poles. Paris had become the haven of Polish emigrants seeking to escape Russian reprisals, and companies of insurgents had marched across half of Europe to France. The French government received them with fears, the people of the streets with enthusiasm. The excitable Paris populace even demanded a war against Russia on behalf of Poland, and a war against England on behalf of Belgium. The name of Poland was on everyone's lips; for many it was a symbol of freedom, to others it brought at least a tinge of remorse. The masses, dissatisfied with their revolution, craved examples of heroism. Decidedly, the atmosphere here was different from that of Vienna, where God was criticized for having created the Poles. In Paris, theatrical posters featured an attraction entitled *Poland Has Not Yet Perished*, the Dombrowski mazurka that had been the anthem of the Polish insurgents. Chopin became increasingly attached to this city. He wrote to Kumelski: "Perhaps I'll stay here for a long time." He no longer wondered what would happen to him next; the future lay open before him.

Of the musicians whom he met through Paër, he was most impressed not by Rossini, his favorite composer, not by Cherubini, director of the Conservatoire, nor by Baillot, the teacher of Slavik, but by Kalkbrenner. Upon hearing him play, Chopin wrote to Tytus: "I am not worthy even of tying his shoelace."

Friedrich Kalkbrenner was then at the height of his fame. It was said of him that he was to the piano what Cicero was to the Latin language. His situation was imposing; he was considered the foremost pianist and piano teacher of the day, and he owned shares in the piano factory of Pleyel & Cie. Born in Germany, he had settled in Paris and become an integral part of the artistic world of the capital. Now forty-three years old, he was known for his boundless vanity; but although he was personally unpopular, he was universally admired for his masterful playing. His art was cold but flawless; he never abused his strength, and he captivated his listeners with his pure and even tone. He was less felicitous as a composer, despite his great ambition and productivity in this field. As a teacher, however, he had no equal in Europe. He used a method of his own, aiming primarily to improve the work of the fingers. For this purpose he devised the so-called *guide-mains*, a kind of railing parallel to the keyboard and supporting the forearm at a point near the wrist. This device made it possible to train the fingers independently of the muscles of the hand, which resulted in an improved touch and tone. Kalkbrenner set forth the principles of his method in a book entitled *Méthode pour apprendre le pianoforte à l'aide de guide-mains,* published in 1830.

Chopin described his meeting with Kalkbrenner in a letter to Tytus:

You won't believe how curious I was about Herz, Liszt, Hiller, etc. —but all of them are ciphers beside Kalkbrenner. I'll confess to you that I played like Herz, but that I should like to play like Kalkbrenner. If Paganini is perfection, Kalkbrenner is his equal, but in an entirely different style. It is difficult to describe his calm, his magical touch, his extraordinary evenness, and the mastery displayed in his every note. He is a giant merely trampling over such players as Herz, Czerny, and consequently myself.

What, then, has happened? When I was introduced to Kalkbrenner, he asked me to play something to him. Willy-nilly, not having heard him before, and knowing how Heiz plays, I doffed my pride and sat down. I played my E minor, for which all the Lindpaintners, Bergs, Stunzs, the Schunkes in the Rhineland, and all Bavaria could not find praise enough. I amazed Kalkbrenner, who immediately asked me whether I was not a pupil of Field, saying that I played in the style of Cramer and had the Field touch. I was greatly pleased, the more so when Kalkbrenner sat down at the piano and, trying to show off to me, made a mistake and was forced to stop! But you should have heard him when he started again. I had never imagined anything like it.

Since then we have been meeting every day, in my place or at his, and now, having come to know me, he has proposed that I should study with him for three years; thus he would make something out of me, something quite special. I told him that I knew how much I still had to learn, but that I did not wish to imitate anybody and that three years was too much. In the meantime he convinced me that I play beautifully when I am inspired, and poorly when I am not—and this never happens to him. He told me, after close observation, that I lack schooling, that I am on the road to excellence but that I might go astray, that there will be no representative of a great piano school after he dies or ceases playing, that I could not found a new school, even if I wanted to, without knowing the old one—in brief, that I am not a perfect machine, and as a result I hinder the free course of my thoughts. He also said that my compositions have character, that it would be a pity if I did not become what I promise to be, etc., etc.

Kalkbrenner's proposal amazed everyone who heard about it. The very fact that this inaccessible and solemn magus took an interest in the newly arrived pianist, that he saw him daily, honoring his fourth-story flat with his visits, was extraordinary. He even offered to teach Chopin free of charge and guaranteed him the use of the Pleyel hall for his concerts.

Frederic hastened to share this exciting news with his parents and, as usual, asked them for advice. At first the whole family was dazzled by Kalkbrenner's magnificent gesture. Izabela wrote that after receiving Frederic's letter she and Ludwika could not sleep for sheer joy. But this enthusiasm was short-lived. The next day the sisters read the letter to Elsner, who, upon hearing it, cried out, "This is pure jealousy! Three years!"

This reaction took Ludwika unawares. "Surprised at the fact that he was immediately of an opinion almost exactly the opposite of ours," she wrote to Frederic, "I extolled Kalkbrenner's merits and his love for art, and reread several times the passage in which you state that he is not motivated by a desire for personal advantage, etc. All this was of no avail. Elsner made a wry face and said that he would write to you himself, adding, 'I know Frederic. He is kindhearted and has no vanity.' "

Elsner showed the Chopin family his letter to Frederic, but he wrote it with more caution than he had displayed in his conversation with the girls. In some places he shifted to French, as if expecting Frederic to show the letter to his friends, perhaps to Lesueur, as Ludwika urged him to do, or even to Kalkbrenner himself.

I learn with great pleasure [wrote Elsner] that the foremost pianofortist (as you said), that is, Kalkbrenner, received you so well. (I knew his father in Paris in 1805, and even then his young son was considered one of the foremost virtuosos.)

I am even more gratified to learn that he promised to reveal the secrets of his art to you. But I am surprised that he fixes a period of three years for this. How could he know, after seeing and hearing you only once, that you would need all that time to grasp his method, etc., that you should devote your musical genius only to the clavichord and your artistic talent only to this kind of composition? I hope that he will change his verdict when he knows you more intimately.

In the science of composition, one must not set down rules, especially for pupils whose talents are obvious; let them discover these rules for themselves, to the end that they may at some time surpass themselves; let them have means for discovering what has not yet been discovered. In the mechanics of art, for its advancement even as regards performance, it is imperative not only that the pupil should equal and surpass his master, but also that he should have something of his own—something that will enable him too to distinguish himself.

Nicolas Chopin also expressed some reservations as to the requirement of three years, but left the final decision to Frederic. He wrote:

The friendship Kalkbrenner has shown you is very flattering, and as your father I am most obliged to him for it. But, my dear son, I don't understand how, considering your talent, which he says he appreciates, he can think that three years are needed to make an artist of you under his eyes, and to give you schooling. I am unable to understand this latter word, and I asked your true friend Elsner to tell me its meaning, and I shall refer you to his letter. You know that I have done everything in my power to foster your ability and to develop your talent, that I have never opposed you in anything, and you also know that your mind has worked more intensely than your fingers. While others spend whole days at the piano, you seldom spend an hour performing works of others. In view of all these facts, this three-year term passes my understanding. However, I do not wish to oppose you in anything, and I will say only that you will please me if you do not make a decision until you have thought it over carefully and heard other people's opinions.

All these letters failed to change Frederic's opinion of Kalk-brenner. He refused to believe that jealousy could be a motive. He wrote to Elsner:

Three years is much, too much (Kalkbrenner himself admits it after observing me more closely, and this should prove to you that a true virtuoso who deserves his fame does not know jealousy). Nevertheless, I would agree to work even for three years if I could in this way achieve a big step forward in my plans. I am intelligent enough not to become a copy of Kalkbrenner: nothing can ever eradicate my perhaps overbold but pure desire and intention to create a new world for myself, and if I work, it will be only for the purpose of standing on stronger feet. . . . I hope that you will not refuse me your blessing, since you know with what motives and what intentions I act.

Not only Elsner and the Chopin family were opposed to the unexpected idea of a further period of study; Frederic's new friends also spoke against it. In spite of all this, he decided to sit down at the piano as a pupil of Kalkbrenner. He closed his eyes to the amusing mannerisms of the master and listened attentively to his instructions. But the lessons did not continue for three years, or even for a few months; soon they ceased to be lessons at all, turning to an exchange of ideas between two musicians of whom each respected the other's individuality.

Chopin could not fail to realize that the Parisian Cicero was indeed a classicist, but that his classicism belonged to an outdated school. He must also have realized that the career of a pianist, which might have seemed attractive in the first flush of his excitement on arriving in Paris, could not be a substitute for the joy of creation that he had so often experienced in his lonely hours in Warsaw, Vienna, and Stuttgart. "I ride in my own coach —I have only hired a coachman for the horses," he said, referring to his fingers guided by the inventor of the *guide-mains*.

Kalkbrenner, for his part, whether his eagerness reflected sincere admiration for Chopin or only ambition to count him among his pupils, or both, gave many proofs of his friendship. He opened his salon and his snobbish home to his pupil, he often improvised on themes from Chopin's works, dedicated to him his Opus 120, *Variations brillantes pour le piano sur une mazourka de Chopin,* and suggested that Chopin give a concert at the Pleyel hall in which he himself would appear.

As for Elsner's violent opposition to Kalkbrenner, it can be variously interpreted. Perhaps the director of the Warsaw Conservatory himself felt a twinge of the jealousy that he suspected in Kalkbrenner. Perhaps he feared that his brilliant pupil might someday be called the pupil of someone else, and perhaps he also feared that piano technique would divert Frederic from what he had always thought should be the young artist's main objective— to write an opera, and to go beyond the piano.

These dreams never left Elsner, and even from a distance he strove to inculcate in Chopin the principles that he had not succeeded in implanting in his pupil at the Conservatory. The arguments he used do not sound overly convincing:

The fame that Mozart and after him Beethoven enjoyed as pianists has long died away, and their piano compositions, in spite of their enduring classical virtues, have had to yield to the taste of a more recent fashion. But their other works, which are not confined to one instrument exclusively—such as operas, songs, symphonies—are still alive among us and exist beside modern works, as if contemporary with them. *Sapienti pauca.*

The Chopin family shared Elsner's views. "Your genius must not confine itself to the piano and to concerts," wrote Ludwika. "You must immortalize yourself by operas." She also repeated Elsner's advice that her brother should write "a play about the time when we were separated." She was referring to the national uprising, using veiled language because of the Russian censorship.

Frederic remembered Elsner's suggestions and mentioned them in a letter to the composer of the opera *King Ladislas the Dwarf:*

In 1830, although I realized how much I lacked and how far I was from being able to emulate you as a model, I was nevertheless bold enough to think: I will at least make an attempt to come close to him, and if not a dwarf, then perhaps some spindle-legs may emerge from my brain.

Such operatic ideas haunted him for a long time, but never were strong enough to change his old conviction that the piano was his exclusive medium.

The speed with which Chopin found his way to the heart of the great city that had seemed so mysterious to him when he first gazed at it from his balcony was indeed astounding. What others strove to obtain by unremitting effort, he won casually, as it were, in two or three months. The world of music and the theater, the favor of formal salons and of close friendships—everything seemed to have been waiting for him. A brilliant connoisseur of the opera and of singing, he became the favorite of the greatest Paris vocal artists, such as Nourrit and Lablache or Madame Damoreau-Cinti, whom he admired more than Madame Malibran. The sixty-year-old Baillot nimbly climbed the four flights to Chopin's apartment for impromptu visits. Zimmerman, an old teacher whose home served as a meeting place for all the pianists of Paris, worshiped Chopin's playing. The reserved Meyerbeer— his opera *Robert le Diable* was at that time being acclaimed by Paris—did not conceal his great admiration for Frederic, which especially gratified his father in Warsaw. He mixed with bohemians and met several rising stars among them—Auguste-Joseph Franchomme, a cellist, Brodt, an oboe player, Tulon, a flutist, and, among pianists, George Osborne, Camille Stamaty, Ferdinand Hiller, and Franz Liszt.

Chopin developed an especially close relation with Hiller and Liszt, who soon advanced in his estimation to a point far above the "cipher" classification he had at first too rashly given them in a comparison with Kalkbrenner. Hiller and Liszt were also violently opposed to Chopin's taking lessons. When Mendelssohn, a friend of Hiller's, came to Paris and joined the group, the opposition acquired a new member. Mendelssohn disliked Kalkbrenner and told Chopin bluntly, "You won't learn anything from him. You play better than he does."

Frederic admired Hiller, leader in this group, and compared him to Beethoven. His relationship with Liszt also developed into a genuine friendship that endured for many years. The passionate and explosive Hungarian, whose entire life was a quest of himself, and who would coolly at any time desert mystical philosophy for the embrace of a woman, saw in Chopin an example of concentration, discipline, and self-control. The études came as a great experience to Liszt, and Hiller was unjust in suspecting him of looking upon this composition as a challenge to his own prestige, as an omen of "the rising sun of Chopin." Liszt, as a militant pianist who tried to contend with the orchestra while playing a Weber concerto, and who pounded his fortissimos on the keys in the manner of a percussionist beating a drum, was deeply impressed by Chopin's proud and exclusive music. As for Frederic, he found in Liszt what he had once found in Tytus, a contrast and complement to himself—virility, exuberance, will—and greatly enjoyed his new friend's company.

Hiller introduced still another celebrity into their circle— Heinrich Heine. This confraternity of foreigners roamed Paris together and often met at No. 5 Rue de la Chaussée d'Antin, in the home of Dr. Hermann Franck, a German scholar, writer, and music lover. His soirées attracted many young people; such evenings seethed with temperament and the sound of music. The host, after discharging his duties, would usually sit down to a game of chess with Mendelssohn.

About this time there appeared an extraordinary review of Chopin's Variations (Opus 2). He wrote about it in a letter to Tytus:

One German in Cassel, enthusiastic about these Variations, sent me a ten-page review, in which after long-winded preliminaries he proceeds to analyze them, bar by bar, explaining that they are not variations like any others, but that they are some kind of fanciful *tableau.*

One sentence of this review read, *"Hut ab, ihr Herren, ein Genie! (Hats off, gentlemen, a genius!)"* and the article concluded: "Although Chopin needs no encouragement, I bow my head to such a genius, to such aspirations, to such mastery." It was with these words that Chopin was saluted by Robert Schumann, then an obscure twenty-year-old critic and musician.

Chopin read this dithyramb with a feeling of curiosity, and agreed with Hiller that "instead of being intelligent, it is very stupid." He was even glad that Hiller kept it from being reprinted in the *Revue musicale.* But did he not in the depth of his soul wish to be saluted with such words not just by "one German," but by the whole of young Romanticist Europe?

Thanks to Chopin, this close-knit group of young musicians began to frequent the homes of Polish aristocrats. The Mondays at Prince Adam Czartoryski's and the Thursdays at Count Ludwik Plater's were an institution, regardless of whether the gathering was given over to politics, a concert, or a dance. The Platers in particular were devoted to music. During one of their soirées, Chopin remarked that only a Pole could fully render the gaiety or melancholy of a Polish national air. Liszt and Hiller contradicted him, and it was decided that the three pianists should each in turn play *Poland Has Not Yet Perished*. Liszt performed it first, then Hiller, and finally Chopin. When he finished, the others were forced to admit that his rendition of the mazurka had been the most poignant and dramatic.

Chopin soon became an intimate of the Platers'. Their daughter Pauline was his first piano pupil in Paris. In their house he would often play for dancing parties and give his imitations. The Countess sensed that Frederic was seeking a warm familial haven in her home, and, displaying remarkable understanding of the characters of the three friends, she once said to Frederic, "If I were young and pretty, my little Chopin, I would choose you for my husband, Hiller for my friend, and Liszt for my lover."

In reality Chopin constantly longed for his family, despite the cordial atmosphere in which he lived, despite his success and the attractive prospects opening before him. Throughout his life, which was full of sudden changes, his attachment to his family, his old friends, and his homeland never weakened, and next to his love for music claimed his deepest feeling. Tytus Woyciechowski once again served as the recipient of Chopin's confidences:

I wish that you were here—you won't believe how sad I am because I have no one to pour out my heart to. You know how easily I make friends, how I like to talk with them about nothing at all—and I have such friends, more than I can count, but no one with whom I can sigh. In contact with these others my feelings are always in syncopated rhythm. That's why I get tired, and you won't believe how much I crave some respite, a whole day when no one will be talking to me.

And this is what the voice of his distant friend meant to him:

At this moment, just when I am about to describe to you a ball at which one divinity with a rose in her black hair bewitched me, I receive your letter. All these "modern" things leave my head at once, I come even closer to you, I take you by the hand, and I weep. I have received your letter from Lwow; so we'll meet only later, or perhaps not at all, for, seriously speaking, my health is poor. I am gay on the outside, especially among my own ("my own" are Poles), but inside me something gnaws at me—premonitions, anxieties, dreams or sleeplessness, nostalgia or indifference. The will to live and a moment later a desire to die—a wish for some kind of sweet peace, torpor, unconsciousness—and sometimes sharp memories torment me. I feel sour, bitter, salty, some kind of vile mixture of emotions tosses me about. I am more stupid than before. My Life—forgive me!

[margin note: Sluggishness]

Chopin undoubtedly realized that one period of his life was closing and another beginning. Warsaw was receding in the distance, becoming ever more remote in contrast to Paris. His former musical world was growing even dimmer. Another world was arising, radiant with the ardent ideas of Romanticism.

At this time he also bade farewell to his dream of Konstancja. The secrecy with which he had surrounded this love had in course of time loosened, and one day Izabela, of all persons, wrote him that Konstancja had married. In her letter his sister observed that Konstancja was a cold and calculating young woman, and that all her emotion went into her singing. He did not protest or despair. He had never succeeded in establishing a sustained correspondence with Konstancja or in strengthening their fragile relationship. He had never been certain that his love was requited; in the end he had come to doubt his own feeling and had wandered far from the person he had once called his ideal. His glances now lingered not only on the divinity with a rose in her black hair;

he met many others who gazed at him more tenderly than had his blue-eyed love in the Krakowskie Przedmiescie. In the very house in which he lived, his fifth-story neighbor, neglected by her husband, invited him for chats by her fireside and asked (in vain) for a rendezvous. Pixis had brought from Stuttgart a fifteen-year-old orphan whom he wished to marry, and Chopin justly claimed that she "looked more sweetly at me than at him." Nor did he conceal his ardent interest in the seductive and unhappily married Delphine Potocka. And this beautiful demon usually did not confine her feeling for artists to concern with art alone.

"Mademoiselle Gladkowska has married one Grabowski, but this does not exclude platonic sentiments," he wrote to Tytus, as if closing the subject that had once taken so large a place in his life and his letters. Thus ended the romance that found a more lasting record in the romantic lover's two concertos than in his heart. Konstancja had met Jozef Grabowski, a generally respected landowner, while Frederic was in Vienna. She was happy in her married life, but at the age of thirty-five, when she had borne five children, she lost her sight as the result of a sudden affection of the optical nerve. She died in 1889. A few days before her death she destroyed all the souvenirs of her youthful love, among them an ivory miniature of Chopin that she had kept through all the years, although she could no longer see the features on it.

CHAPTER

16

At the Crossroads

Duning the eighteen years of his life in Paris, Chopin played in only four concerts in which he was the chief performer and made only fifteen other public appearances. This modest total essentially reveals the character of the man whose fame was to spread from the French capital to the entire world. He was not a virtuoso of the concert hall; he did not dream of adulating throngs or crave applause. He liked to play before select audiences in private homes. And it is to be recalled that the salons of that time were more than the scene of idle social diversion. These luxurious drawing rooms were centers of discussion of all the ideas of the epoch—an elegant forum of the intellectual and the artistic élite of the time.

At the beginning of his career Chopin naturally could not do without the concert hall, and he made a great effort toward arranging a Paris debut. He planned to give a concert on December 25, 1831, but was forced to postpone it to January 15, 1832, because he encountered difficulties in securing singers, despite the assistance given him by Rossini, Paër, and Norblin. In January, Kalkbrenner fell ill, and the concert had again to be postponed; this brought some anxiety to the Chopin family in Warsaw, who feared that Frederic's failure in Vienna might be repeated in Paris. It was not until February 26th that the Paris public had an opportunity of hearing him. Chopin came to the

At the Crossroads

Pleyel hall that evening pale and nervous, having fasted since the morning. While he warmed his cold hands, he tried to find in himself that spur which rose within him from the conflict of despair with resolve.

The hall was not filled to capacity, although the advance sale of tickets at ten francs apiece had been satisfactory. The majority of the audience were Poles—aristocrats headed by the Czartoryskis and the Platers, and other exiles who thirsted for some sort of Polish success after so many defeats. Among them were Chopin's old friends—Niemcewicz, Witwicki, Grzymala, and Fontana. There were many musicians attracted by curiosity; the press too was largely represented, but the general Parisian public was absent.

The program offered eight numbers: the Beethoven Quintet for strings (Opus 29), performed by Baillot, Vidal, Urban, Tilmant, and Norblin; a duet by Mesdemoiselles Toméoni and Isambert; Chopin's F minor concerto; an aria by Mademoiselle Toméoni; Kalkbrenner's Grand Polonaise with introduction and march for six pianos played by Kalkbrenner, Chopin, Hiller, Osborne, Stamaty, and Sowinski; an aria by Mademoiselle Isambert; an oboe solo by Brod; and Chopin's Variations on *Là ci darem la mano*.

The well-known names of the guest virtuosos of that evening meant less than that of the newcomer featured in the announcements as *M. Frédéric Chopin de Varsovie*. The debutant's unique style and the poetic beauty of his compositions, his spontaneity and warmth, deeply impressed the listeners. The loudest applause came from the first row, where Liszt and Mendelssohn sat. Years later Liszt wrote of this concert: "The endlessly renewed applause did not seem sufficiently to express our enchantment at the demonstration of this talent, which disclosed a new level in the expression of poetic feeling and such felicitous innovations in artistic form." Antoni Orlowski reported to Warsaw that "our dear Frycek gave a concert that earned him great reputation and a bit of money. He killed all the local pianists. All Paris is stunned."

The Life and Death of Chopin

François Fétis, founder of the *Revue musicale* and an authoritative critic, wrote on March 3, 1832:

Here is a young man who is true to his natural impressions and follows no model. Even though he has not brought about a complete reform of piano music, he has at least partially achieved something that has long been sought after in vain, namely, an abundance of original ideas, of a kind not encountered anywhere else.

Of the F minor concerto he wrote:

The audience was equally amazed and delighted by it. There is soul in its melodies, imagination in its figurations, and originality in everything. An excess of modulation, a certain lack of order in the linking of phrases, so that occasionally the effect is one of improvisation and not of written music—these are the flaws mingled with the aforementioned qualities. But such defects can be attributed to the artist's youth, and they will disappear as he acquires experience. If Monsieur Chopin's subsequent work fulfills the promise of the debut, there is not the slightest doubt that he will win a brilliant and well-deserved reputation. The young artist deserves praise also as a performer. His playing is elegant, free, graceful, effective, and pure.

Chopin had every right to be gratified with such a reception. After five months of private successes, which seemed a somewhat too protracted preliminary to his father, he was now definitely entered in the ranks of Paris virtuosos. This fact was important because Frederic had made up his mind to settle in Paris, where his passport gave him only transient status. The financial returns of the concert were considerable, since he had not had to pay for the use of the hall. This money represented his first serious earnings since he had left Warsaw. But they lasted him only a short time, and soon he could repeat what he had said upon his arrival in Paris: "I am advancing in the world, but I have only one ducat in my purse." And one of the entries in his whimsical diary is signed: "Frederic Chopin, pauper." He bore his privations with nonchalance, knowing that in an emergency he could count on help from home. Nevertheless, it was time to give serious thought to his financial situation, particularly because securing pupils had turned out to be more difficult than he had anticipated.

He willingly consented to appear in a charity concert sponsored by the Princess de la Moscova, widow of Marshal Ney, in which several prominent artists were to participate. The organizers counted on wealthy and aristocratic subscribers, and Chopin hoped that his appearance would bring him a few well-paying pupils. The concert did indeed come up to the expectations of everyone except Frederic. On May 20, 1832, in the beautiful hall of the Conservatoire, he played the first movement of his F minor concerto before a select audience. He was received warmly, although the *Revue musicale* criticized him for the weakness of his tone. His name reached the most exclusive salons, but not one new pupil applied at the fourth-story address in the Boulevard Poissonière.

The summer of 1832 brought a new period of depression in Chopin's life. Paris did not escape the epidemic that was spreading panic throughout Europe. The cholera that the Russians had brought to Poland had penetrated to Germany and Austria, where one of its victims was Kandler. He died in 1831; his farewell to the world and to music was an article on Chopin.

From his window Frederic witnessed the tragic processions of hearses unaccompanied by the families of the deceased. Victims of the plague were counted by tens of thousands. Riots broke out in the capital, and in June the smoldering embers of the revolution flared up once again in street battles. The *Garde Nationale* fired upon the crowds, and the rioters met death with the cry, "Long live the republic!" There were incidents of inhuman savagery. On one occasion, a revolutionary unit was wiped out to the last man, and the bodies of the rebels were quartered and thrown into the Seine.

Referring to Chopin's state of mind at this time, Orlowski wrote to his family:

He is so gloomy that occasionally I visit him and leave without exchanging one word with him. The cause of this is his homesickness.

Please don't tell anything of this to his parents, because they would be too much upset. The situation in Paris is bad. There is poverty among the artists; cholera has driven all the rich people into the provinces.

Frederic's artist friends had also left Paris. Osborne had gone to London, Kalkbrenner to Meudon, Pixis to Boulogne, Rossini to Bordeaux; Hiller, too, was away. The news from Poland was distressing. The estates of insurrectionists were being confiscated; Polish men and women were being deported to distant parts of Russia, and four million members of the Uniat church had been forcibly converted to the Orthodox faith. The cruel conqueror wreaked vengeance even on children. By a special decree imposed on the people of Warsaw, the orphans of fallen revolutionaries and the children of emigrants had to be registered with the police. Thousands of these innocent victims were deported to Siberia, many of them dying on the way.

Living without money or any hope of making money, left to himself in the turbulent city, dejected by the new misfortunes of Poland and France, Chopin was threatened with a new breakdown. Like many other Polish emigrants, he conceived the plan of leaving for America. America was often discussed in Polish circles. Niemcewicz, who had accompanied Kosciuszko across the Atlantic, was consulted; the seventy-five-year-old poet would discourse at length on the New World, beginning with the celebrated Constitution of the United States and ending with the red-breasted birds that the Americans called robins.

Chopin, more irresolute than ever before, turned this plan over in his mind, abandoned it, returned to it, and consulted his family. The idea of his taking such a long journey caused almost a panic in the Chopin home. Everyone was against it, most of all Monsieur Nicolas, who even urged his son to return to Warsaw. Frederic knew how much alarm his project was causing his family, but was not convinced by their arguments. He refused to put himself under the Russian yoke, and his preparations for the journey went so far that he even wrote a letter of farewell to his family. Then, most unexpectedly, and at the last moment, events took a different turn.

One day while strolling on the boulevards he met Prince Walenty Radziwill. They exchanged some gossip about *Robert le Diable*, which had recently been staged in London and had, surprisingly, proved a fiasco, and voiced their customary admiration for Malibran and Damoreau-Cinti. Then Chopin confided his plan to his friend and was about to say good-by to him. The Prince, taken aback by this sudden news, at once guessed the whole truth. He stayed with Chopin a little longer and persuaded him to come along to a soirée at the house of Baron James de Rothschild.

The soirée was exceptionally brilliant. The Prince knew what he was doing in introducing his young compatriot to this salon frequented by the foremost personalities in French aristocratic, diplomatic, and financial circles. The hostess, who played the piano, was a passionate music lover. Chopin met several of his titled Polish friends; his spirits rose, and when he was asked to play, he gave an enchanting performance. And Radziwill lost no time in whispering the proper words to his friends. When Chopin rose from his seat to face an ovation from his hearers, his future was assured. Princess de Vaudemont, Prince Adam Czartoryski, Count Apponyi, and Marshal Lannes took the young pianist under their protection. He was deluged with requests for lessons, the Baroness de Rothschild being the first to apply. He no longer had any thought of going to America.

He immediately informed his parents of his change of mind, about which he probably had fewer qualms than he had had about any other of his many short-lived projects. Warsaw now began to receive cheerful reports from Paris. Orlowski wrote: "Chopin is well and strong. He turns the heads of all women and makes all men jealous. I prophesied to him this would be the case. He is the fashion now, and soon you will see gloves à la Chopin. Only homesickness torments him."

The news from Warsaw was pleasant too. Ludwika was about to marry Kalasanty Jedrzejewicz, an old friend of the Chopins'. The

famous brother bestowed his blessing on the young couple in an
affectionate letter and sent them a polonaise and a mazurka, so
that they might "dance and be really merry" at their wedding.
The marriage ceremony took place at the Brochow church near
Żelazowa Wola, which had seen the marriage of Nicolas and
Justyna and the baptism of Frederic. The wedding reception
was held in the Skarbek manor house. Monsieur Nicolas informed
his son about it with a tender *envoi*: "And so, my child, you are
all scattered now. Only Izabela is still at home. But in the hearts
of your father and mother you will always be together."

They were also together in the heart of Frederic. He informed
them of his successes, quoted to them what was written and said
about him, listed the places he frequented and the people he met.
He wanted to compensate them for all their previous anxieties
about him, to repay them for all their solicitude. And he had
enough topics to wipe out the old debt.

Hector Berlioz came from Rome to Paris and at once saw
Chopin, but somewhat frightened him by the rugged character of
his music. The celebrated John Field, composer of eighteen nocturnes, came to the city for a guest appearance and gave two concerts, one of which was received warmly, the other coldly. He
showered Chopin with compliments, although he described the
young pianist behind his back as *un talent de chambre de malade*
("a sickroom talent"). This appraisal failed to register in Paris;
Field took it with him on his further journeys, where it had
greater effect.

Orlowski was right: Chopin became the fashion in Paris. He
had many pupils and charged twenty francs an hour. The struggling bohemian had become a celebrity. The most exclusive salons
vied with each other for the honor of entertaining the distinguished maestro. In the home of the beautiful Delphine Potocka
he enjoyed such special favors that he became the subject of
gossip and invidious remarks. He was a constant guest in the
palace of the Princess Belgiojoso, and the daughter of the Prince
de Noailles was his pupil. The Marquis Astolphe de Custine
affectionately called him *Polonaisseur*; this friend, who had a

weakness for young men, wrote him adulating letters full of veiled confessions.

La vie mondaine, that elixir of great cities, which had always stimulated Chopin, did not make him dizzy. He judged his situation soberly. He was aware of the fact that his social contacts served a specific purpose, and he wrote about it without illusions to Dominik Dziewanowski, his boyhood playmate at Szafarnia:

I have entered the highest society. I sit among ambassadors, princes, ministers, and I don't know by what miracle this came to pass, because I myself made no effort to get there. It is the most important thing for me, because good taste is supposed to originate there; the moment you have been heard at the English or Austrian embassy, you have a greater talent. . . . If I were more stupid than I am, I would think that I am at the peak of my career; but I realize how much remains to be done, and I realize it all the more because I am close to the foremost artists and I know what each of them is lacking. I am almost ashamed to write such banalities. I have boasted like a child, or like the boy in the story who feels guilty and gives himself away by defending himself before he is accused. I would cross out what I have said, but I have no time to write a new sheet. Moreover, if you haven't forgotten what I'm like, you will know that I am the same today as I was yesterday, with this difference— that I have one side whisker, while the other stubbornly refuses to grow. I have to give five lessons today. You'd think I am making a fortune. But a carriage and white gloves, without which a man has no *bon ton*, cost more than I have. I love the Carlists, I can't stand the Philippists, I myself am a revolutionary; hence I care not at all for money but only for friendship, which I implore and beg you for.

Chopin was not vain; he was not motivated by snobbishness, and he did not pretend that he was anything that he was not. He knew how to assume a pose when he thought it was useful. He maintained formality toward strangers mainly to protect himself against intrusion. He revealed his true self only to his closest friends.

At the end of this memorable year of 1832, Chopin published

The Life and Death of Chopin

two works—his first to appear in France. They were the Four
Mazurkas, Opus 6, dedicated to Pauline Plater, and the Five
Mazurkas, Opus 7. Both bore the imprint of the publishing house
of Maurice Schlesinger. A new source of income was thus added
to the teaching that brought him about one hundred francs a
day. He actually cared little for money and spent it freely, partly
amused by his good fortune, partly succumbing to his weakness
for luxury and elegance. He left his fourth-story room on the
Boulevard Poissonière and moved to another house near by, at
No. 4 Cité Bergère. 2

Ernest Legouvé, a friend of Berlioz and a well-known writer,
who visited the young teacher-composer in his new apartment, has
given us, in his *Soixante ans de souvenirs*, a most credible portrait
of Chopin:

We climbed to the second floor of a small house and there I found
myself in front of an elegant, pale, sad young man, with brown eyes
of an incomparably pure and gentle expression, with chestnut hair
almost as long as Berlioz's and falling on his forehead in the same
way. . . . Chopin can best be defined as a *trinité charmante*. His personality, his playing, and his compositions were in such harmony that
they could no more be separated than can the features of one face.

CHAPTER

17

Delphine Potocka (polish)

F<small>RANÇOIS</small> X<small>AVIER</small> W<small>INTERHALTER</small>, German by birth and French-man by choice, portraitist of emperors and empresses, kings and queens, princes, counts, barons, and artists, a good draftsman, a weak colorist, elegant and banal master of the art of catching a likeness, made Delphine Potocka so bewitching that his con-temporaries were filled with admiration. One of them wrote:

This portrait represents a woman with the figure of a queen, with blond hair falling in curls on a bust like that of a Greek goddess. . . . The face in three-quarter view shows delicately pure features, with a nuance of severity. . . . In contrast to this the mouth is full of grace and sweetness and has a sensual expression. . . . The forehead of this woman emanates the coldness of a classical statue; her deep-set dark eyes have a piercing gaze, but to make up for it her mouth seems to promise forgiveness and reward to the audacious worshiper.

The real Delphine aroused no lesser enthusiasm. One of her admirers wrote:

Here is a woman in the prime of her years, stately as a Greek statue; her nose has a strangely delicate contour, her eyes are gentle and sweet, on her lips there is a passionate desire for kisses that promise a heaven of delight, and above all this, a somber, high fore-head, as though veiled by a cloud of mourning; whether it is furrowed by a whim or by the thorn of disappointment remains an unsolved and all the more tempting mystery.

Zygmunt Krasinski, one of the greatest Polish Romanticists, having met Delphine Potocka in 1838 (he never afterward ceased loving her) wrote to her in the language fashionable at the time:

The rainbow is daughter of the storm—and when I met you, you were already a rainbow, you had suffered, you had emerged from primordial calm, crucified on the clouds, glowing with all the variety of hues, all the multitude of gifts developed by anguishing pain and constant longing and the desire for something better than this world, which revealed itself to you as evil, treacherous, vile, in discord with itself and unequal to the aspirations of your mind. For of necessity, that which the anguish of life develops in man is his most precious jewel.

To Soltan, his friend, the poet described Delphine on his first meeting with her in less romantic terms:

She is a strange being. She has transcended the abyss; she is a woman whose ardent, strong soul, truly endowed in highest measure with all the gifts that God has lavished upon Polish women, has been spoiled by Paris and London, by the Duc d'Orléans and Monsieur Flahaut, by her unworthy husband and the vanity of fashion, that most wretched of all vanities. Nevertheless, in this soul there remain smoldering fires that become volcanic explosions when memory or some very strong pain fans them; there remains a passionate long desire—long as a note sustained by a perfect singer—the desire for a higher condition in the world, a nobler sphere for the mind, some kind of radiant serenity after so many errors and true misfortunes. But when these fires die out or slumber, she is unbearably capricious, incapable of uttering two serious words, obsessed with a need to laugh and joke in order to escape the terrible boredom that gnaws at her; then she is like a pampered child, a badly brought-up girl, or à Don Juan in petticoats, who has experienced everything and now cries, "Give me the moon! I want to find out whether it tastes like good marzipan, because there is nothing left on earth!"

Delphine Potocka

Chopin was twenty-two years old when he fell in love with Delphine. He had met her two years before in Dresden, where he had stopped on his way from Warsaw to Vienna. When he came to Paris, he went to see her immediately upon his arrival. This fact seemed so important to him that he mentioned it in the very first letter he wrote from Paris, to Kumelski, on September 18, 1831: "Yesterday I dined in the house of Madame Potocka, the beautiful wife of Mieczyslaw."

Indeed, Delphine was most often referred to as a beauty. Frederic admired her when he saw her in society, slender and graceful, splendidly dressed, with little adornment—her favorite jewels were pearls. She held her head high, looking over the heads of other people with melancholy dark-blue eyes framed in long black lashes. To all persons she seemed proud, inaccessible, indifferent. But not to Chopin. He found a new path to her heart—a path that led not through drawing rooms but through music.

She played the piano brilliantly, wrote small compositions, and was a really distinguished singer. Her well-trained soprano voice, with its wide range, could have graced concert halls or the operatic stage, but she had no such ambitions. She knew how to accompany herself, but preferred to have someone else at the keyboard. She felt more confident when she could stand beside the instrument, calm and cold as a statue, fascinating her listeners by the charm of her voice and her figure, and concealing her only defect, her hands, which she considered too large. Gradually Chopin became her habitual accompanist.

She was too beautiful and too much exposed to flattery not to be vain. But this fault did not diminish her charm, for she was aware of her weaknesses and did not think herself a saint. When her famous accompanist became a daily guest in her salon, she showed herself to him without her customary stylized pose and dazzled him all the more. He realized that her coldness, hauteur, and inaccessibility were only a mask.

Her triumphs were as spectacular as her beauty, and her favors as capricious as her moods. Self-centered, she was little concerned with other people's opinions, and soon certain names known throughout France were associated with her in a dubious way. The tales told about her, not always favorable but always interesting, linked her not only with the mansions on the Boulevard St. Germain but with the royal court as well. The aging Count Flahaut was unable to hold her love, and the Duc d'Orléans, son of Louis Philippe, was compelled to share her favors with the Duc de Montfort, nephew of Napoleon I. She was considered a demon who even in love lost her heart last of all. But Frederic could claim that this demon was defenseless against him.

One night, when he was amusing the company by imitating his friends, she said to him, "Now show how you imagine me." Instead of trying to imitate her, he took her scarf from her shoulders, spread it over the keyboard, and improvised a charming, melancholy tune, as though trying to tell her that he could discover her true self through all the veils that separated her from the world.

Delphine worshiped his art and was eager for his comment on her singing and playing. In her home he improvised more willingly than anywhere else, and he would invite her to spend evenings in his apartment, where she met Liszt, Heine, and Franchomme. His friends became her friends; she went with them to the opera, to concerts and cafés. Their wit, fantasy, and way of life seemed to her far more attractive than the atmosphere of the palace of Count Flahaut or the Duc d'Orléans. The salons receded into the background. A dormant gypsy awakened in her.

Before they had time to realize what was happening to them, Frederic and Delphine were seized by a headlong passion. When she stretched out her hands to him, she did not have to fear that he would think them too big or that he would forget their clasp. Three years older than he, she easily divined that she was his first mistress.

She had been only eighteen when she married Count Mieczyslaw Potocki, whose family was notorious in Poland for having betrayed their country and selling out to the Russians. Delphine was not concerned with these political matters; she did not even

Delphine Potocka

like to speak Polish, holding that only the French language was fit for conversation and writing.

Her own family, the Komars, styled themselves counts; their fortune was of recent acquisition, and Delphine's marriage had allied them with one of the wealthiest families in Europe. The young woman had married for love, and the magnificent jewels she received from her husband seemed to her all the more precious for this reason.

Mieczyslaw seems to have been a handsome, gay, empty-headed youth. He became Delphine's first disappointment. She did not have long to wait to discover his brutish disposition, his explosive moods, and his inborn cruelty. He tortured his peasants, tyrannized over his servants, and behaved like a wild beast in his home. She feared him by night and day. The couple had five children, all of whom died in infancy. Mieczyslaw was said to be an epileptic.

After seven years of marital life she left her husband and returned to her parental home, where she was received with surprise but not with sympathy. Once again disappointed, she went abroad, traveled throughout Europe, and settled in Paris. The annual allowance of one hundred thousand francs paid to her by her husband made it possible for her to live as a woman of fashion and to visit London during the season. She was received in the most aristocratic company and resumed the singing and piano playing that she had neglected. But at heart she was restless and dissatisfied: the salons diverted her from art, and art diverted her from the salons. Her unsuccessful experiments in love, which became notorious, probably intensified her inner conflicts.

Her family's arrival in Paris only made matters worse. Her mother tried to persuade her to return to her husband; her sisters were preoccupied with their own problems—Ludmila wondered whether she should marry old Prince Beauvau, and Natalie whether she should enter a convent. Delphine betrayed her emotional instability by her changing moods; sometimes she was proud and reserved, sometimes whimsical and irresponsible, but always she was artificial and lost.

The Life and Death of Chopin

Suddenly Chopin appeared—young, famous, charming, and an incomparable artist. His music bewitched her like good tidings from another, better world. A mistress of conversation, an art she had studied as diligently as she had practiced painting, harp playing, and riding, she also knew how to listen. When Frederic improvised, he always knew whether she was smiling or weeping at the prompting of his fingers on the keys.

When they had to be apart, Frederic wrote to her in a language dictated by his boundless passion. He called her "Findelka," an anagram of "Delfinka," the Polish diminutive of her name. He caressed her in endless words. His allusions to her beautiful body were clothed in musical terms.

If anything in her irritated him, as was the case with her mania for French, he wrote frankly to her:

I have told you before, I won't accept any French letters from you, nor will I answer in French, because I won't be able to do so correctly. We may know other languages, but between ourselves why should we write or speak a foreign tongue? I am tired of babbling French in salons, and I am happy when I can write or talk my own language. At most I shall permit you only a little French seasoning in your letters.

What brought Delphine closest to Frederic was the fact that he confided to her all the secrets of his own world, that he was more open with her than with anyone else. When he was working on his études (Opus 10), he wrote to her: "I spend entire nights with beloved women, women who sing—for, after all, are not my études women? You surely won't be jealous of them. The études are my daughters. I love most of all the A minor and the C minor. These two are the last I have composed. Parents always love their youngest children best."

In another letter he wrote:

When I am assailed by musical themes—now this is happening more than ever before—it is best for me to stay at home. They don't give me a moment's respite, and tug at me as though I were a dog on a leash. Then I sometimes lose my mind, and act so much like a madman that I fear what people may say about me. Recently I was asked whether I am not subject to epileptic fits; apparently that's the impression I give, but I answered sharply. I owe my life to the careful driving of the Parisian coachmen; it is a miracle that I haven't been run over a hundred times. But it's true that they often curse me. Surely they think I'm crazy.

Delphine was alarmed by such reports, but he reassured her:

Don't worry about me, my love. In all seriousness, I tell you that the études have not ruined my health. It's only you women who die sometimes after giving birth to a child. I am sure I'll live after giving birth to my exercises.

When Delphine had gone to her summer home at Enghien, he wrote:

I won't send my finished études to your lake. I'll play them to you myself the first time. I want to see whether any of them will turn out to be special favorites of both of us, as the E major is. Do you remember the piece I improvised when we had quarreled and made up, three days before you left? It has become my Etude in E-flat major; I am sure you'll like it.

At last he was able to write to her:

I have finished the études, and I am again pregnant. For my happiness I lack only you, my love. True, I have grown thin, my nose is like a razor, my eyes are entirely sunken in their sockets; but in the salons I am admired and complimented for my good looks and arresting air. Women cling to me like flies to honey. You know I'm not exaggerating, and I wish you would be as faithful to me as I am to you, although I am sometimes exposed to cruel temptations.

He intended to compose a simpler set of études, for beginners, and he wrote to her about this:

In writing my études I tried to put not only science but also art into them. Since a virtuoso must practice for a long time, he should be given exercises in which he will find proper food for his ears and his soul, lest he be bored to death. I am disturbed because there are no beautiful exercises for beginners. A virtuoso has everything open to him; when he is bored by exercises, he can reach out for the most beautiful music. But a poor fellow who cannot play anything except exercises, whose fingers are as though tied, needs beautiful exercises that will save him from becoming disgusted with music. I have tried to write something of this kind, but I haven't been successful, because for the beginner anything is too difficult. Perhaps I'll postpone this work until later, or maybe someone else will forestall me and do the trick. It's quite difficult.

When Delphine asked him for the études, he warned her of the difficulties of this work:

Once again I repeat—don't play more than two hours a day; that is quite enough during the summer. I won't send you my études; you must play them for the first time with me, after hearing how Liszt plays them. That will be best, my love, because if you interpret them incorrectly, you'll have to unlearn them; but after listening to Liszt, you'll have the ideal picture. And I fear that by playing the études you'll tire your hands for good, which may easily happen. You see, my études are a new method in exercise, and it can be treacherous and dangerous for the uninitiated.

He lectured her on technical details in playful metaphors:

Be careful, Findelka, with the pedal, because this is a sensitive and awfully noisy rascal. You must treat it politely and delicately—as a friend it is most helpful, but not easily does one win its friendship and love. Like a great lady anxious about her reputation, it won't yield to the first comer. But when it does yield, it can perform true miracles, like an experienced lover.

What could be more charming than preparing such a lesson at a distance for a mistress? Even during their separations, the teacher felt close to his pupil—whom he regarded as a virtuoso—and continued to initiate her into his method of work, his secrets of fingering, and his love for Bach. One of the expositions reads:

Delphine Potocka

To an accomplished virtuoso all tricks are permitted. He should use his own methods by all means. You may put your thumb under your little finger. If necessary, take two white or even two black keys with one finger. If you put the third finger over the fourth or even the fifth, you won't be committing a mortal sin either. Don't tire the fourth finger too much; it is so closely connected with the third that you'll never succeed in making it quite free. My fourth finger is completely untrained, yet I can manage it in such a way that no one would guess it. Each finger is built differently; each has a different strength and function. One mustn't destroy but on the contrary develop the finesse of the touch that is proper and natural to each finger. Play Bach's preludes and fugues every day. This is the highest and best school; no one will ever create a more ideal one. If you have plenty of time, memorize Bach; only by memorizing a work does one become able to play it perfectly. Without Bach you cannot have freedom in the fingers, nor a clear and beautiful tone. Without Bach there is no true pianist. A pianist who doesn't recognize Bach is a bungler and a charlatan.

For Bach he always had words of the greatest admiration:

Bach will never become old. His works are structured like those ideally conceived geometric figures in which everything is in its proper place and not a line is superfluous. . . . When I play another composer's works, I often think that I would have solved or written this or that point in a different way. But when I play Bach, I never think like this. Everything he does is perfect; it is not even possible to imagine it otherwise, and the slightest change would spoil everything.

From these lessons Chopin himself was learning, as is shown in the following passage referring to his planned *Method of Methods*:

Do you know, Findelka, these letters to you are the beginning of another, perhaps greater work. I want to write about music and the art of the piano, because we lack such books, but I don't know whether I am equal to such a great task, because it is easier for me to write notes than letters. In writing to you I practice writing about music.

The Life and Death of Chopin

As the years passed, Chopin's letters to Delphine grew into a kind of artistic diary. After composing the études, he conceived the idea of his cycle of preludes, the first of which he had written before his arrival in Paris. About this new project he wrote to Delphine:

Themes have begun to beset me like a hive of bees. I keep noting and noting. You'd laugh at these little things, but I decided not to paste them together, for they will be preludes. Only I don't know whether I'll scratch up forty-eight of them like Bach. I don't think I'll reach that number, for it is too much for my Polish patience. The fact that they are small doesn't mean that they aren't giving me a lot of trouble. You won't believe that the day before yesterday I labored less on my ballade* than on the Prelude in F-sharp minor. Often a large work comes to me faster and more easily than a little one. I don't know myself what this means.

But not only the piano echoes in these love letters. Chopin's friends and admirers are also portrayed here, with the candor characteristic of a man's confidences to a trusted woman.

Liszt and Schumann are reflected in these letters as in a magic mirror. Chopin admired Liszt the virtuoso, but regarded Liszt the composer as negligible:

When I think of Liszt as a creative artist, he appears before my eyes rouged, on stilts, and blowing into Jericho trumpets fortissimo and pianissimo—or I see him discoursing on art, on the nature of creativeness and on how one should create. Yet as a creator he is an ass. He knows everything better than anyone. He wants to attain Parnassus on another man's Pegasus. This is *entre nous*—he is an excellent binder who puts other people's works between his covers.

On another occasion he wrote:

Liszt suggested that he should write variations on the themes of some of my études; I advised him politely to concern himself with something else. He has complained to all sorts of people that I did not

* Probably the Ballade in G minor (Opus 23).

Delphine Potocka

object when Kalkbrenner composed variations on one of my mazurkas, while I refuse to grant the same privilege to my friend Liszt. He
talks and talks in this way to others, but face to face with me he is
extremely polite, and I am the same with him. He is a strange man;
he is unable to wring from his own brain any least thing that has
worth before God or man, but his mouth waters for other men's
work as a cat lusts for cream. You know, Liszt takes an enema tube
instead of a telescope to look at the stars. Then he pulls his chosen
star down from the heavens, dresses it up in an ill-tailored garment
with ribbons and frills and an enormous wig, and launches this
scarecrow upon the world. There are people who admire him, but I
still say that he is a clever craftsman without a vestige of talent. It
would be difficult to find a more dexterous musician than Liszt; he
covers up his poverty of inspiration with clever tricks, and he will so
bedazzle and bewitch you with his acrobatics that you'd swear he is
an artist of genius, whereas actually he is only a most adroit trickster.
But he compensates his creative lack through his great gift for re-
producing the ideas and the achievements of other composers.

Schumann had distressed Chopin with his extravagant review
of the Variations. Chopin could not forgive him his "imaginary
Florestans"; his German colleague's enthusiasm "nauseated" him
as though he had "eaten a pot of honey." He wrote in irritation:

Schumann praises me most highly, and even when he criticizes me
he immediately makes up for it with a tribute, but what he writes is
nonsense and gibberish, not criticism. I am constantly afraid that,
with the best of intentions, he will write something that will make me
ridiculous forever. I'd prefer it if he kept quiet, but it is I who must
keep quiet, thank him, and pretend that I'm happy about what he
has written.

Chopin even begged of Delphine: "Pray to God, my dearest,
my life, that I may get rid of him someday!" Then he mourned:
"Why didn't I live when Bach and Mozart lived? I would have
valued their criticism above everything—I would have thrown all
my nonsense into the fire if they hadn't thought it good."

Apparently no others among the supreme geniuses of music held equal rank with these two in his recognition. Of Beethoven he wrote:

There are few geniuses capable of understanding all instruments and bringing out all the potentialities of each one. I know of only two such men—Bach and Mozart. Even Beethoven is not so universal in scope; he is at his best with the orchestra and the string quartet, but in writing for the piano he sometimes forgets that the piano is not an orchestra. In his sonatas he is sometimes obviously annoyed because the piano is not an orchestra. As for myself, I understand the piano best. This is the ground on which I have the firmest footing.

Chopin's romance with Delphine endured for three years, despite betrayals and storms that came and passed. The lovers separated in 1835; later, love was to bring them together again. In these years they tried to conceal their relationship from the world—Delphine because she had learned a lesson from earlier experiences, Frederic because of his innate discretion. They were successful—in a way. Although the whole Polish colony knew about their love, and it was discussed in many French salons, it remained a secret to their descendants. It was so impetuous and free that almost all account of it was lost in a conspiracy of silence. Its story is preserved only in Chopin's letters. These remained hidden for a hundred years; their passion and frank language ostracized them from the light of day. Moreover, perhaps fearing the judgment of other people, Chopin wrote to his beloved:

If anyone tried to get me to talk about music as you do, I'd refuse. But I know you and I know that you can keep a secret, and that everything I am writing to you will remain between us and this paper. Destroy my letters, because if anyone got hold of them, you'd be compromised and I'd be exposed to great anxiety and unpleasantness.

Apparently Delphine did not heed Chopin's instructions, for a highly interesting portion of these letters has recently come to light. The whole tenor of the preserved fragments shows that

Delphine Potocka

Delphine occupies a special place among the women who aroused Chopin's deeper personal feelings. There can be little doubt that this was the only love relationship of his life in which he was neither dependent nor passive, and in which he could assert himself as the creative male. With her, he seems always to have felt at ease, he was not afraid to touch upon the most intimate feelings, and at times even ventured a Rabelaisian frankness as though to offset his innate timidity.

In one of his letters he outlined a highly personal theory of artistic creation that fairly anticipates the Freudian concept of sublimation:

Findelka, my beloved, my only one!—Once again I shall bore you with a letter about my inspiration and my works, but you'll see that all this concerns you a great deal.

I have given much thought to inspiration and creative work and slowly, very slowly, I have come upon what is the crux of the matter. Inspiration and new ideas come to me only after I haven't had a woman for a long time. When I have spent myself on a woman, inspiration runs away from me, and no new ideas arise in my head.

Think how strange and marvelous it is. The identical energies are used for fertilizing a woman, that is to say, for creating a *man*, and for creating a work of art. It is the life-giving essence, so precious, which a male squanders for the sake of a moment of pleasure! . . .

Think of it—the tempting force that attracts us to woman can be transformed into inspiration. . . . But this holds only for those who are capable and have plenty of talent—for if any good-for-nothing spent his life without women, he would only suffer . . . and would produce nothing for the honor of God and mankind.

He teasingly accused Delphine of having distracted him from composing:

God alone knows how many of my best inspirations and musical inventions have been lost in the process. *Operam et oleum perdidi.* . . . What ballades, polonaises, and for all I know maybe even a

The Life and Death of Chopin

whole concerto were engulfed . . . hence you're full of music, and in a family way with my works. It's a crazy idea, but you must admit it's original.

Just as he opened his whole heart to his mistress in love, so he opened to her his thoughts and feelings in relation to his music. She must have been an exceptional woman, capable of understanding his art. She never offended his sensitive and fastidious nature.

Only once in his life, and to Delphine, did Chopin say, "My longing for you begot in me many musical ideas." And only once in his life did he want to have a child, and he asked Delphine to give him one.

Admirers and Detractors

THE wheel of fortune had brought an auspicious turn, and Chopin now entered upon an unclouded period of intense activity, renown, prosperity, and gratifying love relationships. Inwardly he remained the same man he had been during the difficult years in Vienna and in his first experiences in Paris. Nor did his success affect the nature of his art, which obeyed its own laws and logic, and which remained the most inaccessible secret of the carefree favorite of the salons.

To be sure, the outward circumstances of his life were changed. In the evening Chopin, impeccably tailored, white-gloved, drove forth to dine with Lord Rothsay Stuart, ambassador of Great Britain, or Baron Stockhausen, the Netherlands ambassador, or with Baron Nathaniel de Rothschild, or with Léo, another banker. By day he was occupied at home, giving lessons to gifted ladies of fashion, or improving the technique of more accomplished artists, former pupils of Moscheles and Kalkbrenner. The ladies, having discovered their teacher's weakness for flowers, would bring him violets.

He gave public performances more often than before, for the sole reason that he considered this activity essential to his career. On April 2, 1833, he appeared with Liszt in a benefit concert centering about Miss Henrietta Smithson, an Irish actress who in that same year became Mme. Hector Berlioz. The next day he played with Liszt and the two Herz brothers in a concert in which the four pianists performed compositions for two pianos. Chopin also played several times in concerts of the kind he liked best, namely, performances in private salons.

At this time he received from home the amusing news that his sisters, far from giving up their literary pursuits, had written a new book for children. Its theme, as was clear from the title, *Little Joseph's Journey from Warsaw to the Spas of Silesia, as Told by Himself,* drew upon childhood memories. Little Joseph was Frederic's sister Ludwika, who had made the trip with him, their mother, and Emilia, seven years before. Izabela only assisted in the writing. As before, the young authors curbed their desire for fame and published their work anonymously.

He received another sort of message from home when it became known in Warsaw that the young musician was earning a great deal of money and spending all of it. Old Monsieur Nicolas sent him a paternal reprimand:

I will not cease to repeat that unless you try to put aside a few thousand francs, I shall look on you as one who deserves only to be pitied, in spite of your talent and all the compliments showered upon you. May God protect you from an illness that would force you to interrupt your lessons; you would be condemned to misery in a foreign land. I confess that this thought often torments me, because I realize that you are living from day to day.

Frederic tried to calm his parents and promised to economize, but soon after receiving this letter he rented a large apartment at No. 5 Rue de la Chaussée d'Antin. Its former occupant, Dr. Franck, had left Paris for London and Berlin. Chopin was familiar with the apartment and fond of it.

He shared this residence with Alexander Hofman, his childhood playmate, son of Professor Hofman, the old friend of the Chopin family, who had died three years before. Alexander, now a physician, had taken part in the Polish uprising of 1830 and had only recently left Poland. He brought with him everything that Chopin, the Parisian dandy, was homesick for—a fresh impression of his native land and reminiscences of their youth. Alex-

Admirers and Detractors

ander was a fairly good pianist, and Frederic had played with him in his lyceum days. How many moving, tender, and amusing things they had to tell each other! They probably talked about the old professor's cabinet with its minerals and its wax plants molded in exact facsimile of nature; they recalled also the aeolomelodicon, the fantastic invention that was to revolutionize music. Their reminiscences must have carried them back to their walks in the Botanical Garden, to their schoolrooms, and to the homes of their friends, bright and warm at the evocation of memory. Hofman told stories of the uprising, of forests resounding with gunfire, of cavalry charges darkening the heavens with clouds of dust, and of tragic battlefields where he had treated the wounded. Often those Parisian nights of nostalgic talk found Frederic in the end at the piano, spinning in music his dreams of Poland and Warsaw.

These musical reveries proved attractive to many Polish exiles who roamed about in Paris in quest of the ghost of their lost homeland. A galaxy of poets—Niemcewicz, Zaleski, Witwicki, and the greatest of them all, Adam Mickiewicz, Poland's Homer and Tyrtaeus as well—were spellbound by the wizardry of those improvising hands. Franchomme often brought his cello to the apartment in the Chaussée d'Antin, Delphine sang there, Berlioz played, and Heine sat and listened. Liszt, having mastered the études, so delighted their author with his performances of them that after one such concert Chopin wrote to Hiller: "I wish I could steal from him his manner of playing them."

Hofman, a cheerful, stocky man—Chopin nicknamed him "Fatty"— was ruthless when the visitors stayed too late into the night. He had appointed himself Chopin's personal physician, watched over his health, saw to it that he observed his dietary regimen and prescribed rest hours. He made his friend go on a vacation, which Chopin badly needed, having spent the previous summer in town. He went with Franchomme to Côteau in the Touraine country, and returned feeling much stronger and full of vitality. He also brought back with him several new compositions. He was always to recall this vacation with delight.

In Paris further new vistas opened for him. The year 1832 had

187

seen two of his compositions published. In 1833 there followed the Introduction and Polonaise for cello and piano, Opus 3, the Three Nocturnes, Opus 9, the Trio in G minor, Opus 8, dedicated to Prince Antoni Radziwill, and the Duet for cello and piano in G minor, written in collaboration with Franchomme, and published without opus number. In August came the momentous Twelve Grand Etudes, Opus 10, dedicated to Liszt—a work that unmistakably combined boldness of conception with flawless taste, wealth of imagination with forceful expression, and inventive genius with intrepid faith in his own artistic truth. September of 1833 brought the Grand Concerto for piano and orchestra in E minor, Opus 11, dedicated to Kalkbrenner; November saw the publication of the Variations for piano on a theme of the aria "Je vends des scapulaires" from Herold's opera *Ludovic* (Opus 12).

The majority of these works had been composed in former years and had come to Paris in Chopin's trunks; before publication, however, they underwent countless revisions. The composer was haunted by an ideal of perfection. Inspiration was neither the beginning nor the end of his art. Although he composed without constraint and trusted his inspiration, he did not consider his work finished when he had written down all that he had heard within himself. He returned time and again to the written passages, judging them coolly and severely. He polished his works patiently, indefatigably, and never stopped until his mysterious selective sense had prompted him to choose the best and only possible solution among a thousand. Yet his technical revisions never essentially modified the original score; they never dimmed that freshness of his work which was so greatly admired and which gave his compositions the character of improvisations. On this subject he wrote to Delphine:

I toil devilishly on each of my compositions, and if a man has no facility for creative work, no one can give or teach it to him. Composing is to me what giving birth to a child is to you women—some suffer mortal pains, while others spit out a baby like a cherry pit. I can give birth only in great pain. I always have the feeling that I have a beautiful idea all ready in my head, but after I have written it down, I realize that it is full of holes. One phrase is wrong, another looks entirely different on paper, so much so that I am overcome with despair, and then I begin to torture my memory. Or I have several themes, and I don't know which to choose.

On another occasion he confessed to Delphine: "I can never finish anything at one stroke." When he felt unable to master his material, he made notations of the main motifs and laid them aside:

The best thing for me to do in such cases is to throw such a premature baby into a corner and forget about it. After some time a theme appears suddenly as though out of the blue, and it fits exactly into one of the holes. Then another theme, and so on, until the whole is assembled like a mosaic. But if you think this is the end, you're mistaken. Before I have said my last word, I must go through horrible pangs and tribulations, with many tears and sleepless nights.

His last public appearance in 1833 was on December 15th, at the Conservatoire. He played Bach's Concerto for three pianos with Hiller and Liszt as his partners. The critics reported that the three artists "executed the work with full understanding of its character and with perfect delicacy."

New compositions followed one another in rapid succession. The record for 1834 includes the following works: Three Nocturnes, Opus 15, dedicated to Hiller; Rondo for piano in E-flat major, Opus 16; Grand Fantasia on Polish Airs in A major, Opus 13; Krakowiak, Opus 14, dedicated to Princess Adam Czartoryska; Four Mazurkas, Opus 17; Grande Valse in E-flat major, Opus 18; Bolero, Opus 19. In the same year there also appeared the Paris edition of the Variations on *Là ci darem la mano*.

Chopin was adding ever greater luster to his name. Revolutionary as his ideas were, he not only vindicated his innovations but also won increasing popularity. His works were performed by

The Life and Death of Chopin

Kalkbrenner, Liszt, Hiller, Osborne, Stamaty, Clara Wieck, and Edward Wolff. Painters were eager to make portraits of him; sculptors modeled his exquisite profile in relief, and in Poland etchings of his face sold at ten zlotys apiece.

There was much journalistic writing about him, usually in superlatives. Dr. François Stoepel, a critic well known in Germany and France, enthusiastically reviewed his new works in Schlesinger's *Gazette musicale*. He referred to Chopin as "one of the few geniuses who dauntlessly and energetically strive to achieve their goal, ignoring the demands of the common herd and of fashion." He also stressed the fact that from his early youth on, Chopin had "developed an individual manner of playing and composing for the piano, radically different from that of his contemporaries, inaugurating a new era in composition and technique." To the E minor concerto Stoepel devoted a long essay that concluded as follows: "Both in the elaboration of piano technique and in musical poetry, Chopin has far surpassed all his rivals."

While his stature was universally acknowledged, no critic could as yet explain the significance of his achievement. The *Revue musicale* expressed its opinion as follows:

Chopin has broken new trails for himself. His playing and his composition, from the very beginning, have won such high standing that in the eyes of many he has become an inexplicable phenomenon. . . . No one as yet has tried to define the special character and merit of these works, what distinguishes them from others, and why they occupy such a high place.

Chopin for his part held a rather low opinion of music critics. He wrote to Delphine:

The critics are ridiculous—they want to know everything about everything. Such a connoisseur will discourse learnedly about how love or despair impelled you to create this or that work. And if I were to tell him how it actually was, namely, that I composed the piece because it was raining, because I had no place to go and I felt sad and empty to the point of going crazy, he wouldn't believe that it all arose from the rain. As a matter of fact, Beethoven may have written his Funeral March because he had a stomach ache. . . . Critics frequently see in a work all sorts of things that its author never even dreamed of putting into it. However, a critic will sometimes help a composer to understand something that came to him as out of the blue in the fever of his inspiration, something that he merely felt but failed to edit in the light of cold reason and reflection. Such passages unspoiled by reflection are the best part of a work. But there are few critics endowed with true intelligence. Most of them are asses who care nothing for the artist or his works, who want to show off with their fanciful elaborations as singers do. They talk much, but there is no way of sifting anything intelligent out of their talk.

Among musicians he had fanatical followers and also adversaries; others could not at first make up their minds but were gradually won over by his music. Among the latter were Mendelssohn and Moscheles. The first mazurkas (fourteen had by then been published) seemed to Mendelssohn, who ardently admired Chopin as a virtuoso, "affected to the point of being almost unbearable." Moscheles failed to respond even to the études. He wrote in his diary:

I gladly take advantage of some of my free evening hours to get better acquainted with Chopin's études and other compositions, and I find great charm in their originality and the national flavor of the motifs. However, my thoughts, and hence my fingers, still stumble at certain difficult, inartistic modulations that I simply cannot understand. The whole often seems to me excessively sentimental, unworthy of an educated musician and man.

Among the detractors of his music, there was one so biased, strident, and vulgar that Chopin regarded his criticisms as a curiosity. His name was Heinrich Friedrich Rellstab; he was a retired Prussian officer, a man of violent passions, and something of an adventurer. He had been sentenced to three months' imprisonment for having written a libelous pamphlet about Henrietta Sontag; as a result of another of his violent campaigns, Gasparo

The Life and Death of Chopin

Spontini, the well-known composer, was forced to resign from the Berlin opera. Later Rellstab admitted contritely that he had gone too far in his vituperations. He was the son of a musician, wrote novels and librettos, and as the critic of the *Vossische Zeitung* had become the musical oracle of Berlin. Intelligent but emotionally unbalanced, extremely conservative in taste, he detested romanticism, and any departure from the classical rules enraged him.

He wrote several passionate articles assailing Chopin in *Iris im Gebiete der Tonkunst,* a magazine that he owned and edited. The campaign opened with a review of the Variations (Opus 2), which bore the dedication to Tytus Woyciechowski. Rellstab did not shrink from writing: "Chopin is probably a Pole—at least we may assume this from the fact that his work is dedicated to a Pole—but the vandalism with which he treats a Mozart theme is enough to show that the work stems from the raw Slavic soil."

In reviewing the mazurkas (Opus 7), he accused Chopin of straining after originality and indulging in effects and ear-splitting dissonances. He concluded: "If Monsieur Chopin shows this composition to some master, it may be expected that the latter will tear it to pieces and throw it at the composer's feet, which we hereby are doing symbolically."

Chopin was not disturbed by these venomous attacks. On the publication of his études he expected a new assault. He wrote to Delphine Potocka: "Rellstab criticizes me for putting too much pepper in my works. After these études he will cough and sneeze and spit like a madman. They are certainly different from Czerny's licorice."

He was not far wrong. Rellstab concluded his review of the first series of the études as follows: "Those whose fingers are twisted can straighten them by practicing these études, but others should not play them unless they have a surgeon at hand." He went so far as to recommend two prominent local surgeons as capable of operating on Chopin's victims.

Somewhat later there appeared in *Iris* a letter to the editor, written in bad German, full of invective against Rellstab, and signed "Chopin." Obviously a forgery (for instance, it alluded to a trip of the writer's to Germany in 1833, although Chopin had not left Paris that year), this letter aroused much discussion. Some maintained that it was written by Friedrich Wieck, Clara's impetuous father. Most probably its author was Rellstab himself.

Referring to this unpleasant incident, Monsieur Nicolas wrote to his son:

Some people have maintained that you replied to Rellstab in a letter written in very poor German, and that the taste of the letter was even poorer than its German. These gentlemen seem to forget that you have been well brought up and that your time was not completely taken up with reading music. I am convinced that you have kept silent in this matter; your compositions speak loudly enough for you, since you already have imitators, in spite of their habituation to the old routine, and this means a great deal. Just keep on getting under the skin of this progeny of Zoilus, and you will prove to them that it is impossible to set limits to art.

Soon other German critics came to Chopin's defense, among them Karl August Kahlert, a friend of Schumann's, who was also on good terms with Rellstab. His article was greeted with great satisfaction by the Chopin family, especially by Izabela, who urged her brother to be sure to read it. But Chopin in Paris was indifferent to these attacks from Berlin. They continued for a long time; finally Rellstab came to regret his attitude toward Chopin, as he had once regretted his campaign against Spontini. Several years later, he was conquered by Chopin's music and in 1843, before going to Paris, asked Liszt for a letter of introduction to the composer whose works he had once symbolically torn to pieces. Liszt wrote such a letter, but it is not known whether a meeting between Chopin and Rellstab ever took place.

CHAPTER

——————

19

"Happiness, Happiness"

CHOPIN's home was now a favorite meeting place of Polish émigrés, and often served as temporary quarters for exiled veterans of the 1831 uprising. Frederic was known never to refuse help to persons in need, and he gave his aid readily and discreetly. The émigrés brought him news from Poland, listened to his improvisations on Polish themes, and during such evenings often buried their tearful faces in their hands.

The circle of his musician friends was now enlarged by the addition of Vincenzo Bellini, Sicilian composer, in whom Chopin discovered a fastidious personality and musical tastes similar to his own. Both Chopin and Bellini loved Mozart; to the minds of both of them, poetry and lyricism were the soul of music. They were often together at musical soirées given by Madame Freppa, a well-known singer and teacher, to whom Chopin dedicated his Mazurkas, Opus 17. Chopin was very fond of Bellini's music, and Hiller wrote that he had rarely seen Chopin so moved as he was during a performance of *Norma*; at the end of the second act, he said, he saw tears in his friend's eyes. Among his pupils he developed a special liking for Adolf Gutmann, a fifteen-year-old boy who had been brought by his father from Heidelberg to the celebrated Paris teacher. Frederic, having too many pupils, had received them without enthusiasm. However, when the boy began to improvise, Chopin was struck by his unusual talent and decided to take him under his tutelage.

"Happiness, Happiness"

An important change in his household came with the departure of Alexander Hofman, who left Paris to take a position in Silesia. But Chopin did not remain alone for long. Jas Matuszynski appeared in Paris. After the failure of the uprising, he had left Poland for Germany, resumed his medical studies, and obtained a doctor's degree in Tübingen. "In Paris," Matuszynski wrote to his family, "I made it my first business to look up Chopin. I cannot express the happiness we both felt after five years of separation. He is stouter and taller; I hardly recognized him."

Overjoyed at the arrival of his old friend, Chopin insisted that he occupy the quarters vacated by Hofman. Unlike Tytus, Jas did not dominate his friend. On the other hand, Frederic's homesickness was appeased by the very presence of a friend of his youth. Matuszynski soon established himself as a physician in Paris, and later became a professor at the Ecole de Médecine.

In May, 1834, Chopin went with Hiller to attend the Lower Rhine Music Festival at Aachen. He heard performances of Mozart's *Jupiter* Symphony, fragments of Beethoven's Ninth Symphony, and Handel's *Deborah*; Hiller had translated the text of this oratorio from English into German. In Aachen the two friends met Mendelssohn, who was then director of the Düsseldorf orchestra. On May 23rd, Mendelssohn wrote to his mother: "The two have improved their playing, and Chopin as a pianist is now one of the very first. Like another Paganini, he achieves all kinds of impossible things, such as no one could have thought playable before."

Mendelssohn took his friends to Düsseldorf, where they spent the morning over music. In the afternoon they went to a café for bowling, and at night they visited the home of Schadow, director of the local art school. "There we met several prominent painters," Hiller later wrote about this visit, and went on to describe it thus:

The conversation was quite animated, and everything would have been fine, had it not been for poor Chopin, who sat timidly in a corner, unnoticed by anyone. But Mendelssohn and I knew that he would soon have his turn, and we anticipated it with pleasure. Somehow the piano was opened; I played, and then Mendelssohn. When we asked Chopin to give a sample of his art too, everyone looked at us and at him with surprise. But the moment he had played a few bars, everyone present, and above all Schadow, stared with amazement at Chopin—there was no doubt that they had never heard anything like it. When he finished, all were entranced and implored him to play again and again.

Mendelssohn accompanied his guests to Cologne; from here they went off to Coblenz by steamer. They came back to Paris in high spirits, full of new impressions and with delighted recollections of the beautiful Rhine landscape.

Soon after his return Chopin received another invitation. It came quite unexpectedly and stirred up a new whirl of memories in him. The Countess Teresa Wodzinska, mother of the three boys who had been his close friends in his father's boardinghouse and of Maria, his childhood pupil, asked him to visit her in Geneva. The Countess's letter contained a surprising enclosure—a composition by Maria.

"I was immensely pleased with it," Chopin wrote to Felix Wodzinski, her brother.

That very same evening I improvised on the pretty little theme of that Marynia whom I used to chase through your apartment in the good old days. . . . And today! I take the liberty of sending my esteemed colleague Mademoiselle Marie a little waltz that I have just published.* May it give her at least one-hundredth part of the pleasure I felt on receiving her variations. . . . Make a very elegant, respectful bow to Mademoiselle Marie. Be filled with wonderment, and say to yourself, "Heavens, how big this little thing has grown!"

Chopin was moved by the fact that the Countess remembered him, but could not go to Geneva, because of his preoccupation with his work. He was being importuned on all sides to write an opera. The arguments of his Polish friends were seconded by those of Elsner, who once again took up his cherished dream, and on September 14, 1834, wrote to his former pupil: "While I still live *in hac lacrimarum valle* I should like to see an opera composed

* Opus 18.

by you, not only for the sake of the increase of fame it will win for you but also for the benefit it may bring to musical art as a whole, particularly if the content of the opera is based on Polish history." Influenced by these urgings, Chopin actually discussed with Stanislas Kozmian, who had rendered Shakespeare in Polish verse, a libretto from Polish history, but that was as far as he went. To Mickiewicz, who also urged him to write an opera, he said, "Leave me to my piano, *c'est mon affaire.*"

He complained about this understandable insistence of his countrymen in a letter to Delphine Potocka:

Mozart encompasses the entire domain of musical creation, but I've got only the keyboard in my poor head. I know my limitations, and I know that I'd make a fool of myself if I tried to climb too high without having the ability to do it. They plague me to death urging me to write symphonies and operas, and they want me to be everything in one, a Polish Rossini and a Mozart and a Beethoven. But I just laugh under my breath and think to myself that one must start from small things. I'm only a pianist, and if I'm worth anything, this is good too—after me there will be musicians whose interests will be broader, and in them Polish music will expand and bloom. I think it's better to do only a little but to do that as well as possible, rather than to try to do all things and do them poorly. I'll never change my mind on this score. I swear by my love for you, I don't even consider myself a John the Baptist of Polish music. I'd like only to write and to leave behind the ABC of that which is truly Polish and to teach my followers to reject pseudo-Polishness. Perhaps I'll succeed.

In the meantime the Chopin family was bereft of another of its members. Izabela married Antoni Barcinski, who had been a tutor in her father's boardinghouse. The lonely parents now dreamed only of Frederic and actively concerned themselves with every step, every detail of his life. Monsieur Nicolas reminded his son that his passport was expiring; Madame Justyna worried about his apartment, which turned out to be too cold.

When the season opened Chopin gave a number of concerts; afterward he came to the conclusion that public performances were only a torture to him, and he began to avoid them. On December 7, 1834, he took part in a concert given by Berlioz, who conducted his overtures to *Les Francs-Juges* and *King Lear*, and his symphony *Harold en Italie*. Berlioz's tumultuous and grandiose music, which Chopin heartily disliked, formed an unpleasant setting for the whispers, dreams, and languors of the larghetto of his F minor concerto. Chopin felt discouraged both during and after the concert.

On Christmas Day he played in a benefit matinee organized by Stoepel, which featured Mademoiselle Heinefetter, the Viennese diva, and Heinrich Ernst, a violinist of whom it was said that, dazzled by Paganini, he once followed the latter from town to town to spy out the secret of his technique. Liszt and Chopin performed two duets, one by Moscheles, the other by Liszt. The two friends were acclaimed by the audience and the press.

In the early months of 1835, Chopin made four public appearances. On February 25th he and Hiller played Hiller's new duet for two pianos in Erard Hall, and in March, in the Pleyel hall, he performed with Hiller, Osborne, Stamaty, Herz, and Anton Reicha. He never refused to play in concerts arranged by his friends, and in turn met with no refusal when he arranged a concert for the benefit of Polish exiles.

This concert took place on April 4, 1835, in the Théâtre des Italiens. The program was spectacular; it included Nourrit and Falcon as vocalists, Ernst as violinist, Liszt, Hiller, and Chopin as pianists. The orchestra, conducted by Habeneck, played the overtures to *William Tell* and *Oberon*. Hiller played his duet with Liszt, Chopin his own E minor concerto. The theater was filled to capacity and the proceeds came up to expectations, but the vast hall was not suited to Chopin's delicate playing. He left the keyboard with the realization that he had not succeeded in capturing the attention of his audience. Three weeks later, on April 26th, playing his *Andante spianato* he did electrify a select public assembled at the Conservatoire for a concert given by Habeneck. Nevertheless he told Liszt: "I am not fit for concerts. Crowds intimidate me. I feel poisoned by their breath, paralyzed by curious glances, and confused by the sight of strange faces."

These words were without doubt sincerely spoken. In any event, the period of his public concerts had come to an end, and from then on he appeared on the platform only when he could not avoid it.

About this time he sent his parents two new publications—the Scherzo in B minor, Opus 20, and Four Mazurkas, Opus 24. In June he left for a vacation in Enghien, a favorite resort of Delphine's. He rented rooms on the lake, rested, and took the baths prescribed by Matuszynski. He enjoyed driving around the lovely countryside; he could visit Niemcewicz in near-by Montmorency, and in only an hour could reach the castle of the Marquis de Custine in St. Gratien, where he was sure to be cordially welcomed.

He was in Enghien when he received word that his parents had decided to go to Karlsbad for a cure they had long been planning to take. It would be their first trip abroad after the uprising; he had not seen them for nearly five years. He calculated that they would be about halfway between Warsaw and Paris, and that he would be separated from them by a stagecoach journey of only a few nights. He did not hesitate. By the beginning of August he was on his way, reaching Karlsbad on the fifteenth. His parents arrived on the same day, unaware that their son was there.

Frederic at once began to look for them, but without success. Their name was not on the visitors' list. He questioned various Poles of his acquaintance, but none knew the address of his parents. The following morning he was awakened at seven o'clock by a knock on his door. He opened it to find his father standing before him. Monsieur Nicolas had learned of Frederic's arrival through friends. They wept with joy and hastened to Madame Justyna. That day a letter was dispatched to the rest of the family —the father wrote in French, the son in Polish. Frederic poured out his joy to his sisters:

My dear children, this is the first letter you have ever received written both by Papa and myself. Our joy is indescribable! We hug and hug each other—and what else can one do? It's a pity we're not all together. What I write is disorderly; it's better not to think

filled up

today, but to enjoy the happiness that we have lived to see. This is the only thing that exists for me today. The same parents, always the same, only they've aged a little. We walk with Madame Little Mother on our arm, we talk about you, we tell one another how often we have thought of one another. We drink and eat together; we pamper and scold each other. I am *au comble de mon bonheur*. The same habits, the same gestures with which I grew up, the same hand that I have not kissed for so long. Well, my children, I embrace you—and forgive me for being unable to collect my thoughts and write you about anything except our happiness at this moment, except the fact that I have always hoped for this happiness, and that today I really have it, this happiness, happiness.

Frederic's parents were filled with the same happiness. They were not troubled even about their son's health, which was better than ever after his rest at Enghien. His father said that he had not changed at all, that he looked exactly as he had on leaving Warsaw.

They stayed together at the Yellow Rose Inn. Frederic played for them and told them about Paris, and they told him about Warsaw. His most beloved city seemed unrecognizable from their accounts. The house in which they had all lived together no longer existed; the Russians had closed the university and the Conservatory, and his friends and schoolmates were dispersed.

During the three weeks of his stay in Karlsbad he probably continued to feel as he had on that first day when he wrote to his sisters. He was surrounded by the old home habits, the familiar gestures, the beloved faces. The hands of the clock of life had been moved back and stopped at the happiest hour.

Chopin accompanied his parents to Cieszyn, where they visited the Thun-Hohenstein family. The sleepy little town with its arched gates, hidden in verdure, seemed to be part of the fairy tale they had lived since they were reunited. But Cieszyn was on the border of Poland, and here they had to part. The parents continued their journey via Wroclaw to Warsaw, and Frederic returned to Paris by a route through Dresden. They bade each other farewell on September 14th. Frederic was never to see his parents again.

Maria Wodzinska

O<small>N HIS</small> first day in Dresden, Chopin visited the Wodzinskis. He found almost all of them gathered together—Count Wincenty and Countess Teresa, who were pleasantly surprised by his arrival, their sons Felix and Casimir, his former schoolmates, their daughter Maria and her two little sisters, Jozefa and Teresa. Only Antoni, the oldest son, was absent.

The young people welcomed him cordially both as a childhood friend and as one who had taken the way to greatness out of that sheltered small world of their childhood camaraderie. The parents looked tenderly on this schoolteacher's son, who by dint of his own resources had won access to a society whose doors opened to the Wodzinskis as a matter of course.

Wincenty Wodzinski owned an estimated fifty thousand acres of land, a great part of which was in the Kujawy region, the most fertile area of Poland. The Wodzinskis had always been prominent in the army, in politics, and in the church. One branch of their genealogical tree reached to Italy, to the Orsetti palace in Milan. Their noble Italian ancestors had come to Poland in the sixteenth century in the retinue of Buona Sforza, who had married Sigismond the Old, King of Poland. Maria's black hair and eyes, inherited from her grandmother, were living proof of her descent from Italian aristocrats.

Countess Teresa had a marked weakness for all kinds of splendor. She boasted friendships with royalty; she liked to surround herself with celebrities and collected autographs of noted personages. After the Polish uprising of 1830, the Wodzinskis had settled in Switzerland. In their salon in Geneva they entertained Queen Hortense of Holland and her son Louis Napoleon (later Emperor Napoleon III), and many prominent scholars and artists, among them Juliusz Slowacki, the great Polish poet. The family's present sojourn in Dresden was a year's interlude on their journey back to Warsaw.

In their apartment in the Rampische Strasse, Chopin found something of the atmosphere he had described to his sisters in his letter from Karlsbad—a Polish home, familiar faces, habits, and gestures. And there was still another surprise. The passage of time had magically transformed little Maria into a beautiful young lady. Frederic's lessons with her when she was a child, his romps with her through the apartment in Warsaw, when he pursued her shouting that he loved her, must have seemed almost unreal.

Maria was now sixteen and mature beyond her years. She had been brought up by a retinue of governesses, studying everything that was required by fashion and her mother's ambition. She had a lovely alto voice and had successfully appeared as a pianist at charity concerts in Geneva. The portraits she painted were lauded for their likeness, and her copies of ancient masterpieces were admired even beyond the circle of her family and friends. She was thoroughly familiar with contemporary literature, had a special predilection for poetry, and could quote verses from memory in many languages. It was no secret that in Geneva she had been the inspiration of Slowacki and that she was the heroine of his poem "In Switzerland." She was nicknamed *la brune fille d'Euterpe.*

Dazzled by her charm, Chopin forgot Klengel and the other friends he had planned to see in Dresden. He spent his few days in this city in a state of continuous rapture. Maria and Frederic roamed through Dresden, showing each other their favorite streets, buildings, and views. From the high terrace of the Brühl Palace they watched the Elbe flowing below. They were attracted by the Grossgarten, where they walked in the tree-lined avenues, conversing intimately. Chopin had had similar walks with Tytus, and Maria now added a new charm to these memories. He also went with her to the picture gallery, and showed her the paintings that he loved and that had given him inspiration.

In the evenings he played; he did not have to be asked, but hastened to the piano of his own accord. In addition to the Wodzinskis there were invited guests in his audience. But above all there was Maria. When he rose from the piano the clock of the Frauenkirche tower had already struck the late hours. The guests would leave, but he would linger for a while in the drawing room. He had a place there that was never used by anyone else, and there he would sit and talk with Maria; it was called "Frycek's corner." The girl's throaty voice had a sensuous timbre. She had an olive complexion and full lips, and her gleaming black hair was parted smoothly above her high forehead and was coiled below her ears.

She was less attractive than Delphine; with her strongly chiseled features, lovely from certain angles but too pronounced from others, she was very different from his Parisian mistress, who had both classical beauty and sensuous vitality. But Delphine lacked one trait that Maria had in the highest degree—a charming girlishness. Moreover, Delphine was alone, living for herself and paying for her freedom with suffering, while Maria was surrounded by an atmosphere of family warmth.

Home and family, which in Frederic's eyes stood simply for a consecrated bond, an unworldly, inward fealty, meant something entirely different for the Wodzinskis. They were associated with ideas of an aristocratic hierarchy that dictated a certain policy. Not only Maria lived under this roof—but also principles and traditions that were hostile to his dreams.

Occasionally the Wodzinskis spent an evening with Maciej Wodzinski, Maria's uncle. This dried-up old man, whose former splendor was now attested only by a collection of etchings and a lordly pride, was a connoisseur of old books and a lover of painting; and if he had not been deaf to music, he might have been less annoyed by Frederic's long conversations with his niece. He noticed their attraction for each other and had no compunction about demanding that his brother and sister-in-law put a stop to what he considered an improper idyl.

Count Wincenty, who was very submissive to his brother and somewhat in awe of him, assented at once. But Countess Teresa had her own opinion in the matter. Frederic had won her heart; she called him her son and regarded him as a brother to all her children. Moreover, she decided, there was no reason for uneasiness since Chopin was to remain in Dresden for only a short time. She had a dominant influence on her daughter and shared her feelings over her extraordinary reunion with Frederic after so many years. Her feminine heart throbbed as did Maria's at the thought that this artist whom the world acclaimed as a genius, and to whom all the palaces of Europe stood open, felt at his best in her home, in "Frycek's corner."

Before this delightful intoxication had run a week's course, Frederic had to leave. September was drawing to a close, and the vacation he had begun in June had been protracted beyond bounds. En route to Paris he intended to stop in Leipzig to see Mendelssohn, hear Clara Wieck, and meet Schumann. He had to hurry.

He spent the night before his departure over music sheets. The next day he played a new waltz for Maria (Opus 69, No. 1), which was their farewell. In it rang the chimes of the Frauenkirche, and one could hear the sounds of a departing carriage. When he finished playing he offered her the manuscript. At the top it bore the inscription *Pour Mademoiselle Marie*, and at the bottom there was the date—*Dresde, Septembre, 1835*. Maria took a rose from a vase and handed it to Frederic. Before noon the diligence was on its way.

Shortly after Chopin's departure Maria wrote him the following letter:

On Saturday, after you left us, all of us were sad, with eyes full of tears, sitting in that drawing room where only a few minutes before you had been one of us. Father joined us a little later and was sorry that he had been unable to say good-by to you. Mother, with tears in her eyes, every now and then reminded us of some jest of Frederic's, her "fourth son" (as she says). Felix looked utterly dejected; Casimir wanted to play his tricks as usual, but that day they somehow did not come off, for he was unable to suppress his tears while pretending to be a clown.

At eleven o'clock the singing teacher came; the lesson didn't go well at all—we could not sing. You were the subject of all our conversations. Felix kept asking me to play your waltz—the very last thing that remains with us. We took great pleasure in it—I playing it and the others listening, for it reminded us of our brother who has just left us. I took it to the bookbinder, who raised his eyebrows on seeing only one sheet of paper (this German did not know who it was that had written on that sheet). Nobody ate his dinner; everyone glanced at your usual place at the table, and then at Frycek's corner. The little chair is still where it was and surely will remain there as long as we stay in this apartment.

In the evening we were taken to our aunt's to escape the sadness of this first evening on which you would not be with us. Father followed us saying that it would be inconceivable for him, as it was for us, to stay at home that night. We were relieved when we were away from the place that too vividly reminded us of our grief. Mother talks with me only about you and Antoni. . . .

We still regret that your name is not Chopinski, or that there is no other sign showing that you are a Pole, for the way it is the French may try to take from us the glory of being your countrymen. But my letter is growing too long. Your time is so precious that it is a real crime to make you waste it on reading my scribbles. However, I am sure you won't read all of them. Little Marynia's letter will be thrown into a corner after you have read the first few words. So after all I don't have to reproach myself for stealing your time. Adieu (quite simply). A childhood friend needs no big words. Mother kisses you tenderly. Father and my brothers embrace you tenderly (no, this is not enough), most . . . I don't know myself how to say it. Adieu . . .

CHAPTER

21

The Companions of David

C HOPIN arrived in Leipzig presumably on the night of September 26th and put up at the Hotel de Saxe. The extant accounts of his brief sojourn in this city are unreliable, but it is certain that its high point was his visit to the home of Friedrich Wieck, where he met Clara Wieck and Schumann.

Some time before, Wieck had written to his friend Gustave Nauenburg in Halle:

Tomorrow or the day after Chopin is due here from Dresden. But most likely he won't give a concert, for he is a great lazybones. However, he may stay here for some time if he is not dissuaded from becoming acquainted with Leipzig and its musical world by a false friend, a certain Polish dog. It seems that in Dresden Chopin declared that he did not believe that there is a woman in Germany capable of playing his compositions properly. We'll see what Clara can do!

Chopin had apprised Schumann in advance of his visit, but postponed it to the last moment. It was known that he had arrived in Leipzig and had visited Mendelssohn, who had just been appointed conductor of the Gewandhaus orchestra. But the Wieck household at No. 36 Grimmaische Strasse awaited him in vain.

For Chopin the days had sped unnoticed on the wings of music in the circle of Mendelssohn and his friends. He had played his new études, a fragment of his Concerto in F minor, and one of his nocturnes; he had also listened to the compositions of his host. Finally, on the day of his departure from Leipzig, he set out for the Wiecks', but he took a dangerous route, for he stopped at the house of Mendelssohn, who was supposed to take him to the Grimmaische Strasse. There he sat down at the piano and once again he and his host became lost to all the addresses and clocks in this world.

When they came out of this preoccupation it was afternoon. Chopin's stagecoach was to leave in a few hours. They hurried to the Wiecks'. Mendelssohn knocked at the door; when it was opened he called out, "Here is Chopin!" and fled.

The only persons there to receive him were Frau Wieck, her sister-in-law, Schumann, and three of Wieck's young pupils who stared at Chopin with admiration, awe, and some consternation. They feared a scene, because Wieck had deliberately left the house, taking Clara with him.

Schumann saved the situation. He was timid by nature, a man who wrote more easily than he could speak; but now he found warm words at once to greet the man whom he admired so much and whom he was so eager to meet.

A short time before, Schumann had become the owner and editor of the *Neue Zeitschrift für Musik*, a weekly organ of militant young musicians. Schumann had organized his imaginary confreres into a society that he named the *Davidsbündler,* or Companions of David. This group declared war on the Philistines—that is to say, mediocrity, routine, and dullness in music. Schumann staffed his periodical with fictitious figures that voiced his various opinions. The rough-hewn Florestan debated with the refined Eusebius, and the wise Rado reconciled the antagonists. Some of the names designated real people; Clara Wieck appeared as Chiara or Zilia, and Felix Mendelssohn as Felix Meritis.

Schumann's nervous and unassuming manner concealed an ardent love for music, a passionate idealism, and genuine temperament. Chopin must have listened to him with interest. He now was able to see his admirer as he was in reality—an ardent, inspired musician and poet. He must have thought of Schumann's

Carnaval, about which he had many reservations, but in which the author had added only Paganini and Chopin to the fantasy figures symbolizing his dreams. It was difficult to ask for a greater proof of devotion.

After some time Wieck and Clara came back. Apparently the old man had not expected to find Chopin, because he seemed embarrassed, not knowing whether to be angry or pleased. Music smoothed out everything. At Frederic's request, Clara played Schumann's recently completed Sonata in F-sharp minor, two Chopin études, and a composition of her own. The subtle skill of this adolescent artist deeply impressed Chopin; it is said that tears came to his eyes. At Clara's invitation he sat down at the piano and the Companions of David at last heard in his own performance the artist whose works they had long considered exemplary. Chopin played for them his Nocturne in E-flat major (Opus 9, No. 2) and a fragment of a Schubert march.

At the end of two hours Chopin had to leave. Schumann was bewitched; Wieck had forgiven his guest for his unpunctuality, and Clara was delighted with a new composition that Chopin presented to her. All of them accompanied the visitor to the stage-coach depot. The three young pupils had the feeling that they had witnessed a historic meeting. One of them, Wenzel, later wrote: "He reminded one somewhat of Mendelssohn. Only he was more slender and more distinguished in manner. He spoke German fluently but with a foreign accent."

Frederic was in haste to get to Paris, but several nights spent in diligences had exhausted him. When he reached Heidelberg he was ill. He stopped there for a few days that he later recalled with pleasure, thanks to the hospitality shown him by the parents of Adolf Gutmann and by Frau Diller. He arrived in Paris in mid-October.

At about this time Mendelssohn wrote to his father and his sister Fanny:

Chopin was here. I cannot conceal from you, dear Fanny, that you have judged him unfairly. Perhaps he was not in the right mood when you heard him; this often happens to him. As for myself, I was again enchanted by his playing, and I am convinced that if you and Father heard some of the better pieces played as he played them to me, you would say the same thing. There is something utterly original in his playing, and at the same time it is so masterful that he can be called the perfect virtuoso. Because I like and value all perfection, it was a most pleasant day for me. I was happy to meet a true musician once again, a musician who has a clearly defined and perfect goal, so unlike those half virtuosos and half classicists who like to combine in their music *les honneurs de la vertu et les plaisirs du vice.* Although our styles are as different as heaven and earth, it is easier for me to communicate with such a man than with those semi-demi-people.

In the *Neue Zeitschrift für Musik* of October 6, 1835, Schumann published the following item: "Chopin was in Leipzig but stayed only for a few hours, which he spent in a circle of close friends. The style of his playing is exactly like that of his compositions—that is to say, unique."

But two weeks later Schumann was again carried away by his enthusiasm. In one of the *Schwärmbriefe,* Eusebius wrote to Chiara: "Chopin came. Florestan rushed to meet him. I saw them walking arm and arm, but it was as though they were floating on clouds, not walking." And then, not quite faithful to the facts, but expressing all his timid admiration for Chopin, he added, "I did not talk with him. The very thought of it overwhelmed me."

"Gray Hour"

O<small>N HIS</small> return to Paris, Chopin learned with grief that Bellini had died. But he was soon engrossed by the approaching musical season. Discussion centered predominantly on Sigismond Thalberg, the new sensation of the pianoforte. His concerts were hailed with enthusiasm; an elegant, handsome virtuoso, he bewitched the packed concert halls. But the musicians were divided into two camps regarding his merits. Fétis, Kalkbrenner, and Pixis headed the ranks of Thalberg's admirers; Chopin and Berlioz gave primacy to Liszt, who became the official rival of the Austrian pianist.

Thalberg, a natural son of Count Moritz von Dietrichstein and the Baroness Wetzlar, had been famous from childhood in the salons of Vienna. At the age of fourteen he played before Metternich, and after studying with Hummel he rose quickly to public success. His fantastic technique and skillful exploitation of the pedal enabled him to achieve striking effects; it was commonly said of him that he played as if he had three hands. He captivated his audiences by his beautiful sensuous tone, but he was an artist of little sensitivity or poetic feeling. Chopin, who had met Thalberg in Vienna, and whose opinion of him had not changed since that time, was indifferent to the new idol's Parisian triumphs. He was confirmed in his feeling by his natural reluctance to follow the dictates of fashion. Moreover, he was irri-

"Gray Hour"

tated by Thalberg's habit—Liszt was guilty of a similar practice —of arbitrarily changing other composers' works. It was said that one evening when Thalberg had been playing one of Chopin's nocturnes at a private soirée, the composer of the piece, who had remained silent during the performance, approached him, congratulated him, and asked, "Whose composition was this?"

Chopin was not interested in the rivalry between Liszt and Thalberg. He kept aloof, perhaps feeling that his art was above such contests. Heine, who despite his enthusiasm for Liszt was a partisan of Thalberg, said, "There is only one man whom I would place above Thalberg. That is Chopin, but he is much more of a composer than a virtuoso."

Emotionally, Frederic was still under the spell of his experiences in Karlsbad and Dresden. His feelings for his family and his feelings for Maria converged into one powerful current that carried him in a direction he had never explored. He thought of marriage; he dreamed of having his own home. His romance with Delphine was drawing to an undramatic close. The Countess intended to return to her husband. Frederic himself approved of this plan, seeing in it the only course by which she could save herself from further shock and disappointment. In August, 1836, she sold her household effects and left Paris. Balzac wrote to Madame Hanska that all that Delphine left behind were debts and rumors that he did not wish to repeat.

Chopin dedicated to Delphine his F minor concerto, which was now to be published. This was a kind of farewell to his mistress. The concerto had been written under the impetus of his love for Konstancja; but Konstancja had become for him a memory without resonance. And now everything that had been frustrated in his adolescent love—his hunger for dreams and his need for an intimate companion—quickened again when he thought of Maria.

About this time Antoni Wodzinski, Maria's light-minded brother, came to Paris to squander his time and his money with blithe recklessness. Through him Frederic heard about everything that was going on at the Wodzinskis', and he began to make his plans. He decided to go to Dresden the following year and to invite his mother to join him and to help him in his designs. He thought that she would know better than he how to approach the Count and Countess on such a vital matter. He wrote to his parents, revealing his secret dreams to them.

Frederic's plans caused a great stir in the family, and would doubtless have seemed to them the most important thing that had happened in many years, if he had not suddenly fallen ill. In November, 1835, he caught a cold that assumed a disquieting form. He had a high fever and coughed up blood; the doctors feared that the consequences would be grave. Exhausted by his illness, Chopin became depressed and ceased writing home. He suffered hallucinations, was obsessed by the thought of death, and even made a will.

The news of his illness soon spread in Paris and found its way to Warsaw in the form of a rumor that Chopin had died. This rumor was so persistent that on January 8, 1836, the Warsaw *Courier* published the following announcement: "We inform the many friends and admirers of the sublime talent of the virtuoso Frederic Chopin that the rumors about his death that have been circulating for several days have no foundation whatsoever."

The Chopins learned of their son's illness before Christmas, and their holidays were blighted by anxiety. Friends brought them the hearsay news that Frederic had recovered; but the troubled parents were somewhat reassured only when they heard that the Christmas issue of the *Journal des Débats* had reported that Chopin had played improvisations at a private soirée. Monsieur Nicolas at once hastened to the Lourse café and asked for the Paris newspaper, to read the comforting item with his own eyes. "It was enough to ease the minds of many persons," he wrote to his son. "But the hearts of your nearest are still haunted by doubt."

On January 9th a letter from Frederic, after a long period of silence, finally dispelled the parents' anxiety. The father in an answering letter adjured his son to pay more attention to his health; he also wrote to Matuszynski, asking him to take Frederic under his medical care, "even though this should result in a quarrel."

"Gray Hour"

Monsieur Nicolas reacted to his son's Dresden projects calmly and with understanding. He had no objection to Frederic's plans; he consented to let Justyna go, but advised his son to arrange a concert tour to cover the traveling expenses of both.

However that may be, it is a beautiful castle in Spain [he wrote]. But I'll say never mind, let us keep building it. I think that if it can be made to come true at all, you cannot have better support than with your mother at your side. I shall bear temporary separation from her with patience when I think of its purpose. But all this requires health and money, and you must begin to think of one and the other. This is the only way for you to see Dresden again and that which may interest you there, if your original impression does not change.

Happy over his father's assent, Frederic disregarded the nuance of skepticism in this letter. He was absorbed in his plans, eager to leave as soon as possible. He learned from Antoni that the Wodzinskis intended to go to Sluzewo, where the reconstruction of their country residence was almost completed. In connection with this plan Count Wincenty went to Poland and while in Warsaw called on the Chopins. He questioned them with particular concern about Frederic's health. The Countess and Maria were still in Dresden, and Frederic kept sending them collections of autographs and his newly published compositions.

Mendelssohn and Schumann urged Chopin to come to Düsseldorf again to attend the musical festival, but he declined on account of his plans. However, it became known in Leipzig that he intended to go to Dresden in the summer, and Clara Wieck, meeting the Countess Wodzinska at one of her concerts, repeated the news to her. "Is this true?" the Countess wrote to Frederic. Apparently his intended trip was a surprise to her.

Frederic was living in a state of excitement; he worked a great deal, drafting new polonaises, nocturnes, and mazurkas, correcting the proofs of his compositions now being printed, and preparing for a concert with Liszt, who was about to leave Paris. This concert took place in Erard Hall on April 9, 1836. Liszt achieved a great triumph. Chopin, too, had many reasons for satisfaction.

His friend gave a brilliant performance of several of his new études of the second series, and in the last number of the program they appeared together, playing Liszt's Grande Valse and enrapturing the audience.

The first of Chopin's five compositions published in 1836—the Concerto in F minor, Opus 21—appeared in April. It was followed by two Nocturnes, Opus 27, the Ballade in G minor, Opus 23, Two Polonaises, Opus 26, and the *Andante spianato* and Polonaise, Opus 22. By July all of these works were on sale. Chopin was free to leave.

In addition to his lessons, his compositions were becoming an increasingly important source of income. They were published in France, Germany, and later in England, and often he was paid several times over for one work. While in his everyday life he had little regard for money and spent it openhandedly, he was exacting and unyielding in his dealings with publishers. He sold his smaller compositions, such as nocturnes or mazurkas, for from three to five hundred francs each, and larger works—polonaises, ballades, or scherzos—for a thousand or more apiece. Such high fees were his particular ambition, and he no doubt thought with satisfaction that he could boast of more than glory and fame when visiting his wealthy friends.

He had no time to prepare the tour which his father had suggested to him, and for this reason he did not dare insist on his mother's joining him. On learning from Antoni Wodzinski that Countess Teresa was about to go to Marienbad, he got on a stagecoach and left for the country where he had met his parents a year before and had spent an unforgettable month with them.

By the end of July, 1836, he found himself in Marienbad, happy and excited. There he met Countess Teresa and her daughters; the Count and his son Felix and Casimir were in Poland. He took quarters in the same villa as the Wodzinskis, who received him warmly. Maria did not conceal her joy. From the first day on they resumed their Dresden intimacy just as though they had not been separated for a year. Frederic played for them in the evenings, and soon found a new corner for himself in their drawing room. He sat for hours in the garden with Maria, posing for a portrait she was painting.

Chopin's intimacy with the Wodzinskis began to attract the attention of friends. Frederic realized that he should declare his intentions and regretted that his mother was not with him. He somehow could not bring himself to make a formal proposal.

Maria was genuinely interested in him. In Dresden the Wodzinskis had spent a dull year, missing the company of celebrities that frequented their salon in Geneva, and now their Parisian friend had brought with him a breath of the great world. His conversation was interesting, and he made the most of his talent for mimicry when he sat at the piano playing like the disheveled Liszt, the stiff Kalkbrenner, or the aristocratic Thalberg, whom he had nicknamed "the Emperor."

During all this time in Marienbad, Frederic was actually treated like a son by the Countess Wodzinska. She discussed family matters with him, including the prospective marriage of Felix and the reconstruction of the palace in Sluzewo. He was asked to keep an eye on Antoni in Paris and to select a piano for the Wodzinskis at Pleyel's. These happy days stimulated his wit; he became the favorite of Maria's little sisters, and only his cough, an aftermath of his illness, gave pause to Countess Teresa.

In the first days of September the ladies returned to Dresden, accompanied by Chopin. He told himself that he was only taking them home, but in fact he hoped that in Dresden he would at last find the courage to ask for Maria's hand. He had little time left, for he would shortly be obliged to return to Paris.

The distractions of life in Dresden did not favor the task he had set for himself. Maciej Wodzinski disapproved of Frederic, and again pointed out to the Countess the impropriety of his courtship of Maria. Schumann wrote to Chopin that he wished to visit him. The King of Saxony expressed a wish to hear the famous pianist, a request that caused great excitement throughout the Polish colony. But Frederic did not even answer Schumann's letter and refused the King's request. He was in an antagonistic mood and not even Maria could prevail upon him to attend the royal reception. He counted the few days he would still have in Dresden; he had reserved a seat in the coach for September 10th.

Only on the eve of his departure did he succeed in rousing within himself the old spur of determination. He contrived to be alone with Maria and found the words to express his dream. It was at nightfall, in the twilight hour that is called in Poland the "gray hour." Maria accepted his proposal, but added that Frederic must obtain the consent of her parents and that everything depended on them.

Maria had been taught from childhood on to cultivate perfect social manners, and to distrust spontaneous impulses of the heart. Her family was rigidly patriarchal; she had only as much freedom as her parents granted her. She did not rebel; on the contrary, she felt instinctively that passivity may be made a feminine charm.

Chopin went to her mother. The moment he chose turned out to be unpropitious—the Countess was suffering from toothache. Her attitude was kind, although she received him only for a very brief moment. She promised him the hand of her daughter provided that her husband did not oppose the marriage. It was agreed that the engagement should be kept a secret until the final decision, which was postponed to the spring or summer of the next year. The Countess gave Frederic some motherly advice concerning his health. He was to retire at eleven at the latest, drink *eau de gomme* for his cough, and wear woolen stockings.

He had no choice but to accept the Countess's decision. After all, the turn of the year was not too far off. The secrecy about the betrothal seemed justified, even if only on account of Maciej Wodzinski's influence on Wincenty. Moreover, the ladies were about to go to Poland, and the marriage would have to be postponed in any event. Maria was looking forward to seeing Frederic's parents; she promised to give them the portrait she had painted in Marienbad. She also showed herself solicitous about his health and promised to embroider a pair of warm slippers for him.

CHAPTER

23

Shadow Play

CHOPIN journeyed back to Paris by the same route he had taken the year before, and once again stopped in Leipzig; here he visited the Wiecks, saw Schumann, listened to the playing of Clara Wieck, and played his own compositions to them. He enjoyed the atmosphere in the circle of these enthusiastic lovers of music, among whom were his most devoted friends outside of Warsaw and Paris. Clara fully rendered the poetic quality of his compositions, following the text with absolute fidelity, which he always considered the noblest practice in a virtuoso. Frederic left Leipzig with regret. Shortly after his departure, Schumann, in a letter dated September 14, 1836, wrote to Heinrich Dorn, his former teacher of counterpoint:

The day before yesterday, just when I had received your letter and was sitting down to answer it, who should come in? Chopin. I was overjoyed. We spent a beautiful day together and yesterday we celebrated. . . . I have his new ballade [Opus 23]; it seems to me a work of supreme genius. I told him that I liked it more than any of his other compositions. After thinking a long while he said, "I am very glad of that because I too like it best." He also played several new études, nocturnes, and mazurkas, all of them incomparable. One feels moved even as one sees him sitting down at the piano. You would like him enormously. But it seems to me that Clara is a greater virtuoso and that she interprets his compositions with deeper feeling.

The Life and Death of Chopin

This time, remembering how stagecoach traveling had exhausted him the year before, Chopin traveled slowly. He stopped at Kassel, where he visited Louis Spohr, and at Heidelberg, where he took a short rest. Then he hastened on to Paris.

At home he was met by Matuszynski, who handed him two letters from Dresden that had preceded him. One was from Countess Wodzinska, the other from Casimir, with a postscript from Maria, who wrote:

We are inconsolable after your departure. The three days past have seemed like centuries to us. Did they seem so to you, too? Do you miss your friends even a little bit? I shall venture to answer yes for you, and I think that I am not mistaken—or at least this is what I want to believe. I am trying to convince myself that this yes comes from you (for surely this would be your answer, wouldn't it?). . . . Mother had her tooth extracted; she has been much weakened as a result. She has been confined to her bed since. In two weeks we shall leave for Poland. I shall see your parents—what a joy for me! I wonder whether dear Ludwika will recognize me. Adieu, *mio carissimo maestro,* don't forget Dresden, and later Poland. Adieu. Good-by for the present. Ah, may we see each other again very soon! . . . Casimir told me that the piano in Sluzewo is completely wrecked and that it is impossible to play on it. Therefore I am asking you to remember the Pleyel. I hope I'll hear you play on it in happier days than the present (in so far as concerns us). Good-by, good-by, good-by! This word holds some hope.

The style of this letter does not seem too elegant for a "daughter of Euterpe." But it is a warm letter, and Frederic could read in it that Maria constantly thought of him, longed for him, and wished to see him "in happier days."

He must have read the Countess's letter with anxiety; after all, more depended on her than on Maria. She wrote:

I cannot cease regretting the fact that you left on Saturday; on that day I was ill, and I was unable to give sufficient thought to the event of the gray hour. We spoke about it too briefly. Our conversation might have been longer the next day. . . . Do not think that I retract what I said. No. . . . I shall ask you to keep silent. . . .

Keep yourself in good health; after all, everything depends on that. . . . Casimir arrived on Sunday. I found that he had changed a great deal since he left. What a prospect this opens for Maria! Who can tell what she will be like in a year? . . . When I see your parents and sisters, I shall tell them that you are in good health and spirits, although I won't mention the secret of the gray hour. But be sure of my favor. . . . Adieu. Go to bed at eleven, always drink *eau de gomme*. Dr. Matuszynski will agree with me. Good-by, beloved Frederic. I bless you in my soul as your loving m. . .

P.S. Maria is sending you the slippers. They are a little too big, but I add that you should wear woolen stockings. . . . I assume that you'll be obedient, since you promised. Finally, remember that this is the time of probation. . . .

The signature "Your loving m . . ." is odd. Was it intended to express the writer's usual cordiality toward her "fourth son," or something more? Why did she warn Frederic that Maria might change? Why did she stress so much the secrecy enjoined on him in regard to the engagement? Was this secrecy the most important thing about it? And was it really true that everything depended on his health?

He kept the secret, but made one exception—his parents. He wanted them to know about his engagement before they saw the Wodzinskis, who on their return to Poland would come to Warsaw to attend the wedding of Felix. Possibly he hoped that despite everything the Countess would allude to the engagement, and that his affairs might take an unexpected turn.

The meeting between the Wodzinskis and the Chopins in Warsaw was cordial enough, although marked with the usual formality. Maria presented Frederic's parents with an engraved copy of the portrait she had made of him. She had inscribed it, "To his parents, grateful for their kindness, Maria." She gave another copy of it to Ludwika. The two families visited each other several times and discussed everything except the matter that certainly most occupied their thoughts. Nothing unexpected took place. Then the Wodzinskis left Warsaw for their permanent home in Sluzewo.

The Life and Death of Chopin

All that Frederic could hope for now was letters. A correspondence did develop between him and the Wodzinskis, but it was quite different from what he might have hoped for. Its main and practically only theme was Antoni Wodzinski, who found nothing better to do in Paris than to enlist in a regiment of Polish lancers formed by the French government for support of the Bourbons during the period of dynastic conflict in Spain. Antoni was wounded in the fighting near Huesca. Frederic lent him money, transmitted to him the sums sent by Countess Teresa, and served as his go-between in his correspondence with his family.

He did not forget the piano for Sluzewo; he selected an instrument at Pleyel's and ordered it to be shipped by sea to Danzig. Despite his intimacy with the Wodzinskis, his relations with them were so formal that he did not mention the price of the piano that he had arranged with his friend Pleyel. Only after the piano reached its destination did the Countess recall this detail, remarking that "We'll have to raise the money." Chopin also sent new autographs to Sluzewo, reported gossip about friends, and waited for some warmer word from the people who, he hoped, would soon be related to him by marriage.

While their first letters were relatively cordial, those that followed rarely contained even a single sentence that went beyond conventional amiability. On one occasion the Countess signed her communication "Gray Hour," and Maria added in a postscript, "Good-by till May or June or later." That was as far as she went. She never wrote him a letter of her own. She merely added a few lines to the letters written by her mother. Her love was confined to postscripts.

He answered them in the same restrained style. "I can think only of the slippers, and at the gray hour I play." Such were the pantomime exchanges carried on between these persons separated by a distance of many hundred miles. To the consistently matter-of-fact gestures of the Wodzinskis, Frederic consistently countered with supine tenuousness. It was a correspondence devoid of feeling or insight; there was no room in it even for expression of mood.

Shadow Play

In these letters Frederic found the very opposite of what he sought—doubt instead of hope, disappointment instead of joy. He wondered whether the secrecy imposed upon him in the matter of his engagement was only a subtle way of rebuking him. In his uncertainty, he even consulted a celebrated fortuneteller named Madame Lenormand, who in her filthy dark room in the Rue Tournon foretold a bright and happy future for him.

He did not take too much to heart the Countess Wodzinska's therapeutic suggestions about *eau de gomme* and sleeping hours. The Countess had friends in Paris who kept her informed about every detail of Chopin's life. Perhaps she was worried about his amorous propensities, which were the subject of gossip among his friends; perhaps about his former relations with Delphine; or perhaps she was really concerned about his health. At all events, when she heard that Frederic spent his evenings in salons as of old, and did not follow the treatment she had prescribed, she reprimanded him quite sharply.

He could not understand what connection there was between *eau de gomme* and love. He could not understand the purpose of a correspondence that avoided the theme most important to the correspondents. He could not understand what was going on behind his back, but he knew that it was something that boded ill for him. The more he was tormented by the vicissitudes of his love, the more he sought consolation in music. He recorded everything that he felt in the language of his art, which the echoes of human confusion and chaos could not reach. In the realm to which he soared, he could not be disappointed by the Countess's letters or by Maria's unresponsiveness; there delusive hopes did not die. Music, the sister of dream, reacted to happiness and grief in its own way, giving them a new content inexpressible in words.

As was his wont, he composed several works simultaneously, putting them aside to be polished later. The fruits of this period of tormented love were the Four Mazurkas, Opus 30; the Scherzo in B-flat minor, Opus 31; the Two Nocturnes, Opus 32; and the two first études of the second series, in A flat and F minor. These last, according to contemporary opinion, were most closely associated in his mind with his feeling for Maria.

CHAPTER 24

A Soirée in the Chaussée d'Antin

IN THE fall of 1836, Chopin moved to a new apartment at No. 38 Rue de la Chaussée d'Antin. He would get up late and begin his day with a session with his barber, who shaved him and dressed his hair before breakfast. Until noon he worked at his compositions or dawdled in the house; then began his lessons, which lasted till evening. He reduced his social life to a minimum, seeing only his closest friends. He now had a servant, an exiled Pole, who, in bad French but with soldierly determination, kept out visitors, explaining that his master was not at home or was not receiving. In front of the house stood a cabriolet. At six o'clock, Chopin, dressed in a dark-blue frock coat with gold buttons and wearing a broad cravat with a diamond pin, donned his white gloves, threw a cape over his shoulders, and drove to dinner or to the home of a friend.

It was only a short distance to the Hôtel de France on the Rue Laffitte, where Franz Liszt lived with the Countess Marie d'Agoult. Frederic had not seen Liszt for a year, and since Madame d'Agoult liked him, he visited them often and stayed many hours. He was fond of these attractive lovers, although their liaison, which had aroused a great deal of comment two years before, offended his sense of discretion. They flaunted their love too ostentatiously for his taste. On the other hand, how could he help envying Liszt for having a mistress who had courageously broken with her former life and followed the summons of love? The omniscient Madame Lenormand had foretold the Countess's stormy career, and Madame d'Agoult, six years older than Liszt, had not quavered before an uncertain fate. She had deserted her husband and children, taking with her only her husband's aristocratic title.

Fair-headed and smiling, she was a person of great beauty and sparkling intelligence, but it was said by one of her contemporaries that her feminine warmth was hidden beneath "a twenty-foot layer of cold lava and a six-foot layer of snow." Her dream was to become a famous novelist. She spent long hours over sheets of paper, covered with minute calligraphic handwriting, which she signed "Daniel Stern." She was happy at the side of Liszt, but she would have been willing to enhance her romantic splendor with an additional worshiper. The favors she showed Chopin might have suggested to him that she destined him for this role.

Chopin, usually prone to flirtation, at this time was gloomy and self-absorbed. He did not come to Rue Laffitte for the sake of Madame d'Agoult; he was attracted by the atmosphere of this home. Liszt and the Countess had recently returned from Switzerland and spoke of their life there as though it had been a series of adolescent adventures. Geneva society had refused to recognize their liaison and had boycotted their home, although all the exiled kings and ministers living in Switzerland had acclaimed Liszt at charity concerts. When their daughter Blandine was born, their purse was empty, but nothing could disturb their serenity or rob them of their insouciance. When Liszt came to Chamonix on an excursion, he wrote in the hotel register that he had been born on Parnassus, that he was coming from the Land of Doubt, and was on his way to the Land of Truth.

In Switzerland the couple had been visited by George Sand, with whom, after their return to Paris, they took quarters at the Hôtel de France. They had a common salon and received friends together. Among their visitors were Lamennais, Nourrit, Pierre Leroux, Sainte-Beuve, Eugène Sue, Mickiewicz, and Chopin's inseparable pair of friends, Hiller and Heine.

The Life and Death of Chopin

In the little salon in the Hôtel de France, Chopin also was introduced to George Sand. He met her there in the company of her son Maurice and her daughter Solange, all three of them in trousers. At that time, women were supposed to treat this article of masculine attire as *inexprimable*; that is, it was considered improper for women to speak about it, let alone wear it. But Madame Sand was known as a revolutionist and did not spare tradition even in its trivial aspects. Chopin had naturally heard about the famous novelist's amorous adventures and extravagant way of life, which contrasted strangely with the unassuming figure before which he bowed for the first time one winter evening. Small in size (she was less than five feet tall), she smoked cigars continually and only rarely took part in the conversation. Her olive complexion, her dark eyes, and smoothly combed black hair, something Southern in her face, may have reminded him of Maria. But she seemed to him unpleasant, common, even forbidding. "What an antipathetic person, this Sand," he said to Hiller one night on leaving Liszt. "Is it really a woman? I am inclined to doubt it."

On December 13, 1836, Chopin invited Liszt with Madame d'Agoult and George Sand to a party of his own. Liszt accepted the invitation all the more eagerly because for some time he had been trying in vain to interest Chopin in Madame Sand. That night the two virtuosos were to play Moscheles' Sonata in E-flat major for four hands.

Liszt had been at Chopin's receptions before. He recalled how Heine used to tell Chopin about imaginary lands, about green-haired nymphs wrapped in silvery shawls, about amorous gods chasing after naiads, and how Chopin echoed these marvelous stories with melodies and chords. In Chopin's house Liszt had met many friends, including Meyerbeer, Hiller, Mickiewicz, whom he called the Dante of the North, and Niemcewicz, author of *Historical Songs*. In these poems Chopin found endless themes for improvisation. On such occasions, he liked to have his listeners near him, closely clustered around the piano, some even, as George Sand said later, resting their elbows on it. After each improvisation he would pass his fingers over the entire keyboard, partly as a

A Soirée in the Chaussée d'Antin

jest, partly to break the mood he had created. He hated sentimentality.

The ladies came to Chopin for the first time. The drawing-room floor was covered with rugs; the windows were heavily curtained. Yellow candles were lighted next to the piano, and a fire flickered in the fireplace, but the corners of the large room were plunged in shadow. There was a fragrance of violets, the host's favorite flowers. Bouquets of these were arranged in low vases.

Madame d'Agoult voiced her admiration for the décor of the apartment. Every piece had been carefully selected. She knew that Chopin was pleased at the interest she displayed in his pictures—among them a portrait of Copernicus—in his antique Polish palace chair, in the consoles, the whatnots, and the mirrors that reflected her beautiful head and bare arms.

George Sand, perhaps deliberately or perhaps simply because she was fond of fantastic garb, appeared in Polish colors—a white dress with a scarlet sash and crimson buttons, and a frogged jacket. She immediately found a place for herself on the settee by the fireplace, lighted a cigar, and entered into a conversation with the pale and slender Eugène Sue.

The drawing room was filled with guests. There was Adolphe Nourrit, the great singer, the idol of Paris, a paragon of elegance and a master of wit; there were the distinguished Marquis de Custine, Pixis, and Berryer, the renowned attorney. The rest of the company consisted of Poles—Wlodzimierz Potocki and his brother Bernard, who was in love with Madame d'Agoult, Albert Grzymala, a close friend of George Sand, and Jozef Brzowski, a musician who had recently arrived from Warsaw.

The king of the gathering was Liszt. Always brilliant in such a setting, he related countless anecdotes, jumped from subject to subject, shook his golden hair, and teased Chopin. When Frederic retorted with his customary aptness and wit, Liszt would burst out laughing, and exclaim, "Ah, mazurka, mazurka!"

Finally they sat down at the piano—Liszt at the right, and Chopin at the left. Pixis turned the pages. All conversation stopped.

Brzowski, who had never before heard Liszt, recounted in his memoirs that he felt feverish. The technique of the players and the effects they were able to achieve amazed him. The piano seemed to come alive. "It stopped my breath," he wrote.

When they had finished playing, ices were served; then Madame d'Agoult made tea and offered it to the guests. Only George Sand remained pensive and taciturn in her place, gazing at the fire.

The conversation stopped again when Liszt and Adolphe Nourrit approached the piano. The brilliant tenor sang several songs of Schubert, among them *Der Erlkönig*. "The effect was indescribable," commented Brzowski.

The Polish guest wanted to hear Liszt alone and asked him to play, but in vain. Liszt had begun a philosophical discussion, trying to draw the entire company into it. Philosophy was his passion; in Geneva he had even registered for a series of lectures on this subject. But there was always an element of dilettante display in his expeditions from the Land of Doubt to the Land of Truth; his way of defining dogmas led to chaos, and in his quest for faith the prophets changed with the fashions. Chopin disliked such discussions, which seemed pretentious to him, and never took part in them. He would shrug his shoulders at the word God, which Liszt brought in at every turn; he was annoyed by this drawing-room mysticism.

Liszt succeeded in focusing the attention of all the gathering on him, until he began to bore them. The hours passed, but his vigor was inexhaustible. George Sand's face grew gloomy, and even Madame d'Agoult's beauty paled. Chopin became more and more impatient. Only Bernard Potocki kept pace with Liszt and debated stubbornly, bent on impressing Liszt or perhaps Madame d'Agoult.

Finally the lateness of the hour quenched the ardor of the philosophers, and the visitors began to leave. Chopin remained alone with Jas Matuszynski. Next to the fireplace was a heap of ashes dropped by the strange, pensive lady who throughout the evening had smoked cigars and gazed at the fire.

CHAPTER

───────♪───────

25

"My Misery"

Early in 1837 an epidemic of influenza broke out in Paris. In February, Chopin fell ill; he had a high fever and he coughed and spewed up blood. Exhausted, listless, he was confined to his bed for several weeks. And the letter he had received from Countess Wodzinska, with a postscript from Maria, had only contributed to his low spirits.

The Wodzinskis were bored in their residence at Sluzewo. "We spend lonely days in the castle. The clock strikes the hours more loudly than ever, reminding us that it is time to have a meal or retire," wrote the Countess. And, referring to Frederic's veiled complaint that her previous letter had failed to "mention anyone," she commented: "I don't know what my last letter was, but if I didn't mention anyone, it was because I had to dispatch this letter sooner than I had expected; this is always the case when the forester comes, and everyone cries, 'Hurry!' for the post is three miles away. This is also the case today."

Maria in her postscript thanked him for new compositions and autographs, among which was a line by Heine, and added, "When we see each other, I'll thank you even more nicely." In this strangest of all notes ever written to a fiancé, she took occasion to declare herself "a very lazy letter writer." The other items were equally unsensational. "Mother described our routine, and so I have nothing new to report, except perhaps that we are having a thaw. Great news, isn't it?"

Wearied by his doctors, who were unable to determine whether he was suffering from influenza or from consumption, Frederic got rid of them as soon as he could. He preferred to be alone. With his subtle sense of irony he must have bestowed a bitter smile on Maria's little-girlishness. Nor could he overlook the fact that Countess Wodzinska, who had so much leisure and wrote to him only once every few months, always concluded her letters when the forester hurried her.

Yet his thoughts centered around the distant castle. He recalled that Maria had said to him in the previous fall that they would see each other abroad, in May or June, and the time seemed to him intolerably long. When he recovered, his doctors advised him to go to the spa at Ems; Tytus Woyciechowski informed him that he intended to go to Germany, and suggested that they meet there. George Sand, who had gone to her estate in Nohant, repeatedly invited him, through Liszt and Madame d'Agoult, to visit her. She feared that her rustic country seat might strike the Countess as somewhat like a Cossack encampment, and asked her to bring anyone she pleased—all the Mickiewiczs and Grzymalas in the world, as she wrote, and Chopin as well, *"Chopin que j'idolâtre."*

Frederic refused to commit himself either to a meeting with Tytus or to a treatment at Ems. He made up his mind to drop in for a few days at Nohant, but as was his wont in complicated situations, he did not keep his resolution. To the Wodzinskis he wrote chiefly about Antoni, the feather-brained warrior in Spain, and he forwarded their letters to him. About other things he spoke with reticence: "Today I should like to be in Sluzewo rather than to be writing to Sluzewo. I would have said more than I have written."

Thus April passed, then May, when he was supposed to see Maria. The Sluzewo castle was silent as though under a spell. Finally June came in this calendar of torment. Once again Frederic wrote discreet, wretched words. "Is the summer beautiful

228

in Sluzewo? Is there much shade? Can one sit under a tree and paint?" he asked, referring no doubt to the garden in Marienbad where he had sat for Maria. "It has become difficult for me to remain in Paris. The doctor orders me to go to Ems, but I don't know as yet where and when I'll go."

At this time the Sluzewo forester took no foreign mail to the post, and Chopin stayed in the hot city and waited. Paris was deserted and the plan for meeting Tytus had not materialized. Liszt and Madame d'Agoult, after spending two months in Nohant, left for Bellagio on Lake Como. Chopin had the impression that something had gone wrong between Liszt and Madame Sand, but did not try to find out what it was.

He was absorbed in his own tribulations. Apparently he refused to resign himself to the idea that the failure of the Wodzinskis to answer was itself an answer. He even ignored the fact that Maria had long ago ceased to add postscripts to her mother's letters. Her last words to him had been about the weather.

In this state of mind he suddenly had an access of determination. Camille Pleyel suggested that Chopin accompany him to London. Chopin agreed at once, on condition that no one should know it.

They set about clearing up the matter of Frederic's passport, which he had neglected to renew or extend after arriving in France. Since he associated with Polish exiles, he was exposed to the wrath of the Russian authorities and actually should have been on their blacklist. But Count Pozzo di Borgo, the Tsar's ambassador in Paris, had different designs on Chopin. He offered the composer the title of court pianist to the Russian emperor, which carried with it a salary, a pension, and all kinds of honors. But to accept such a position was for a Pole equivalent to betraying the cause of his country. Chopin's answer was clear and proud: "Although I did not take part in the revolution of 1830, my heart was with those who did. Therefore I consider myself an exile, and this title does not permit me to accept any other."

He left with a French passport on July 11, 1837. Stanislas

Kozmian, who had never had an opportunity to write the libretto of Chopin's projected opera, reported to his family from London:

Chopin has been here incognito for two weeks. He does not know anybody, he refuses to see anyone, and so he is entirely available to me. I spend whole days with him, and even—as yesterday—whole nights. He is here with Pleyel, renowned for his pianos and his wife's adventures. They have come *pour se régaler de Londres*. They have put up at one of the best hotels, they have a carriage, and are plainly looking for ways to spend money. I often go to the opera. Pasta is marvelous in *Medea* and *Romeo*. I haven't yet seen *Ildegonda*, because Chopin refuses to listen to boring music. Devrient sang in *Fidelio*, and Moscheles played a long concerto. Chopin says that his playing is fearfully baroque.

Chopin appeared at a reception given by Broadwood, the well-known piano manufacturer, to whom Pleyel introduced him as Monsieur Fritz of Paris. He maintained his incognito throughout the dinner and during the first part of the concert in the drawing room where the visitors played and sang informally. Then "Monsieur Fritz" was invited to the piano. After the very first bars a murmur swept the gathering; the amazement grew, and then there were whispers: "Chopin, Chopin!" The rest of the evening was given to Frederic, playing his compositions and improvising.

In a letter that bears no superscription or date but that beyond any doubt belongs to his correspondence with Fontana, Chopin sums up his impressions of London as follows:

My Life, thank you for Kozmian—without him there would be no London for me. Thank you for your letters—without them I wouldn't be sighing and sighing. But the whole host of devils take you together with the mud here, which you thought was dry. . . . I'll tell you some other time how many pleasant thoughts and unpleasant tastes the sea gave me, and I'll also tell you the impressions that this soot-smeared Italian sky makes on my nose, which is hard put to it to bear the weight of such columns of gray air. . . . Now I'll tell you only that all this amuses me in a most decorous way; and you may tell Jas that it is easy to amuse oneself discreetly here if one is staying only for a

to have a good time

short time. There are tremendous things here! Grand urinals, and yet there isn't a place to piddle. But the Englishwomen! And the horses! And the palaces! And the carriages! And the riches! And the splendor! And the squares! And the trees! Everything, from the soap to the razors—everything is extraordinary, everything is of a pattern, everything is well-behaved, everything is washed clean and nevertheless is black as a nobleman's posterior! ! ! . . . . . Now go and praise London!

In the last days of July, Chopin returned to Paris. Kozmian had escorted him as far as Brighton. At about this time Moscheles made the following entry in his diary: "Chopin, who spent a few days in London, was the only one of the visiting artists who did not call on anyone. Not only that—he did not even wish anyone to come to see him, because each visit makes his suffering worse." Mendelssohn wrote in similar terms to Hiller a short time later, adding, Chopin "played very beautifully at Broadwood's one evening. . . . He is still suffering and sick."

Frederic did not feel physically ill, but he was spiritually broken. In London he had received a letter from the Countess Wodzinska, forwarded to him from Paris, that canceled his last weak hope: she informed him that she was not going abroad at all. It became evident that he would not see Maria, that his mock betrothal had come to an end, and that his dreams of a wife and a home of his own had vanished in thin air.

His letter replying to Maria's mother, posted from Paris, was devoted to the affairs of Antoni. There were only a few resigned words about himself: "Your last letter reached me in London. . . . I thought that from there I would go to Germany via Holland. I returned home. The season is advanced, and as for me, I shall probably wait for its end in my apartment." Thus he spent the rest of this unhappy summer in Paris. In the fall he once again received an envelope from Sluzewo. The letter it contained was intended for Antoni, but the Countess availed herself of the opportunity to inquire about Frederic's health. They had nothing more to say to each other.

The emptiness that came now was certainly more difficult to

bear than the previous uncertainty. Chopin tried to save himself by concentrated work on his compositions, by giving concerts, by contact with people. Ironically, the fate that denied him even a crumb of happiness was not niggardly of public recognition and honors.

Schumann wrote a lengthy characterization of the Polish composer in an essay devoted to his two concertos. He maintained that Chopin represented a continuation of the spirit of Beethoven and Schubert; he defined his place in contemporary music and stressed the essentially Polish quality of his compositions, at the same time urging him to transcend the boundaries of patriotic inspiration. "If the powerful autocratic monarch of the North only knew what a formidable and dangerous enemy he has in the work of Chopin, in his simple mazurkas, he would outlaw music. Chopin's compositions are cannon hidden in flowers," wrote Schumann-Eusebius.

At any other time of his life Frederic would have derived pride and happiness from the new compositions he was now publishing. In October, 1837, there appeared his second series of the Etudes, Opus 25, dedicated to the Countess d'Agoult—another Orphean book comprising twelve songs of happiness and grief, with the heavenly melody of the seventh étude, the heroic bravura of the eleventh, and the Polish despair of the twelfth. In December came four more compositions: the rapturous Impromptu in A-flat major, Opus 29; Four Mazurkas, Opus 30, including the beautiful Mazurka in C-sharp minor; the stormy, and, as Schumann wrote, "Byronic" Scherzo in B-flat minor, Opus 31; and the Two Nocturnes, Opus 32.

In 1838 he published only the Four Mazurkas, Opus 33, and the Three Waltzes, Opus 34. The early part of this year brought him the signal distinction of being invited to play his compositions and to improvise before King Louis Philippe, his family, and numerous royal guests at the Tuileries. The soirée was extremely successful. Chopin enchanted the gathering and the King rewarded him with a precious memento.

The London *Musical World*, which had been unfriendly to

Chopin, published a warm appraisal of the Two Nocturnes and the Scherzo, which had been published by Wessel under the inept titles *Il lamento e la consolazione* and *La méditation*. The London journal also commented on the soirée at Broadwood: "If M. Chopin was not, perhaps, the most retiring and unambitious of all living musicians, he would, before this time, have been celebrated as the inventor of a new style, or school of pianoforte composition. During his short visit to the metropolis, last season, but few had the high gratification of hearing his extemporaneous performance. Those who experienced this pleasure will not readily lose its remembrance. He is, perhaps, *par éminence,* the most delightful of pianists for the drawing room."

In March, 1838, Chopin made two public appearances. On the first of these occasions, he played Beethoven's Seventh Symphony in a piano arrangement for eight hands by Valentine Alkan, the chief pianist of the evening; the other pianists were Pierre Zimmermann and Adolf Gutmann. The second appearance was at a benefit concert in Rouen, given by Antoni Orlowski, where he performed his E minor concerto. Ernest Legouvé wrote about him in the *Gazette musicale* as follows:

Chopin, who for several years had not appeared in public— Chopin, who usually displays his splendid genius to audiences of five or six persons—Chopin who brings to mind enchanted isles rich in marvels beyond description—Chopin, whom one cannot forget after one has heard him even once, appeared in Rouen to support the cause of a certain Polish professor by means of a concert that brought together five hundred persons. His desire to do a good deed must have been linked in his mind with the memory of his homeland, because he overcame his aversion to public appearances. Needless to say, the success was tremendous, tremendous! The enchanting melodies, the indescribable subtleties of execution, the melancholy, passionate inspiration, the poetry of the playing and of the compositions, moving the imagination and the heart equally, dazzled and deeply moved these five hundred persons, just as they have always enraptured the eight or nine elect who have been accustomed to admire him for hours on end in the greatest absorption. Throughout this time one could feel that the hall was electrified and hear the murmur of rapture and amazement that may be considered the unconscious utterance of souls carried away by enthusiasm. Chopin, awaken! May this triumph become decisive for you! Do not persist in your selfishness, but allow your genius to shine for all. Reveal at last what you are in truth, and decide the dispute that has divided the artists. Then, to the question, Who is the foremost artist of Europe, Liszt or Thalberg? the whole world will answer as do those who have heard you: "Chopin!"

At about this time Chopin had one of the most flattering encounters of his entire artistic career. One day Paganini unexpectedly appeared at his door, accompanied by one of his pupils, Madame Peruzzi. The two virtuosos had not met before, and Chopin pressed the bony hand of the maestro with emotion. At the request of Paganini, who had never heard him before, he sat at the piano, realizing while he played that the great artist who had once been his model and ideal was now in turn listening to him in wordless rapture.

But at bottom Chopin remained indifferent to his success. He was not interested in the enthusiasm of crowds, and he cared little whether or not he was acclaimed as the world's first pianist. His inner pride had received a deeper hurt than any outward success could assuage.

He did not try to conceal his love before such intimate friends as Matuszynski, Fontana, or Grzymala. The latter-day role of the girl who had played a part in Chopin's youth became known outside his closest circle, and at the very time Frederic was saying farewell in his mind to Maria, it was rumored that he was suing for her hand. Even George Sand, when in the spring of 1838 she came from Nohant to Paris, learned about it. She saw Chopin in the home of a friend, Madame Marliani, and received him at the Hôtel de France. He did not look like a man happily in love. Gloomy, irritable, fairly misanthropic, he was paradoxically somewhat relieved by the hypocrisy of the salons. He was himself only at the piano. He did not conceal his grief when he was in the sanctuary of his art—which offers this boon, that the personal expression is cloaked under the various forms in which it is apprehended by the hearers.

Usually when he began to play he was pale, with a distraught look in his eyes; when he finished his face was excited, flushed. His emaciated profile had grown sharper; his tired eyes were framed in dark rings. His elegance and his meticulous manners formed a strange contrast to the indifference he displayed toward everything that was not art. Music became sublimated in him into an ideal untainted by the ills of life. In his eyes music was the supreme reality—it was beauty inaccessible to falseness, morality without fragile constraints, a service that was difficult but consecrated to infallible truth as to a divinity.

"He is a poor melancholy angel," George Sand said of him, moved by the charm of this man who had human weaknesses and by this genius that was without a flaw.

Frederic soon felt that he had ceased to be merely one of her thousand acquaintances and friends. He no longer avoided her and gradually became accustomed to the peculiar ways of this lady who wore trousers and smoked cigars. He was so shattered inwardly that her unexpected tenderness attracted him more strongly at this time than it could have at any other. Into his album, which had formerly served him as his notebook, he pasted a little billet from George Sand that read: *On vous adore.*

But he was moving closer to her without passion, and did not expect to go beyond the boundaries of sympathy, however ardent. In this he merely obeyed his instinct of self-preservation; he was not seeking a new love, he only wanted to forget the old one.

Suddenly the silent castle spoke again. There arrived a letter from Countess Wodzinska, insignificant in content as usual, and this time Frederic gave it scant thought. This letter was the last of that shadow-play in which his unhappy love had been bandied about for so long.

As had happened in his relations with Konstancja, only a few real events had given sustenance to Chopin's love for Maria. He had spent one week with her in Dresden, and then, after a separation of one year, a month in Marienbad. This had sufficed to transform his feeling for his childhood companion into dreams of love; but it was not enough to keep these dreams alive after three years.

What it was actually that frustrated Chopin's plans is veiled in mystery and can be only a matter of speculation. It is certain that Maria was not indifferent to him, but it is equally certain that the girl had no will to oppose her parents. Considerations of caste certainly did not favor a marriage between Maria and a musician without title or wealth. This was probably the reason why her mother preferred to keep their betrothal a secret.

It is possible, however, that the parents' opposition would not have been so great if another, more serious factor had not arisen to complicate matters. During the years in which the Wodzinskis were interested in everything affecting Frederic, his health failed him; he went through two serious illnesses, and once they, with his other friends, even experienced the shock of rumors that he had died. As aristocrats they might have sanctioned the marriage of their daughter to a musician of genius; yet as parents they could with good reason oppose her union with a man who was suspected of having tuberculosis, then an incurable disease.

Be that as it may, Chopin expected greater sincerity on the part of Countess Wodzinska and her daughter. His resentment grew as time passed and the final decision continued to be put off. He may have ascribed the behavior of the Wodzinskis to various motives; but probably he laid it at the door of their patrician pride. He felt this not only to be an insult to his own pride but a slight to his art, which in his view stood supreme among all values.

Maria's subsequent life was marked by a number of vicissitudes. In 1841 she married Count Jozef Skarbek, son of Frederic Skarbek of Zelazowa Wola, who was Chopin's godfather. Ludwika reported this marriage to her brother with bitterness: "May God be kind to them and forget." This wish did not come true.

"My Misery"

Maria was not happy; she could not have children, and it was said that her health failed owing to her husband's inadequacy. After some years her marriage with Skarbek was annulled and she later became the wife of a man named Wladyslaw Orpi-szewski. She remained faithful to the memory of Chopin and it is recorded that as a patroness-performer in charity concerts she often played his compositions.

Frederic, on taking leave of his unhappy love, did not destroy his mementos of it. He placed the letters from the Wodzinskis, together with the rose that Maria had given him in Dresden, in an envelope and tied it with a pink ribbon. On this little sepulcher of his lost hopes he wrote the words *Moja bieda*— "My misery." (or sorrow)

George Sand

Mᴏʀᴇ fascinating than anything that George Sand has written in any of the one hundred and nine volumes comprising her works is the story of her own life. She entered the world with a contradictory heritage. Her father was a descendant of a king; her mother was a child of the Paris gutter.

Her paternal great-grandfather was Maurice of Saxony, natural son of August II, Elector of Saxony and King of Poland, and Aurore Königsmark, a Swedish countess. Born in 1696, Maurice became a famous *condottiere*, fought under various flags, conquered armies and surrendered to women, and ended his adventurous career as a marshal of France. Among his many mistresses was Victoire de Verrières, a well-known Parisian opera singer, who bore him an illegitimate daughter. The girl was baptized Marie Aurore; posterity knows her as George Sand's grandmother.

Marie Aurore's career was as extraordinary as her father's. The French courts by a special decree legalized her birth and granted her permission to call herself by the name of De Saxe. She was brought up by her cousin, mother of three French kings—Louis XVI, Louis XVIII, and Charles X. Her education was interrupted when at the age of fifteen she married Count de Horn, a natural son of Louis XV. The Count suffered from an incurable disease, and the young wife was warned betimes that she must take care not to be alone with her husband even for a moment.

She succeeded in avoiding contact with him rather easily, because three weeks after her marriage she buried the Count, fallen in a duel.

The following fifteen years were spent in her mother's house, and as a thirty-year-old virgin she married Claude Dupin de Francueil, the sixty-year-old lover of her aunt. By him she had a son, Maurice, who became her greatest love and greatest torment. Marie Aurore dreamed of bringing him up as a paragon of chivalry; she gave him an artistic education, forced him to study the violin, amassed a fortune for him, and looked for a suitable wife for him among wealthy aristocrats.

Her dreams were dispelled slowly but thoroughly. During the French Revolution, Madame Dupin de Francueil lost the fortune she had inherited from her husband, and managed to save for her son only a house in Paris and a small estate she had bought in Nohant in the province of Berry. At the age of twenty, Maurice interrupted his studies and joined Napoleon's army in Italy, leaving his afflicted mother an embarrassing souvenir—an illegitimate son by a servant girl. This son was given the name of Hippolyte Châtiron, and he was brought up in Nohant.

During the Italian campaign, Lieutenant Dupin became acquainted with a young woman who accompanied the troops, ostensibly as the general's wife but actually his mistress. Sophie Victoire Delaborde was the daughter of a Parisian dealer in birds, and when Maurice met her in Milan, she was the mother of a child, Caroline, whose father was unknown. By her liaison with Maurice she had other children, who died. Sophie won great influence over Maurice and demanded that he marry her. The frightened officer managed to resist only his mother's objections; he obediently took his mistress to the church and the *mairie*, whence Mademoiselle Delaborde walked forth as Madame Dupin.

The couple took an apartment in Paris at No. 46 Rue Meslay. Exactly one month after their wedding, on July 1, 1804, several of their friends gathered in their modest home to celebrate the engagement of Sophie's sister to a friend of Maurice. The company were dancing quadrilles; Maurice played the violin, and

Sophie in a pink dress conversed pleasantly with her guests. At a certain moment she nodded to her sister and left the room. Before the last figure of the quadrille was over, the sister appeared at the door and called out, "Maurice, you have a girl."

Out of deference to his disappointed and lonely mother in Nohant, Maurice gave his daughter the name of Aurore, to which Sophie added, for the sake of elegance, Amantine and Lucile. This was the name of the woman who came to be known as George Sand.

Aurore Dupin had a stormy childhood. At the age of four she found herself in Madrid, then just fallen to the French; a short time later parents and child were forced to flee to the French border, across a country shaken by revolution, amidst horrors worthy of the brush of Goya—fires and corpses, ambushes and pestilence. The fugitives found peace and rest only on reaching Nohant.

Madame Dupin de Francueil, although dejected by her son's *mésalliance*, opened her heart and home to him and his family. Their life began to be tolerable. But in September, 1809, Maurice, returning from a visit to friends in La Châtre, fell from his horse and was killed. Sophie and her mother-in-law soon began to compete for influence over the five-year-old Aurore; each wanted in her own way to dominate the girl's upbringing. The grandmother urged her to study music and singing, the mother to cook and sew. For two years alternately each wrested the frightened child from the arms of the other; but little Aurore preferred the loud and hysterical caresses of her mother to the dignified tenderness of her jealous grandmother. When the vexed Madame Dupin de Francueil noticed also that her daughter-in-law suffered from her loneliness and widowhood, she made up her mind to take a drastic step. She offered Sophie an annuity of fifteen hundred francs on condition that she leave Nohant and renounce her right to rear Aurore. The little girl slipped into her mother's bed at night, begging her not to sell her. Sophie hugged the trembling child and wept with her, but her maternal feelings proved weaker than her thirst for life and her love of money.

George Sand

After the mother's departure, the education of the future heiress of Nohant began in earnest. The organist of La Châtre taught her to play the clavichord and the harp; Mademoiselle Greuze, who claimed to be the daughter of the famous painter, gave her drawing lessons; and Deschartres, an ex-priest in residence at the manor house of Nohant, taught her Latin, Greek, history, and mathematics. The young student also made use of the rich library accumulated by her grandparents, choosing as her mentors Homer, Tasso, Racine, and Molière. Her greatest passion, however, was to go to the village, play with the children of the servants and peasants, and walk in the fields and the woods. The grandmother considered such pastimes improper, and she regretted that her granddaughter's inseparable companion was Hippolyte, the fruit of Maurice's careless youth. She was also upset by the fact that Aurore, in a religious confusion resulting from the teachings of a rebellious priest and her own influence as an unbeliever—had invented a deity of her own, whom she called Corambé. This deity was conceived of as a female figure, and probably symbolized her frustrated love for her mother.

Madame Dupin de Francueil's aversion to her daughter-in-law persisted even with distance separating them. She tried to root out the child's attachment to her mother, even resorting to punishments. On one occasion she locked Aurore in her room for three days and did not shrink from explaining to the child her mother's past, sparing no details. The result in the thirteen-year-old girl was an attack of convulsions.

The grandmother decided that the only way out of this difficult situation was to send the girl to a convent. She chose the famous Couvent des Anglaises in Paris, so named because it was conducted by English and Scottish nuns. Aurore spent two years in this establishment, which had windows screened from the street. She did not learn much there except English, but she recovered her faith. She became a zealous Catholic, dreamed of St. Theresa, and was soon absorbed in prayer and meditation. After some time she made up her mind to become a nun.

Madame Dupin de Francueil was again terrified. This time

she acted with lightning speed. Aurore, then fifteen, was taken out of the convent. She stayed with her grandmother in Paris. Here she began to frequent aristocratic homes and was considered a marriageable young lady. But she manifested little interest in young men, and continued to yearn for the habit of a nun. The grandmother ordered their trunks packed and took her charge to her country residence.

In Nohant, Aurore fell from religious ecstasy into the ecstasy of unrestrained youth. She galloped over the fields, mounted astride in the masculine manner; she attended the hunts, and once more she sat for hours in peasants' houses, listening to folk legends and songs. She acquired a love for nature, plants, trees, and birds that became lifelong. With her young friend Stéphane de Grandsaigne she studied anatomy and the rudiments of medicine, and with the aged Deschartres she visited sick peasants and helped in treating their ailments. The rest of her time was spent in reading in the library.

This exuberant life made her forget her alleged religious vocation. Her grandmother breathed with relief, feeling herself victorious. But she was not fated to enjoy for long her conquest and her grandchild's growing attachment. Ill and deaf, Madame Dupin de Francueil died on Christmas Day of 1821.

At the age of seventeen, Aurore became the owner of the estate in Nohant and the house in Paris. She did not want to stay in the country alone. Deschartres in his old age had become an eccentric; formerly a materialist, he was now a mystic. On the eve of the grandmother's funeral he awakened his charge in the dark of night, took her to the cemetery, to the opened family vault, and removed her father's skull from the coffin, saying, "Kiss this relic. You will remember this all your life."

Aurore went to her mother in Paris. With her went her servant, her dog, and her books. But Sophie continued her contest with Madame Dupin de Francueil even after the latter's death; now she waged war against the shade of her rival. She could not endure Aurore's fine manners and ridiculed her education. Her tenderness often yielded to fits of anger, during which she beat her daughter. She dismissed the girl's servant, chased her dog away, and burned her books. Aurore was now obsessed with one idea—how to get out of this house, where her presence proved a hindrance in her mother's free life.

She found her only pleasure in visits to the family of James Duplessis, who had been a friend of her father's, and lived near Paris in a château surrounded by a beautiful park. Madame Duplessis, twenty-seven-year-old mother of five daughters, received Aurore with maternal warmth. The young provincial was often taken to concerts and plays, which she always enjoyed immensely. One day after a performance the whole company stopped at a café for ices on the terrace. A young man went by in the street, and Madame Duplessis called to him, "Casimir!" He sat down at their table and at once Aurore attracted his attention. He was tall, good-looking, and of pleasant manner. He was invited to the château and soon became a frequent guest there. He took part in games and entertained the young ladies in the park. His easy and friendly demeanor did not in any way suggest that he had matrimonial intentions.

The young man's name was Casimir Dudevant. He was the illegitimate son of a colonel in Napoleon's army, but his father had taken the necessary steps by which the boy had been given the right to bear his name and the title of baron. Having served his term in the army, Casimir had studied law, and was wondering what to do next. Aurore was little interested in all this. The young man seemed to her a pleasant companion, and without hesitation she consented to become his wife. Her mother thought him not sufficiently attractive, and for this reason made some difficulties at the beginning, but in the end she signed the *contrat de mariage*. It was agreed that the husband-to-be should administer Aurore's property, which was worth about half a million francs, but without right to dispose of her capital or to sell her land. Moreover, he undertook to pay Aurore an annuity of three thousand francs.

The wedding took place on September 10, 1822. Aurore entered upon this union without love, without dreams, and without demands. She felt happy because she had left her mother's house and returned to Nohant—that was all. Nor did Casimir try to arouse any illusion in her. He did not think her pretty and told her so openly. He was attracted by her vivacity, humor, health, and tenderness toward children. He also appreciated the size of her fortune (but this he never mentioned), and immediately upon his arrival in Nohant he threw himself with gusto into the work of administration. This gave him opportunity to gratify two of his instincts—possessiveness and will to domineer.

He began with chopping down trees, redesigning the garden, and rearranging the furniture. Then he gave orders for putting to death the old dogs and the parrot that used to eat strawberries from the grandmother's hand. Aurore looked on with regret as century-old linden trees fell in the park and the thickets where she had once worshiped her childhood god, Corambé, began to disappear. But she bore these changes without protesting, bewildered by her husband's energy, although she felt that her beloved Nohant had ceased to be her personal possession. She attempted to check the exuberant administrator by keeping him in the library as much as possible, and even succeeded in making him read with her. She would read Pascal to her husband, but he usually fell asleep.

The young wife lost all interest in her once pleasant companion, who now seemed to her annoying and enervating, and gradually moved away from him, preoccupied with herself, especially after she became pregnant. On June 30, 1823, in Paris, she gave birth to a son and named him Maurice. She had yearned for a son so ardently that when she awoke after her delivery and saw the baby sleeping next to her, she closed her eyes again in order not to interrupt her wonderful dream.

The infant Maurice now occupied all her thoughts. Husband and wife were so bored by each other that more and more often they left their country home to visit friends. Among friends, especially with the Duplessis family, Aurore would recover her former vivacity and humor. This fact annoyed Casimir and aroused his hatred. On one occasion he tried to call his wife away from a group; when she continued to amuse herself with her friends, happy and laughing, he slapped her in the face. This incident had a shattering effect on Aurore. Her depression was such that her health was affected, and it was feared that she had consumption. She decided that "marriage is only self-sacrifice." She lost her interest in life; she wanted to forget everything. But fate decided otherwise.

On a sojourn away from home for treatment, she met a young lawyer of Bordeaux, Aurélien de Sèze, who dazzled her by his intelligence, erudition, and sensibility—traits that Casimir lacked. The emotion aroused in her was so strong that after short-lived scruples she threw herself into the new friend's arms. But their first kiss did not remain their secret. By accident Casimir saw them; and, surprisingly enough, Aurélien was much more upset by this than Baron Dudevant. The philosophically minded young lawyer did not wish to renounce his feeling, and he made a formal agreement with Aurore concerning their future relationship. This agreement was based on lofty principles, though it was somewhat complicated and rather unpractical. They decided that they might love each other, but since marriage was sanctioned by law, their love must respect this institution, be transformed into friendship, and serve to consolidate the marriage.

Aurore accepted this agreement as a matter of course. She wrote Casimir a letter of eighteen pages, asking him for permission to be a friend of Aurélien. She explained to her husband that he suffered from certain spiritual deficiencies, which her correspondence with Aurélien would compensate for, and in her eagerness she listed as many of them as she could discover. Her sincerity was no doubt unconsciously motivated by her disappointments and resentments.

Casimir agreed to everything, all the more willingly because he was increasingly estranged from his wife. At home he had fits of anger over every trifle; at a distance from home, in Bordeaux, he found a mistress, and often took trips to the city for "urgent reasons." In Nohant, he organized drunken parties with Hippolyte; to these orgies he invited guests from the village and the near-by town. As for Aurore, she renewed her old acquaintance with Stéphane de Grandsaigne, to whom she now began to pour out the thoughts and feelings for which she could not find room in her letters to the platonic Aurélien. Stéphane was an attractive young man, who did not try to make any formal agreement with Aurore, and who often during Casimir's drunken parties gave company to the neglected wife. After three years of correspondence, Aurélien came to visit Aurore in Nohant and found her pregnant and sewing on garments for the expected baby. Despite the principles of his agreement, he was surprised, but he did not discuss his feelings with anyone, neither with Aurore nor with Casimir or Stéphane. They always kept silent concerning the paternity of the child.

Solange was born on September 13, 1828. Although the confinement was premature, Aurore left her bed after two days. Her healthy and vigorous nature was in great need of activity. Life in Nohant had become empty; Casimir had eliminated her completely from the administration of the estate, and Maurice was in charge of a tutor. Friends often came to visit at Nohant; there were discussions of literature and politics, and the visitors paid tribute to Aurore's intellect. But all this was not enough for her. She revived somewhat when Jules Sandeau, a young student of law in Paris, began to take part in these gatherings. He had long golden curls, his face and his heart were fresh, and he had a passion for literature. Aurore nicknamed him "Colibri."

Because the letters between Aurore and Aurélien became less frequent, and because Aurore had to keep on writing even without having a correspondent, she shifted to poetry. Her verses on love, which she drenched with her tears, proved inferior. She began a novel, *Aimée,* but she was not sure of herself as a novelist either. She drew no pleasure from her portraits and water colors, her attempts at interior decoration disappointed her, and needle work bored her. There seemed to be no outlet for her vitality. She began to feel suffocated by her empty life and dreamed of going away.

An accident helped her make up her mind. Rummaging in her

husband's desk, she discovered an envelope addressed to her and bearing the inscription, "Open after my death." Of course she opened it at once. It contained the strangest will in the world. Her husband bequeathed to her his hatred and contempt; his letter listed all her faults, accused her of evil deeds, branded her as an evil character, and intimated that she was a pervert. Probably it did not occur to her that this was a belated answer to her own long letter to Casimir, in which she had listed his faults and praised Aurélien's qualities. She snatched up the envelope, rushed to her husband, and demanded her freedom and her annuity.

This was the crucial event of her life. She had no hesitation as to where she would go. She thought of the golden-haired Jules, who lived in Paris, and advised him that she was coming to the city at once. On a frosty night in January, 1831, she alighted from the stagecoach and found her friend awaiting her. Paris intoxicated her. She felt free; life had a new flavor. Her happiness was completed by her romance with Jules, who was seven years younger than she. It seemed that she could not ask for anything more. But she missed her children; she dreamed that Maurice was ill, and she awakened crying in the arms of her frightened lover.

She soon discovered that her annuity was inadequate. With inexhaustible energy she began to look for work, changing occupations in rapid succession. She tried translations from English, which proved unprofitable; she sewed dresses and made hats for sixteen and eighteen hours a day, at the most wretched wages; she returned to painting, but the portrait she exhibited in the concierge's window waited in vain for a buyer. With Sandeau she tried journalism and worked on the staff of *Figaro*, whose editor Delatouche was like herself a native of Berry. But her articles were too long, they lacked wit, and despite the fact that the editor favored her, they were usually thrown into the wastebasket. In an entire month she earned only fifteen francs.

Poverty stole into the happy lovers' mansard. For the sake of economy Aurore began to dress like a man and to wear iron-tipped shoes. She worked to the point of exhaustion, and kept herself going by drinking coffee, smoking cigarettes, and taking snuff. During that period of ferreting out earnings, she wrote, in collaboration with Sandeau, a short story entitled "Prima Donna," which was published in the *Revue de Paris*. The story was signed "Jules Sand." Cheered by this success, the pair of authors wrote a novel, *Rose et Blanche*. Contrary to their expectation, the work found a publisher and brought them four hundred francs. There was no doubt that literature was more profitable than millinery.

Aurore and Jules hurriedly planned a new novel and divided the work between them. Aurore wrote her part in Nohant, where she went to visit her children. Three months later she returned to Paris, bringing with her not a section but a whole novel, entitled *Indiana*. Jules's manuscript consisted only of some blank sheets. That night he comforted his disappointed collaborator by exclaiming, after reading *Indiana*, "You have produced a masterpiece!"

Aurore did not suspect that she was a writer; she had no literary ambitions, and was amazed when Jules declared that he would not sign the book. He thought that *Indiana* would achieve great fame, which should go exclusively to Aurore. She tried to change his attitude, all the more so because the publisher insisted on printing the novel under a name already known to the public. But Jules was adamant, even Delatouche failing to convince him. Finally the publisher proposed a compromise. He said to Aurore, "Today is St. George's Day. Add the name George to Sand, and we'll go to press."

Thus was born the famous nom de plume. *Indiana* was received with enthusiasm. Sainte-Beuve welcomed the new talent and predicted a great future for George Sand. Her fee amounted to eight hundred francs. François Buloz, editor of the *Revue des Deux Mondes*, engaged her as a regular contributor.

At first George Sand was frightened by her success. She had always written for money and for pleasure; now she was crushed by a sense of responsibility. "Never again shall I enjoy writing," she declared bitterly, but apparently she did not yet know herself. Three months later, she had a new novel ready—*Valentine*. Such was the beginning of that immense cycle of work which she carried on without interruption for the remaining forty-four years of her life.

She gradually realized how much the world fascinated her, what depths of passion she could discover in people. She was so absorbed and attracted by everything around her that she copied her works from life. Unable to create characters, she reproduced them, like a painter portraying a model. She wrote in an objective style, colorful, inventive, and natural, that never failed her but on the contrary took hold of her and often carried her as on a potent wave. Although she fell short of being a genius, her style had the breadth of greatness. Love was for her a continual surprise, and she devoted all her literary energies to elucidating its hypnotic power and defining its place in the social life. She fearlessly explored the private world of marriage and even its intimate retreats. This vexed some of her readers and gratified others, but aroused the curiosity of all. She was not afraid of shocking people; perhaps she even liked to do so. Her masculine daring enabled her to flout public opinion, and her inexhaustible vitality spurred her to fight.

At this time she made another discovery about herself, one that had little to do with literature. It was a dramatic discovery, and it probably came to her as a shattering revelation. The full happiness that she sought in love proved accessible to her only in a fragmentary way. Formerly she had suspected that her lack of satisfaction was due to the physical deficiency of her mates; her cohabitation with Jules convinced her that she herself was deficient. Though she had resilient health and vitality, she was physically slow in erotic response and unable to experience full gratification. This exhausted both her and her lovers. About Jules she wrote to one of his friends that he had fainted a hundred times in her embrace in the course of three months: "How anguishing it is, how guilty one feels to see in one's arms a dying man for whom one would gladly give one's life!" In her emotional confusion she attempted to protect him against her own love, but he did not consent to this, declaring that he wished just such a death. Her joy yielded to anxiety, her passion to self-sacrifice, her erotic impulse to motherly solicitude.

But whatever the results of her own detailed and somewhat rhetorical analyses of such situations may have been, she did not in the least renounce love. A militant libertine on paper, fighting for her right to love, she became a martyr to love in actual life.

Her adolescent-maternal romance with Jules Sandeau lasted two years; its epilogue has something of the triviality of her marriage with Dudevant. One day, returning unexpectedly from Nohant, she found her Colibri *en flagrant délit* with the laundress, and she broke with him on the spot. But she was unable to live alone, and her pursuit of inaccessible happiness led her along paths of the most painful experience. She had a seven-day romance with the handsome, cold, arrogant Prosper Mérimée; it ended brutally and suddenly. The poet walked out of her house leaving five francs on the mantelpiece, and told everyone in Paris that George was a dissolute woman who indulged in love from curiosity. She spoke of him differently: "If he had loved me, he could have dominated me. If I had been able to surrender to any man, I should have been saved. My independence consumes and kills me." She must have recalled him once more when she learned that he had become the lover of Marie Dorval, a famous actress whose friendship with Aurore was the subject of invidious conversations in the salons.

For some time, upset by her experiences, George Sand avoided men; she was content with her work and with the platonic love of Sainte-Beuve, to whom she opened her heart in her letters. When the great critic wanted to introduce de Musset to her, she said, "No. He is too much of a dandy. I prefer Dumas."

At a dinner arranged by Buloz for the contributors of his *Revue des Deux Mondes,* George Sand, the only woman guest, had Alfred de Musset at her left. This was on June 20, 1833. A short time afterward he sent her a poem and a letter: "I must tell you something crazy and ridiculous. I love you." And again: "George, I love you like a child." She asked him to come to her at midnight; he left her in the morning. In his notebook he merely recorded the date—July 29, 1833.

"Mademoiselle Byron," as he was called, or "Spring in Person," as Sainte-Beuve aphorized him, was tall, pale, and sickly. He had chiseled features and the piercing gaze of a man whose eyes have no brows or lashes. A viscount without fortune, a royalist without interest in politics, a frequenter of salons and of bordellos, a sensitive poet and a common drunkard, a dreamer in love with love, and a skeptic scoffing at dreams, a combination of subtlety and cynicism, wit and bitterness, grace and grimace—this strange human paradox kindled the strongest feeling in George Sand's life. "I am happy," she wrote to Sainte-Beuve. "Thank God for me." The author of *Indiana* and *Valentine* now added *Lélia* to the roster of names that became famous as the titles of her books. Her renown grew; her heart was filled with joy. De Musset moved to her apartment on the Quai Malaquais; he wrote poems and drew portraits of her that Delacroix valued above his poetry.

In September the two left for Fontainebleau, intending to live only on nature and love, but just when Aurore thought that she was growing more attached to him with each day, their sufferings began. De Musset, who was only twenty, could not forget the past of his twenty-six-year-old mistress. He was obsessively jealous, questioning her about his predecessors, wanting to know every detail, and tormenting her and himself. In vain did George Sand invoke her right to happiness and freedom; the importunate lover persisted until, amid the tears and the despair of both, he had learned about everything.

George Sand's sincerity and loyalty failed to dispel the nightmares thus precipitated. Their romance was shaken. They felt Paris to be banal and decided to run away to Italy. George Sand took an advance of four thousand francs from Buloz for a new novel; de Musset also undertook some writing commissions. In December, 1833, they left for Florence via Genoa, Leghorn, and Pisa. They were thrilled by the miracle of Italy, but the blue sky did not brighten their love. Aurore worked every day, and de

Musset found her soberness and self-control intolerable. What kind of romantic was she if she could think of Buloz when looking at Cellini's dreams in gold and silver! Then there was her correspondence with Nohant and her longing for Maurice. De Musset wandered in the sinister alleys of Florence. In Venice, after a few happy days, he returned to his old addictions. Aurore fell ill with dysentery; de Musset was impatient, spent much time in brothels, drank, and played cards and lost. When he returned, Aurore raised her sad face to him from her manuscripts, reminded him of his obligations, and reprimanded him like a mother. He probably found her boring, and one day he burst out, "George, all this was a mistake. Forgive me. I don't love you."

This dramatic confession was not the end of their martyrdom. De Musset fell ill; he had an attack of delirium tremens and came close to death. During a fit he almost choked Aurore. For three weeks she nursed the unconscious poet, jumping up each time he stirred, and when he fell asleep, she took out her manuscripts and wrote. Her only helper was Dr. Pagello, calm and blond, and quite unlike an Italian. During the crisis of de Musset's illness he did not leave their hotel, staying night and day with George Sand.

Upon his recovery de Musset fell into a paroxysm of jealousy over the Doctor, and the spring that followed was nothing but one long torment. The lovers could no longer stay under one roof; George Sand, having spent ten thousand francs to pay the poet's gambling debts, sent him to Paris. She remained in Venice with Pagello, went on excursions with him, and wrote a novel, *Jacques*, for Buloz; but her unconquered love for de Musset pursued her everywhere. Unable to part from Pagello, who revealed to her the secret of gratification in love, she came with him to Paris, where the honest and frightened Italian, expecting to fight a duel with de Musset, practiced pistol shooting, until his comedy role was concluded by a quiet disappearance from George Sand's life.

Her romance with de Musset lasted two years more. They returned to each other and separated again; de Musset was torn by the contradictions of his nature, and Aurore thought of suicide. She was saved by Nohant, her old world, and her new cares. Casimir was an incapable administrator; he had fallen into debt and the estate was threatened with ruin. But because of this situation George Sand was forced to act, and this helped to lift her out of her vicious circle. She decided to recover her house and her children, and to divorce her husband. The affair dragged on for a long time but ended propitiously for her. Her lawyer was Michel de Bourges, a passionate republican and leftist leader. George Sand was surrounded by new people and new ideas; she was fascinated by the imperious Michel, and because she understood the world only through love, she entered a new sphere through his embraces.

Public affairs and politics did not interest her. Even after becoming intimate with de Bourges, she wrote: "My devotion to Michel has not yet made me read the newspapers, but I am seeing him every day, which amounts to the same thing." Nevertheless, the new environment freed her from her excessive egocentricity and directed her attention outward. She had, up to that point, waged her struggle for woman's happiness and freedom in love only on the basis of her own experiences, and had not identified herself with any ideological movement. De Bourges revealed to her the subcutaneous nerves of the epoch, and showed her how the pulse of time was beating. The daughter of the Parisian proletarian now joined the cause of the people, the republic, and radicalism.

Her new lover could have become her established, perhaps permanent mate, could have won mastery over her self-willed character; she had dreamed of such a man ever since her liaison with Prosper Mérimée. But Michel had no respect for art, and he had a low opinion of literature. He thought a writer's worth was measurable by his contribution to the struggle for the people's future, and that he should work for mankind as an artisan of the pen. This ran counter to her artistic nature, which had been refined by de Musset. Franz Liszt—whom she had met earlier—and Madame d'Agoult, inflamed by the ideas of Lamennais, believed in man's regeneration through art, and as George Sand moved away from

Michel, she became increasingly attached to these companions, who were enthusiasts, philosophers, and gypsies all at the same time. After a trip to Switzerland and a stay with Liszt and Madame d'Agoult, she considered herself one of their circle, and for some time they became her closest and most trusted friends.

Having recovered Nohant, she dreamed of establishing there a summer colony for her friends, a house of rest and work, a kind of village salon with windows giving on the fragrant garden. She went about furnishing the rooms, and when Liszt announced that he was coming and bringing Chopin with him, she bought an expensive piano at Pleyel's. She worked with incredible discipline, writing at night, usually from nine in the evening to five or six o'clock in the morning. Her average output was twelve manuscript sheets exclusive of her correspondence.

The children were in charge of a new tutor, Félicien Malefille. This tall young man, who had a big black beard and a walleye, had tasks beyond those of teaching Maurice and Solange. In his extra-tutorial time he devoted his heart and his thoughts to the lady of the house. He also tried his prowess in literature, and George Sand even lent her name for the cover of his book, *Le dernier sauvage*, to insure its success. Their romance flowed calmly and happily. Malefille was modest and faithful. When the beautiful Madame d'Agoult came with Liszt to Nohant, and, annoyed at the virtuoso's friendship with George Sand, began to intrigue in order to estrange Malefille from his mistress, the young man proved impervious to intrigue. Only the relationship between the two ladies was undermined; the lover's devotion remained intact.

George Sand did not seek out temptations, although she often took trips to Paris. But the spring and the hot summer of 1838 disturbed her serenity. Chopin, a sad, reserved man, who had not said a word about love, took hold of her thoughts. One might have imagined that he was absent from the world, that he was filled with indifference and contempt; but when he opened the piano, it seemed that he raised the lid under which his true life was asleep. He ran over the keys with his fingers not only in order to play but also to live, and when he closed the piano it was as though he had removed himself from the world again. His art listened only to his own conscience, and he lived only to be loyal to his art. George Sand had never before met with such artistic asceticism, and she was amazed at the fact that this Parisian dandy was capable of it. Her vivid, amorous imagination did the rest.

At first she did not know what to do with her feeling; she concealed it, alluding to it in misty terms only in writing to her friend Madame Marliani: "In times of love the weather is variable. For a week's time one says yes and no, if and but. In the morning one says, This is unbearable; in the evening one says, This is real happiness."

In the summer she came to Paris for a longer period than usual, and spent the evenings in the deserted city with Madame Marliani and Chopin.

She was made curious by Chopin's mysterious feeling for his childhood friend. This expert in love could not be mistaken. She divined his distress. She thought a great deal of him and herself, before she made up her mind to say to herself, "I am used to loving only men who love me, and I am truly dismayed by the impression he has made on me."

She was afraid of this love; she feared disappointment. She was ready to repress and destroy her feeling. She was strong and farsighted enough to do so. Finally, unable to come to a decision, she addressed herself to Grzymala, her trusted friend, and asked him for advice.

A curiosity of epistolography, written with a sincerity that is almost repellent and an inconceivable coldness, her letter to Grzymala was in fact a dissection of everything that she felt might happen or not happen between her and Chopin. This dissertation of five thousand words was centered around one question: Was she to repress her love for Chopin in consideration of his feeling for his childhood friend, or could she love him and trust in her passion?

The Life and Death of Chopin

Grzymala's answer has not come down to us, but it is easy to guess it. Chopin no longer was preoccupied with Wodzinska. George Sand must have learned this fact with joy. What Liszt had not achieved was now brought about by Grzymala. Aurore and Frederic had good reasons this summer of 1838 for not leaving Paris.

Majorca

(al' ō)

I AM in Palma, among palms, cedars, cactuses, olives, oranges, lemons, aloes, figs, pomegranates, etc.—everything that the *Jardin des Plantes* has in its hothouses. The sky is like turquoise, the sea like lapis lazuli, the mountains emerald, the air is heavenly. Sun all day, everyone wears summer clothes, it is hot; at night guitars and singing for hours on end. Enormous balconies with grapevines overhead, Moorish walls. Everything turns its face toward Africa, as the whole town does. In a word, a marvelous life. Love me!"

This was what Chopin wrote to Fontana on November 15, 1838. He had left Paris without telling anyone where he was going, with whom, or for how long. Only his closest friends—Matuszynski, Grzymala, Fontana, and Pleyel—had been initiated in regard to details. Because Matuszynski was not too energetic, and Grzymala was ill, Chopin had entrusted all his commissions to Fontana —the bald, prematurely faded lyceum schoolmate whom he had for a long time supported, and the only pianist who was allowed a voice in all his affairs and interests and even in his compositions.

"I am close to what is most beautiful. I am better," he wrote, intoxicated with love and with his surroundings. He lived in a villa from which he had a view over the enchanting blue and green landscape. Before him spread a garden full of unfading flowers and a huge valley reaching down to the sea, and in the distance there gleamed the golden walls of Palma and its enormous cathedral. It was a place of serene beauty. The pines and oaks on the hills rustled gently; the wind drove the clouds slowly before it.

Chopin and George Sand had decided to go to Majorca in the summer. Maurice, now sixteen, was suffering from rheumatism. His mother expressed a wish to take her son to the South for the winter, and Chopin remarked that if he were in Maurice's place, he would recover at once. And Dr. Gaubert, Chopin's physician, had found that his patient was not suffering from tuberculosis, but had frankly told George Sand that if she made it possible for Chopin to spend some time in a mild climate, he would owe her his life.

At first Aurore considered Italy; then her friends advised Majorca. The distant island seemed to the lovers an ideal refuge, where they might conceal from the world what George Sand wanted to keep exclusively for herself, and what Chopin wanted to keep a secret at all costs.

George Sand left Paris on October 15, 1838, taking with her Maurice, Solange, her servant Amélie, and heavy cases of books. Chopin obtained an advance of five hundred francs for his preludes, which he had sold to Pleyel for two thousand francs, promising to send him the manuscript in a short time. He borrowed an additional one thousand francs from his friend Léo, and a few days after Aurore's departure quietly left town. Pleyel sent a piano to follow him. Traveling for four days without interruption, he arrived at the Spanish border and met George Sand at Perpignan. She greeted him happily and thought that he looked "fresh as a rose and rosy as a carrot."

From Port-Vendres, a French port near the Spanish frontier, they sailed for Barcelona. Here they spent a few days in excursions and in visiting the city (they naturally did not miss the occasion to attend an Italian opera). On the night of November 7th, they boarded the steamer "El Mallorquín." On the ship's first-class passenger list they were identified as follows: "Mme Dudevant, married; Maurice, her son, minor; Solange, her daughter, minor; M. Frederic Chopin, artist." Amélie was a second-class passenger.

Majorca

The sea was phosphorescent in the darkness, the steersman sang monotonous songs, there was a gentle, warm breeze. They were glad that they had run away from Paris. They no longer feared Malefille, who, upon hearing from Aurore that she was leaving him, lay in wait for her with a dagger near Chopin's apartment, and threatened him with a duel. The trip was untroubled, and only Solange complained. They saw the shores of Majorca against the rising sun. They looked on the scene happily, and when they disembarked it seemed to them like a paradise. In Palma they found all the beauties and enchantments of the world except comforts. There were no hotels in the town, and they stopped at the only accessible inn, which smelled of garlic and teemed with insects, and where a scorpion in the soup would not disturb the appetite of a native.

Such a welcome might have discouraged others, but not George Sand. With the help of the French consul, she found the villa Son-Vent, near the town, rented it from the rather unpleasant owner, and moved in with her brood. They were amused by the modesty of this refuge—the unpolished tables, the straw chairs, the cots instead of beds, the bare walls. The house lacked even windows and doors, which were considered the personal appurtenances of tenants, and George Sand had to obtain these necessities by her own devices. Everything here was different from what they had known in France—the people, the customs, the plants. The children were happy even with the stones on the roads, and brought back from their walks fragments of marble and quartz, which they packed in their traveling bags.

Most of all they were enchanted by their discovery, during an excursion, of the former Carthusian monastery of Valdemosa. This strange hermitage, situated high in the mountains, so that it appeared suspended between heaven and earth, seemed to them so romantic that George Sand immediately leased three cells (communicating and forming one apartment) for the extraordinary price of thirty-five francs a year.

In Palma Chopin forgot big-city fashions and the cabriolet; he now went on foot, and he tore his elegant Parisian shoes to pieces on the stony paths. All he lacked for his happiness was the Pleyel piano, which had not yet arrived, and when they sat admiring the magnificent view that opened before them from the villa, he dreamed of the delights of playing here at night.

On the day after he wrote his cheerful letter to Fontana, Frederic fell ill. One imprudent excursion, during which he got a chill, weakened him so severely that he had to stay in bed. To make things worse, the weather shifted to rain, and the rest was done by Son-Vent, which turned out to be a real house of winds. The villa was cold; dampness penetrated the walls; the plaster was saturated with moisture like a sponge. The only stove, installed by the tenants, smoked unbearably. The rains were interminable. The patient coughed more and more, and began to spit blood.

George Sand was full of anxiety. The three best physicians in the town, summoned in turn, failed to relieve Chopin's sufferings. They recommended bloodletting, but the patient and his guardian opposed this treatment. George Sand began to treat him herself, trusting her instinct more than she did the Majorca physicians. "I nurse him like a child," she wrote to Madame Marliani. "He is an angel of sweetness and kindness."

The crisis was over, and on December 3rd, Frederic wrote about his illness to Fontana in the past tense, and in a carefree tone:

These two weeks past I was sick as a dog: I got a chill, despite the temperature of 70, amidst roses, oranges, palms, and fig trees. Of the three most famous doctors on the island, one sniffed at what I spewed up, the other tapped at the place from where I spewed it, the third poked and listened while I spewed. The first said that I was dead, the second that I was dying, and the third that I would die.

Chopin had begun to regain strength when the news of his illness spread in the neighborhood, causing a panic among the natives. They regarded all pulmonary diseases as incurable and infectious, something like cholera. As a result, the newcomers were confronted with a further disaster. Their landlord demanded (in writing, for he feared to come near his tenants) that they should leave his house at once. He insisted that their furniture must be burned and the house disinfected, at their own expense.

They were forced to remove to Valdemosa. The French consul harbored them for four days, which they spent warming themselves at the fireplace.

Chopin was glad of the prospect of moving to Valdemosa, and on December 14th wrote to Fontana: "Tomorrow I go to that wonderful monastery of Valdemosa, to compose in the cell of some old monk who perhaps had more fire in his soul than I have. . . . I think I'll soon send you my preludes and the ballade."

They set out caravan-like in two wheeled carts, Chopin covered with plasters, the children amused by the new adventure, Amélie frightened at the fancy of her masters, and George Sand supervising everything. Valdemosa was only three miles from Palma, but the trip took three hours. The road led continually uphill, at first through a steep defile, then up a slope through thickets, a veritable jungle. It seemed as though these forsaken stretches had never been trodden by man, as though the rocks had fallen from heaven; the oaks and pines might have been molding for centuries, and the luxuriant honeysuckle and mint might have been sown by God himself. It was a difficult trip, and not altogether safe. Even the native horses and mules did not feel at ease here, seeking what was called a path over precipices and through the bush—a path that after each rain was buried under gravel and sand.

Finally they broke through this barrier created by an unrestrained nature, and reached the peak of Valdemosa. The wildest fantasy could not have chosen a spot more entrancing to human eyes and hearts. The high plateau ended abruptly on two sides and opened an immense view on the colorful and fertile valleys, edged by two silvery strips of sea; on two other sides, it was banked by even higher wooded vistas. The whole world here seemed to be open through and through, and at the same time under the protection of mountain arms. Below, in the valleys filled with sun, the wind swayed the oaks, poplars, and cypresses as in a cradle; above, eagles and vultures circled over the great crests of the woods. "A smile and melancholia," commented George Sand.

In this strange wilderness, the enormous edifice, which also looked as though dropped there from heaven, seemed strangest of all. The monastery was surrounded by a wall and buttressed on a terrace above the precipice. When they passed through its gate, they entered a world of solitude and oblivion. The various buildings, the towers and colonnades, stood in undisturbed silence, which was interrupted only by the loud echo of the new inmates' steps. As during their previous occasional visits, they were struck by the immense area of this uninhabited place—George Sand said that it could house a whole army corps. There were actually three monasteries, connected by courtyards, dead and silent. The oldest of them, with its Gothic windows, dated from the fifteenth century. In the adjoining burial plot, in graves without tablets or inscriptions, rested the remains of hermits forgotten both in life and in death. The two other structures contained the ancient cells of the abbot, as well as the church and twelve chapels. A government decree of 1836 had expelled the Carthusians from this monastery, and Valdemosa had been government property for two years. The cells were leased to occasional tourists. Only three persons inhabited the place—the former monastery pharmacist, who by some miracle had escaped eviction, the porter, and Maria Antonia, the cook who prepared meals for the visitors.

Maria led the newcomers to their apartment. In a low-vaulted and narrow corridor, twelve identical doors gave access through mysterious three-foot-thick walls. Each apartment consisted of three rooms; in one of these suites, situated next to Maria Antonia's, the new tenants unpacked their baggage.

"My cell has the shape of a tall coffin." Thus Chopin described his room in a letter to Fontana. "The enormous vaulting is covered with dust; the window is small. Outside the window there are orange trees, palms, cypresses. Opposite the window there is my bed on thongs, under a Moorish filigree rosette. Next to the bed there is an old *nitouchable* square writing desk that I can scarcely use; on it a leaden candlestick (this is a great *luxe* here) with a candle. Bach, my scribblings, and old papers (not mine)—silence. One can yell. . . . Still silence."

In this environment they spent almost two months. Here their love found a refuge. Indeed, nothing could disturb their happiness and seclusion. The children ran about the monastery buildings and went on excursions into the mountains. The only visitors they had were eagles, high up in the air, under the clouds. Heaven and earth had conspired to surround and saturate them with poetry.

This sequestered life brought the lovers supremely close to each other. While still in Palma, George Sand had written to Madame Marliani: "We are coming closer to each other with ever greater cordiality and happiness. What can one complain about if one's heart is alive?"

Frederic probably had similar feelings, and, analyzing his love, he must have marveled how suddenly and completely it had taken hold of him. The lovers were unlike in every possible way—in age, nationality, character, inclinations. George Sand was six years older than Chopin. She identified herself with her time and her country, while he felt deeply for Poland and its misfortunes. The French language, which was the medium of her art, was always alien to him; he spoke it with an accent and wrote it incorrectly. George Sand was distinguished for her frankness; Chopin was rather secretive. She lacked that instinctive discretion which was his peculiar characteristic. She said of herself that she had cheap, plebeian tastes and could do without luxuries, while he was refined and liked luxury. They moved in different circles: in the aristocratic salons she was hated and he was worshiped. He did not tolerate ugliness or eccentricity in any shape or form, beginning with clothes and ending with personalities; she was indifferent to such matters. Even their views on art were different: she employed art for temporal purposes; he exalted art above everything else, as an end in itself. Finally, their methods of work were radically opposed. Frederic sometimes spent years on a composition in order to perfect it, and it was inconceivable to him that one could finish a manuscript at night and send it to the publisher in the morning. Incidentally, he was prejudiced against woman writers and had only recently referred to them contemptuously as *bas bleu.*

And now the tiny person who embodied all these rejected qualities filled his darkness with light and his disillusioned heart with an immense yearning. Whenever Aurore took her children for a long walk, he waited for her return with nervous impatience. At night when she went out, with a candle in her hand, to look at the monastery in the moonlight, he was jealous of the moon and the walls. Only her intelligent black eyes could appease him, and only her low unhurried voice whispered to him confessions that he desired to hear.

Probably their very unlikeness accounted for his love. Just as his friendship with Tytus had once given him fulfillment, this love now complemented his being with everything he lacked. George Sand with her resoluteness and energy radiated self-assurance and strength. No effort was excessive for her, no obstacle insurmountable. She could cope with any situation; she knew no fear before the world, from which he sought refuge in seclusion, and against which he protected himself by contempt.

In addition to these qualities that Chopin lacked, George possessed a strong family sense. With Frederic, the desire for a home life had developed into a kind of *idée fixe*; for her, these things were taken for granted. Her maternal instinct was not spent entirely on Maurice, and she was not exaggerating when she said that she nursed Frederic as though he were her second son. He must have been deeply moved at the realization that she protected him so completely, that she wished to make him feel secure, safe against all evil. Not to be alone, to have a place on earth that was his own, something like his place in the house in the Krakowskie Przedmiescie in Warsaw, something like his childhood with his parents and sisters—the best world he had ever known, and the only one in which he had been happy—became his deepest, his irrepressible longing. If only he could regain that old world or create something just as perfect in its likeness! He would transpose all his dreams there; he would entirely give himself to music. He did not want to escape from life; he wanted only to economize energy as much as possible. He knew only too well how much toil his art required, how absorbing it was and how inseparable from absolute self-sacrifice. Weak and ailing, he wanted nothing but this heroic work, which was both an effort and a joy.

He seemed to come closer to this inaccessible world thanks to George Sand. He looked upon her with admiration. After six hours of lessons with her children each day, she found time for housekeeping, for trips to Palma, and at night for writing. Following her example, he set to work at polishing his preludes.

From December 20th on the Pleyel piano had been in Palma, held up by the customs officials, who demanded five hundred francs before releasing the instrument. "Nature here is beneficent," Chopin wrote to Fontana, "but the people are thieves, for they never see foreigners, so they do not know how much to ask for anything. Oranges come gratis, but a trouser button costs a fabulous sum. Yet all that is but a grain of sand—with this sky, the poetry that breathes in everything here, the color of this marvelous place, which human eyes have not yet rubbed off."

But nature was not as beneficent as Frederic thought. Winter came even to Majorca; pouring rains alternated with snowfalls, burying the flowering bushes; violent winds were unleashed and blew bitter chill through the monastery galleries. The noise of rivulets swollen to torrents and the distant echo of the surging seas were added to this wild orchestra. Sometimes the fog was so dense that even the sea birds lost their way in it, and knocked their heads wildly against the low vaults of the colonnades.

Strange, mysterious things began to happen in the monastery, deepening the mood it created. At night there appeared a half-crazed old man, a former monastery servant, who made a tour of the empty corridors, knocking at the doors with a shepherd's crook, and calling out the names of the long-gone monks as if to summon them to their rites. He knocked also at the door of the rooms occupied by Chopin and George Sand, and called, "Nicolas! Nicolas!"

Frederic must have shuddered on hearing his father's name called out in the darkness and re-echoing in the colonnades. It proved impossible to stop the old man's visits; he was often drunk, and the porter tried in vain to keep him away from the gate.

The Life and Death of Chopin

The intruder entered the monastery as his own demesne and persisted in his eerie tours. After each one he would lie down in a corridor and fall asleep holding a knife in one hand and a <u>rosary</u> in the other. Everyone was afraid of him, and George Sand forbade her children to leave the apartment after sunset.

One night they were aroused by a strange noise; it made them think, as George Sand said, that someone was pouring out thousands of bags of nuts on the floor. They ran out into the corridor, but no one was there. The courtyard and the colonnades were deserted; the mysterious noise was coming nearer and growing more distinct. After a while a most extraordinary procession passed through the gate; amidst the looming monasteries, it seemed to them an invasion from another world. A cortege of ghosts was advancing; the figures wore bird beaks and horse tails, and were surrounded by torches. In the center strode a black-robed monster with horns on his head, and with a terrifying face that had the color of blood. They stared at this apparition in amazement, and George Sand later admitted that it was only after some minutes that she realized what she was seeing. It was a carnival masquerade organized by the peasants of the neighborhood; marching to the sound of castanets, they were proceeding to a village ball in the apartment of Maria Antonia.

Such incidents had an enervating effect on Chopin. He suffered from insomnia. Once again he had chest pains, and the idea of being ill in this remote corner of the world filled him with tormenting fear. He went to bed, then arose again; he had good and bad days, forced himself to work, and sought help from his understanding mistress in his struggle to control his depression.

Unfortunately, all this was too much for him. The monastery still fascinated him, but this was now the fascination of horror. He wished he could find refuge from the sight of the low, sodden clouds and the oppressive, monotonous murmur of the torrents and the sea. Before his windows, starved eagles and vultures swooped down on sparrows, tearing their wretched prey to pieces with blood-curdling screams. The cemetery of the monks loomed in the fog like a reminder of death, and the continuous howl of the wind was like the wail of lost souls in torment.

Frederic could not face these daily incidents. Any trifle was sufficient to disrupt his composure. He spent the greater part of the day in the apartment; he did not join the others in their walks, but remained always within the walls of the monastery buildings. He waited impatiently for the evening, when the whole family gathered around the fire, and when he could listen to the laughter of the children and the calm voice of George Sand.

With the advent of the season of rains and storms, the so-called roads vanished from the surface of Valdemosa. Communication with the continent by way of Palma was cut off. The inhabitants of the monastery found themselves isolated from the world, and their previous discomforts now were complicated by unexpected difficulties connected with provisioning.

Majorca was famous for its pigs and for its two hundred native dishes made of pork, which Chopin could not stand. Butter was unobtainable, the olive oil was stale, bread when it reached the monastery was soggy with moisture, and everyone was sick from eating unrefined sugar. George Sand had to make her purchases through the cook employed by the French consul—the only person in Majorca whose feelings toward the foreigners were friendly. The local population was hostile toward them, held them to be damned because they did not attend church, and regarded them as eccentrics who were not in full possession of their faculties. They were asked to pay incredible sums for anything they bought; a peasant near Valdemosa demanded the equivalent of three French centimes apiece for wild violets needed for infusions. Maria Antonia, who merrily sang boleros, stole part of their food reserves and the goat's milk that George Sand had bought in the delusive hope that with its help she might revive Frederic and the children. Upset and worried over her lover's health, she often wished that she could give him a bowl of bouillon and a cup of claret.

Frederic's condition grew worse. He had fever and did not leave his room. He no longer had the strength to control himself, to chase away his nightmares and thoughts about death. Maria Antonia openly accused him of spreading an infectious disease, and told him that after his death he would not be buried in consecrated ground and would go to hell. These walls that he could not escape, this solitude that had become unbearable, seemed to enclose him like a trap. No one had ever visited them except for a friend of Chopin's named Dembowski. He arrived unexpectedly in Valdemosa, was horrified by the conditions in which his hosts were living, and hastened back to Palma.

In January, 1839, the arrival of the Pleyel piano, finally wrested from the hands of the customs officers, brought Frederic real relief. The evenings now gained a new meaning, and the preludes passed their final test. But even the excellent instrument and the possibility of lighter work no longer could reconcile him to the monastery. Disappointed and depressed, he hoped for better weather and looked forward to departure as his salvation.

Only the children continued to make excursions to the mountains. The health of Maurice especially benefited from these winter expeditions. George Sand rejoiced over the transformation of the sickly boy into a tall young man. She took walks with him; he accompanied her to Palma, and she found in him a companion and helper. Maurice was her smiling day, Frederic her anguished night.

One day when she was in Palma with her son, a sudden downpour cut them off from return. They were able to set out for Valdemosa only after sunset. Their coachman deserted them on the road, refusing to drive in the darkness, and they continued on foot. In the flooded defile, the sharp stones tortured their feet, and their clothes were torn in the wooded thickets. They made their way uphill along steep slopes, under pouring rain, for six hours. They reached the monastery late at night, drenched to the bone, shoeless, exhausted by their trip. As they stood in the doorway, Chopin gazed at them from his piano with unseeing eyes. "Ah," he said, jumping up from his chair, "I knew that you were no longer alive."

He was as though in a trance and only after some time recovered his balance. He had awaited their return with such tenseness that he had fallen into a kind of hypnosis. He told them that thinking of the dangers threatening them, he could no longer distinguish reality from the nightmares that beset him. He had sat at the piano and played, but it seemed to him that he had drowned in a lake and that icy drops of water were falling on his chest in a regular rhythm.

"That was the rain drumming on the roof," George Sand said.

"I did not hear it," he answered. He returned to his piano and began to play.

Years later, recalling this incident, George Sand aptly wrote about her friend: "His soul was full of the mysterious harmonies of nature, which he translated into sublime equivalents in his musical thought, not into servile duplication of external sounds." It seems vain to speculate as to what particular prelude Chopin played for George Sand that night. Biographers interested in that question have variously identified it as the sixth prelude, in B minor, the eighth, in F-sharp minor, the fifteenth, in D-flat major, the seventeenth, in A-flat major, or the nineteenth, in E-flat minor. Actually it seems that only the sixth or the famous fifteenth should be considered as offering a likelihood. The fifteenth prelude was popularly christened the "Raindrop" Prelude, in the face of the composer's explicit protests. It is not certain, however, whether it came into being on that stormy day on which his mind was obsessed by fantasies of his loved one's dying. Probably Chopin did not compose a single new prelude on Majorca, although according to his custom he reworked and perfected all of them during his sojourn there. The only new composition written on Majorca was the Mazurka in E minor, which he called the "Palman" Mazurka.

When he had finished the polishing of the manuscript of the preludes, he immediately wrote to Fontana: "I am sending you the preludes. You and Wolff copy it. I think there are no errors."

The great lyrical monument of many years of his life stood ready. Here, in this remote corner of the world, lost amid mountains and fogs, while he struggled against his illness and his visions of death, he had completed his long and difficult work. The preludes are considered the most poetic work of the greatest poet among composers. Like a collection of poems, the series presents an interplay of darkness and light, of miniatures and broad expanses, of heroic rhapsody and tragic frustration. Mingled with reminiscences of the études and nocturnes, these twenty-four compositions contain anticipations of Wagner. This immense treasure, embellished with an unsurpassed delicacy of detail, closes with the powerful final Prelude in D minor, in which Chopin once again reminded the world of embattled Warsaw.

After the preludes he finished the Ballade in F major and two polonaises (A major, C minor), which he sent to Fontana for Pleyel, asking five hundred francs for each of these three compositions.

During the first days of February, when spring was coming to the mountains, Chopin despite his exhaustion found strength to work on his third Scherzo, in C-sharp minor, the great Sonata in B-flat minor, and the Two Nocturnes (G minor, G major)—all of which he had brought with him from Paris.

More than ever before he now longed for that city, for its people, its light and warmth. It seemed that only in Paris could he get what he had come to seek on Majorca. He implored George Sand to consent to flee from these howling winds, the nightly apparitions, the evil predictions of Maria Antonia. Finally they received news from Palma that "El Mallorquín" had resumed its weekly trips to Barcelona. 'Amélie was the first to speed her departure, asking George Sand to release her from service. George Sand, notwithstanding everything that had happened, took leave of Valdemosa with regret, and later declared (probably with a good deal of exaggeration) that she could have remained there for years.

They decided to leave on February 12th. They sold their piano to a local banker; this was a great relief in the midst of their evacuation difficulties. George Sand made vain efforts in Palma to obtain a comfortable vehicle for Chopin. The town, in which she had never visited anyone—only once did she appear in the theater—turned a deaf ear to her requests. On the final day an ordinary two-wheel peasant cart drove up before the monastery. Thus they began their return journey, which was another nightmare. The cart jolted from cobble to cobble, bumping on its axle, and the travelers were thoroughly shaken. This ordeal lasted for three hours. Upon arriving in Palma, Chopin suffered a hemorrhage.

They found themselves in a hopeless situation. It seemed impossible to continue the trip; yet what could they expect from the Palma physicians? Frederic refused to envisage an interruption of the journey and another week of waiting for the boat. He spent a tormenting night in Palma; on the following day the party drove to the port and Chopin was carried aboard ship. At the last moment he received three letters from home.

"El Mallorquín" was now quite a different ship. On this sailing it carried a cargo of swine penned on deck, and these were continuously lashed with whips to keep them from falling asleep. An unbearable stench filled the cabin, and Chopin had to listen to the squealing of the beaten beasts. The sick man was given the worst mattress that could be found aboard, which was to be burned after he had used it (and after he had been made to pay for it). He did not sleep a wink throughout the night, and the bleeding could not be stopped. He reached Barcelona half dead.

George Sand was on the verge of despair. Then she noticed the French warship "Méléagre" lying in the harbor, and wrote to its captain asking him for help. The famous writer's letter had the desired effect, and a short time later the travelers were aboard the "Méléagre," feeling like people rescued from certain death. The children shouted, *"Vive la France!"* The ship's physicians immediately attended to Chopin and succeeded in stopping the bleeding after twenty-four hours.

Moved to a hotel room, Frederic slowly recovered. George Sand nursed him day and night. After a week's rest he was strong enough to board the steamer "Phénicien," which took them to Marseille. The captain gave the invalid his own cabin.

Thus ended one of the best-known and saddest of lovers' journeys. The pair had sought what they hoped would be best for them; what they had found was the worst. They had wanted to be only with each other, but solitude had proved hard to bear.

The Life and Death of Chopin

They had chosen an enchanting country, but it became for them a hostile ambush. They had longed for the sun, but nature had overwhelmed them with its inimical aspect. They had set out to improve their health, and they returned in the shadow of death. Their love had withstood this severe test and continued alive in their hearts, but it had undergone changes that were to cause complications later.

CHAPTER

28

Marseille

CONSIDERABLY weakened upon his departure from Majorca and saved by dint of heroic effort in Barcelona, Chopin recovered quickly during his sojourn in Marseille. He arrived there with George Sand on February 25, 1839. "One more month, and both Chopin and I should have died, he of melancholy and disgust, and I of anger and indignation," she wrote to Madame Marliani the next day.

Suddenly everything took on a changed aspect. Dr. Cauvières, an old friend of George Sand and an admirer of her writings, took Chopin under his care and assured her that he was threatened with nothing serious. The physician merely advised against a return to Paris, recommending that the convalescent should stay some time in the country, and George Sand planned to move him to Nohant. Frederic himself, a few days later, wrote to Fontana: "I cough little, only in the morning, and as yet I'm not considered a consumptive. I drink neither coffee nor wine, but only milk. I keep warm and I look like a girl."

Soon he was engaged in an unusually intensive correspondence; this was the surest sign that he had returned to health. He charged Fontana with a large number of errands of all kinds, concerning his compositions, his debts, his tailor, and his glove maker. He asked his friend to dispose of his apartment at the earliest opportunity and to store his furniture with friends. In this connection he wrote: "I once told you that in the first drawer of my desk on the side nearest the door there is a sheet of paper that you or Grzymala or Jas may unseal. Now I am asking you to remove and destroy it without reading it. Do this, I conjure you in the name of our friendship." He was probably referring to the will he had written in Paris several years before, during an illness. "This sheet of paper is no longer of any use," he added.

He expatiated on his finances and his troubles with publishers at great length. He disliked being financially dependent on George Sand; moreover, publishers were his pet aversion. He regarded them as sharks, cheats, liars. In Majorca he had referred to them as scoundrels and dogs, but there, feeling far removed from them, he wrote: "All these lice bite me less now." In Marseille he used Fontana as an agent in bargaining with Pleyel, Schlesinger, and Probst for larger fees, and in his correspondence with his friend, he aired his resentment by showering his publishers with a stream of abuse, in which such a term as "scoundrel" was the least drastic of his epithets. He grumbled in this way for two months, and then wrote a friendly letter to Pleyel.

Liszt mentions that he never heard Chopin use a sharp word. He would have been surprised had he looked into the virtuoso's correspondence with his closest friends. Possibly Chopin disliked inelegancies in using the French language; when he wrote in Polish, he had no such inhibition.

Chopin's passionate angers in these matters seem all the more incomprehensible because he was not in the least avid for money. His behavior might be explained as a paradoxical reaction of an oversensitive man. He entered the sphere of money through his art, for him the most intimate substance of life, and this fact alone sufficed to arouse resentments in him that easily gave rise to quarrels. After some time he would grow tired of contention, and would suddenly resign himself to everything. He could give no thought to money when he fell under the spell of music.

He was returning to music as he recovered strength and moved away from the ghosts of Majorca. George Sand wrote that "at the piano he conjured away all cares and brought poetry back home." They were lodged at the Hôtel de Beauveau in the Old Port, closing their doors to crowds of admirers who, upon the news of their arrival, invaded the hotel with sheafs of manuscript under their arms or at least with albums for autographs. Marseille bored them and except for Dr. Cauvières and the poet Gaszynski, they saw no one. George Sand continued to give lessons to her children. Frederic translated for her Mickiewicz's *Forefathers*, and she wrote an article comparing the Polish poet with Goethe and Byron. Chopin thought of her with tenderness, and in a letter to Grzymala for the first time referred to her as his beloved: "My angel is finishing her new novel, *Gabriel*. Today she is in bed all day, writing. Do you know, you would love her even more if you knew her as I know her now."

They eagerly followed the reports from Paris, and impatiently opened the letters that Chopin received at the hotel. George Sand, by way of precaution, had hers directed to the care of Dr. Cauvières. Frederic rejoiced over the success of Clara Wieck, who was giving a series of concerts in Paris. Of her playing he wrote that "one couldn't do better," although he regretted that she had chosen to perform as a selection from among his works the Etude in G-flat major (Opus 10, No. 5). "How could she choose, instead of something better, the étude least interesting for those who do not know that it was written for the black keys!"

They were jolted out of this secluded life by the sudden and tragic news of the death of Adolphe Nourrit. The great tenor had left Paris two years before, unwilling to share first honors with a newly engaged singer, Duprez, and had gone to Italy. He sang in Naples, where he was received enthusiastically; but the blow inflicted upon his ambitions and his fear of losing his voice plunged him into melancholia. On March 8th, after singing in a benefit concert, he jumped from a window and died instantly. His relatives disguised the fact of suicide, and explained his death as accidental. His widow, traveling through Marseille to bring her husband's body back to Paris, asked Chopin to play at a memorial service in his honor in the city. Chopin agreed.

The Life and Death of Chopin

During the Elevation, the old and rather dilapidated organ of the church of Notre-Dame-du-Mont intoned Schubert's *Die Gestirne*, a favorite with Nourrit, who had often sung it. According to George Sand, Chopin played it with an accent so sweet and sad that it sounded like an echo from another world. The audience listened somewhat disappointed because no one could see Chopin nor George Sand, who was hidden near him in the organ loft.

Both of them remembered Nourrit with deep grief. He left behind six children, and George Sand feared that she would burst into tears when meeting the widow.

Besides this tragic and upsetting incident, Frederic at this time had other reasons for being dejected, reasons that he kept deeply concealed in his heart. Something that he certainly had not reckoned with had taken place. His liaison with George Sand had ceased to be a relationship of lovers.

Aurore continued to care for him with the greatest tenderness; she gave him countless proofs of her devotion, but now her love consisted only of admiration, friendship, and motherly feeling. She was doubtless wearied by Chopin's moodiness, about which she wrote:

Gentle, cheerful, and charming, Chopin could bring his intimates to despair when he was ill. There was no nobler, more delicate, nor disinterested soul, there was no man more loyal and faithful in daily relationships. No one could surpass him in wit and gaiety; no one had a fuller or deeper understanding of his art. But unfortunately no one ever had a temperament so uneven, an imagination so deranged and gloomy, a sensitivity so easily wounded, and emotional demands so impossible to satisfy. Nothing of this was his fault; it was all the fault of his illness.

The shocks of the experience in Majorca had left their imprint on her. It must have been a fearful thing for her to see this fragile man tossing in fever, choked with coughing, calling for help with blood on his lips. If the very sight of the sufferer did not blunt her passion, she mastered her love by force of her cold reason and

276

her masculine will. This woman in whose embrace lovers had fainted, who remembered how close Jules Sandeau had come to death, could not doubt that if she continued to live with Frederic it would be fatal for him.

She was in the habit of clearly and openly formulating such ticklish questions, and she surely did not conceal her decision from him. It did not mean that they were to separate: she was deeply concerned for him, and she knew all too well how much he needed her. Moreover, she felt wearied by her avatars; she longed for peace and feared new complications and shocks. She adjusted herself to the idea that their love must evolve into something else, and she waited until Frederic for his part could reconcile himself to the change. It was not easy for him; upon his recovery he wanted to return to his old amorous ways, he was tormented by his frustration, and he was prone to jealousy. He drew comfort from the continued kindness of his mistress, from their plans for spending the summer in Nohant, and most of all from his piano. Only music never disappointed him; only music reconciled him to everything, took him away from human misfortune, and brought him back where he belonged.

His mistress was always deeply moved by his unearthliness. When he was transported by his art, he seemed to her a being of another world, unfathomable, and this attached her to him most of all.

This Chopin is an angel [she wrote]. His kindness, tenderness, and patience worry me sometimes—I imagine that he is too delicate, too refined, and too perfect by nature to live for a long time our coarse and heavy earthly life. In Majorca, while he was mortally ill, he composed music that was full of the perfumes of paradise. But I have become accustomed to seeing him in heaven, and I have come to think that in his case being alive or being dead does not matter. He does not quite know himself in which planet he exists; he has no idea of life as we conceive of it and feel it.

In an interval of their sojourn in Marseille, Chopin and George Sand and her children went on a short trip to Genoa. Perhaps

Aurore wanted to divert the thoughts of both from the new secrets of their hearts, or perhaps she was drawn by old memories. Six years before, she had been with de Musset in this city of roseate houses; now she was looking at them again through the sadness of time and of her latest, troubled love. Frederic liked Genoa; he was particularly impressed by the historical relics associated with Christopher Columbus. But he did not join George Sand in all her excursions. She was busy showing her children the familiar places, and happy to see Maurice absorbing everything with youthful curiosity.

The return was unpropitious. Because of stormy seas they traveled forty hours instead of the normal twenty. Chopin disembarked in Marseille so worn out that Dr. Cauvières took him to his own apartment. When he had rested and returned to the hotel, George Sand began to prepare for their departure. May was ending; the weather was hot; they were wearied by the city. They were to go together to Nohant.

They set out for Arles, where Madame Sand's own carriage was waiting for them. This was perhaps the most pleasant part of the whole hapless pilgrimage they had entered upon in the fall of the previous year. They traveled only by day; the nights were spent at inns, to give Frederic an opportunity of resting. Their way led through Provence, the land of red soil, glaring light, plane trees, and cypresses, but George Sand preferred the vistas of her fertile Berry to these parched fields and dusty roads. The travelers talked only about Nohant, which Frederic was now to see for the first time after hearing so much about it for the past three years.

All of them were excited when after a week's journey the carriage turned from the main road into a narrow side road. They went by the village and the little church hidden among elm and walnut trees, and drove up in front of the wrought-iron gate. They were received by the whole corps of retainers amid merry tumult. Frederic entered the spacious courtyard and stood before the two-story house with its hospitably open shutters. At the back of the house he could see the garden. Then they went indoors and upstairs. Here the guest room had been made ready for him.

Nohant

THE first neighbor invited to Nohant was Dr. Gustave Papet, an old friend of Madame George Sand. He examined Chopin and said, "You are not tubercular, but you have a chronic inflammation of the larynx. I don't promise to cure you, but I don't see any cause for alarm. A stay in the country will benefit you a great deal."

This diagnosis was the best medicine for Frederic. He recovered his poise and his humor and began to forget the nightmare of Majorca. His sensitive, intense nature did not need strong impressions; one rustling plane tree could enchant him more than a wooded wilderness, a curving path through the fields more than a mountain panorama, and the smooth-flowing Indre River more than all the oceans. "The countryside is beautiful," he wrote to Grzymala, "nightingales, larks—only you, my bird, are missing." He drove in a phaeton through peaceful villages, over rolling hills and into valleys, passing by luxuriant fields and meadows with browsing sheep, and he would return home enraptured by the fragrance of the earth, as he had been many years before.

For the first time in many years he was in the country again. How far behind him he had left Szafarnia, Poturzyn, Zelazowa Wola, the manor houses of Poland, the evening improvisations, and the early friends! Tytus had married; he had a second son now whom he had named Frederic. Yet to his old friend at this distance he seemed unchanged.

"Write an oratorio," Tytus urged his friend in a letter.

But Frederic smiled at such adolescent taste. "And why don't you establish a Camaldolite monastery instead of a sugar refinery?" he wrote in reply.

Chopin easily adjusted himself to the routine of his new environment, all the more so because he was left completely free. He rose late, had breakfast in his room, and did as he pleased until dinner time. At five o'clock a bell summoned the household to the dining room or, in good weather, to the terrace. The piano stood in the drawing room and here he played in the evening. He gave lessons to Solange and ordered music sheets for her from Paris; together they played compositions for four hands, and he became attached to her. He had no such feeling for Maurice, but was not unduly upset about it. The handsome boy often scrutinized him with searching eyes, as though wondering how his mother had become so intimate with a man who was not even his tutor.

George Sand's neighbors liked Chopin from the moment they met him; since they were accustomed to her ways with men, they took his presence in her house as a matter of course. His greatest admirer was Hippolyte Châtiron, Aurore's natural half-brother, who lived near Nohant; he was a gay reveler, usually in a state of slight intoxication, and always ready for pranks. In this company Frederic too was full of humor and fantasy. Just as he had done with his sisters in his childhood, he organized charades, pantomimes, and theatrical spectacles; about these spectacles George Sand later wrote an essay. They consisted largely of improvised scenes, constituting a kind of domestic *commedia dell'arte*; they followed a general pattern established in advance but abounded in the most unexpected effects. The improvisations of the actors were accompanied by those of Chopin on the piano, who was the leading spirit in this theater. After the spectacles he went to bed about the same time as Maurice and Solange, and according to George Sand, he fell asleep like a child.

Chopin's love for the countryside was that of the typical city dweller. The village meant for him primarily rest, quiet, and an opportunity to concentrate on his work; beyond the fact that it had these charms, it meant boredom. He was not very much interested in what was going on outside the house and the park, and he was not absorbed in the contemplation of nature. In his view, hunting parties, riding, and fishing were invented for the guests who were never lacking at Nohant. He did not play billiards, which George Sand had introduced as a pastime for her familiars in bad weather.

To offset all this, the evenings were exclusively his when he was alone with George Sand. She understood him completely, and Heine called her a "perfect listener." He discussed his new compositions with her and received her comments. According to Niemcewicz, George Sand spoke sparingly but always to the point. She was well versed in musical matters, she played tolerably well on the piano, and sang in an alto voice, but Niemcewicz's appraisal does not apply to all of her judgments.

A day will come [she wrote about Chopin], when his music will be faithfully orchestrated, and then the whole world will know that this genius, as comprehensive, complete, and learned as that of the greatest masters whose art he has assimilated, has maintained an individuality more exquisite than that of Johann Sebastian Bach, more powerful than that of Beethoven, and more dramatic than that of Weber.

That summer Chopin completed all the compositions for which he had had no energy or time in Majorca. They included the Sonata in B-flat minor, Opus 35, with the funeral march (the latter had been finished long before); the Impromptu in F-sharp major, Opus 36; the Two Nocturnes, Opus 37, and the third Scherzo in C-sharp minor, Opus 39. He also wrote three new mazurkas, in B major, A-flat major, and C-sharp minor respectively, which, together with that in E minor composed in Palma, form Opus 41. While engaged in this difficult task, which he spoke of casually, he did not neglect one of the most abiding interests of his life, and wrote about it to Fontana: "In moments of leisure

The Life and Death of Chopin

I correct the Paris edition of Bach, not only the engraver's errors, but all the errors sanctioned by those who supposedly understand Bach (I do not claim that I understand him better, but I am convinced that sometimes I can divine him)."

Aurore observed his industry, thoroughgoing and scrupulous in every detail. She admired his will and his clarity about his creative goals, the dauntless artistic character, which amazed her in this man devoid of any ability to make a decision when it came to trivial everyday matters. She wrote:

His music was spontaneous, miraculous. He found it without seeking it, without previous intimation of it. It came upon his piano sudden, complete, sublime, or it sang in his head during a walk, and he was impatient to hear it himself with the help of the instrument. But then began the most desperate labor that I have ever witnessed. It was a succession of efforts, hesitations, and moments of impatience to recapture certain details of the theme he could hear; what he had conceived as one piece, he analyzed too much in trying to write it down, and his dismay at his inability to rediscover it in what he thought was its original purity threw him into a kind of despair. He would lock himself up in his room for whole days, weeping, pacing back and forth, breaking his pens, repeating or changing one bar a hundred times, writing and erasing it as many times, and beginning again the next day with an infinite and desperate perseverance. He sometimes spent six weeks on one page, only in the end to write it exactly as he had sketched it at the first draft.

With every detail, with every recopied page, Frederic came in the evening to George Sand, who used to say that he consulted her as Molière consulted his servant.

She tried to be his surest help, support, and judge. The lover from whom she had become estranged was still for her a great artist, and his art filled her with admiration. As she expressed it:

The genius of Chopin is the most profound and the most feelingful that has ever existed. He succeeds in making one instrument speak the language of the infinite, and often sums up in ten lines that any child could play a poem of immense exaltation, a drama of unparalleled force.

Frederic knew that although his intimate relation with her had changed, he still possessed her heart so far as music was concerned. This change had taken place not without violent or painful scenes. They often discussed the matter; but George Sand was unflinching in her resolve, and if Frederic wanted to remain at her side, he was compelled to agree to her terms. Her indifference toward him as a male was manifested by her complete tolerance. She was not even concerned with his amours in the village—adventures he indulged in perhaps as a goad to her. Rumors about his relations with a peasant girl in Nohant left her unperturbed.

As the summer passed, and their guests, Madame Dorval, Grzymala, and Emanuel Arago, left one after the other, Chopin and George Sand were obliged to face the question of what their plans were to be for the future. If we are to believe the highly slanted later account by George Sand in her *Histoire de ma vie*, they debated the question at length and very seriously. George Sand thought, or perhaps only tried to convince herself, that if Frederic were to return to Paris alone, he would forget her after six months, as she said; if they were separated by distance, their pleasant but difficult relationship would evolve into a normal and safe friendship. She also thought that she was at an age when love is easily aroused in a woman's heart, and he for his part did not conceal from her that in Paris he intended to resume an interrupted romance. What purpose, then, was to be served by their staying together?

All this might have been an argument for a definite separation. But there remained her picture of the melancholy angel, a helpless man whose genius dazzled her, who longed for a home, for family warmth, and for the materialization of his unfulfilled dream of a place of his own on earth. She was not indifferent to these considerations, and for all this she loved him. In the end, it was the angel who won in this dispute about the future, and George Sand made up her mind to move to Paris. Frederic welcomed her decision with enthusiasm.

There began a search for two apartments, one for her and one for him. Fontana, Grzymala, and Arago scoured entire city districts, according to a list of streets sent them from Nohant.

In a lively correspondence the friends discussed every detail. Frederic drew a plan for an apartment for George Sand, and warned Fontana that it must be seemly, quiet, comfortable, without trumpeters, blacksmiths, or bad odors in the neighborhood, "for she cannot live just any old way."

An apartment for Frederic was found first, at No. 5 Rue Tronchet. Fontana was buried under a mass of commissions. "Choose the same kind of paper as I had before—it was *tourterelle* [dove-colored]—but bright, glossy for both rooms, with a narrow dark-green gadroon for a border. For the entrance hall, something different, but nice. However, if prettier and more modern papers are available, papers that you like and that you know that I would like too, take them. I'd rather have something simple, modest, and neat than the ordinary stuff of the *épiciers*."

Frederic also asked him to have his bed and desk sent to the cabinetmaker, to have the mattresses renovated and the chairs cleaned, to hire a manservant. On another occasion he reminded his friend that his gray curtains must be transferred from the study to the entrance hall and asked him to order a red sofa with a white cover of the same material as the chair covers. Finally Fontana was directed to order a hat at Dupont's, and trousers and a black velvet vest at Dautremont's.

Poor Fontana! And he was so diligent! He carried out all the commissions and then found an apartment for George Sand. It consisted of two pavilions at No. 16 Rue Pigalle, and its plan was exactly as she desired. "Take it, don't ask. Hurry," Frederic urged him.

Everything was ready at last. Frederic packed his new manuscripts—six compositions revised for the printer, and an impromptu that he had finished shortly before his departure. In the Rue Tronchet a valet was waiting for him.

In his last letter from Nohant, he asked Fontana for one more thing:

Since you are so efficient, my dear, see to it that in my new apartment no black thoughts or choking cough come to me. Give some thought to my health, and if you can, change many episodes of my past. It wouldn't be bad either if I could find there a few years of completed work—a great deal of it. I shall be much obliged to you if you yourself become younger, or if you can manage to void our having been born.

Chopin left Nohant with George Sand's family on October 10th, at five o'clock in the morning. They spent the night at Orléans, and the following night Chopin was in the Rue Tronchet and George Sand in the Hôtel de France, where she stopped for a few days while her house in the Rue Pigalle was being prepared for her.

CHAPTER

30

En Famille

WHEN Chopin returned to Paris after almost a year's absence, he found himself the center of attention in the salons. His mysterious journey, his liaison with the famous novelist, his illness, which was held to be tuberculosis (a "fashionable" disease at that time), the recent publication of his Preludes (Opus 28)— all this aroused curiosity, sycophantic or genuine. Each evening he visited one of the twenty or thirty great houses in which he was received as a friend, often leaving with some beautiful woman who was happy at the thought of any sort of intimacy with the great artist. And every day he went to see George Sand.

"How do you feel?" she would ask him, always anxious about his health.

"Couldn't feel better," he would answer, pale and tired.

George Sand's house in the Rue Pigalle had become the head-quarters of the republicans and socialists. Cavaignac, Louis Blanc, and above all Pierre Leroux came there to discuss how they could destroy the old world and build a new one. Indeed, they discussed every subject under the sun, but always returned with passionate concentration to the project of dethroning Louis Philippe.

Unlike George Sand's friends, the King's entourage at St. Cloud was more concerned with music than with revolution. On October 29, 1839, Count Perthuis, the royal aide-de-camp, escorted Chopin and Moscheles, under a pouring rain, to St. Cloud. In the brightly illumined *salon carré* they found the King, the Queen with her sewing basket, the Princesse d'Orléans, and the ladies of the court. The artists were cordially welcomed; the Queen asked Chopin with great solicitude whether the piano had been tuned properly, whether he liked the lights, and whether the stool was high enough. Chopin opened the concert by playing several of his études and nocturnes. The high point of the program was Moscheles' Sonata in E-flat major, for four hands, which was one of Frederic's favorite pieces.

"Divine, delicious," the ladies whispered, distinctly enough to be heard by the pianists, who were asked to repeat the slow movement. Later Moscheles wrote of this concert: "I am convinced that Chopin's playing, full of a fire and élan that did not weaken for a moment throughout the performance, must have had a very stimulating effect on his listeners."

To close the concert each pianist offered an improvisation. When they left the palace, it was almost midnight. The rain had ceased, and a starry sky spread out over the lights of Paris. Chopin ordered the coachman to take him to the city in a hurry; he wanted to say good night to Madame Sand, and probably cared little that in her salon he might find men who were conspiring against the monarch for whom he had just played. A few days later, he placed on one of his shelves a silver goblet that he had received as a gift from Louis Philippe.

Chopin had met Moscheles at the house of Léo, and for six weeks afterward, until Moscheles' departure from Paris, the two pianists remained inseparable. Moscheles, who had formerly complained that his fingers got inextricably mixed up when he tried to play Chopin's études, was full of enthusiasm after he had heard Chopin play these compositions. Of his new attitude to Chopin he wrote:

The sudden modulations that I could not grasp when I played his works no longer bother me. His *piano* is so ethereal that no strong *forte* is needed to create the necessary contrast. Listening to him, one yields with one's whole soul, as to a singer who, oblivious of accompaniment, lets himself be carried away by his emotion. In short, he is unique among pianists.

After the years of mutual recrimination that had preceded their meeting, the two men parted as friends. Chopin promised to compose three short études for a book on piano method that Moscheles and Fétis were preparing, and he kept his word. Before the year was out he sent the manuscript of *Trois nouvelles études* to London.

Apart from this he wrote little; his lessons and his social life hardly left time for composing. One of his best pupils, Fredericke Müller (later Madame Streicher), to whom he dedicated his *Allegro de Concert*, wrote that Chopin once played for her fourteen Bach preludes and fugues from memory, remarking, "These things can never be forgotten. For a year I have not practiced a quarter of an hour on end. I have not the strength or the energy. I wait for a little health in order to take up all this again, but— I am still waiting."

He disliked his new apartment. Despite its southern exposure, it turned out to be dark and damp. More and more frequently he invited himself for dinner at George Sand's, and each time returned home reluctantly.

"How do you feel?" she would ask him, constantly more worried by his pallor and coughing fits.

"Couldn't be better," he would answer in a broken voice.

There was only one solution, and it was not long before it was adopted. Chopin moved to the Rue Pigalle, although he retained his own apartment in the Rue Tronchet. In George Sand's house, she and Solange occupied one pavilion, and Maurice and Frederic the other. Her house had this great advantage, that in it one could be cloistered from the world while living in the very heart of Paris. The pavilions were in a garden, walled off from the street. To a certain extent Frederic's old dream had come true—George Sand and he now had one household.

George had written a play entitled *Cosima*—so named in honor of the second daughter of Liszt and Madame d'Agoult, and was busy trying to get it staged. Frederic again gave lessons to Solange, who was growing up to be a pretty and capricious child, troublesome to her mother and brother and to her governesses and teachers. Maurice was studying painting with Delacroix and spent his spare time in the garden, flirting with his distant cousin, Augustine Brault, who was more and more often invited to the Rue Pigalle.

George Sand had two beautiful drawing rooms and throngs of friends. Some canvases by Delacroix, an engraved portrait of the hostess by Calamatta, magnificent Chinese vases, green-upholstered furniture, and a rosewood piano attracted the notice of Balzac. Since he was a keen observer, he also noticed George Sand's double chin and her hands, tiny as a child's. One of her favorite visitors, Delacroix, reputedly a natural son of Talleyrand, was very fond of Chopin, whom he admired as pianist and composer. A pale and sickly dandy, worried about his lungs as Frederic was, he was also like Chopin in temperament. The painter's young friend Charles Baudelaire found in him skepticism, courtesy, a stubborn will, a very special kindness, and sensibility—the same qualities that Delacroix probably perceived in Chopin. Delacroix was a great student and lover of music and ranked Chopin next to his favorite Mozart, but he had to resign himself to the fact that Chopin did not appreciate his paintings. This may be the reason why a portrait by Delacroix showing Chopin at the piano and George Sand standing next to him, which was begun in 1838, was never completed. Chopin was somewhat afraid of Delacroix's grandiose conceptions, rich colors, and dramatic action. It was for similar reasons that Chopin did not feel affinity with Beethoven, Shakespeare, or Michelangelo. But he delighted in discussions with Delacroix, valued his intelligent judgment, and shared his refined tastes. He felt it a relief to be with this radical artist after the radical politicians had left the salon.

Among the revolutionaries, idealists, and mystics attracted to George Sand's iconoclastic milieu, Frederic became intimate only with Louis Blanc and Cavaignac, a young republican. The disheveled, unwashed Leroux seemed to him repellent. He looked with disapproval on the growing intimacy between George Sand and this new director of her literary conscience, as Heine called him.

Chopin's own drawing room in the other pavilion was as usual frequented by Polish exiles, among them political leaders and poets. Of this circle he particularly liked Zaleski, who had once lived near Zelazowa Wola, and Witwicki. The aristocratic Poles, at first scandalized by his liaison with George Sand, came to overlook her radicalism and sought contact with the influential novelist through their distinguished compatriot. Balzac, who used to say of Chopin that he was more Polish than all of Poland, soon had to admit that George Sand too was "stuffed with Poles." In December, 1839, the *Revue des Deux Mondes* published her *Essai sur le drame fantastique: Goethe, Byron, et Mickiewicz,* which she had written in Marseille. In the eyes of George Sand, Poland was associated with the mystical doctrine of Leroux, the preacher of "eternal and continually progressing truth." He held that in the course of evolution truth passes from nation to nation, and he thought that in his time it was incarnate in Poland, which must become the propagator of Christianity, equality, and fraternity.

In the spring of 1840 there was a painful moment for the family in the two pavilions: *Cosima* failed after one disastrous performance. Madame d'Agoult, sitting in her box with Liszt, listened to the jeers and hisses of the audience with a smile of satisfaction, which vanished only after the lights went on. The old friendship between the two ladies had come to an end—killed by the jealousy of the vain and ambitious Countess. Chopin also lost favor with her; she now called him "an oyster powdered with sugar."

In the midst of these disappointments a crisis arose in the friendship between Chopin and Liszt. The affair was discussed with relish by the gossips. Liszt, it was whispered, had had a tryst with one of his enthusiastic feminine admirers (it was perhaps Madame Pleyel) in Chopin's bedroom, and had forgotten to remove the traces of his escapade or even to inform his host about it. Frederic could not forgive him this bold improvisation.

The summer of 1840 was passed without much gratification. George Sand did not want to go to Nohant unless she had four thousand francs to spend. She complained to her brother that in Nohant, "even before she had time to get up in the morning, twelve persons were installed in the house." Finally she decided to stay in Paris—probably because she did not want to be separated from Leroux.

Chopin, too, stayed in town. In lieu of a vacation in the country he had to content himself with drives in the Champs Élysées or the Bois de Boulogne. Sometimes George Sand and Solange rode their horses beside his coach; sometimes he took only Solange, whose whims and fancies amused him. As a memento of one such drive there remains a curious little document—a record of their weights. The thirty-year-old Chopin weighed ninety-seven pounds, the twelve-year-old Solange eighty-four.

But in this weak organism there raged a violent and unsatisfied hunger, the need for love. Chopin had now become accustomed to a situation that only a short time before had seemed to him inconceivable: his feelings for his mistress had become platonic, but his heart, freed as it was, clamored for its rights. George Sand remarked that he fell in love with three women every night; he would succeed in persuading each that she was the only one, and then forget them all when he returned home.

There was one woman who would have smiled at these words and who might have had quite other thoughts of him. For several months Delphine Potocka had been back in Paris. She had lived through painful experiences and wore her beauty with a melancholy that was easier to understand now than in earlier days. Her attempt to resume marital life had ended in failure. Her husband, seconded by her own family, had implored her to return to him; when she did, he displayed the same brutality as before. "It is sad and boring here," she wrote to Chopin from her country residence at Tulczyn, "but life for me is everywhere the same. May it pass without worse sufferings and ordeals—what I have endured is enough. Somehow, I too have failed to be happy in this world. Each time that I have wished somebody well, I have been repaid with ingratitude and tribulation. *Au total*, this life is an enormous dissonance."

Delphine's stay in Tulczyn was short-lived. After stormy scenes she left her husband, this time forever. She went to Rome, where her mother was living, and where she tried to forget her misfortune and to obtain an annulment of her marriage.

Her romance with Krasinski, whom she had met in Italy, was a subject of great interest in the Polish colony in Paris, especially after Delphine's return to the city. While still in Nohant, when he was striving to reconquer George Sand, Chopin tried—in vain— to arouse jealousy in his unyielding mistress by telling her that he knew someone in Paris with whom he might renew a broken romance. Having lost Aurore, he thought of Delphine with so much the more tenderness.

Delphine was one of the visitors to the Rue Pigalle. Frederic again admired her beautiful singing and took his place at the piano to accompany her. It seemed that despite five years of separation, they were as close to each other in feeling as ever. Old memories must have revived, and the past returned not to frighten them away from each other but to bring them together. Delphine resisted a renewal of her liaison with Chopin; she did not understand why he wanted to return to her since he was George Sand's lover—as everyone thought. On November 19, 1840, he wrote her a letter explaining everything:

My life, my dearest! You want me to write an explanation and apology, and although I live only a few steps away from you in Paris, you nevertheless want it sealed in writing. The master gives orders, the servant must obey. But I must remind you of your promise that, if my explanation is good, I shall be granted forgiveness and the highest favor. Therefore I shall explain everything to you.

As for Madame Sand, people invent more lies than truths. My liaison with her lasted less than a year; it came to an end when I fell ill on Majorca. I swear by my love for you and by my love for my mother—what I have just said is the sacred truth. Apparently I wasn't enough for her. My illness served her as a pretext for a break with me. Then she proved to me at great length and with learned arguments that my health did not permit an amorous liaison. . . .

From that time on she has given me only maternal love. She takes care of me devotedly—you wouldn't believe how good she is to me —and I accept her kindness, for you know how much I need tenderness and protection.

So the talk that I have been her lover for all these years is just a lie. All those who go to Nohant know about her lovers, and in Paris too it is known who is her favorite. . . . This unquenched passion of hers is a real disease, something that must be understood and forgiven. After our break I still loved her, I had a passion and a taste for her. . . . Today I feel friendship for her, and a great deal of gratitude, and I love her as one loves one's mother.

After breaking with Sand, I had a few brief affairs, but these were passions without love, and are not worth mentioning. Don't believe it if you are told that I am quick to fall in love. You knew me so well once—after all, I haven't changed. . . . Only you and Sand have had my heart, and you are more than Sand to me, because I have had more passion for you, and because you know and understand me as no one else does. I haven't opened my soul to her; she is a foreigner and wouldn't understand me.

The other women in my life are either youthful dreams buried long ago or winds of hot passion that blew only for a short while. . . . When a great love overwhelms me, when passion seizes me, and temptations tear me like dogs, I forget about the world—as I once did with you—and I am ready to give everything to a woman, to sacrifice my life and my work. With other women it wasn't so, with them I never lost my head. . . .

So you see that aside from Sand there has never been another love or even a great passion in my life. But you will be best convinced by my works. When we were together, I only polished up work in my old albums, preparing for the printer things that had been lying around for some time; or if I wrote new works, it was only when you were away for a long time. . . . Now, these last years, see how many works, and not insignificant ones, I have thrown off—it's clear that not love but art has taken my energy.

And if in all these years I have loved only you and Aurore, admit that I do not have a heart that easily and quickly falls in love. I hope I have already convinced you, having made everything so clear that even a child would understand it. I had an important mistress, and then lighter affairs. You too took a famous lover after me, and surely there has been no lack of light affairs with you, so I consider that we're even.

I have made my general confession. I bitterly regret my sins and humbly await the return of your favor. Findelka, I've never loved anyone as I love you. You have always had the warmest place in my heart and memory. I have never lost my passion and my taste for you. In Sand's embraces, I have always thought that I would rather have you.

Consign to oblivion all the lies and slanders that separate us. I will be better now, I swear, for my difficult life has taught me forbearance, and never will I torment you with jealousy as before. I have never loved anyone as deeply and strongly as I love you. You were my first mistress, so be my last—after you I won't take any other. I think I have convinced you and that you will let me come to you tonight. . . .

The Years of Fruition

fruitful   *zenith*

THE years that now followed were the happiest in Chopin's life. He enjoyed peace and good health in his adoptive home, sheltered in a family group, and tended by Madame Sand, while carrying on his secret liaison with Delphine. These years were also fecund of work. In 1840 he published a sequence of compositions that mark the apogee of his art—the Sonata in B-flat minor (Opus 35), the Impromptu in F-sharp major (Opus 36), the Nocturne in G minor and the Nocturne in G Major (Opus 37), the Ballade in F major (Opus 38), the Scherzo in C-sharp minor (Opus 39), the Polonaises in A major and C minor (Opus 40), the Four Mazurkas in C-sharp minor, E minor, B major, and A-flat major respectively (Opus 41), the Waltz in A-flat major (Opus 42), and the Three New Etudes (without opus number).

The Sonata in B-flat minor surprised everyone by its originality. Even Schumann, keen expert that he was, felt disturbed by it and saw in it "a sphinxlike smile." Its irresistible emotional dynamic, and its all-powerful lyricism represented a new departure in sonata writing. This composition holds within it everything that human tragedy is made of—all the nights, the autumns, the trampled loves, the grief and pathos of death.

In the Impromptu in F-sharp major he was once again listening with all his soul to Poland. He was suffused in a nostalgic melodious happiness. The same yearning mood darkens the reli-

Le Lac de Willis

gious Nocturne in G minor; this and the Nocturne in G major are among the most beautiful of compositions in this supremely Chopinesque genre.

A new poetic imagery came to expression in the Ballade in F major, dedicated to Schumann. It was inspired by a poem of Mickiewicz entitled *Switez* ("The Enchanted Lake"), and serves as an example of a musical work drawing upon a theme of literature, though its provenance seems unimportant in relation to its musical beauties. Chopin, who liked to associate idyl with tragedy, and hope with despair, nowhere else succeeded in expressing these contrasts as sharply as he does here.

A different kind of vigor emanates from the Scherzo in C-sharp minor. It surges with anger, protest, and fighting spirit; it seems as though the creator of this drama is struggling in combat with all the evil then besetting his steps. Powerful chords storm the heavens in Promethean rebellion, the prayerlike choral in D-flat major heralds supernatural help, and the whole demonic poem throbs with the conflict of these two titanic forces. The Scherzo is dedicated to Adolf Gutmann, who, in the words of Lenz, was strong enough to "punch a hole through the table" with these chords.

The two polonaises that constitute Opus 40 come directly from Chopin's Polish heart. The contrasting keys and the fact that the two works are published together reveal the composer's design, which was to symbolize the destinies of Poland, her greatness and her tragedy.

The form of the polonaise was known two hundred years before Chopin's time; it is said to have its source in old Polish Christmas carols. Its stately measures resounded for the first time in Cracow in 1574, when the Polish nobles filed in procession before their newly elected king, Henry III of Valois; from then on, it became customary for a polonaise to accompany the coronation solemnities. In Poland the polonaise was played as dance music in the castles of the magnates and the manor houses of the gentry. In the course of time, this dance made its way from the Polish palaces and the court to France and other European countries.

It was a kind of promenade, in which the dancing pair moved around the hall with gliding steps and graceful gestures. The polonaise continued to be popular until Napoleonic times, but for Polish ears its rhythms always held the overtones of splendid ceremonials, wedding feasts, court balls—an echo of bygone times. This was how Chopin heard it; before his time polonaises had been written by Bach, Mozart, Beethoven, Weber, Schubert, and many Polish composers. All of them were interested in the form. Chopin fell under the spell of the spirit of the polonaise.

The polonaise in A major is a triumphant processional, that in C minor a song of mourning. It is said that Chopin referred to the former as "the Sobieski polonaise," and expressed the wish that it might be played at the crowning of a new king in a free Poland. Actually, it resounds with majestic splendor and the accents of a lofty triumphal. The second polonaise also breathes an exalted dignity, but it is the dignity of grief and despair, perhaps more moving than the fanfares of the first. These two contradictory moods manifested themselves whenever Chopin sought to give expression to his feelings about Poland. Joy and sorrow, rapture and dejection, heroic resolve and melancholy were the fixed poles between which he moved. Their magnetic currents did not repel each other—rather, it was the interaction of the two that gave rise to that Polish *żal* (sorrow) which Liszt emphasized so strongly.

In addition to the aristocratic Poland of the polonaise, there was also for Chopin the peasant Poland of the mazurka. In his hands this dance became a sublimation not of the Polish past and its legend, but of what he himself had heard in his country and of what he liked best to hear. He did not literally repeat the melodies of the folk songs; he touched upon them only occasionally, but he preserved the rhythm of the form unchanged, and knew how to bend it to the requirements of his most etherealized inspirations. Thus this spiritual aristocrat drew the sustenance of his art from the common sources of music in the life of the people.

In this period Chopin's thoughts about Poland were conditioned by his association with Mickiewicz. The great poet's revolutionary drama *Forefathers* certainly influenced Chopin's fantasies in the realm of the heroic, and the epopee *Pan Tadeusz* stirred his memories of idyllic Polish scenes.

Mickiewicz was regarded in Paris as an extraordinary being. The Polish colony endlessly bruited the story of his poetic duel with Slowacki, in which Mickiewicz improvised verses that entranced his listeners. They sobbed, wept, and some were hysterically moved. No one recalled whether he spoke for five minutes or half an hour; no one recalled the content of his improvisation, but all maintained that his words had carried them away.

George Sand met Mickiewicz as early as 1836, and became sufficiently interested in the Polish poet to support his efforts to stage his play, *The Confederates of Bar*. In 1840 Mickiewicz returned to Paris after a year's sojourn in Lausanne, where, as an instructor in Latin literature, he had amazed his students "by the freshness of his approach to a seemingly stale subject." This statement appeared in the report of the university authorities to the Swiss ministry of public education. In December, 1840—he was then forty-two—he was appointed professor of Slavonic literature at the Collège de France. He lectured to audiences that comprised not only French, German, Polish, and Russian students but also such intellectual notables as Sainte-Beuve, Lamartine, Lamennais, Montalembert, and Michelet. Chopin attended these lectures in the company of Madame Sand, who was greeted with applause when she entered the auditorium to occupy a seat next to Mickiewicz.

This poet-teacher, of slight stature, with ardent black eyes under heavy eyebrows, held his audiences spellbound from his very first words. He spoke on a little-known subject; the Slavs were at that time regarded as an exotic race and the history of their literature was not widely studied. Mickiewicz spoke twelve languages, and his memory was prodigious. Unfolding his broad pictures of unfamiliar civilizations, he would be carried away by his own interest, and his hearers would be transported likewise under the stimulus of his magnetic power and élan. At such moments, when his pale face was flushed, and his long black hair fell in wild disorder about his head, people sensed in this professor something of the spirit of a prophet. George Sand declared that he was an ecstatic, a personality of the same type as Jeanne d'Arc, Dante, and Socrates.

In this period, which was given over to a mystical quest for a means to fellowship among men and for a spiritual foundation on which to erect the structure of earthly government, Mickiewicz was advocating a kind of religion of freedom. He believed that mankind must be regenerated not through political movements but through morality, and that nations must reach a common understanding transcending the authority of their rulers. He also held that Poland was suffering in expiation of the evils of the world and in order to redeem humanity: Poland was the Christ of the nations, and Polish liberation would insure the freedom of all subjugated peoples. Consequently he demanded that all things be sacrificed to Poland, even art. He himself had given up poetry for many years, devoting himself to political and social causes, and he often reprimanded Chopin for his failure to write operas that would further the prestige of Poland. This asceticism of the poet-apostle was in constant conflict with the asceticism of Chopin, the artist par excellence. They were brought together by their patriotism, but they were far apart in their relation to art.

One evening Chopin was playing in Madame Sand's drawing room for her, Maurice, and Delacroix. It was after supper, during which they had talked about the parallels between painting and music. Chopin had spoken little and reluctantly, as was usual when such topics were discussed. He had contented himself with declaring that he was working on his own method of playing and his own theory of music, and then had gone to the piano. The others were listening to him in absorption when suddenly the doorbell rang. Chopin was startled and stopped playing.

"I am not at home," Madame Sand told her servant.

"No, you're in for him," Chopin interrupted her.

"For him? Who is it?"

"Mickiewicz."

"How do you know?"

"I am sure of it. I was just thinking of him."

Chopin often spoke of premonitions, unconscious whisperings, and inexplicable anticipations, and was even given to superstition: he feared the numbers seven and thirteen, and Mondays and Fridays. Madame Sand treated such ideas with complaisance and probably smiled also at this instance. But Chopin turned out to be right. Mickiewicz entered the room with timid courtesies to his hosts, sat down in a corner, and asked Chopin to continue playing. The new listener seemed to stimulate the pianist. "He played splendidly," George Sand wrote later.

Chopin's playing was suddenly interrupted when the servant rushed into the drawing room crying that the house was on fire. The fire was in Madame Sand's bedroom and was easily extinguished, but the incident occupied almost an hour. At that moment everyone remembered Mickiewicz. In the drawing room the candles had gone out, but the poet was sitting in the same chair and in the same corner as before. He had not moved from his place, unaware of the lapse of time. "If it had been someone else," George Sand wrote in her memoirs, "one might have suspected him of striking a pose. But there was nothing artificial in Mickiewicz. He was still listening to Chopin."

The poet, who was sensitive to Chopin's playing, failed to understand his psychological make-up, just as he had failed to divine the genius of Slowacki. He was irritated by Chopin's way of life; he reproached the composer with wasting his time in salons and thought that he lacked warmth of feeling. He was inwardly closer to the active Madame Sand and thought that Chopin could not give her the happiness she deserved. Later he even went so far as to maintain that Chopin was her evil genius and a vampire, that he was torturing her, and that in the end he might kill her.

These harsh words were not repeated to Chopin, who never lost his sympathy and respect for Mickiewicz, and moved away from him only when the poet gave himself over to extreme mysticism. Thus the two greatest Poles of that era never became truly intimate, although their friendship lasted for years, and although their names were often associated. At one point it was even rumored that Mickiewicz was writing a work that Chopin was to set to music. These rumors reached Warsaw, and Ludwika questioned her brother about them, but they turned out to be entirely unfounded.

As for Chopin's liaison with George Sand, its true nature remained concealed not only to Mickiewicz but also to all other persons of the Polish colony. Chopin had ceased paying any attention to what was said about it, and except for his confidences to Delphine, he never tried to explain it to anyone.

It would have been most difficult for him to explain it to his parents. He confined himself to vague references, until his father broached the subject. In January, 1841, Monsieur Nicolas wrote to Frederic: "I am glad to hear from you that you are in good care, but we are curious to know more about this close friend of yours."

Although there was some talk in Warsaw about it, the Chopin family were convinced that his association with the famous novelist was only one of friendly intimacy. Frederic left them in this conviction; in 1841 he could do so without being untruthful.

On April 26, 1841, Chopin, overcoming his repugnance to appearing in public performances, arranged a concert at the Pleyel hall. He invited Madame Damoreau-Cinti and Ernst to appear with him. Before the concert he played a great deal of Bach, which he considered the best preparation. The tickets, at fifteen and twenty francs each, were sold out within a short time to a select group comprising royal and aristocratic patrons and friends and pupils of Chopin.

Pleyel prepared his auditorium for something intermediate between a concert and a private soirée. The staircase was covered with carpeting and decked out with flowers; the concertgoers entered between banks of fragrant verdure and were greeted as though at a reception. At eight o'clock the hall was filled to capacity; there were some seats on the platform, close to the artist, who was so fond of intimacy.

Chopin was in high spirits. In the first rows he could see

The Life and Death of Chopin

Madame Sand, Heine, Liszt, Delacroix, Franchomme, Legouvé, Mickiewicz, and Witwicki. He played only his own compositions —études, preludes, nocturnes, mazurkas, the Polonaise in A major and the Ballade in F major. The Ballade and two études were encored. During the intermission he was visited by Ernest Legouvé of the *Gazette musicale*, who came to tell him that the concert would be reported by Liszt instead of by himself. Chopin received this news without enthusiasm. "It's a pity," he said. "I should have preferred a critique by you."

"You must not think that. An article by Liszt will be of great moment. He will proclaim you a king," said Legouvé.

"Yes, but within his own empire," Chopin answered.

His suspicion proved unfounded. Liszt was carried away by enthusiasm, although as usual he expressed it in an excessive emphasis on purely external effects. He was dazzled by the audience, in which he saw "the most elegant women, the most fashionable young men, the richest financiers, the most illustrious *grands seigneurs*, a complete élite society, a full aristocracy of birth, wealth, talent, and beauty." He described the mood of the hearers, who "fixed their ears in advance, prepared to concentrate, said to themselves that they must not miss a chord, a note, an intention, a thought." He characterized the pianist as follows:

It has been only rarely, at very long intervals, that Chopin has played in public; but this, which in the case of any other artist would have led with certainty to obscurity and oblivion, has been the very thing that has secured for him a reputation above the whims of fashion, that has protected him from rivalries, jealousies, and injustice. Chopin, who has remained outside the extreme activity that for several years has crowded performing artists from all parts of the globe upon one another, has constantly been surrounded by faithful disciples, enthusiastic pupils, and ardent friends, who have guarded him against annoying quarrels and painful vexations and at the same time never ceased to promote his works and, with them, admiration for his genius and respect for his name. Thus, this exquisite, exalted, eminently aristocratic celebrity has remained free from all attack.

Every criticism of him has been silenced, as though posterity had already given its judgment. And in the brilliant audience that hastened to be with the poet who had been silent so long, there was not a single hesitant response, not one reservation: one paean of praise was on the lips of all.

All the newspapers and weeklies spoke of the concert in the highest terms. *Le Ménestrel* voiced the opinion that one listened to Chopin as one read the stanzas of Lamartine, but that only those capable of poetic feeling could truly appreciate him. In *La France musicale* he was compared to Schubert:

The one has done for the pianoforte what the other has done for the voice. . . . Chopin is a pianist of conviction. He composes for himself, plays for himself . . . and everyone listens with interest, with delight, with infinite pleasure. Listen how he dreams, how he weeps, with what sweetness, tenderness, and melancholy he sings, how perfectly he expresses the gentlest and loftiest feelings. Chopin is the pianist of sentiment par excellence. He may be said to have created a school of playing and a school of composition. Nothing indeed equals the lightness and sweetness of his preluding on the piano, nothing compares with his works in originality, distinction, and grace. Chopin is unique as a pianist—he should not and cannot be compared with anyone.

The concert brought in six thousand francs. Upon hearing this, Witwicki sighed, "Just try to recite verse for three quarters of an hour—for he surely didn't play longer—and try to get six thousand francs for that!"

Reports of this concert reached the Chopin household in Warsaw, but not through letters from Frederic. His mother wrote to him reproachfully:

You gave a concert, we knew from the papers that you were to give it and then that you had given it, and it was unpleasant that we didn't hear all this from you. It is impossible that you should not for such a long time be able to find a free hour in which to report to your parents about yourself and to inquire about them. You have thus caused us grief, no doubt unwittingly. You forget, my dear child, that your old parents live only in the thought of you and that every day they pray God to give you health and blessings, and they never cease to thank Him for the favors He has showered upon you. Your health, your good name, the fame that is yours, all this comes from His Most Holy Providence; therefore you together with us must be thankful to Him, and you will see that He will help you in all your good designs and that you will be happy.

Chopin had not written to his parents for three months. It was as though his adoptive family had drawn him away from his natural one. He now habitually discussed all his plans with George Sand, happy not to have to decide anything himself. She had been successful in straightening out her financial affairs; she had also concluded a profitable agreement concerning an edition of her collected works, and was preparing to go to Nohant for the summer. Chopin followed her there, as he did each summer for the next five years.

They left with Maurice and a new manservant of Chopin's in the middle of June; Solange was placed in a boardinghouse, where she was to stay until her school vacation began. Chopin occupied the same room he had had two years before, and once again he had an environment conducive to concentration and work. However, the weather was rainy and cold, the storms were so violent that trees were uprooted, and Chopin did not feel at his best. He spent the greater part of the day in his room, trying to compose. Touched by his mother's reproaches, he wrote at length to his parents, and waited for the piano that Pleyel had promised to send him.

After a month and a half of this monotonous life, he hailed with joy the arrival of Pauline Viardot-Garcia and her husband. This daughter of a great Spanish tenor, Manuel del Popolo Vicente Garcia, and sister of Malibran was an outstanding artist and a fascinating personality. She was only twenty, but had already acquired a reputation as a singer of genius, whose mezzo-soprano voice had a range of more than three octaves. Her musical erudition derived from the best sources: her father had taught her singing, Liszt had been her instructor on the piano, and Reicha had been her teacher of composition. Her marriage to Louis Viardot, a friend of Leroux's, had been arranged by George Sand, who had thus rescued her from a dangerous involvement with de Musset. No wonder, then, that at Nohant the whole company made up an intimate family circle. Chopin took Pauline for walks and even to the billiard room, which he otherwise avoided. In the evenings they read scores and played Bach and Mozart, and their conversations about music were protracted late into the night. It was probably during that summer that Madame Viardot-Garcia conceived the idea of vocalizing some of Chopin's mazurkas and études, a project that she later carried out.

At this time Frederic received the Pleyel piano he was awaiting, and it was set up in a room on the second floor. Although he did not think much of this instrument, he preferred to have it near at hand. He became more and more absorbed in work, and after the departure of the Viardots he did not wrest himself away from his manuscripts even at night. "Three o'clock in the morning —stars," he wrote in a letter to Fontana, forgetting to add the date, and asking his friend to undertake several errands for him. The first composition he sent to Fontana was the Tarantelle in A-flat major (Opus 43). He referred to this work in deprecating terms: "I hope that I shall not write anything worse for a long time to come." He asked Fontana to copy the manuscript and to insert the opus number, for he had forgotten what it should be. Nor was he sure of the proper measure for a tarantelle: "Go to Schlesinger's or Troupenas's and look up Rossini's collection of songs. . . . It contains a tarantelle (in A), I don't know whether the measure is 6/8 or 12/8. It is written both ways, but I'd rather have it as does Rossini."

He was also absorbed in other compositions that he considered more important. Among these was the Polonaise in F-sharp minor (Opus 44), a moving poem about Poland and one of his masterpieces. He wrote it at a moment when the Polish colony in Paris was indulging in sudden and unfounded hopes for a better future, as reported to him by Fontana. The unappeasable homesickness of these exiles fed on fictions, created legends, continually needed new mirages. It was rumored among the émigrés that the world was about to do something for Poland, that a great change was to take place shortly, and some of them even prepared to return home. Chopin was never indifferent to such moods, but he feared disappointment and was skeptical about Fontana's reports, to which he replied, "What you are writing me about Poland surprises me. May it be true, but I don't think so." On another occasion he exclaimed, "May we hope to return to Poland? Have you gone completely crazy?"

This inner conflict, this passionate longing and bitter disillusionment, and above all, this desperate, tragic love for country, are expressed in the Polonaise in F-sharp minor with powerful accents. After a stormy introduction, followed by passages that may suggest echoes of the 1830 uprising, there comes an enchanting mazurka, like a sweet dream of youth and happiness.

The sheets on which he wrote the Polonaise must have been lying next to those on which he was writing his Fantasia in F minor (Opus 49). These two utterly different compositions were close to each other in the poet-composer's thoughts. They are the fruit of the same industrious nights and days in Nohant, and they are examples of the same absolute perfection. The content of the Fantasia seems to take us beyond human affairs, beyond the Polish tragedy and Chopin's personal feelings—or perhaps it is so saturated with these that it could express them only in the purest music.

After the tremendous creative exertion of these compositions Chopin sought relaxation, and his Ballade in A-flat major (Opus 47) is probably the fruit of this need for escape into a dream. While he was writing it, he may have had in mind his half-facetious poetic talks with Heine about naiads or the legends of Lorelei, or perhaps he was longing for his sweet, caressing Delphine. This new ballade, so unlike the preceding ballades, has a quality of grace and elegance that later made it immensely popular.

The Years of Fruition

It is permissible to think that in seeking relaxation Chopin also returned to his old manuscripts, some of them dating from the months he spent in Vienna, when he projected compositions in collaboration with Slavik and Nidecki. On the basis of these fragments he now composed his Allegro de Concert in A major (Opus 46). Then he proceeded to attempts at new harmonizations. Many passages of his Prelude in C-sharp minor (Opus 45) must have sounded to his contemporaries like a voyage of discovery; years later some of its phrases were re-echoed by Brahms and Wagner. The same virile and triumphant accents characterize the splendid Two Nocturnes (Opus 48).

He now worked with greater facility and speed than ever, no longer beset by his old hesitations and doubts. Occasionally he would run downstairs to play a passage or a whole composition to George Sand, but on the whole the other residents of Nohant saw little of him. He was now less interested even in his beloved pantomimes, and if he still took part in them it was only as a relaxation from work. He tenderly greeted his favorite, Solange, when she arrived from Paris, and then left her to her own devices. He drew some satisfaction from the fact that she annoyed Maurice, who was growing increasingly arrogant and unpleasant.

The daily bustle of Nohant did not reach his room on the second floor, but if anything happened to disturb his mood or interfere with his work, he fell into uncontrollable anger. There was, for instance, an unpleasant affair brought about by the doltish Fontana and the prying Mademoiselle de Rozières. Chopin had for a time given lessons to her in Paris, and had even recommended her to George Sand as a piano teacher for Solange. Now this sentimental and pretentious creature proved intrusive and meddlesome. She showered George Sand with letters and won the favor of this kindhearted and easily moved woman by disclosing a life secret: she had fallen in love with—of all people—Antoni Wodzinski. Frederic had almost forgotten what the name of the Wodzinskis had meant to him; he referred to Antoni as an amiable harebrained boy who had failed to pay him back money he owed him. Then he had received the unexpected news that

Maria Wodzinska was about to marry Jozef Skarbek, and for the first time realized that he had become indifferent to the whole situation. Much water had flowed under the bridge since the "gray hour." It seemed of no concern to him that Maria was marrying a boy several years younger than herself, of whom Chopin knew only that he was the son of his godfather, merely a reminder of Zelazowa Wola.

But at that very time he received from Fontana a piece of news that upset him considerably. His Paris factotum had given Antoni Wodzinski, who was about to go to Poland for his sister's wedding, a most improper souvenir: it was a portrait of Chopin by Danton. Frederic openly communicated his misgivings to his kind but blundering friend:

They won't believe that it has not come from me. In Antoni's home I am listed otherwise than as a pianist. Some persons will interpret your gift in a completely false way. You don't know them! It will all come back to me here, in a completely different light. These are very delicate matters that one mustn't touch. But it's done, it's too late. Please, my dear, don't tell anyone what I have written here; let it remain between ourselves. If I don't erase it, it is because I am sure you will understand me. Don't reproach yourself in any way. Love me and write. If Antek hasn't gone yet, please leave things as they are, for otherwise it will be worse; he will tell Mademoiselle de Rozières everything, for he is kind but weak. And she is indiscreet, eager to show off her *intimité* with him, always ready to meddle in other people's business, and she will make a mountain out of an anthill. It won't be the first time she does this. She is (between ourselves) an unbearable pig, who by some strange means has dug her way into my enclosure and digs and digs, looking for truffles among roses.

These were sharp words. And there was further trouble in store. Upon his arrival in Poland, Antoni Wodzinski fell ill, and Mademoiselle de Rozières contemplated the distant journey to Poland, "to save his life." Chopin was irritated by this zeal and indiscretion; moreover, he feared that this spinster would take to Poland a heavy portmanteau of Parisian gossip, and that she would return with an even heavier load of Warsaw gossip. "She knows about my past," Chopin complained to Fontana, probably referring to his liaisons with George Sand and with Delphine. But most of all he was angered by Mademoiselle de Rozières' efforts to obtrude her attentions on George Sand, by her long letters about her unfortunate romance with Antoni, and by the result of her confidences—George Sand's friendship for her. He was jealous of what he thought belonged to him in this woman so occupied by her work, by politics, friends, children, and her household. He wanted her tenderness and sympathy to be his exclusive possession, and the importunate Mademoiselle de Rozières was striving to appropriate that sympathy for herself. "A stick, a stick, that's what she needs, the old hag," he wrote in a rage.

Such incidents filled him with disgust and impatience. He needed indulgence, special consideration, and help, to enable him to cope with his difficult tasks. This feeling reflected not only his weak constitution but also his lofty ideas of his art. He took it for granted that George Sand should remember every detail concerning his medicines and his diet, that she should regularly send his chocolate to his room in the morning and his bouillon at noon. He was constantly charging Fontana with new commissions. He asked him to liquidate his apartment in the Rue Tronchet; he sent his valet back to him from Nohant, asking him to hire a new one. Fontana had to buy perfumes, gloves, and pastries; in addition, he served as Chopin's agent in dealing with publishers and as his copyist. "For heaven's sake, I beg you," the composer wrote to Fontana, "take good care of my manuscript, don't bend it, smear it, or tear it (all of which you don't know how to do, but I am writing because I love my boring compositions)."

Fontana scrupulously carried out all of Chopin's commissions. In October he closed the apartment in the Rue Tronchet and moved the furniture to the Rue Pigalle. In November, Chopin returned from Nohant to his pavilion. He lived there with Matuszynski, his physician-in-ordinary, who was now more gravely ill than his patient.

The manuscripts had been copied, the agreements with the

publishers signed. Before the close of 1841 there appeared the Prelude in C-sharp minor, the Polonaise in F-sharp minor (dedicated to Princesse Charles de Beauvau, Delphine's sister), the Tarantelle, and the Variation on the march in Bellini's *I Puritani* (in the *Hexameron* collection, without opus number).

At this point the faithful services of Fontana came to an end. A good friend and a fair pianist, he was unable to support himself in France; he tried his luck in Bordeaux and gave a concert in Paris, but in the end he decided to go to America, like many other Poles to whom the homeland remained closed.

Frederic was now absorbed in the life of the city, in the salons, and in his lessons. Among his pupils was an extraordinarily gifted eleven-year-old boy named Karl Filtsch, a German-Hungarian from Transylvania, for whom he predicted a future that would equal the careers of the greatest geniuses. In the evenings Chopin went to the opera or to the theater, or to visit in the homes of the Czartoryskis, the Platers, the de Rothschilds, or other great houses. His cabriolet also stopped in the Rue des Mathurins, where Delphine had her Paris residence. Frederic was a regular guest in her theater box, while she in turn dazzled the gatherings in his salon. Once again the exiled Polish aristocrats had material for gossip and disapproval. Delphine's friends counted her lovers; her enemies counted her years. But Delphine seemed to preserve her youth: in her thirty-fifth year her beauty was even more alluring than before. Her singing, too, was greatly improved, and Frederic always had an authoritative favoring word for the artistry of his friend, which left many princesses and countesses inconsolable.

On February 21, 1842, all these illustrious friends and acquaintances attended a concert given by Chopin at the Pleyel hall. This time he was supported by Madame Viardot-Garcia and Franchomme. The famous names and famous beauties, and all the elegance of their costumes and their rich jewels, did not eclipse the arrival of George Sand with her daughter Solange and Augustine Brault. The critic of *France musicale* commented that any other woman, on finding herself the object of as many glances as there are stars in the sky, would have been upset, but that Madame Sand only smiled and nodded with ease.

Chopin accompanied Madame Viardot-Garcia at the piano. For his solo performances he played his *Andante spianato*, the Mazurkas in A-flat major, B major, and A minor, the Ballade in A-flat major, three études from Opus 25 (those in A-flat major, F minor, and C minor), the Prelude in D-flat major, four nocturnes, and the Impromptu in G-flat major. The concert was extremely successful: it aroused the enthusiasm of the audience and received excellent reviews, and the returns were considerable.

During the night on which Paris was acclaiming Chopin in the Pleyel hall, Wojciech Zywny died in Warsaw at the age of eighty-six. It was hard for Frederic to become accustomed to the idea that he would never see again the owner of the yellow wig and the enormous snuffbox, who had had for so long a place at his parents' table. The man who was the symbol of an epoch in his life, who had discovered Bach to him, who had been the first to record his compositions, who had so often covered his eyes with his checkered handkerchief while he listened to his young pupil, was gone. As Frederic went back in thought to his old teacher, his longing to see his parents and his Polish friends was rekindled in him. He contemplated visiting the Wiesiolowskis. They were living in Poznan province, under Prussian rule; thus he could be on Polish soil without having to come in contact with the Russians.

His plans came to nothing because of a new blow. On April 20, 1842, Jas Matuszynski died. He had been ill of pulmonary tuberculosis a long time and had suffered hemorrhages, but no one had expected him to die so soon. Frederic had become as much accustomed to his friend's illness as he was to his own. Many a week when they lived together they had stayed in bed in their rooms comforting and nursing each other.

Jas's death had a destructive effect on Chopin. He was panic-stricken. Ever since his childhood he had been referring to Jas as a man "made of the same clay" as himself. He had the feeling that his apartment was haunted. He could not bear the sight of the corpse. There was no way of quieting him.

The Life and Death of Chopin

George Sand acted at once. On April 21st, Matuszynski was buried in the Montmartre cemetery, and a week later she took Chopin to Nohant. She had made up her mind not to return to the Rue Pigalle.

Her guests that summer were chosen from among the people whom Chopin liked best. Delacroix arrived early in June. He had just recovered from a severe cold and was exhausted after a two-day stagecoach trip over bad roads. He set up a studio in the attic, gave lessons to Maurice, and spent many hours with his *ami angélique*. He wrote about Nohant as follows:

This place is quite pleasant, and the hosts are most amiable. When we are not together at dinner, lunch, or billiards, or on a walk, each of us stays in his room, reading or resting. Sometimes, through the windows opened on the park, there come to us breaths of Chopin's music that mingle with the song of nightingales and the fragrance of the rose shrubs.

Delacroix drew a portrait of Chopin à la Dante, in profile, and at the end of his four-week sojourn, he wrote:

I spent some time tête à tête with Chopin, whom I like very much; he is a man of exceptional distinction and the most genuine artist I ever met. He is one of the few whom one can admire and respect.

After Delacroix left, Witwicki came for a few days, then Mademoiselle de Rozières, with whom Chopin's relations had improved, and finally the Viardots. The presence of friends had a comforting effect on Chopin, who shook off his depression and returned to work, although it seemed to be beyond his strength. He began to compose his Polonaise in A-flat major (Opus 53). He referred to it as "the Battle of Grochow." It is a gallopade of ghostly warriors fighting for Poland. The powerful rhythms and fierce emotional force of this work produce an almost painful tension. It is the most literal music among all of Chopin's works that convey the echoes of war; in it the most literal patriotism and the most characteristically Polish heroism are expressed in a universally understandable language.

This greatest of all the polonaises taxed its creator to such an extent that he had hallucinations; he would jump up from the piano dazed and run to George Sand to tell her about his visions. Alarmed, she moved her bed to her study, which was next to Frederic's room, in order to watch over him at night.

Among the other compositions written that summer were the magnificent Ballade in F minor (Opus 52), a true musical novel, boundlessly rich, and the Scherzo in E major (Opus 54), which embodies an emotion so perfectly sublimated that one can find in it what one pleases, joy or grief, happiness or despair.

In July, George Sand and Chopin went to Paris for a short time. They found ideal apartments for themselves in the Square d'Orléans, whither they moved toward the end of September, 1842.

The Square d'Orléans, a rectangular court with a lawn, trees, and a central fountain, was situated in the heart of Paris, isolated from street traffic, and protected from noise. The peaceful environment had attracted many artists; Kalkbrenner, Zimmermann, Alkan, Danton, Alexandre Dumas père, and the Viardots all lived in this "little Athens." It was Madame Marliani who found this charming place for her friends. George Sand rented a large apartment on the second floor at No. 5 for three thousand francs, Chopin had a drawing room and bedroom on the street floor at No. 9 for six hundred francs. Madame Marliani lived between them at No. 7.

The three households formed a kind of community. Madame Marliani was charged with the housekeeping, and luncheons and dinners were served in her apartment. "In this sad Paris we live as at Nohant," George Sand wrote. In the evening they would cross the courtyard to visit each other, "like good neighbors in the provinces." Once again Chopin gave concerts in his home, and George Sand organized discussions. Maurice was studying painting with Delacroix, *con furia,* as his mother said; he had a studio above her apartment, but no one could say with certainty whether his talent matched his zest. Solange, ever more beautiful and more malicious, who had been boarding in Chaillot, was given a little room of her own in her mother's apartment.

Frederic described his new apartment at length to his parents but did not mention Madame Sand. His father answered him: "By your last letter we are pleased to hear that the country air has improved your health, that you hope for a good winter, and that you have moved to a new apartment. But will you not be lonely if other persons do not move with you? You don't say anything about that."

Though he failed to explain, he did not feel lonely in the least. On the contrary, he was in high spirits. On invitations from Louis Philippe, he drove forth to give court concerts and to receive the mementos bestowed on him in royal tribute. In the Rue des Mathurins he feared surprises less than ever before; Krasinski, although still in love with Delphine, had yielded to his stern father and made up his mind to marry the Countess Eliza Branicka. Chopin found a new servant, a Pole by the name of Jan, with whom he could speak his native tongue. He accepted only gifted pupils and only such as were highly recommended. Liszt sent him a talented Russian bearing the German name of Wilhelm von Lenz, who at once quarreled with George Sand; he made several guesses as to the nature of her liaison with Chopin and left behind some rather subjectively colored memoirs. Frederic's greatest joy and pride was Filtsch. This favored pupil would play the E minor concerto with Chopin performing the orchestral score on another piano. The young prodigy enraptured not only the other listeners but the author of the concerto himself, who was known to be exacting when it came to the performance of his own works. After one such soirée Madame Sand kissed the boy, and Liszt said: "If this youngster begins a concert tour, I'll close my shop."

The year of 1842 saw the publication of two compositions, the Three Mazurkas (Opus 50) and the Mazurka in A minor, printed without opus number in the album *Notre temps*.

In 1843, the following works were published in Paris and Leipzig: the Impromptu in G-flat major (Opus 51), the Ballade in F minor (Opus 52), the Polonaise in A-flat major (Opus 53), and the Scherzo in E major (Opus 54). The Ballade was dedicated to the Baroness de Rothschild, and the Polonaise to Auguste Léo. Both were close friends of Chopin.

All of these works had been written in Nohant. According to George Sand, Chopin always longed for the countryside, but once he was there he hated it. If this is true, it does not seem to apply to Nohant during those years. In 1843 he went there as early as April. He wrote five new compositions—two nocturnes (in F minor and E-flat major) and three mazurkas (in B major, C major, and C minor). Deprived of the services of Fontana, he wrote to his publishers himself at the same time trying by tactful persuasion to charge his friend Grzymala with this task, which he found unbearable. The summer passed pleasantly; the guest rooms of the château were occupied successively by the Marlianis, Madame Viardot, and Delacroix, whom Chopin liked best. He made an excursion with George Sand to the valley of the Creuse River; they rode on donkeys, slept on straw, laughed at the primitive inns, and fared none the worse for all these discomforts. In August, Chopin went to Paris to fetch Solange, who tyrannized over everyone at home, and with whom he alone was charmed. In October he returned to the Square d'Orléans.

The severe autumn and winter of 1843 affected Chopin's health. Often ill, and always pretending that he felt fine, he tried to find some time for composition amidst the absorptions of his social life. He wrote the Berceuse in D-flat major; his friends were enraptured with its sweetness. Bohdan Zaleski entered in his diary, under date of February 2, 1844, a striking pen picture of an evening on which Chopin's friends gathered to hear him play.

At four o'clock I went to Chopin. . . . Pale, suffering, but in good spirits, inspired, he greeted me cordially, and sat down at the piano. It is impossible to relate what and how he played. For the first time in my life I felt the beauty of music so intensely that I burst into tears. I caught all the nuances of the master's emotions, and I perfectly remember the themes and impressions of each piece. He played first a marvelous prelude, then the berceuse, then a mazurka, then again the berceuse, then a magnificent polonaise, and finally, in my honor, an improvisation in which he evoked all the joyful and sorrowful voices of the past, leading them over into a mournful song, and ending with *Poland Has Not Yet Perished*, in all moods, from the warlike to the childlike and angelic. I could write a book about this improvisation.

Soon after this Chopin fell gravely ill. He was beset by gloomy thoughts, and once again the shadow of death fell on his own close circle. Camille Pleyel's mother died, and Frederic dragged himself from his bed to follow the funeral procession to the cemetery. At the grave, Chopin and Pleyel, with their arms around each other, wept together. Heine considered Chopin's state so disquieting that he mentioned it in his letters to the *Augsburger Allgemeine Zeitung*.

In the spring Chopin recovered and even took part in a concert given by Alkan. Chopin, Alkan, Pixis, and Zimmermann played parts of Beethoven's Seventh Symphony in an arrangement for four pianos.

This was his last show of energy in this period. A short time afterward a devastating shock came to him. His father died in Warsaw. Nicolas Chopin, at seventy-three, had fallen ill of a lung disease and his weakened heart had proved unequal to the strain. His thoughts were often on Frederic; he would gaze at the portraits and the busts placed next to his bed, and he expressed the wish that his absent son bear his death with resignation. He died on May 3, 1844, with Izabela and her husband, Barcinski, at his bedside. His last moments were calm; he died fully conscious. He asked that his body be opened after death, "lest he be subject to the sad fate of reviving in his coffin," as Barcinski wrote to Frederic. He said farewell to his family, and added, "I thank the Lord that he has permitted me to bring up such good, virtuous, and tender children."

Frederic was in the throes of grave crisis. Dejected, losing strength, falling from despair into apathy, he was unable even to write a letter to his family; he became ill and stayed in bed for two weeks. There is no doubt that in this misfortune George

Sand's kindness and devotion were his only comfort. She wrote a cordial letter to Frederic's mother, doffing her incognito for the first time, and began a friendly correspondence with Ludwika, expressing her maternal solicitude for Frederic. "This is my most pleasant task, which I have undertaken with joy and in which I have never failed," she wrote to Madame Justyna. As soon as Chopin recovered somewhat, she took him to Nohant.

Madame Sand's letters reassured Chopin's family in Warsaw, and his two sisters spoke with emotion of her friendly feeling for him. Nevertheless, it was decided that Ludwika should go to France to be with her brother at this difficult moment.

The news of her intended coming roused Frederic from his depression, and he even returned to work. He drafted his Sonata in B minor, and through Franchomme arranged for the publication of the Two Nocturnes (Opus 55) and the Three Mazurkas (Opus 56).

Madame Sand immediately wrote to Ludwika, offering the Jedrzejewiczs her Paris apartment and inviting them to Nohant. Foreseeing that Ludwika might be upset by Frederic's appearance, George Sand prepared her gently:

You will find my dear boy weak and much changed since you last saw him, but please don't be alarmed about his health. It has not been greatly different over the last six years, during which I have seen him every day. In the morning he has a fairly severe coughing spell. During the winter he has two or three more serious crises lasting two or three days each, and from time to time he suffers a little from neuralgia—this is his normal state. For the rest his chest is in good condition, and despite his delicate constitution, he has no lesion.

George Sand was genuinely glad that Ludwika was coming, and she felt that Frederic would be stimulated by his sister's presence:

His joy at seeing you, although mingled with deep and painful emotions that may weaken him the first day, will do him a great deal of good. I am so happy because of this that I bless you for your decision. . . . And so come, both of you. Please believe me that I love you in advance like a sister. Your husband, too, will be a friend whom I shall receive as though I had known him for a long time. I am only advising you that little Chopin—so we call the great Chopin, your brother—should have a good rest before you allow him to go to Nohant. It is a trip of two hundred miles, and somewhat tiring for him.

George Sand was not mistaken; seeing Ludwika meant for Frederic not only happiness but a return to life. Under the care of his servant Jan, he hastened to Paris to meet Ludwika at the stagecoach depot. Brother and sister did not conceal their tears when they fell into each other's arms early in August, 1844, after fourteen years of separation. Frederic settled the new arrivals in Madame Sand's apartment and did not leave them for a moment. They went sightseeing, attended performances at the theater and opera (where they heard *Les Huguenots*), visited friends from Warsaw, and placed a wreath of flowers on the grave of Jas Matuszynski. To honor his guests, Frederic arranged a reception and musical evening at his home, to which he invited many of his friends. But all this seemed to him not enough, and he took the Jedrzejewiczs to the Franchommes, the Léos, the Marlianis, and Mademoiselle de Rozières. Thus two weeks passed, and then they left for Nohant.

Madame Sand gave them a hearty welcome. She lodged the visitors in her study, that is to say, as close as possible to Frederic. In Ludwika she found an intelligent reader of her works and something of a writer; Kalasanty proved an educated and kind-hearted man. The couple were at once treated as friends and were liked by all the members of the household. Madame Sand read aloud to them from *La Mare au diable,* the novel she was then at work on, Solange was inseparable from Ludwika, and even the usually unsociable Maurice asked Kalasanty to teach him Polish.

The weather was beautiful. The little company went on excursions in the neighborhood, and in the evening the young people danced on the lawn and engaged in dramatic improvisations. On the piano rack in the drawing room there was the recently published Two Nocturnes, which Chopin had dedicated to his friend and pupil, Jane Stirling. He played a great deal, sometimes joining in four-handed performances with his sister or Solange. He was gay and serene, and enjoyed the animation in the house which had never seemed more pleasant to him.

He now felt that he was the most important person at Nohant. Toward Ludwika he acted the host. He had transferred some small part of Warsaw to French soil; he had linked a portion of his heritage with the values he had accrued in his own life. He passed from memories and dreams to reality as from one room to another.

Early in September he had to say farewell to this brief happiness. He escorted Ludwika and her husband to Paris. The Franchommes gave them a farewell party and concert; then the Jedrzejewiczs left for Warsaw via Vienna and Cracow, and Frederic returned to Nohant. Ludwika's luggage contained many gifts, among them a pencil drawing of her brother, made by George Sand, and a rosary, a gracious souvenir for her mother from her freethinking hostess.

"I assure you," George Sand wrote to Ludwika, "that you are the best physician he has ever had, because merely speaking to him about you is enough to restore to him his love for life." Chopin continued his work on the Sonata in B minor, but his thoughts were constantly with his sister, and his letters reached her at every station of her journey.

I am trying to find some trace that you have left, and all I see is the place on the sofa where you used to drink your chocolate, and the drawings that Kalasanty copied. You have left more of yourself in my room, and on my table lies your embroidery for my slippers, wrapped in tissue paper, and on my piano a little pencil that you had in your purse and that comes in quite handy.

He sent her his songs, described at length the life at Nohant, the work in the garden, the plans for remodeling the house. Concerning the children he added:

The Life and Death of Chopin

Solange is slightly indisposed today; she is staying in my room, and asks me to send her cordial regards to you. Her brother (kindness is not part of his nature, so don't be surprised that he has no word of thanks to your husband for the cigar clipper) will go to see his father next month, taking his uncle with him, lest he be bored.

He could now write about everything openly; he did not have to conceal or pretend anything. Ludwika's visit brought him closer to George Sand; emotionally it marked for him the linking of the two families. He referred to her in his letters as the "lady of the house," and this perhaps deliberate conventional designation embodied a more profound truth than he consciously realized. George Sand's house was his place on earth; it had become the indispensable condition of his existence. The lady of this house was the mistress of his life. Everything depended on her—his peace, his sense of security, his creative work, and even his health. On her also depended the freedom that both needed.

Their peculiar union was never more cordial than during those years. When Chopin late in autumn returned to Paris alone, he wrote to George Sand with the warmth of a friend, the solicitude of a guardian, the respect of an admirer, and the humor of a happy man. For her part, George Sand, as always when he left Nohant without her, wrote about him to her friends, with numerous commissions, counsels, and requests; she always asked them not to let him know that she was concerned about him. Thus she surrounded Chopin with a conspiratorial organization for solicitous care, which sometimes included even servants. When he failed to write, she worried about his health and asked her friends to find out how he felt. "I could not do without these preoccupations, which constitute my happiness and my life," she wrote to Madame Marliani toward the end of 1844.

Only one other person occupied a place comparable to Chopin's in her thoughts and emotions. This was Maurice, who knew it. George Sand wrote to her son: "Decidedly, I couldn't live without you and without my poor ailing friend."

CHAPTER

32

Storms

AFTER the summer holidays of 1844, Solange did not return to the boardinghouse in Chaillot but stayed with her mother in the Square d'Orléans. This seemingly unimportant fact had far-reaching consequences. It brought brother and sister, two individuals of radically different character, under the same roof. The two had opposite tastes, opinions, sympathies, and antipathies. The incompatibility of their natures had been evident from their childhood, which was marked by violent conflicts and by extreme indiscretions on the part of their parents.

Their upbringing had been erratic. Maurice left school at the age of fifteen, and although he had many tutors, his education and his manners alike failed to raise him above the common level. He began to consider himself an artist and eagerly studied painting, with the encouragement of his mother. Solange had grown up in less favorable circumstances. She had been first under the care of her mother, then of her father, then of her grandmother, and then again of her mother. At one point, Baron Dudevant had kidnaped the child from Nohant while George Sand was away, taking her to his house in Guillery; the mother was able to get her back only with the help of the police.

After 1838, when Dudevant, who had been separated from his wife for two years, finally renounced his right to have Maurice, the children had only one parent—a mother who was absorbed in her work and her personal life. Each child wanted to have as much of her attention as possible, and brother and sister engaged in a jealous rivalry for her favors. But their chances were not equal.

Solange had heard her mother say that she was pretty and wicked, and that Maurice was handsome and good. Most often Solange was told that she was wrong and Maurice that he was right. Whatever Solange did was judged coldly and objectively; whatever Maurice did met with enthusiasm or at least complaisance. The mother said of him, "Not only our hearts but also our characters are so completely in accord that we cannot live one day without each other."

George Sand was unable to conceal her preference for her son. Just as her grandmother had idealized her son, Aurore's father, so she idealized Maurice. When he was only nine she wrote to him: "I dreamed last night that you were as big as I am. I could not recognize you. You came to embrace me, and I was so happy because of it that I wept. When I awakened, I found Solange at my side; she had climbed into my bed and it was she who was kissing me." This dream symbolizes George Sand's relationship with her children: Solange yearned for her mother's love, but her mother craved her son's caresses and in her dreams loved him like an adult.

Deprived of paternal affection—Dudevant had never liked her— and unloved by her mother, Solange had a feeling of inferiority. She was increasingly resentful of her brother, hostile to her mother, and obsessed with a desire to wreak her frustration on them both. This led to violent clashes in the household.

George Sand made vain attempts to conciliate her daughter; she appealed to the girl's good sense and to her vanity, and in the end sent her off to a boardinghouse. Solange became calmer for a time and developed a great attachment to Madame Bascans, the owner of the boardinghouse. But upon her return to her mother's home, the old resentments and conflicts flared up again.

Solange, at sixteen, had grown tall and alluring; she was vivacious and coquettish, child and woman in one. She had blond hair and beautiful black eyes; she knew how to please and was eager to be liked. Except for Madame Viardot, everyone in George Sand's entourage preferred her to her brother. Maurice was then twenty-one years of age; he was black-haired, of olive complexion, with rosy cheeks and a small, carefully groomed mustache. In appearance he resembled his mother. In disposition he was like his father—he was domineering and inclined to self-worship, and had a passion for elegance. He was self-assured in relation with others, and in his dealings with his sister did not disguise his innate callowness.

After her return from the boardinghouse, Solange had to contend with an additional rival. George Sand, disappointed in her own daughter and motivated by her love for children, had adopted Augustine Brault, a distant cousin, in whom she found the qualities that Solange lacked—submissiveness and devotion. She paid for the girl's education, took her to Nohant, and was overjoyed when she realized that this pretty and meek poor relation was not indifferent to Maurice. Solange disliked Augustine, taunted her about her lowly origin, and tyrannized over her. As Maurice's feeling for Augustine grew, Solange came to see in her an enemy, all the more so because in their daily conflicts these two were in league against her. Realizing that she was engaged in an unequal struggle, she began to look for an ally; she did not have far to seek.

Chopin was aware of everything that was going on among the young people. At first his only wish was to work in peace and to be spared the intolerable distraction of petty family squabbles. But when the situation grew so tense that even George Sand proved unable to cope with the daily civil war, he abandoned his neutral attitude.

He did not wish to be a third party in the struggle of the two children fighting for their mother's affections, but in fact he was. He considered his position to be something like that of a father, though Maurice for his part refused to grant him such authority. Jealous of his mother, he had long nurtured a hidden hostility to Frederic, which in the end came into the open. He made no obeisance to Chopin's genius; he was not impressed by the composer's fame or attracted by his grace and humor. Excursions, vacations, and amusements they all shared, even gifts from Chopin, among them a gold watch, failed to soften the young man's growing resentment. "Nurse him if he is sick," his mother wrote to him. "Take my place for a little while. If you were sick, he would gladly take my place at your side." Yet no one has recorded that Maurice ever showed any concern for the invalid Chopin.

Frederic easily made his choice between the contestants in this situation. Solange had always been his favorite, while Maurice had long seemed antipathetic to him. His animosity toward the youth might have remained suppressed for a long time, had it not been for the presence of Solange. Her restlessness, her excitability, her critical mind, and her will to resist suddenly bared all the conflicts latent in this precariously built family structure.

Chopin had many reasons for concerning himself with other matters. During the winter of 1844-45 he was ill several times. He had many pupils, and he was at work on new compositions. Nevertheless, he felt that the atmosphere in the household was deteriorating from day to day. At first he personally seemed to be unaffected; only his Polish servant became the target of criticisms.

"Jan is devoted but stupid," Madame Sand had opined. Maurice and Augustine eagerly seized upon this remark. They scoffed at the servant's broken French, ridiculed his obsequious manners, and generally treated him with contempt. Chopin preferred to close his eyes to these manifestations of malice, which for all their unpleasantness were trifling. But more serious trouble was brewing.

George Sand conceived the idea of legalizing her adoption of Augustine, which Frederic considered unfortunate. He looked with a suspicious eye on Maurice's flirtations with his cousin, and he thought that George's unavowed hope that Augustine would become Maurice's wife was naïve. His arguments failed to convince George Sand, whose disagreement with Chopin further encouraged Maurice's aggressiveness. The atmosphere in the household in the Square d'Orléans became tense. After his years of fruitful work, at a time when his friendship with George Sand seemed most cordial, Chopin found himself confronted with a crisis that was mounting slowly but irresistibly.

In May, 1845, Chopin published his Berceuse (Opus 57) and the Sonata in B minor (Opus 58), and in June he hastened to Nohant, perhaps hoping that the domestic clouds darkening his life in the city would be dispersed in the country.

Actually, the first weeks of his stay in Nohant proved happy ones. He was examined by Dr. Papet, whose opinion was reassuring. George Sand wrote to Madame Marliani: "He [Dr. Papet] found all his organs perfectly sound, but thinks that he has a tendency to hypochondria and that he will continue to worry until he reaches the age of forty and his nerves lose their excessive sensitiveness."

Despite a long period of bad weather, Frederic's health was not impaired. He enjoyed the visits of Madame Viardot and of Adolf Gutmann, who was about to begin a concert tour and who intended to visit Chopin's family in Warsaw. As usual, Chopin was most pleased by the visit of Delacroix and wrote about him to Franchomme in enthusiastic terms: "He is the most admirable of all artists. I spent delightful moments with him. He adores Mozart and knows all of his operas by heart." Madame Sand added warm words to his letters to Ludwika, to whom she offered as a memento the manuscript of *La Mare au diable,* which she had read aloud to the Jedrzejewiczs a year before.

Yet the atmosphere in the household continued tense. Maurice and Augustine became openly hostile, and their petty persecution of Jan now assumed the character of an indirect attack on Chopin. Solange had frequent quarrels with Maurice, and whenever she failed to win the upper hand she would burst into tears. Chopin was particularly annoyed by Maurice's rudeness and the vulgar abuse he heaped on his sister. And whenever he defended Solange, he himself became the butt of Maurice's attacks. Day after day passed amid sarcastic altercations and chicaneries.   *trickeries*

"There is a great storm outside and in the kitchen too," Frederic wrote to Ludwika, referring to his poor Jan, who finally became

(shik ā ɴ eries)

a scapegoat not only to Maurice but also to his fellow-domestics. Even Madame Sand reprimanded Jan, and Frederic thought that he might have to dismiss his faithful retainer for the sake of peace.

It was true that the reverberations of the family conflict reached him through the back door. There was something thoroughly trivial and humiliating in this situation. At bottom he cared little for Maurice and Augustine and their pseudo-love, or even the liaison they had perhaps entered upon under the mother's protective wing. Why was he involved in all this offensive rivalry, these tactless affronts, this cheap hatred? He fled to his room, but the place that had formerly witnessed his loftiest flights was now the scene of discomforts and anxieties of the most earthly kind. He tried to absorb himself in his work, but found no relief in it. He wrote the mazurkas in A minor, A-flat major, and F-sharp minor that later were published as his Opus 59, and he set down the preliminary drafts of his Barcarolle and of the Sonata for cello and piano, the Polonaise-Fantaisie, and the music for two songs by Zaleski—all this with great effort and with shaken confidence in his strength. "I don't play much, for my piano is out of tune, and I compose even less," he wrote to his family soon after his arrival in Nohant.

He spent most of his time in his room, where he was visited only by George Sand and Solange. Madame Sand often found her daughter with Chopin and could not help noticing that in his presence this rude and aggressive girl was the embodiment of refinement and serenity. It is not clear what brought these two together—possibly their pastimes, such as music, long drives, walks in the park and fields with George Sand's dogs, all described by Chopin in his letters to his family. Perhaps there were still other things that he did not mention. "Yesterday Solange interrupted my work by asking me to play on the piano with her; today she wanted me to watch the cutting of a tree," he wrote. On another occasion he reported: "Solange, who has just brought me some chocolate for a snack, asks me to write that she embraces Ludwika. She is very kindhearted."

He desperately needed the presence of a kindhearted partisan. George Sand more and more often sided with Maurice; Frederic felt hurt by this and was all the more eager to welcome Solange when she ran to him. They probably exchanged complaints and comforted each other, and it must have gratified Solange to have won over to her side the man who up until then had belonged exclusively to her mother. Now a young woman of seventeen, she had grown even prettier; George Sand said that she looked "beautiful as the day" when she was mounting her horse. Solange had not known love, and her sympathy for Chopin may have been her first substitute for it. Frederic probably also allowed himself some wishful dreams, and it is not impossible that occasionally he thought that this child to whom he wanted to be a father might become his wife. This much is certain, that their intimacy attracted attention, that it gave rise to speculation and gossip, even to the implausible legend that Chopin had asked George Sand for Solange's hand and had been rejected. The fact remains that George Sand looked unfavorably on their friendship, and that Maurice found in it a new stimulus for his animosity toward them.

The changes taking place in the life of this family had become so marked that even strangers noticed them. Mademoiselle de Rozières mentioned them in her letters, and even Ludwika questioned her brother as to the truth of the rumors that had apparently reached Warsaw.

George Sand, too, must have become aware of these changes. In her memoirs she wrote that Chopin was "beginning to lose his confidence" in her, and these words probably refer to the year 1845. Her own surmise may not have been apt, but it seems certain that Chopin had begun to feel out of place in her home. As he realized his growing estrangement from his adoptive family, his thoughts were increasingly with his own. This is best proved by his correspondence, which was addressed to Ludwika but was destined to reach all his relatives in Warsaw. Although rather unskilled as a writer, he began at that time to write great letters of two thousand words or more each, which it took him a day or two, sometimes a whole week, to compose. They constituted a kind of diary; he would break off a passage on any occasion, at any point, and begin again without transition. "I must shave, because I have a long beard, so I will stop this letter again." And then, "I have shaved," and so on.

In these letters he discussed all sorts of things—important, unimportant, amusing, sad. He quoted anecdotes, reports from Paris, piquant gossip about Victor Hugo, puns; he mentioned "the electromagnetic telegraph between Baltimore and Washington," the first railroad, gondolas on the Seine, the tunnel under the Thames, monuments and fireworks, Meyerbeer, Liszt, Mendelssohn, princes and country fairs, persons living and dead, his own family and strangers, servants and dogs. He recorded all the details of his everyday life, every idea that occurred to him. At bottom these letters reflected his need to converse with someone close to him, his perennial yearning for a home.

I feel strange this year; in the morning I often look into the room adjoining mine, but no one is there. Sometimes it is occupied by a friend who has come for a few days. And I no longer drink chocolate in the morning, and I have placed my piano differently. . . . I am always with one foot in your abode, and with the other in the adjoining room, where the lady of the house is working, and I am not at all in my own place at this moment, but as usual in some strange space. These are surely those *espaces imaginaires*, but I am not at all ashamed of this; after all, we have an old proverb, "Through his imagination he went to a coronation," and I am a real blind man of Mazovia. And so, without looking very far, I have written three new mazurkas that will probably be published in Berlin.

His sojourn in the *espaces imaginaires* did not bring more fruit that year. At the end of the summer Frederic wrote to Ludwika more or less as he had written after his arrival in Nohant:

I don't know why, but I am unable to do anything serious; yet I am not lazy. I don't go about as I did with you, and for whole days and nights I stay in my room. But I must finish some of my manuscripts before my departure from here, because I cannot write in the winter.

Storms

He did not succeed in this, and the manuscripts he spoke of, including the Barcarolle and the Polonaise-Fantaisie, returned with him unfinished to Paris, where he arrived on November 28, 1845. But before the close of the year there were published in Berlin (and in January, 1846, in Paris) the Three Mazurkas (Opus 59), which are especially notable for their fresh and innovational quality.

Life in the Square d'Orléans proceeded as before—that is to say, amidst "storms outside" and within. Only the kitchen had quieted down. Chopin had dismissed Jan, who was replaced by Pierre, a Frenchman. "I would never have dismissed him," Frederic wrote to Ludwika, "except that he had begun to irritate the others. The children made too much fun of him, so I couldn't keep him, as I would have done if I could have considered only myself."

George Sand's household was increased by two persons. Augustine had moved in to stay, and at the same time Lucie, daughter of the old servant Françoise, had come from Nohant as Solange's *dame de compagnie*. The entire household went as a unit to the theater, the opera, the ballet (though there was no room for Chopin in their box), quarreled internally as a unit, and as a unit suffered a siege of influenza.

Frederic was inwardly torn and for the first time ventured a critical remark about George Sand: "The lady of the house has such a bad cold and sore throat that she must not leave her room, which makes her very impatient. The better the health one has, the less patience with physical suffering. There is no medicine for this in the world; even reason is of no avail."

In Paris there were storms, "thunder, lightning, hail, and snow" all at once. The bad weather continued through the Christmas holidays, and led Frederic to write to his sister:

Our beautiful Christmas! It is not known here. Christmas Eve was sad, because they're sick and refuse to see a doctor. They have extremely severe colds; they have gone to bed for good. Everyone curses Paris for its climate, but they forget that in winter the country is even worse and that winter is winter everywhere. It's a few bad months to live through. I often wonder how impatient people could live under a sky even less kind than the one here. Sometimes I'd give a couple of years of my life for a few hours of sun. I have survived so many persons stronger and younger than myself that I think I'm immortal.

Chopin resumed his lessons and his other activities. The first to report that year was the Baroness de Rothschild, and he did not have to wait long for other pupils. But he no longer had Filtsch, who had died in May, 1845, at the age of fifteen. Chopin was greatly affected by his death.

During lessons, Chopin would sit at the smaller of his two Pleyel instruments and his pupil at the larger. When he did not feel well, he would rub his temples with Eau de Cologne and direct his pupils while reclining on a couch. The metronome was always going during a lesson.

Usually each lesson lasted an hour, but occasionally a session would go on for four or five hours, changing into a concert. There are many references to such lessons in memoirs by Chopin's pupils, but it is difficult to ascertain what is truth and what is legend in such testimony—how much of it is a record of correct observation and how much is fancy stemming from adoration of the master.

On the piano rack there were always several pencils. Chopin used these to mark the texts. He also broke them in pieces during the lessons. The memoirs do not supply us with any details about this destructive habit, but apparently the domestic storms in George Sand's household raged in effigy even in Chopin's drawing room.

image
of a
person

CHAPTER

33

Prince Karol and
Lucrezia Floriani

ON JUNE 25, 1846, the daily *Courrier français* of Paris began
serial publication of George Sand's *Lucrezia Floriani*; a
year later this novel appeared in book form. It recounts the
romance of Prince de Roswald, who bears the Polish name of
Karol, and Lucrezia Floriani, an actress. The character of Karol
was based on the personality of Chopin, and under the name of
Lucrezia, George Sand portrayed herself. Although the plot of
the novel does not parallel the actual course of the relationship
between George Sand and Chopin, the two protagonists, and
especially their psychological portraits, offer likenesses so faithful and apt that there can be no doubt as to their actual proto-
types.

Karol, slender, sickly, weak, "with the beautiful face of an
angel," is six years younger than Lucrezia, who is the mother of
four children and "widow of many lovers"; he has "only one true
passion in his life—filial love." Lucrezia is "rather slight in stature
and somewhat stout," and she has a beautiful voice. The external
resemblance of the characters to Chopin and George Sand carries
through even in details: Karol drinks chocolate instead of coffee,
he dislikes Shakespeare, and Lucrezia concentrates all her affection on her son.

As regards their dispositions and tastes, the two lovers are
separated by a gulf.

331

"See the earth, how beautiful it is," says Lucrezia.

"I don't see the earth, I see only heaven," answers Karol. The two complement each other, and they are seized by a love in which Karol "breathed only with the breath of Lucrezia. . . . He could not understand anything or think anything unless she stood between him and the external world." But soon complications arise. Karol is jealous of his mistress's past, of the servant, the priest, the doctor, and the children. He torments her and himself, and when Lucrezia refuses to become his wife, he begins to draw away from her; he grows indifferent to her and in the end ceases to love her.

The thing that beyond any other makes life with Karol difficult is his reserve. Lucrezia says that no one could "even suspect what was going on in him":

The more exasperated he was, the colder was his manner, and one could have an idea of the degree of his rage only by estimating the degree of his icy courteousness. It was at such moments that he was truly unbearable, because he wanted to reason and to subject real life—of which he had never understood anything—to principles that he could not define. Then he would rise to wit, a false and glittering wit, in order to torture those whom he loved.

Lucrezia suffers a great deal because of Karol's aloofness, and complains that "of all the fits of anger, of all the retaliations, the blackest, most cruel, and most hurtful is that which remains cold and polite." Deserted by the man to whom she wanted to be a mother and a lover, deprived of the last love of her life, aware of the fact that her own feeling is weakening, and wearied beyond her strength by this relationship that has lasted for ten years, Lucrezia dies. The reader must conclude that Karol is the indirect cause of her death. In this respect the novel is not a correct forecast of reality; the real Lucrezia survived the real Karol.

The book had the effect of a bombshell. It aroused countless comments and speculations, and public opinion was almost unanimous in condemning George Sand. Heine wrote a few years later: "She has hideously mistreated my friend Chopin in a repellent book divinely written." Many readers felt that Karol was a caricature of Chopin, and the novel a scurrilous attack on a friend and lover.

These charges seem unjust. There is no trace of conscious malice in the sharply drawn and meticulously analytical portrait of the Prince. He is depicted as a neurasthenic and as a fascinating aesthetic personality, complex but essentially noble. He has his defects and weaknesses, but also uncommon qualities such as a mere caricaturist would never have discerned in him. His reticence may be depressing, he cannot be easily understood, but there is something more than mere literary psychologizing in the insight conveyed in Lucrezia's words: "A microscope would be required to read a soul accessible to so little of the light that the living absorb."

This is possibly the most essential truth that George Sand could utter about Chopin—that after eight years of intimacy he remained inscrutable to her and at bottom a stranger. Her judgment of Frederic is couched in almost the same words as her description of Karol. Of the actual man she wrote: "Nothing was ever manifested of his inner life, whose mysterious and intangible expression was his masterpieces, and whose sufferings were not betrayed by his lips."

Such a discovery must have shocked George Sand, who considered herself a psychologist and a physician capable of healing the wounds of love. It also meant that Chopin, who had entrusted the direction of his daily life to her, had preserved his inner independence, his own character, and above all, his own ideas about art and creation. What, then, was the place of this novel in their life?

Lucrezia Floriani was written during the first five months of 1846, when the relations between George Sand and Chopin were becoming more and more strained, but when it was scarcely to be supposed that they were close to a break. On the other hand, the psychological dissection of Chopin, performed in public, suggests that George Sand's feeling for him could not have been very profound at the time. It seems likely that *Lucrezia Floriani* represents a more or less unconscious attempt on the part of its author to free herself from Chopin. She doubtless wanted to arrive at a clear picture of the nature of this man who was so close to her and yet so distant, thus to lighten the oppressive weight of a liaison that had long since ceased to subsist on passion.

George Sand actually made some effort to deny the significance of her confession. The only person who maintained that Karol had nothing in common with Chopin was herself. In her *Histoire de ma vie*, in which she indisputably wished to present herself in a favorable light, she tried to prove this, but with amazing clumsiness. The most important argument she advanced was that Karol is not an artist, as though this circumstance could have any essential bearing (indeed, the novel ascribes to Karol a *nature d'artiste*—an artistic temperament).

George Sand's denials are all the more strange because the method of transposing personal experiences into more or less discreet fiction, common to many other novelists, was especially characteristic in her case. She was, as has been said, primarily an observer, not a creator of worlds of her own envisioning; she took her themes ready-made from life, and closely modeled her characters on persons she had actually met. This is true of most of her novels; in the best known of them, the identities are patent. In *Consuelo* she portrayed Madame Viardot-Garcia so faithfully—and flatteringly—that her model read the successive installments of the story with the greatest eagerness; and *Elle et lui* was entirely devoted to recounting her relationship with de Musset.

While the charge that she had caricatured Chopin is manifestly unfair, it is true that the fictionalized character is treated with a nuance of hostility, conveyed in tone and atmosphere rather than in words. In any event, the author obviously sympathizes with Lucrezia, who is represented in a favorable light throughout the book.

How Chopin reacted to George Sand's new work is not quite clear. From *Histoire de ma vie* we learn that "every day he read the manuscript of it lying on the desk," and this seems plausible. But the author's remark that Chopin never suspected that Karol was a portrait of himself, and that he came to think so only later under the influence of her enemies, sounds like a bit of wishful thinking.

It is said that one of George Sand's children (perhaps Solange) said to Chopin, "Have you read *Lucrezia Floriani*? Mother put you in there." But even if this anecdote is apocryphal, it is difficult to assume that Chopin, who was a man of exceptional sensitivity and delicacy of feeling, could be blind to something so obvious. It is much more likely that his friend's exhibitionistic novel brought him a violent shock. Possibly, because of his chronic irresolution, he did not know how to cope with the situation confronting him, and in his helplessness waited for the first impact of his realizations to pass; it is also possible that in the end he thought that the best way out for him was to withdraw into himself and keep silent.

All this, however, is a matter of conjecture. The only extant example of any reference made by Chopin to this book is contained in a letter he wrote after the publication of George Sand's next novel, *Piccinino:* "I do not doubt that Ludwika will like this novel better than *Lucrezia,* which here too has aroused less enthusiasm than the others."

In June, 1846, when *Lucrezia Floriani* began to appear in Paris, Chopin was at Nohant. He had time for reflection, and he must have realized by then that he was losing his place in his adoptive home. Augustine Brault was now a full-fledged member of the family; George Sand, after paying the girl's parents to relinquish their rights, had legally adopted her. Maurice had gained complete ascendancy in the household, which he dominated at will, as his father had formerly done. He induced George Sand to dismiss Françoise as well as Pierre, the old gardener, who had served on the estate for forty years. "I hope that the young man and his cousin will look with more favor on the new servants," Chopin wrote.

He felt lonely that summer, despite the presence of many

visitors, including Eugène Lambert, Victor de Laprade, Emmanuel Arago, and Louis Blanc. The only guests he enjoyed were Delacroix and Laura Czosnowska, a friend from Warsaw. After Laura's departure he wrote: "Although they treated her courteously, they were not sorry when she left. The cousin did not like her, hence the son did not either; as a result there were jokes, the jokes led to rudeness, and since I disliked this, there is no longer any question about her." Delacroix, too, found the atmosphere of Nohant unpleasant that summer and left in disgust.

Chopin suggested that George Sand invite Nowakowski, a Polish musician then in Paris, but in vain. "I'd like to see him, but he isn't wanted here," he wrote.

He worked with difficulty, and complained to Franchomme: "I am doing everything I can to work, but without success. If this goes on, my new compositions will no longer suggest the warbling of birds or even the crash of breaking china. I must resign myself to this." In spite of his disturbed state, he completed his Barcarolle (Opus 60), the Polonaise-Fantaisie (Opus 61), and Two Nocturnes (Opus 62), the latter published that year. He also worked on three mazurkas (in B major, F minor, and C-sharp minor) and his Sonata for cello and piano.

One of his letters to his family at this time ran the length of two thousand words, and he returned to it ten times:

I wish I could fill my letter with the most cheering reports, but I know nothing except that I love you and love you. I play a little, and compose a little. With my sonata for cello and piano I am satisfied one day, another not. I lay it aside, then pick it up again. I have three new mazurkas in addition to the old ones [an illegible word follows], but time is needed to have good judgment. While I am composing a piece it seems good to me; otherwise I wouldn't write it down. Only later there comes reflection, rejecting or accepting it. Time is the best censor, patience the most excellent teacher. . . . I expect a letter from you soon, but I am not worried, and I know that being as large a family as you are it is difficult for all of you to gather together to write me a word, all the more so because the pen is not enough for us; I don't even know how many years we would need to talk enough *pour être au bout de notre latin*, as the proverb goes here. Therefore don't be surprised or downcast if you don't have a letter from me. The only reason for this is the same as with you: there is a certain unpleasant feeling mingled with the pleasure of writing to you, namely, the conviction that between us words are meaningless—one might say that even events are hardly meaningful.

"The pen is not enough"—thus Chopin wrote from the house of the author of *Lucrezia Floriani*. Between him and George Sand, too, words were meaningless, although in a different, even opposite, sense. If any "events" took place, it was only further to separate these two. The stuff of their common life, their mutual attachment, their trust, their need for each other, was worn thin. As always in such circumstances, a tense atmosphere prevailed. Any trifle provoked irritation.

"Your sister is a hundred times better than you àre," George Sand said to Chopin.

"Je crois bien," he answered coldly.

At this time there occurred an incident that assumed the significance of a crisis. George Sand mentions it in *Histoire de ma vie* in metaphorical but inaccurate terms. It seems that Chopin offended Maurice in an unexpected way, over some trivial matter. "A minute later they embraced, but a grain of sand had dropped into the calm lake, and then little stones began slowly to fall into it, one after the other." One day Maurice, exasperated by Chopin's scoffing at him, declared that he was ready to leave the house. "This could not come to pass—it would not have been right if it had," George Sand wrote. "Chopin could not endure my just and necessary intervention. He lowered his head and declared that I no longer loved him. What a blasphemy, after the eight years of my maternal devotion to him!"

A friend, Monsieur Péru, described the same incident in less poetic terms. It took place during a meal, at which a chicken was served; Maurice was given the breast, and Chopin a leg. This trifle touched off an explosion. Chopin, we are told, said, "I shall never consent to being treated as an object of charity." Maurice burst out with the declaration that he would leave the house, because he saw that there was no room in it for both of them.

Whatever the exact nature of this incident may have been, it marked the moment when George Sand was confronted with an alternative—Maurice or Chopin. The result of her choice was a foregone conclusion. She sided with Maurice against Chopin. Inwardly their liaison had broken down, although ostensibly it still stood. She wrote: "Chopin's friendship had never been a refuge for me in my sadness. My true strength came to me from my son."

In this atmosphere the summer of 1846 drew to a close. Chopin eliminated himself or was eliminated from the life of the household. Occasionally he would still take part in a pantomime or a *commedia dell'arte*, but most of the time he stayed alone in his room. He wrote:

The whole summer here has passed in various walks and excursions in the unfamiliar region of the *Vallée Noire*. I did not take part in them, because such things give me more fatigue than pleasure. I am tired, cheerless; all this affects my mood, and the young people don't enjoy me very much.

On November 10th he left for Paris. He never returned to Nohant. Madame Sand and her children stayed in the country throughout the winter.

Hence it could not be said in reality that the desertion was on Karol's part. Chopin wrote to George Sand from Paris, sent her souvenirs, and carried out her numerous commissions. This correspondence (six letters have survived) was held to an impeccably courteous style; it was impersonal and contained no reference to the situation that was the source of their conflicts and bitter feelings. In these letters Chopin wrote:

How good it is that your drawing room is warm, that the snow at Nohant is lovely, and that the young people are amusing themselves with the carnival. . . .

Today we have some sun and snow, as in Russia. I am very happy with this weather for your sake, and I imagine that you walk a great deal. . . .

Your letters made me very happy yesterday. This one should reach you on New Year's Day, with the customary bonbons. The weather is cold but pleasant for those who can walk, and I hope that your migraine is gone and that you walk in your garden as before. May you and all your family be happy in this coming year, and when you have an opportunity, please write to me that you are well.

Perhaps Lucrezia was right. Perhaps it is true that of all the possible retaliations, the blackest, most cruel, and most hurtful is that which remains cold and polite.

Romanticism and Common Sense

Aᴛ ᴛʜᴇ very time when George Sand's relations with Chopin were breaking down, two comic-opera marriages were in the making in her family. All these events are so interwoven that it is impossible to separate them.

As early as October, 1846, Chopin wrote to his family:

> There was talk of Italy for this winter, but the young people prefer to stay in the country. Nevertheless, next spring, if Solange takes a husband or Maurice a wife (the two things are on the anvil), ideas will surely change.

The artisan at the anvil was George Sand. The champion of free love, the revolutionist in morals, in this instance fell into the age-old pattern and behaved like a conventional dowager. She had long ago chosen a wife for Maurice; and although Augustine was not the exclusive claimant of his heart, George Sand persisted in her idea that her son should marry her adopted daughter.

She displayed even greater eagerness in trying to provide for the happiness of Solange with a husband of her maternal choice. Solange Dudevant was probably confronted by a situation exactly like that which had faced Aurore Dupin many years earlier: she dreamed of leaving the parental home, which had become intolerable, and she could do it by marrying. And there is some justification for assuming that George Sand for her part was concerned not only for her daughter's happiness but also for the peace of her own household.

The first man upon whom the mother looked with the eyes of a matchmaker was Louis Blanc, an old friend and one of the Nohant guests in the summer of 1846. This was a rather poor choice: the eminent socialist was interested in revolution, not in marriage, and as far as women were concerned, his admiration for George Sand was more ardent than his feeling for Solange. The plan was abandoned as speedily as it had been undertaken.

George Sand's second candidate was another guest of that summer, Victor de Laprade, a poet and a protégé of Pierre Leroux. This time the matchmaking made more headway, and news of it reached even the virtuous, straight-laced Laprade family in Lyon. Horrified at the thought of a close association with the notorious freethinker, they hastened to call their son home from Nohant.

Solange was indifferent to these undertakings, and George Sand was undaunted by her own failures. Only the third act of the comedy seemed to promise attainment of her goal. Fernand de Préault, a local nobleman, fell in love with Solange, and George Sand hastened to report to her friends that her daughter was "very much interested in her beautiful cavalier." Fernand was a handsome, pliable, and pleasant provincial, without much ambition or money, but the son of a respected family, and his solidity engendered confidence. Everything seemed to go well. George Sand watched over the young couple and did her best to make their sojourn at Nohant pleasant. She wrote plays and acted in them in masculine roles, and the *première* of one of these productions, a melodrama entitled *La Caverne ou la Taverne du crime*, was made a Christmas Day entertainment for the whole neighborhood.

Meanwhile, Chopin was freezing in the Square d'Orléans. He did not have the courage to leave his fireplace "even for a moment." When he drove to the Czartoryskis he wrapped himself "in every possible cloak." He continued to write letters to Nohant in the key of Prince Karol's icy politeness.

Early in February, 1847, Madame Sand, together with her

family, which now included Solange's fiancé, came to Paris. Suddenly warmer currents began to flow between George Sand and Chopin. Something like the old family life was resumed; Chopin played in Madame Sand's home, and Delacroix, describing one such gathering, wrote in his journal: "What a charming genius!" George Sand in turn appeared at Chopin's receptions; she was present at a soirée he gave in honor of Delphine Potocka ("You know how much I love her," he wrote to his family). On this occasion he played his sonata with Franchomme as his cellist.

Possibly, for Chopin and George Sand, three months' separation had blunted the edge of the old disagreements; possibly, too, the general excitement in connection with the impending marriage of Solange had relegated the family conflict to the background. Madame Sand had come to Paris to prepare the marriage contract and the bride's trousseau. But the two months that followed shifted events into an unexpected course.

There appeared on the scene an obscure sculptor named Auguste-Jean Clésinger, then thirty-three years old. A year before he had addressed a grandiloquent and ungrammatical letter to George Sand, thanking her for "happiness given him" by her novels; he had also dedicated to her a statue that he named "Melancholia." Won by the young man's enthusiasm, she invited him to her house immediately upon her return to Paris and received him with great kindness. He was a bumptious bohemian, a reckless adventurer, intoxicated with his first successes as an artist, completely uneducated but, according to current opinion, talented. Dark, tall, of athletic build and Herculean strength, he had atrocious manners, and was immediately disliked by Chopin. His past had been stormy. He was born in Besançon, where his father enjoyed a local reputation as a sculptor. Cardinal de Rohan became his patron and wanted to make a priest of him. Half a year later the young student abandoned theology for the chisel and brush. He went to Italy, but had to flee the country because of his debts. His father refused to receive him after his return, and the sculptor enlisted as a cuirassier. He left this service as a noncommissioned officer.

Clésinger soon became an intimate friend of the Sand household. He made a marble bust of the lady of the house and also asked Solange to pose for him. *La grande princesse,* as her mother called her, began to visit the studio of *le beau diable,* as Madame Viardot-Garcia called Clésinger. Solange was impressed by the temperament and picturesque figure of the artist, compared with whom her bread-and-butter fiancé seemed dull and uninteresting. One day she returned from the studio richer by the greatest experience of her life as a maiden; now she could no longer consider herself the betrothed of Fernand. She had a private talk with him and revealed her secret to her mother. Madame Sand, Solange, and Augustine left in haste for Nohant in Chopin's carriage.

Left alone in Paris, Frederic wrote to his family:

Solange is not going to marry yet; when they came here for the signing of the marriage contract, she changed her mind. I regret this and I am sorry for the boy, because he is quite decent and very much in love, but it's better that this has happened before the marriage than if it had happened afterward. The story runs that it is postponed, but I know what's behind all that.

He did know—although not the whole truth. From this point on, Madame Sand did not keep him informed.

Chopin continued his usual life in Paris, although he now occasionally worked at his compositions in the mornings, polishing the last three mazurkas he had written at Nohant. He also worked on three waltzes, in D-flat major, C-sharp minor, and A-flat major respectively, and revised his Sonata for cello and piano.

About this time he received from Poland a collection entitled *Songs of the Polish People,* which comprised nearly one hundred themes prepared by Oscar Kolberg. The book failed to arouse his enthusiasm, and he wrote of it bluntly:

The intention is good, but the shoulders too narrow. I often see similar things, and I think that nothing at all is better than that, because such labors only distort and make more difficult the work of the genius who one day will discover the truth there. Until then, all these beauties will be nothing but rouged puppets with glued-on noses, with legs shortened or on stilts, and they will be the laughing stock of those who behold them.

He gave many lessons, sometimes seven a day. One of his pupils was Madame Marie Kalergis. This beautiful, gifted Egeria, in love with love, might easily have reminded him of Delphine. It was not long before his friends began to couple him with his pupil with meaningful allusions; it is not known whether their guesses were correct.

He posed for portraits by Ary Scheffer, Winterhalter, Lehmann, and Antoni Kolberg, but he thought that the best likeness of him was achieved in a drawing made by George Sand and given by her to Ludwika. His relations with Madame Sand continued warm for the time being. In a letter to his family, begun on April 4th and finished on April 19, 1847, he wrote: "You are asking me about my plans for the summer. They are the same as always: I'll go to Nohant." Thinking of the difficulties that beset Solange's mother, he wrote: "If anyone deserves happiness, it is Madame Sand." He waited for her arrival in Paris, asked her about the date, in order to have her apartment heated, and communicated to Maurice any news he had from her.

Chopin opposed Solange's marriage with Clésinger, expressing his objection to George Sand, and since he was unaware of the actual situation, he tried to persuade her that there was no need to hurry the decision. His concern for Solange was motivated by common sense and his understandable sympathy for his favorite. By means of his participation he was probably trying to save his own increasingly precarious position in the Sand household. Fighting for Solange, he fought for himself, for his past and his future. His attitude doubtless also reflected the instinctive urges of husband and father that had come to frustration in him. George Sand divined this, and her words in a letter to Madame Marliani (the same words are repeated in *Histoire de ma vie*) hit the nail on the head: "Chopin unwittingly, and unable to stop himself, played the part of my lover, my husband, the proprietor of my thoughts and actions."

She looked at Chopin's intervention with hostility. His advice and warnings stirred her resistance all the more because she felt that he was meddling in matters that were no concern of his. And these matters were weighty. Developments followed one upon the other with lightning speed.

Toward the middle of April, Clésinger appeared at La Châtre demanding Solange's definite promise to marry him. *"La grande princesse* has become so human that she said yes," George Sand wrote. And she immediately enjoined upon Maurice: "Not a word of all this to Chopin; this is not his business, and once the Rubicon is crossed, the if's and but's can do only harm."

Thus Solange became the fiancée of Clésinger, and George Sand, while keeping this fact concealed from Chopin, wrote to all her friends about the idyllic happiness of the lovers at Nohant. In a letter to Madame Marliani, dated May 6th, she even indulged in a bit of romantic optimism:

In two weeks Solange will marry Clésinger, a sculptor of great talent, who earns a great deal of money, and who can assure her a brilliant existence. . . . Apparently she has found what she dreamed of. May God make this come true. For my part, I like the boy very much, and so does Maurice. He has little polish at first sight, but he is full of the sacred fire, and for some time I have been observing him without his being aware of it. Thus I know him as well as one can know someone who wants to please. You will tell me that this is not always enough, and you will be right. But what fills me with confidence is the fact that the main feature of his character is a sincerity maintained to the point of rudeness . . . He is industrious, courageous, active, resolute, persevering.

This optimism lasted only for twenty-four hours. On May 7th, Madame Sand wrote to Maurice, then with Baron Dudevant at Guillery: "Come quick, with or without your father. Our position is untenable."

Chopin was unaware of all these anxieties; he was seriously ill. "On May 2nd I had a severe attack of asthma, and for two weeks I was confined to my room, but I didn't suffer much," he wrote to his family afterward. His health was deteriorating, and even when

The Life and Death of Chopin

there were no acute episodes, it must have been a subject of concern to him. He was now unable to climb the stairs and had to be carried to his apartment. The violence of this most recent attack was such that his friends feared the worst.

Princess Marcelina Czartoryska, Grzymala, Gutmann, Madame Marliani, and Mademoiselle de Rozières visited the patient. He was treated by Dr. Molin, and after a week he was out of danger. On May 11th, Delacroix, who had till then not been admitted to the bedside of the "poor sick lad," was allowed to see his friend and to talk to him until "long after midnight."

Chopin's illness came as a shock to George Sand, who was informed of it by Princess Marcelina after the crisis was past. On May 8th she wrote to Mademoiselle de Rozières:

I am quite frightened. Is it true that Chopin was very ill? The Princess wrote to me yesterday that he is out of danger. But why don't you write to me? I am sick with worry and I am dizzy as I write this. I cannot leave my family at this moment, when I don't even have Maurice to save appearances and protect his sister from malicious gossip. I suffer very much, I assure you. Write to me, I implore you. Tell Chopin what you think proper about me. I don't dare write to him; I fear that I might upset him. I fear that Solange's marriage may displease him very much, and that each time I mention it he may suffer an unpleasant shock. Yet I could not conceal it from him, and I had to act as I did. I cannot concede that Chopin should be the head and adviser of my family; my children would not accept this, and the dignity of my life would be lost.

There is some lack of sincerity in George Sand's sudden and belated concern about Solange's reputation, and in her exaggerated attitude regarding possible loss of her dignity. Her concern about Chopin's health, however, was genuine.

Even more revealing is a letter of May 12th to Grzymala, in which she wrote:

I knew in a vague and uncertain way that he was ill, twenty-four hours before receiving the letter from the good Princess. Thank that

346

angel from me, too. It is impossible for me to tell you what I suffered during those twenty-four hours; but whatever might have happened, my circumstances would not have permitted me to move.

Well, this time he is saved once again, but how dark is the future in that quarter!

I do not yet know whether my daughter will be married here in a week or in Paris in two weeks. At all events, I shall be in Paris for a few days at the end of the month, and if Chopin can be moved, I shall bring him back here. My friend, I am as happy as possible about my daughter's marriage, because she is transported with love and joy, and because it seems to me that Clésinger deserves this, that he loves her passionately, and that he will create for her the existence she desires. Nevertheless, one suffers a great deal when one makes such a decision.

I think that Chopin, too, must have suffered in his corner over not knowing, not being informed, and not being able to give any advice. But it is impossible to take into account his advice on the real affairs of life. He has never correctly interpreted facts or understood human nature in any respect; his soul is all poetry and music, and he cannot bear anything that is different from himself. Moreover, his influence in my family affairs would mean for me the loss of all dignity in the eyes of my children, and all their love.

Talk to him and try to make him understand in a general way that he must refrain from being concerned about them. If I tell him that Clésinger (whom he dislikes) deserves our affection, he will only hate him the more and will arouse Solange's hatred. All this is difficult and delicate, and I don't know of any means to calm and restore a sick soul that is irritated by the efforts one makes to cure it. The illness that gnaws at this poor man morally and physically has long been killing me, and I see him go without ever having been able to do him any good, because it is the anxious, jealous, and suspicious affection he has for me that is the principal cause of his misery. For seven years I have lived like a virgin with him and with others; I have aged prematurely, really without effort or sacrifice, I was so weary of passion, so disillusioned—and that irretrievably. If any woman on earth should have inspired him with the most absolute

confidence, it was myself, and he has never realized it; and I know
that many people accuse me, some of having worn him out by the
violence of my passion, others of having reduced him to despair by
my follies. I think you know what is true of all this. As for him, he
complains to me that I have killed him by deprivation, while I was
certain that I should have killed him if I had acted otherwise.

This passage confirms what Chopin wrote to Delphine in 1840
—that his romance with George Sand had been short-lived. Their
relation had been purely platonic for eight years—not seven, as
George Sand states—and her remark that throughout this time
she had lived as a virgin "with others" seems to be a bold lapse
of memory.

Her denial of the accusation that she had been "killing" Chopin
either by the violence of her passion or by "deprivation" sounds
belated. Many years had gone by since that spring in Marseille
and that first summer at Nohant when Chopin had found himself
discarded as a lover. Their "white marriage" had given freedom
to both of them. What might be "killing" Chopin was something
different. It was the realization that he was losing his privileges in
her family—and Madame Sand was depriving him of these deliberately and unyieldingly.

It was decided that Solange's marriage should take place in
Nohant on May 20th. On May 18th, Baron Dudevant came to
Nohant, the marriage contract was drawn up, and Solange received as a dowry the Hôtel de Narbonne in Paris. The property
was valued at one hundred thousand francs and yielded an annual income of six thousand francs.

Everything was done in such haste that there was no time for
informing the neighbors. Solange's name was inscribed in the
marriage register not as Dudevant but as Sand. Her mother had
sprained her ankle and was carried to the church. The following
morning at four o'clock Baron Dudevant left for Guillery. Solange
left at once with her husband for Besançon. "Never has a marriage
been less gay," wrote George Sand.

Three weeks later, on June 7th, she wrote cheerfully to her half-sister Caroline Cazamajou that Augustine was engaged. Her second dream was coming true, although the prospective husband was not Maurice. She had made up her mind that her son's feelings toward Augustine were those of a brother, and when Théodore Rousseau, a gifted painter and a friend of Maurice, asked her for the hand of Augustine, she happily consented.

Thus the man who "never correctly interpreted facts" turned out to be right. Chopin did not taunt George Sand with her mistakes. He congratulated her on her daughter's marriage and later in an affectionate letter wished Solange a happy future. Only to his family did he disclose what he actually thought:

As for Solange's marriage, it took place while I was sick, and I am not sorry, for I don't know how I would have reacted to all this. He, the bridegroom, is devil knows of what family. He was introduced here and no one dreamed that someday it would come to this, up to their last trip to the country. But I at once disliked the fact that the mother praised him to high heaven, that they drove to his atelier almost daily to pose for busts, that every day they accepted flowers and various other gifts, such as little dogs, etc.

The mother is a dear woman, but hasn't got a penny's worth of practical sense, and she invited him to the country. That was all he wanted; he went, and since he is cunning, they had no time to think it over before it was all settled. Solange was impressed with the gifts, because he is supposed to be another Michelangelo, because he is an excellent horseman (he was a cuirassier, so it's no wonder). Maurice, too, sided with him, because he could not stand Préault, who is polite and decent; and this fellow sensed the situation at once and began to flatter him. Moreover, since the mother kept everything secret, they had concerning him only those *renseignements* that he himself gave them, while here all the friends, Marliani, and Arago, and Delacroix, and myself, had the most wretched reports about him —namely, that he is in debt, that he is a brute, and that he beat his mistress, whom he deserted, after making her pregnant, in order to marry now, etc. etc., that he drinks (this all of us knew, but it was excused on account of his genius). In brief, all the artists who know him in Paris as a good-for-nothing can't get over the fact that Madame Sand chose him for a son-in-law.

So far everyone has been very content. He is as polite as he can be. She is happy in her new status, she has cashmeres and rides, but I don't give them a year after the first child comes before the mother has to pay their debts. They were a little ashamed of writing to me about it when they were in the country, and the letters I have are most curious. The son has surely profited most from this affair, because he not only has a brother-in-law whom he can exploit in *certain respects*, but there is also the fact that his father, the worthy Monsieur Dudevant, didn't give Solange even a hairpin as a dowry, so he will get more. Furthermore, that cousin Augustine, whom he was supposed to marry, is now going to marry Rousseau, the famous landscapist, a decent man, who lived in the same house as Clésinger. This, I think, is the wisest thing they can do, because both Madame Sand and her son will get rid of a difficulty—they had both gone much too far. She won't have to support the whole family . . . and he is rid of his promise to enter upon a marriage for which he had not the slightest inclination. The girl is pretty, so he thought he was in love with her, but each time it came to making a decision he withdrew.

So now all of them are here to finish this matter, and the day before yesterday the banns were published at the church of Notre Dame de Lorette and the *mairie*. After that they will go to the country at once. I don't know whether I'll go with them; I really don't want it, because aside from considerations regarding the lady of the house, the son, and the daughter, I should have to get used to new people, and I have had enough of that.

Meanwhile the most surprising events were taking place in Nohant. At the end of June, Solange and Clésinger returned there from their honeymoon trip, which had turned into a flight before creditors. It became known that Clésinger was in debt up to his ears and that he continued to borrow right and left.

Madame Sand now saw him in an entirely different light: his sacred fire had changed into recklessness, his sincerity into vulgarity, his courage into aggressiveness. She wrote about the young couple in far less enthusiastic terms than she had used a few weeks earlier: "The moment they had their independence and their money, they raised their masks and fancied that they were going to dominate me, to ruin me, and torture me at will."

The house became an inferno. Clésinger quarreled with everybody, Solange intrigued to destroy the relations between Augustine and Rousseau, who were helpless, and Maurice realized that he had no weight in the household. At the same time Solange charged that her brother was using a friend named Borie, who was his guest at Nohant, in machinations against herself.

Soon there was an explosion. In the course of some quarrel, Solange told Rousseau that Augustine had been Maurice's mistress. Madame Sand declared this to be a lie and a slander, but Rousseau left Nohant and his fiancée.

One day, in the presence of several friends, a servant, and the parish priest, who happened to be calling, Clésinger lunged toward Maurice with a hammer in his hand. Madame Sand flung herself between the two and struck Clésinger in the face. The sculptor hit her in the breast with his fist. Maurice seized a pistol and "would have killed him on the spot," wrote George Sand, had it not been for the priest and the others, who stopped Maurice in time.

The whole neighborhood was scandalized. For three days George Sand lived in fear of murder. She ordered Solange and Clésinger to leave her house and declared that she wished never to see them again. Solange, who was pregnant, asked her mother for the use of Chopin's carriage to enable them to get to Paris. George Sand refused. The Clésingers left for La Châtre bearing off some candelabras and embroidered bedcovers. George Sand wrote to Mademoiselle de Rozières asking her not to allow them to occupy her apartment in Paris. She stigmatized them as burglars, ready to rob her of everything, down to her last bed, and said further:

I was forced to write part of this to Chopin; I was afraid that he might arrive in the middle of a catastrophe and that he would die of pain and the shock. Don't tell him how far things have gone; we'll conceal it from him if possible.

Meanwhile Chopin received a letter from Solange, who wrote:

I am ill. . . . Would you agree to lend me your carriage to take me back to Paris? Be so kind as to answer me at once. I am waiting for your letter at La Châtre, where I feel very much out of place. I left Nohant forever amidst the most atrocious scenes precipitated by my mother. Please wait for me before leaving Paris. I want to see you at once. I was absolutely refused your carriage. So if you consent to give it to me, please write me a line to this effect, and I will send it to Nohant in order to have the carriage delivered to me.

Three days later Chopin wrote to Solange:

I have been grieved to hear that you are ill. I hasten to inform you that my carriage is at your disposal. I am writing about it at the same time to your mother. Please take care of yourself.

Madame Sand complied with Chopin's request and handed over his carriage to Solange, but never forgave Chopin for his action. Their relation was nearing its end. They exchanged two more letters, which have not been preserved. It is said that Madame Sand demanded of Chopin that he break with the Clésingers, and, if he came to Nohant for the summer, to refrain from defending Solange or speaking of her at all. It is also alleged that Chopin read George Sand's letter—which he called the "famous letter"—to Franchomme and said, "How can I close my door to them when they have only me?"

He also showed the letter to Delacroix, who on July 20th wrote in his journal:

Chopin came in the morning while I was at lunch after my return from the Museum. . . . He told me of the letter he had received; he has read almost the whole of it to me since my return to Paris. . . . It must be granted that it is atrocious. Cruel passions and long-suppressed impatience come to the light of day in it; and, by way of a contrast that would be diverting if the matter were not such a sad one, the writer now and then supplants the woman and launches into tirades that seem borrowed from a novel or a philosophical homily. <sermon>

Chopin answered George Sand probably with no concealment of his opinion on everything that had happened and without promise that he would break with the Clésingers. This letter went unanswered, but did not remain without results. George Sand considered his attitude a betrayal.

I see that as usual I have been the dupe of my stupid heart, and that while I spent six sleepless nights tormenting myself about his health, he was with the Clésingers saying and thinking evil things about me. Very well, then. His letter is of a ridiculous solemnity, and the sermons of this good father of a family will indeed be a good lesson to me. A person forewarned is worth two; I shall keep very quiet from now on.

There are behind all this many things that I can guess, and I know what my daughter is capable of in the way of slander. I know what Chopin's poor brain is capable of in the way of prejudice and credulity. . . . But at last I've seen the light, and I shall act accordingly; I shall no longer give my flesh and blood to feed ingratitude and perversity. From now on I shall be peaceful and withdrawn at Nohant, far from the enemies who pursue me. I shall know how to protect the gate of my fortress against the wicked and the insane. I know that during this time they'll tear me to shreds. Very well! When their hatred is quenched in this direction, they will devour one another. . . .

I think Chopin is magnificent in associating with and approving Clésinger, who struck me because I wrested from his hands a hammer that he had raised against Maurice—Chopin, who, everyone said, was my most faithful and most devoted friend! It is admirable!

On August 14th Madame Sand found calmer and more final words. "I don't hear anything about Chopin," she wrote to Mademoiselle de Rozières. "Please let me know about his health, nothing else. The rest does not interest me at all, and I have no reason for regretting the loss of his affection."

CHAPTER

35

Parting

Wᴴɪʟᴇ George Sand seems to have completely lost her self-control in the crisis of her relationship with Chopin, he displayed in it a striking strength of character. This sick, solitary man, whose irresolution was proverbial, whom George Sand accused of being blind to realities, behaved much more sensibly than the woman who was so full of vitality and who vaunted her capacity to direct the lives of those about her.

Chopin was innocent of the charges she hurled against him. He did not slander her with the Clésingers, nor did he seek to take revenge on her, although he could easily have found a willing partner for such an undertaking in Solange. On the contrary, he was convinced that Solange should conciliate her mother; he bent his efforts in this direction, and he never changed his mind about this. Of course he did not desert the Clésingers and did not refuse Solange his friendship; it was "the only refuge that remained open to her," to quote her biographer Rocheblave. And his help was not confined to words; he lent them money (which they returned later) to pay for Solange's trip to Besançon.

In every letter Chopin wrote at this time to Solange he mentioned her mother. Solange had visited George Sand twice in November and reported to Chopin:

I found her very much changed, but cold as ice, and even cruel. When she greeted me she said that if I would break with my husband,

Parting

I might return to Nohant—that so far as he is concerned she does not know him. What do you think of such a greeting?

Chopin tried to comfort her. He wrote:

The first step has been taken. You have shown affection, a certain rapprochement has taken place, you have been asked to write. Time will do the rest. You also know that one must not take literally everything she says, and that even if it is possible to cease knowing a stranger, as for instance myself, your husband is in a different situation, since he has become a member of the family.

On her father's estate near Nérac, Solange was expecting a child, but even then her mother did not have much to say to her. She had written a letter of nine lines, and Solange complained about it to Chopin. He answered, "Soon you will be receiving ninety lines instead of nine, and the young mother's joy will be also the grandmother's. Both of you will adore the little angel who will come into the world to restore both your hearts to their normal state."

While George Sand's hatred for Solange or Clésinger is understandable, she was unjustified in her accusations of Chopin. She counted him among her enemies. She was full of reproaches against him; she charged him with intentions and acts exactly opposite to his actual intentions and acts. Why this kindhearted woman was overwhelmed by anger to such an extent, why her clear mind was darkened by such an eclipse, how after years of devotion to Chopin she could so abruptly become his antagonist are questions that are difficult to answer. Perhaps she ceased to realize that she herself had contributed to the disasters that had befallen her; perhaps, conscious of her responsibility, she refused to admit it and succumbed to the common human weakness of blaming others.

It is fact, however, that she suffered a great deal, and later considered the year 1847 the worst year of her life. "I know very well that had it not been for Maurice, I should have ended my wretched life," she said on one occasion. This confession may have been no more than a rhetorical gesture, coming as it did from an individual of whom Chopin said with wry insight: "Sometimes she does not speak the truth, but this is permissible in a novelist." She dominated Maurice, he obeyed her willingly—and that was all. She instructed him as follows in the event that he should meet Chopin:

If you run into him, say *bonjour* to him, as though nothing had happened: "You're fine, so much the better"—nothing more, and go your way. Unless he avoids you; if so, do the same. If he asks about me, tell him that I have been very ill as a result of my sorrows. Don't temper this: tell it to him in an abrupt tone, so as not to encourage him to speak to you about Solange. If he speaks to you about her, which I don't believe he will, tell him that you don't have to discuss this with him. There it is; one must foresee everything, and since the slightest word will be repeated and commented on, there they are, all prepared.

She sent Maurice to Madame Marliani and explained why in the following words:

Madame Marliani raises a great cry over the fact that you don't visit her. You know how greedy she is for details, and how curious. Tell her everything she wants to know. Since Clésinger and Chopin blow the trumpet against us, blow the truth into Madame Marliani's trumpet.

George Sand did not return to Paris that year, although if she had come to the Square d'Orléans she certainly would have met Chopin and had an opportunity to find out at least that he did not hate her. She chose to withdraw to her "fortress at Nohant," and to give up her apartment in the Square d'Orléans.

Her irritated and unyielding behavior caused some of her friends to draw away from her. Her correspondence with Mademoiselle de Rozières stopped, Delacroix cooled off toward her, and never returned to Nohant; and Grzymala, her most faithful confidant, broke with her. Even those of her friends who remained attached to her and tried to give her a true picture of events failed to convince her that she was wrong. The charming Madame Viardot-Garcia, who remained devoted to her, wrote to her from Dresden on November 19, 1847:

There is another passage in your letter that I cannot pass over in silence. It is the passage in which you say that Chopin is part of Solange's clique, which represents her as the victim and denigrates you. This is absolutely false, I swear it to you, at least in so far as he is concerned. On the contrary, this dear and excellent friend is obsessed and aggrieved only by one thought—the thought of the suffering all this unfortunate affair must have caused and still causes you. I have not found the slightest change in him. He is as kind, as devoted, as adoring of you as he has always been, rejoicing only over your joys, grieving only over your sorrows. For heaven's sake, my darling, don't ever believe the meddlesome friends who come to report gossip to you. You have learned by a sad experience that one should not always believe gossip, even if it comes from closely related persons; all the more must one distrust it when it comes from other people.

To these warm words Louis Viardot added his opinion:

For the sake of justice and truth I must tell you that the hostility with which you think he ungratefully pursues you has not manifested itself, at least in our presence, by one word, one gesture. This is in all frankness the sense and summary of what he told us: Solange's marriage is a great misfortune for her, her family, her friends. The daughter and the mother were cheated, and they recognized their error too late. But this error, in which both share—why charge it to only one of them? The daughter wanted, demanded, an improper marriage, but does not the mother share in the guilt through having given her consent? With her great mind and great experience, was it not her duty to enlighten a young girl who was impelled by rancor more than by love? If she deluded herself, one must not be pitiless with regard to an error in which one has shared. "And for myself," he added, "pitying them both from the bottom of my heart, I try to give some comfort to the only one of them whom I am allowed to see."

357

The Life and Death of Chopin

There was nothing else, I swear it to you, dear Madame Sand, and this he said without reproach, without bitterness, with deep sadness. Pauline, being the good girl she is, and having only a general idea of this sad affair, offered to see Madame Clésinger with him. Chopin neatly dissuaded her from this intention. "No," he answered, "you will inevitably be accused of siding with the daughter against the mother." You can see for yourself that this is not the behavior or the speech of an enemy. I fear that there is between you only the breath of malicious mouths. May God preserve you from this!

Meanwhile, Chopin was anxious to hear about George Sand. He questioned his friends about her, was surprised that she did not write to them, and took note of the fact that she had not mentioned him when seeing Solange. He lived in solitude, although he was surrounded by throngs of people. Witwicki, his friend, had died after a long illness. Grzymala had great troubles of his own, having lost his fortune, defrauded by his partner. Gutmann was on a tour, Fontana had gone overseas, and Delphine was in Nice. His health was not at its best and he wrote to Solange: "I am choking, I have a headache, so please forgive my corrections and my French"; or, "I choke and wish you the greatest luck." In the summer he went to Ville d'Avray, near Paris, for a brief visit to Albrecht, an attaché of the Saxon legation in Paris, whose daughter he held at her baptism; he also visited the Rothschilds at Ferrière. The rest of the time he stayed in town.

Both his health and his work were affected by the fact that he could not go to Nohant. In June, 1847, he signed a contract with the publishing house of Breitkopf & Härtel in Leipzig, and later an agreement with Brandus et Cie in Paris, for the publication of the Three Mazurkas (Opus 63), the Three Waltzes (Opus 64)— the first of these, in D-flat major, the so-called "Minute Waltz," is dedicated to the Countess Delphine Potocka, and the second, in C-sharp minor, to the Baroness Nathaniel de Rothschild—and the Sonata in G minor for piano and cello (Opus 65), dedicated to Franchomme. These were the last compositions of Chopin published in his lifetime. The Paris edition of them appeared on October 17, 1847, exactly two years before his death.

Parting

In this sad period of his life he could unburden himself only to his family, hundreds of miles away from him. He often spoke about his mother with Madame Obreskov, who went for a time to Warsaw and even planned to bring Madame Justyna to Paris. To Ludwika he wrote at length about everything, and most of all about George Sand. His letters were as of old like an intimate conversation, and they supply additional proof that although Chopin judged George Sand with severity, any feeling of hatred toward her was alien to him. In one of these letters he wrote:

One might think that she wanted at one stroke to get rid of her daughter and of me, because we were inconvenient to her; she will correspond with her daughter, and thus will for the time being calm her maternal heart, which needs at least some news of her child, and with that she will stifle her conscience. She will think that she is just, and will proclaim me an enemy on the ground that I allegedly sided with her son-in-law (whom she cannot stand only because he married her daughter—and I opposed this marriage as much as I could). She is a strange creature for all her intelligence. Some sort of madness has come upon her: she makes a mess of her own life and of her daughter's life; with her son too it will end badly—I predict it and guarantee it. In order to justify herself she would like to discover something invidious in those who wish her well, who had faith in her, who have never treated her unkindly, and whom she cannot endure beside her because they are mirrors of her conscience. That's why she has not written one word more to me, that's why she won't come to Paris this winter, that's why she has not mentioned me to her daughter. I don't regret that I helped her through eight of the most delicate years of her life, when her daughter was growing up and her son was staying with her; I don't regret anything of what I suffered, but I do regret that she has broken her daughter, this well-cultivated plant protected from so many storms by her mother's hand, through an imprudence and frivolity that might be forgiven in a woman of twenty but not in a woman of forty. But it's no use going over what has been and is no longer. Madame Sand can have only a kind memory of me in her soul if she ever stops to think.

But time passed, Madame Sand did not stop to think, and Chopin ceased to wait anxiously for some sign from her. This difficult year closed with a sad Christmas, of which he wrote in a letter to his family: "I spent Christmas Eve in the most prosaic way, but I thought of you." The winter was a severe one; there was much sickness all about him. "I cough, I go out rarely, because it's too cold for me," he wrote to Solange, but despite his caution he fell ill with an "atrocious attack of influenza."

Nevertheless, he took himself in hand, refusing to succumb to his depression, and began to consider a concert:

My friends came to me one morning and told me that I must give a concert, that I shall not have to bother about anything, that I shall only have to sit down and play. Since last week there have been no tickets available, and all tickets are twenty francs apiece. People are subscribing for a second concert (which I am not planning). The royal court asked for forty tickets. The newspapers merely mentioned that I might give a concert, and yet people wrote from Brest and Nantes to my publisher to reserve seats for them. I am surprised at such *empressement,* and today I must play, were it only for the sake of my conscience, because it seems to me that I play worse than ever. I'll play (for curiosity's sake) a Mozart trio, with Franchomme and Alard. There will be no placards and no free tickets. The hall is comfortable; it has room for three hundred persons. Pleyel always makes jokes about my stupidity, and to encourage me to give the concert will decorate the staircase with flowers. I'll be as if at home, and my eyes will encounter for the most part only familiar faces.

All this must have meant a great effort for him—a difficult attempt to rebuild his broken life. Practical matters had always taxed his energy, and now he had to devote all of it to such things. He was unable to compose, and despite all his activity, he must have suffered from a feeling of emptiness. This must have been his meaning when he wrote: "I am very busy on all sides, and with all that I do nothing."

The Square d'Orléans had become deserted. Madame Marliani

had moved out long ago; Madame Sand returned her apartment to the landlord. Maurice took care of her furniture; he came to the Square d'Orléans but did not visit Chopin. The loquacious artist neighbors had a subject for gossip.

"As for myself, I have buried it," Frederic wrote to Ludwika in a letter that once again takes up the subject of George Sand's behavior. "No one could ever keep up with the caprices of such a person. . . . Perhaps this is also the condition of her life, her literary inspirations, her happiness." It is quite possible that with these penetrating words Chopin touched on the very core of the matter. George Sand needed life to write about it. And what had been written ceased to live.

Chopin and George Sand were to meet once again and to converse briefly, but this was a meeting in a blind alley. It is difficult to blame either of them for the break. Life itself led them to part, perhaps against their will. The fact is that their association proved weaker than external obstacles.

For George Sand, this separation marked the culminating point of her life's failures and became an enduring trauma. For Chopin, it meant much more—it was a sentence of death.

CHAPTER

36

"The Sylph Has Kept His Word"

THE friends who had persuaded Chopin to "sit down and play" were Pleyel, Count Perthuis, Léo, and Albrecht. They were thinking not only of his genius but also of his need for money. They were joined by Jane Wilhelmina Stirling, who had been Chopin's pupil for four years. The audience represented a distinguished list of subscribers. Special tickets were engraved. The King, the Queen, the Duchess d'Orléans, and the Duc de Montpensier bought ten tickets each. A subscription for a second concert was opened, but Chopin said, "Even this one bores me." He was thinking of leaving Paris.

Pleyel took care of all preparations, as Chopin wrote to Ludwika; he also sent him, for his use at home, the piano on which he was to play at the concert. Miss Stirling assured him that the greenroom would be heated, and that the auditorium would be aired after he left the platform.

On Wednesday, February 16, 1848, at eight-thirty in the evening, Chopin, who had not been seen in any public performance for six years, began the concert that was to be his last in Paris. The features of the first part of the program were: a Mozart trio played by Chopin with Alard as violinist and Franchomme as cellist; arias sung by Antonia Molina di Mondi; Chopin in a nocturne and the Barcarolle; another aria by Mademoiselle di Mondi; Chopin in an étude and the Berceuse. The second part comprised the scherzo, adagio, and finale of Chopin's G minor sonata, with Franchomme at the cello; the new aria from Meyerbeer's *Robert le diable,* sung by Gustave-Hippolyte Roger; and Chopin in preludes, mazurkas, and a waltz. The accompanists were Aulary and De Garaudé.

In the preliminary moments in the greenroom, Chopin collected his strength, mastered his stage fright, and once again summoned his determination. Perhaps he considered this concert the beginning of a new life. Here he would prove that he would somehow manage to get along without George Sand, who about that time wrote sarcastically to Maurice: "The newspapers report that Chopin is giving a concert before his departure. Do you know where he is going—to Warsaw or simply to Nérac?"

When he came forward on the flower-decked platform he was greeted with an ovation. Dressed with exceptional care (while preparing for the occasion before the concert he had worried a long time about which of his dozen tail coats he should choose), he surprised everyone by his physical fitness. He was only paler than usual, a fact that did not escape his friends' eyes. He played with great energy. He was in complete control of the instrument, and was able to render all the beauties of his works; it was a demonstration of his style at its best. No slightest weakness was detectable in him; he performed the dynamic passages *con brio*, only he took pianissimo the two final passages of the Barcarolle, which are marked forte. It is not known which of his nocturnes, études, preludes, or mazurkas he played, but it is known that each of the works he gave aroused enthusiasm, and that after his performance of the Waltz in D-flat major (Opus 64, No. 1), the ovation reached its climax. He had to repeat this waltz, and he was called back several times. After he left the platform, however, his nerves gave way. In the greenroom he felt so weak that he almost fainted.

On February 20th, the *Gazette musicale* carried a long review of this concert, which ran in part as follows:

The sylph has kept his word. What a success, what enthusiasm! It is easier to tell you what a welcome he was accorded, what raptures he aroused, than to describe, analyze, and make clear the mysteries of a performance that is unlike anything in our earthly regions. If we had at our disposal the delicate pen that pictures the exquisite beauty of Queen Mab . . . we should at most be able to give you some glimpse of a talent that is purely ideal, and in which the tangible counts for practically nothing at all. To interpret Chopin there is only Chopin himself; all those who attended Wednesday's performance are as convinced of this as we are.

Chopin busied himself with preparations for the second concert, which was scheduled for March 10th, and for which six hundred persons subscribed at once. But this concert was never heard. The plans for it were cut short by a sudden contretemps in the life of Paris and of all France.

On February 22nd Chopin felt indisposed; he spent his birthday in bed, and knew little of what was going on in the city. He developed a neuralgic attack that confined him to his room for a week. On the night of that February 22nd the people of Paris held demonstrations in the streets, singing the *Marseillaise* before the royal palace, and clamoring for reforms. It was the beginning of a revolution—of still another of those seasons of popular ferment that had become associated with various stages of Chopin's life.

On the next day the first shots were fired and the first victims fell. Under red flags, by the light of torches, blood-drenched corpses were borne in open carts through the streets. The bells of a church in a slum district rang out; soon these were followed by bells in the rest of the city. The *Garde Nationale* went over to the side of the populace; the government resigned, and the King fled to Saint-Cloud. On February 24th the Republic was proclaimed, with Lamartine as head of the government. Paris was intoxicated with freedom, parades, and songs.

This was the rebellion of the republicans of France against a bourgeois king, the rebellion of romantic aspirations against a program of mediocrity—a rebellion against political hypocrisy, against satrap tyranny everywhere in Europe, and against the misery of the workless proletariat. France, which, as Lamartine put it, had become bored under Louis Philippe, was no longer bored. Street orators proclaimed that the Middle Ages were over, and that modern history would begin with the restoration of freedom to oppressed nations—first of all to Poland.

The émigrés of various nationalities living in Paris took new courage, and the spirit of the crowds once again fired the hearts and minds of the Poles. "All of us are living in the streets like the ancient Athenians. We are asking for news, and there is a mass of news," wrote Bohdan Zaleski.

Chopin was stunned by the new configuration of events. King Louis Philippe, who had been kind to him, had fled from Saint-Cloud and crossed the Channel to Newhaven as Mr. Smith. The new government included some of George Sand's friends. Louis Blanc and Arago headed the workers, and Malefille became governor of Versailles.

Each day brought a new development. Reports on public affairs vied with private news. On March 3rd, Chopin received a letter from Solange announcing that she was the mother of a little girl, born February 28th, six weeks before term.

On the same day Chopin sent her his congratulations:

I cannot refrain from telling you at once my joy at knowing that you are a mother and well. The coming of your little girl has given me joy in even greater measure, as you may suppose, than the coming of the republic. Thank God that your sufferings are over. A new world begins for you. May you be happy. Take care of yourselves.

The next day, March 4th, was a Saturday, the day on which Madame Marliani received. In her salon Chopin met several friends, among them Edouard Combes, French vice-consul at Rabat in Morocco, a man of picturesque personality who had made explorations on the Red Sea coast and in Central Africa. He had also spent a long time in Abyssinia and written an account of that country, which had earned for him the nickname of "the Abyssinian." As Chopin was leaving Madame Marliani's drawing room in his company, he ran into George Sand entering the foyer with Lambert, a painter and a friend of Maurice's. As they greeted each other, George Sand noted that Chopin's hand was cold and trembling. He asked her when she had received her last news of Solange.

"A week ago," she said.

"You did not hear from her yesterday or the day before?"

"No."

"Then I can tell you that you are a grandmother. Solange has a daughter, and I am pleased to be the first to give you the news." With these words he bowed and walked down the stairs with Combes. At the foot of the stairs he stopped, recalling that he had not told George Sand that Solange was well. He asked Combes to go back and tell her this, for he was too weak to attempt the stairs again. He wrote about this to Solange:

I was waiting for the Abyssinian downstairs when your mother came down with him and questioned me with much interest about your health. I answered that you had penciled me a few words yourself the day after the birth of your child, that you have suffered a great deal, but that the sight of your daughter has made you forget it all. She asked whether your husband was with you, and I said that the address on your letter appeared to be in his handwriting.

They did not seem to have anything more to say to each other.

"How do you feel?" George Sand asked him.

"Quite well," he replied, and asked the concierge to open the door. He bowed and walked out with Combes. He never saw George Sand again.

George Sand alludes to this meeting in *Histoire de ma vie:* "I wanted to speak to him, but he evaded it. It was my turn to tell him that he did not love me. I spared him this suffering, and I put everything in the hands of Providence and the future."

Chopin was well informed about George Sand. He knew from Grzymala that she had come to Paris several days before, that she was staying with Maurice, that she was taking her meals in a restaurant, that she had invited Combes to meet her there, and that she planned to leave shortly. Apparently it was easier to part than to forget.

On March 7th, George Sand was back at Nohant. She went there to win over the province of Berry to the side of the revolution, but met with resistance on the part of the native Berrichons. The change she effected did not go beyond replacing the mayor of the little town. The new mayor was Maurice.

Solange's daughter lived only a few days, and the child's death came as a shock to her family and friends. "Courage and calm! Take care of yourself, for the sake of those who remain," Chopin wrote to her, in a letter that concluded as in refrain on the theme of George Sand: "She is to be pitied—it is a great blow to her, I am sure of it, and I do not doubt that she will do for you everything she can."

In reality the relations between mother and daughter did improve, and at the end of March Chopin was able to write to Solange: "I am very glad of the good letters Madame your mother has written to you. Attend to your health now, and everything will go as well as could be."

He was a faithful and sensible friend in good and in bad times. The sylph had indeed kept his word. He had faithfully stood by Solange. As a mediator he evinced a tact that perhaps cost him no effort; but the calm he maintained could certainly have been achieved only with difficulty. If George Sand failed to appreciate his magnanimous demeanor, it is probably because she refused to notice it.

When she returned to Paris, Chopin knew about it at once, but he felt that he no longer existed for her in this city. She was wholly immersed in the revolution. "I live, I am strong, I am active, I am no more than twenty years old!" she exclaimed in rapture.

She belonged to the left wing of the revolutionists, and called herself a Communist, holding that the Gospels were the "true code of Communism." She wrote bulletins for the government and articles for the journal *La Réforme*, which also carried writings by Karl Marx. Her enthusiasm was boundless and uncritical: "We are mad, we are intoxicated, we are happy over the fact that having fallen asleep in the mire, we have awakened in heaven."

But the revolution did not fulfill the promise of this soaring first phase. Just as swiftly as it had achieved its initial victory, it degenerated into chaos and universal disappointment. The nation at large did not follow the lead of radical Paris, and radical Paris compromised its own cause. The public works organized to meet the needs of the unemployed ended in a fiasco. One hundred thousand men dug trenches in the Champ de Mars only to fill them again. The socialists fought the democrats, the conservatives feuded with both the democrats and the socialists. Lamartine lost his hold on public opinion despite his ardor and eloquence. Even the new mayor of Nohant had to face a demonstration of the peasants of his district, who shouted under the windows of his house, "Death to the Communists! Down with Maurice Dudevant! Down with Madame Dudevant!"

The revolutionary élan had spent itself. Only one slogan—"We demand freedom for Poland!"—continued to ring in the streets of Paris with unabated fervor.

The course of history in Poland likewise moved in violent zigzags. This nation, which had embarked on this new struggle for liberation earlier than any other in Europe—as early as 1846—and after two years of heroic hope could only count its dead, hurled itself into a new effort, carried away by the spreading wave of revolution. Mickiewicz founded a Polish freedom legion in Italy, and in Poznan province a rebel leader named Ludwik Mieroslawski rallied twenty thousand peasants to arms. Exiles left France en masse for Poland, expecting that their homeland would become independent at any moment. The French railroads transported them gratis, in groups of three hundred, as far as the German border. They were setting out on the continental highway of freedom, only to find themselves trapped in the dead alley of despair.

Chopin went through the same seesaw of emotions as his fellow-Poles, shifting abruptly from hope to disappointment, from joy to bitterness, from excitement to depression. When he came to the Paris railway station to say farewell to Kozmian, who had come from London on his way to join the Poznan rebels, he was in a resigned mood, and said to his friend, "My public activity is over. If you have a little church in your village, give me a piece of bread, and in return I'll play for you in honor of the Holy Virgin."

On April 4, 1848, when he wrote to Fontana in America, the

springs of resolve had quickened in him again. He was looking into the future with stubborn hope, and this time it was not merely the goad of a just though defeated cause, such as his father had known, but also the hard, never capitulating Polish faith that dictated his words:

Our people are gathering in Poznan province. Czartoryski was the first to go there, but God alone knows in what way a new Poland will arise. . . . What the newspapers write here is lies. There is no republic in Cracow, nor did the Austrian emperor proclaim himself King of Poland. The Prussian King does not contemplate cession of Poznan; he has compromised himself at home, yet the Poznan Germans address him in resolutions declaring that "whereas" this land was conquered at the price of their forefathers' blood, and "whereas" they do not even know the Polish tongue, they do not wish to live under any government but a Prussian one. All this, you see, smells of war, and there is no knowing where it will begin. But once it begins, all Germany will be aflame. Italy has already begun. Milan has driven out the Austrians, but they will sit in the provinces and will surely fight. Probably France will help, because a certain element of the populace must be got rid of here to do any good. . . . The Muscovite will probably have difficulties of his own as soon as the Prussians are given a thrashing. The Galician peasants have set an example to those of Volhynia and Podolia; these things won't come to pass without some horrors, but at the end of it all there is a splendid, great Poland—in brief, Poland. Therefore, despite our impatience, let us wait until the cards are well shuffled, so as not to expend strength in vain, for strength is needed at the right moment. This moment is close, but it is not today. Maybe in a month, maybe in a year. Everyone here is convinced that our prospects will be clearly foreshadowed before the coming fall.

This was the last letter Chopin wrote, as far as is known, before his departure for London. He felt that he had nothing to do in Paris. The aristocratic milieu was gone, his friends were scattered to all parts of the world, and there could be no thought of lessons. Music was silent in the capital of France. On the other hand, the great season was in full course as usual in London.

A London Season

JUDGED in retrospect, Chopin's trip to England appears to have
been an act of folly. In May, 1847, he had suffered a severe
attack of what he called asthma, and in February, 1848, an
equally severe onset of what he called neuralgia. His constitution
was undermined by tuberculosis, and he had for two successive
years been deprived of the beneficent rest he had known in Nohant. The purpose of his English journey was to give concerts—
that is to say, he was sentencing himself to strenuous effort that
was certain to exhaust his dwindling energies. And the climate of
London was the very negation of everything he needed for the
conservation of his imperiled physical resources.

Surprisingly, no one among Chopin's intimates recognized these
dangers. All of his friends—Grzymala, Franchomme, Gutmann,
Mademoiselle de Rozières, the Princess Czartoryska—encouraged
him to undertake the journey; perhaps they were deceived by the
energy and enthusiasm he displayed in making his preparations
for departure. Chopin was not fleeing from the revolution, as
George Sand maintained. He had conceived the idea of going to
England before the time of his Paris concert, when no one sur-
mised the imminence of revolution, not even its leaders-to-be. His
break with George Sand was for him a sufficient motive for leaving Paris.

The coming of the revolution, depriving him of his sources of income, only confirmed him in his project, although it delayed execution of the idea. He had planned to give two concerts in Paris in order to raise the money needed for his trip, then to go to London, and, if it proved possible, to settle there and begin a new life. He collected letters of introduction not only to Englishmen but also to Poles living in London, as though his name were not a sufficient introduction. Yet he apparently thought that he might return to Paris, because he retained his apartment and arranged no farewell party.

He was going to a country where he was known, where he had his publishers, where Moscheles, Madame de Belleville-Oury, Mademoiselle Sophie Bohrer, Henry Field, William Holmes, Edward Pirkhert, F. B. Jewson, H. B. Richards, R. Bernett, and many other virtuosos had performed his works. His compositions figured in the repertory of the Royal Academy of Music, and he had won his first personal friends in England eleven years before. In Paris the *Gazette musicale* mentioned his proposed trip on April 2nd, and H. F. Chorley wrote in the London *Athenaeum* that it was the new French republic that was to be thanked for Chopin's visit. He was also welcomed by a notice in the *Musical World*.

The moving spirit in this project of a journey to England was Jane Stirling, his pupil. She was forty-four years of age and belonged to a well-known Scottish family of merchants that had acquired a great fortune in India. Kindhearted and gentle, extolled by Ary Scheffer as a paragon of beauty, she bestowed boundless admiration and devotion upon Chopin. To these feelings, of which she had given countless proofs, there was added love, the belated love of a lonely life. All these emotions, combined with a marked sentimentality, gave rise to a kind of ecstatic affectation, in which kindness was mixed with imprudence, and protectiveness with obtrusiveness. As regards Chopin's own feelings, this woman who adored him also bored him. Jane's idolatry was in some measure shared by her older sister Catherine, widow of James Erskine, and these two ladies, whom Chopin often referred to as "the Erskines" or *moje Szkotki* ("my Scottish ladies"), took over the guardian role that George Sand had relinquished.

Chopin arrived in London on the night of April 20th, which was shortly before Easter. In the lodgings at No. 10 Bentinck Street rented for him by the two ladies, he was welcomed by moving tokens of their thoughtfulness. "The good Erskines have thought of everything, even of my chocolate," he wrote to Grzymala on Good Friday, the day after his arrival. "You will never believe how kindhearted they are. At this moment I perceive that the paper on which I am writing bears my initials, and I have found a number of other such delicate attentions."

A week later, however, he moved to a spacious and beautiful apartment at No. 48 Dover Street. On May 1st, he saw the sun in the sky of London for the first time and wrote: "Since this morning I have been less choked, but all last week I was indisposed." To Gutmann he wrote: "Erard was most courteous; he has lent me a piano. I also have a Broadwood and a Pleyel. Altogether I have three instruments—but of what use is this, when I have no time to play on them. I have countless visitors, and my days pass with lightning speed. Up until today I have not had a free minute."

London was full of artists. Berlioz was there, Kalkbrenner and Osborne were giving concerts, Thalberg had announced twelve performances, and Charles Halle was planning to settle in England. The two rival opera houses, Covent Garden and the Haymarket, featured the most brilliant singers, who had been lured from the Continent by high salaries or had fled from the turmoil of revolution. Chopin was visited by Madame Viardot-Garcia, who had come to London with her husband. On May 12th she sang some of his mazurkas in her own arrangements in a concert at Covent Garden, and they had to be repeated. At the Haymarket, Chopin heard Jenny Lind; he was introduced to her, and the two became friends. "She is a genuine Swede, moving not in an ordinary light but in a kind of aurora borealis," he wrote. "She sings purely and with extraordinary assurance, and her *piano* is as steady and even as a hair." He invited her to dinner and afterward reported to Grzymala: "Then she sang Swedish folksongs until midnight. Their character is as distinctive as that of our own songs. We have something Slavic; they have something Scandinavian. The two are completely different, but we are closer to each other than Italians are to Spaniards."

He easily established contacts with musicians. He met several of his former pupils; of these, Norweg, Tellefsen, and Lindsay Sloper, an Englishman, were of great help to him in many matters, and gave him pleasant companionship. About the Philharmonic, he wrote to Grzymala:

I was asked to play there but I refused, because it was with the orchestra. There one must play Mozart, Beethoven, or Mendelssohn, and although the directors and others tell me that the Philharmonic also played my own concertos, and with success, I'd rather not play, because nothing can come of this. Their orchestra is like their roast beef or their turtle soup—strong, hearty, but nothing more. All this does not really explain. But this one incredible thing will suffice: they never rehearse in advance, because everyone's time is precious; they have only one general rehearsal, and even this is public.

He used his bad health as an excuse for his refusal to play: nevertheless, his attitude made a bad impression on the Philharmonic. The *Musical World* published a brief note about it, saying that Chopin had been invited to play at the Philharmonic but had refused.

During the three months he stayed in London, he appeared in public five times, giving three performances "at twenty guineas," and two drawing-room concerts—at Lady Gainsborough's, in the home of the Marquess Douglas, and (on May 15th) at the Duchess of Sutherland's in Stafford House, where Queen Victoria and Prince Albert were among his listeners. He described this gathering thus:

The Duchess of Sutherland had the Queen to dinner, and in the evening there were only eighty persons, of the foremost London society. In addition to the Prussian prince and the royal family, there were only such persons as old Wellington and others like him (although it is difficult to find anyone like him). The Duchess introduced me to the Queen, who is courteous; she spoke to me twice, and Prince Albert came to the piano. Everyone says that such distinctions are rare. Italians who also performed that evening were Mario, Lablache, and Tamburini. There was no woman singer.

Chopin played his mazurkas and waltzes, as well as Mozart's variations in G major for two pianos, with Jules Benedict as his partner.

After his soirée he expected to be invited to play at court, but this hope did not materialize. Apparently this was an outcome of his refusing to play at the Philharmonic and of his neglecting to return the call of its director, who was also the court conductor. Despite all this it was rumored in Paris that Queen Victoria was taking lessons incognito from Chopin.

His first public concert in London took place on June 23rd. It was a matinee in the home of Mrs. Adelaide Sartoris, at No. 99 Eaton Place. Of this patron he wrote:

Mrs. Sartoris, née Kemble, is the young daughter of a famous English actor, and she herself is a famous English singer; she was on the stage for only two years, then married Mr. Sartoris, a wealthy man of good family. She has been adopted by all of London high society; she goes everywhere, and everyone goes to her. I met her in Paris.

On this occasion he played some of his nocturnes, études, and mazurkas, two waltzes, and the Berceuse. Giovanni Mario took part in the concert. There were a hundred and fifty tickets at one guinea each. A brilliant audience filled the hall, among them Jenny Lind. The *Athenaeum* published a warm review emphasizing the fact that Chopin's performance and compositions had aroused an enthusiasm of a kind previously unknown in London.

For the second concert, on July 7th, the Earl of Falmouth offered the drawing room of his house. Chopin has left the following sketch of this nobleman:

A London Season

He is a great lover of music, wealthy, a *grand seigneur*. He was very courteous to me. One might give him threepence in the street, and in his house he has a host of lackeys better dressed than himself. I have met his niece in Paris, but I saw her in London only at the concert.

This time there was a soprano, Madame Viardot-Garcia, who included in her program her own arrangements of some of the mazurkas, which were warmly applauded and were again encored. The two hundred seats in the room had all been taken in advance; the reception was enthusiastic, and the press excellent. The *Athenaeum* reported that the second concert was even more successful than the first, that Chopin played with greater spirit, and that the program was richer. According to the *Daily News* of July 10th:

There was a numerous and fashionable assembly, who were delighted with the entertainment provided for them. M. Chopin performed an *andante sostenuto* and a scherzo from his Opus 31, a selection from his celebrated studies, a nocturne and a berceuse and several of his own preludes, mazurkas, and waltzes. In these various pieces he showed very strikingly his original genius as a composer and his transcendental powers as a performer. His music is as strongly marked with individual character as that of any master who has ever lived. It is highly finished, new in its harmonies, full of contrapuntal skill and ingenious contrivance; and yet we have never heard music which has so much the air of unpremeditated effusion. The performer seems to abandon himself to the impulses of his fancy and feeling, to indulge in a reverie and to pour out unconsciously, as it were, the thoughts and emotions that pass through his mind. . . .

He accomplishes enormous difficulties, but so quietly, so smoothly, and with such constant delicacy and refinement that the listener is not sensible of their real magnitude. It is the exquisite delicacy, with the liquid mellowness of his tone, and the pearly roundness of his passages of rapid articulation which are the peculiar features of his execution, while his music is characterized by freedom of thought, varied expression, and a kind of romantic melancholy which seems the natural mood of the artist's mind.

The editor of the *Musical World*, Davison, confined himself to a short notice merely marking the occurrence of the concerts, about which, he said, he was unable to give any details, because he had not attended either of them. Chopin had not sent him tickets.

Such was the outcome of Chopin's feud with the all-powerful critic who directed not only the *Musical World* but also the music section of the London *Times*. The conflict went back over several years. At first Davison had been enthusiastic about Chopin, but in 1836 when he met Mendelssohn and became enraptured with his music, he fell into the erroneous conviction that Chopin hated Mendelssohn, and began to hate Chopin. The *Musical World* published five slipshod articles containing judgments such as this: "The entire works of Chopin present a motley surface of ranting hyperbole and excruciating cacophony." Such extreme denunciation might have reminded Chopin of Rellstab's criticisms. On the other hand, Davison had written flatteringly of Chopin's concert at Broadwood's in 1837. Even more odd, when on an order from Wessel and Stapleton, Chopin's English publishers, Davison had written his "Essay on the Works of Frederic Chopin," he controverted everything he himself had previously written and produced a study not only full of enthusiasm for Chopin's music but actually keen and understanding. He reversed himself similarly again when the publishing firm Boosey and Company paid him for an essay entitled, "The Mazurkas and Valses of Frederic Chopin." His latest attack in the *Musical World* had appeared in December, 1847. In this Chopin had been taken to task for not having joined in a letter of condolence to the widow of Mendelssohn. This letter began with the words: "May we, German artists, living far from our homeland . . ." Chopin had refused to sign a letter purporting to come from Germans exclusively. To the Paris correspondent of the *Musical World* (and no doubt to its London editors), such an attitude seemed unforgivable.

A London Season

Chopin remembered these hysterical or perhaps simply mercenary performances of Davison's, and did not invite him to his concert. He referred to his feud in a letter to his family:

After my matinees several newspapers published favorable reviews, with the exception of the *Times*, whose critic is a certain Davison (a creature of the late Mendelssohn). He does not know me and imagines that I am an enemy of Mendelssohn (so I am told). I don't mind this at all. But you can see that people are always motivated by anything but the truth.

The two concerts brought Chopin about three hundred guineas. The firm of Cramer, Beale and Co., which had previously published some of his works, purchased the D-flat major and C-sharp minor waltzes of his Opus 64. Frugality was the motive imputed to Beale for not buying the third waltz, in A-flat major. Chopin also had some income from lessons. He charged one guinea per hour, a very high fee at that time. Living in London was expensive, as he complained in his letters. His landlord raised his rent to eighty pounds a month; his servant, a lazy Italian, stole from him, and his carriage was a costly item. He was unable however, to reduce his expenses: he could not climb stairs without the help of his servant, and he could not move about the city without a carriage. His second valet, Daniel, a Gallicized Irishman, proved more efficient, and Chopin always had a good word for him.

One may wonder where he found the energy for unending social engagements. Every day he attended some reception or other, meeting prominent personalities, and his letters teem with names and titles (often cited in garbled form), with descriptions of splendors and luxuries, allusions to family and political relationships, quoted compliments and malicious remarks. Whenever he had a free evening, Miss Stirling and Mrs. Erskine pounced on it. He was never alone. He met Lady Byron, of whom he wrote: "We would appear to be greatly attracted to each other, and our conversations are like those of a goose and a piglet— she quacks in English and I squeal in French. I understand why she bored Byron." He listed the celebrities he had met: "Carlyle,

377

the old Rogers, a very famous poet and respected friend of Byron's, Dickens, Hogarth, a close friend of Walter Scott's, etc., etc."

Carlyle, impressed by Chopin's music, wrote to Alexander Scott:

If you see M. Chopin, pray offer him my hearty regards. I hope we shall get some language to speak in by and by, and then get into more plentiful communication. An excellent, gentle, much-suffering human soul, as I can at once see without language.

Jane Welsh Carlyle admired what she termed the "aristocratic reserve" of an art that revealed its essence only to the "elect": "I prefer his music to all others," she wrote to Miss Stirling, on sending her a poem, with the request that she translate it for Chopin.

In this feverish life Chopin was in search of something more than dazzling triumphs, or the company of wealthy and fashionable people, or the pleasures of splendid salons, for all that he liked them so much; he was also seeking an escape from his inner anxiety, from his uncertainty as to the future, and from his bitterness over the past. He was seeking this escape, but was unable to find it. George Sand was constantly in his mind; he talked about her with the Viardots and even with Jenny Lind, and constantly mentioned her in his letters to Grzymala. Once he said to his friend Kozmian, who had returned to London after the failure of the plan of insurrection in Poznan: "I am a poor reed—I clung to a shaky wall, and this wall collapsed; what shall I turn to now?"

His letters reflected in ever increasing measure his anxiety, his constant struggle with illness, to which he refused to yield, and his depression in the face of utter exhaustion. On May 6th he wrote:

I have been breathing more freely only for the last few days. The sun appeared only a few days ago.

In a letter of May 13th he remarked:

A London Season

I cannot get out of bed before eight. My Italian, who takes care of himself and his bills, spoils my mornings. After ten o'clock there begin tribulations that don't bring in any money, and at about one o'clock a few lessons. I can neither walk nor move about much.

On June 1st his report was:

I have not yet been able to get used to the London air, and it is very difficult for me to live in the press of all these visits, dinners, and soirées. I have been spitting blood these last days. I am treating myself with lemons and ice, which do me good.

On June 2nd he wrote:

The weather has been nasty for a week, and this doesn't agree with me at all. If I could drag myself for whole days from Ananias to Caiphas, if I had days free from blood-spitting, if I were younger, if I were not knocked out as I am as a result of my attachment, I should be able to start life anew.

On June 30th he ended a letter thus:

I cannot finish this letter, my nerves are so worn. I suffer from some kind of stupid nostalgia, and despite all my resignation I don't know what I'll do with myself, and I am worried about it.

A note of July without date reads:

I can no longer be sad or glad; my feelings have dried up completely. I am only vegetating and waiting. I hope the end will come soon.

He was unhappy about the failure of the uprising in Poland, and the Cavaignac massacre in Paris. A group of Polish émigrés in London gave a dinner in his honor. When it came to speeches, Chopin rose and said, "Gentlemen, I have no oratorical talent, but if it is agreeable to you, please come to my home. I will play for you."

Thirty guests came to Dover Street. He played mazurkas and polonaises, and then he improvised. Time and distance were obliterated. Until two o'clock in the morning his hearers were in Poland.

Chopin entered upon a cordial friendship with Lord Dudley Stuart, president of the Society of Friends of Poland, with whom he had long conversations. Kozmian described Chopin's mood as follows:

His visit to England was an event in the musical world, and his sojourn a continuous succession of triumphs. But Chopin no longer took any interest in his successes. He was sad and dejected, although his health was surprisingly good. It was difficult to drag him to the piano, unless he had to play. Most often he selected a funeral march. He talked only about Poland.

Yet he met with so much sympathy everywhere that he must have been encouraged. He found in London a new friend as loyal and helpful as Fontana had been. This was an exiled Polish major named Karol Szulczewski. Chopin was also greatly attached to Henry Fowler Broadwood, the son of the world-renowned piano maker. He wrote to his family:

Broadwood, who is the Pleyel of London, has been my best and truest friend. He is a very wealthy and well-bred man, to whom his father handed over his fortune and factory after retiring to the country. To give you an idea of his English politeness: One day he visited me in the morning. I was tired and told him that I had not slept well. At night, upon returning from the Duchess of Somerset's house, I found new elastic mattresses and pillows on my bed. After many questions, my good Daniel admitted that Mr. Broadwood had sent them and had asked him not to tell me anything.

In July, when the season began to decline, many of his English friends invited him to the country. But the claims of Miss Stirling and Mrs. Erskine came first. They might have been saviors to him, but their kindness, for all their good intentions, only did him harm.

My good Scottish ladies show a great deal of friendship to me here; I always dine with them if I am not going into society. But they are used to dragging about all day long in a carriage in London, with their visiting cards, and would like me to pay calls on all their friends, while I can scarcely keep alive.

Miss Stirling could not be a George Sand. Chopin aroused in her something like an ecstasy, which she wished to share with the whole world. She was intoxicated with his success, and she took drawing rôoms, connections, and triumphs too seriously. Whatever benefits Chopin received through her he paid for with the remnants of his declining health, but her loving heart was unaware of the tragic nature of this exchange. George Sand had provided for Chopin a security that gave him life; Miss Stirling drew life from him.

Her indefatigable adoration must have surfeited him. He often spoke of it in exactly the same words: "My Scottish ladies are kind, dear, but sometimes they bore me so much that it's frightful." Toward the end of the season, he wrote to Grzymala:

My Scottish ladies are good, but they bore me so much that I don't know where to turn. They insist that I go to Scotland to their family. It's a beautiful idea, but today I don't feel like doing anything. Here anything that is not boring is not English.

Thus he lingered in the city through July. In the end he decided to avail himself of the hospitality of the Scottish ladies' brother-in-law, Lord Torphichen, near Edinburgh. This was in the first days of August. Broadwood undertook to buy his railroad ticket, but when Chopin appeared at the station, Broadwood's messenger handed him not one but two tickets. His solicitous friend was trying to make the trip as comfortable as possible. The seat next to his was occupied by Mr. Muir Wood, a friend of Broadwood's, who owned bookstores in Edinburgh and Glasgow. A seat in the same car was found for Daniel.

The trip of four hundred and seven miles took twelve hours. When Chopin arrived in Edinburgh he was spitting blood and had to rest for an entire day. He did not attach much importance to this symptom. "My blood has been stirred up a bit. But it's a minor matter," he wrote to Grzymala.

Scottish Mists

IN CALDER HOUSE, twelve miles from Edinburgh, Chopin was greeted by Lord James Sandilands Torphichen and his two sisters-in-law, who had meticulously prepared for their guest's comfort. He was lodged in a room with a beautiful view on an immense park, well-kept lawns, century-old trees, remnants of ancient fortifications, precipices, and mountains. The old castle was steeped in tradition and legend. Everything here stirred the imagination. The walls, far more impressive than those of the Valdemosa monastery, were eight feet thick; there were endless corridors, lined with portraits of family forebears—the ladies in farthingales, the men in armor or in national costumes. Three hundred years earlier, John Knox, the Scottish reformer, had lived and prayed in a room above the one that Chopin now occupied.

Calder House also had its inevitable ghost, and Chopin inspected the family portraits so that he might recognize the nocturnal visitor. But the spectral ancestor, respecting the visitor's peace, did not leave his picture frame, and in the end Frederic was forced to admit: "I haven't yet seen who it is that haunts the castle at night."

In his room he had a Broadwood piano, and in the drawing room Miss Stirling had installed a Pleyel. Every day he received the Paris newspapers. On his desk were music paper, pens, and ink waiting for his compositions. It was evident that the "good Scottish ladies" had done their utmost to please him. The peaceful countryside fascinated him; as he had done in his youth, he listened to folksongs and observed with interest the life of this feudal estate. Every day new visitors arrived at the castle and were at once lost in its immensity. They had at their disposal the libraries and galleries, as well as horses, carriages, and numerous domestics. Breakfast was brought to their rooms; lunch was at noon, dinner at seven. In the evenings they sat in the drawing room into the late hours; the conversations were for the most part in English. Chopin regretted that his knowledge of English was inadequate: "I can understand simple things; I don't let anyone get the best of me, and I won't die of starvation. But this is not enough." The company would fall silent when he sat down at the piano, and then the admiring response obliterated the limitations of language. "I play Scottish songs to the old lord; the dear man hums in unison, and then he pours out his feelings to me as best he can in French."

After his three crowded months in London, Chopin found a respite in Calder House. For the first time since setting foot on British soil he found words of contentment: "I feel peaceful, quiet, and well." Occasionally he spewed up blood. But he had the opportunity of rest and relaxation. Lord Torphichen invited him for the whole summer of the next year, but Chopin, referring to this invitation in a letter to his family, only remarked sadly, "I would gladly stay here all my life, but what purpose would it serve?"

Indeed, what purpose would it serve? The music paper and the pen and ink daily under his eyes lay untouched. "I have not a single musical idea, I am completely out of my groove," he wrote to Franchomme. He wanted to compose, "were it only to please these amiable ladies, Mrs. Erskine and Miss Stirling," but he was unable to write a single measure. He was constantly oppressed by his uncertainty as to the future and by his separation from his dear ones. In his letters he inquired about Warsaw, Solange, the Princess Czartoryska. He had given concerts in order to secure solitude; now he had as much of it as he could wish, and he had it gratis, but it was impossible for him to profit from it. At moments he felt that his situation in this environment was ridiculous: "I am like a donkey at a masked ball, or a violin string on a bass viol—surprised, baffled, out of sorts."

This was not the new life he had dreamed of. He was unable to adjust himself, to get accustomed to the ways of England. To his friends who urged him to spend the winter in London, he replied:

If this London had not been so black, and the people so heavy, and if it had not been for the odor of coal and the fogs, I would have learned English. But these Englishmen are so different from the French, to whom I have become attached as to my own people. Here they compute everything in pounds sterling, and love art because it is a luxury; they are good-natured, but so insular that I can understand how one may become rigid here oneself or change into a machine. If I were younger I might try to become a machine—I would give concerts everywhere and perform the most tasteless pieces (for money only!), but now it is hard to begin making a machine of myself.

To Fontana, who in the meantime had returned from America, he wrote:

If I were in better health, I should go to London tomorrow to embrace you. Perhaps we shall not see each other very soon. We are old cembalos on which time and circumstances have played their wretched little trills. Yes, two old cembalos, although you'll object to such company. This is no reflection on their beauty or decency: the *table d'harmonie* is perfect, but the strings are torn, and some of the little pegs have dropped out. The only trouble is this—that there is no great lutemaker, some kind of Stradivarius *sui generis,* to repair us. We can't bring forth new tones under mediocre hands, and we stifle in ourselves everything that, lacking a lutenist, no one will ever wrest from us.

The thought of George Sand never left him. He questioned his friends in Paris about her, and they supplied him with accurate (or inaccurate) details about everything pertaining to her. These reports were not pleasant. Before leaving Paris, George Sand had suffered every possible defeat in her brief activity as a revolutionary; in addition, she had been subjected to virulent personal attack. In Paris there had appeared scurrilous pamphlets bearing the signature of Augustine Brault's father (though probably published by George Sand's political enemies). George Sand was accused of having made Augustine into Maurice's mistress. The pamphlet contained scandalous letters allegedly written by George Sand. Chopin, who did not know that these letters were spurious, reported the whole thing to his family, and concluded:

There you have the good deed that she thought she was doing, and which I opposed from the very day this girl entered her house. She should have been left with her parents; she should not have been pressed on the son, who will marry only money (and only if he is cajoled into doing it, because he'll have enough money). But he wanted to have his pretty cousin in the house, and he made his mother put her on an equal footing with Solange. She was dressed like Solange, but received more attention, because this was Maurice's wish. The girl's mother was considered a madwoman because she saw things clearly, but in the end the father too saw the light. So Mme Sand has made of this girl *une victime*, pretending that she was persecuted by her own parents. Solange saw all this, so she was a nuisance. Maurice needed his friend Lambert to protect him from Solange and the servants. Borie needed Augustine to protect him from Solange and Maurice. Maurice needed Borie in order to create the impression in the city that Borie had designs on Augustine. The mother felt obstructed by the daughter, who unfortunately saw everything that was going on: hence the lies, the discomfiture, and the rest.

If Chopin had come to Calder House earlier, if he had stayed longer, if he had become accustomed to his new situation, he might have regained his peace of mind and his strength. He might have begun to compose again, and the castle near Edinburgh might have saved him. But after a three-week stay with his friends there, Chopin began to wander from city to city, from one estate to another, trying house after house. He gave three concerts—in Manchester, Glasgow, and Edinburgh—and in the course of the two subsequent months he spent in Scotland, he changed his residence ten or eleven times; in other words, he did everything to exhaust himself to the extreme, physically and mentally.

He went to Manchester after an almost fatal accident. During a drive near the sea the horses bolted, the reins broke, the coachman fell from his seat. "The carriage was smashed up," he wrote. "It was tossed from tree to tree. We would have been thrown over a precipice if one tree had not stopped the carriage." Except for minor contusions, the passengers were unharmed, and Chopin wrote that he "calmly awaited the last hour." Only his preparations for the concert suffered as a result of this accident.

In Manchester, where he arrived after an eight-hour railroad journey, he was the guest of Salis Schwabe, whom he had met in Paris. "He is one of the most important industrialists. He owns the highest chimney in Manchester; it cost him five thousand pounds," Chopin wrote to Grzymala. The Schwabes were friends of Miss Stirling and Mrs. Erskine, who managed to have Chopin invited to the industrialist's suburban residence, Crumpsall House, to save him from the smoke-filled air of the city.

On August 28th the "Gentlemen's Concert" took place in a large hall seating twelve hundred persons. It featured, in addition to Chopin, an orchestra and three singers—Alboni, Corbari, and Salvi. Chopin was surprised to find Osborne there to accompany the singers. "You, my dear Osborne, who have heard me so often in Paris, remain with those impressions," Chopin said to him. "My playing will be lost in such a large room, and my compositions will be ineffective. Your presence at the concert will be painful to both you and me."

Osborne did not heed Chopin's request. He wrote: "I was present, unknown to him, in a remote corner of the room, where I helped to cheer and applaud him. I heard him for the last time, when his prediction was fulfilled in part, for his playing was too delicate to create enthusiasm, and I felt truly sorry for him."

The *Manchester Guardian* reviewed this concert on August 30th:

Scottish Mists

Chopin appears to be about thirty years of age. He is very spare in frame, and there is an almost painful air of feebleness in his appearance and gait. This vanishes when he seats himself at the instrument, in which he seems for the time perfectly absorbed. Chopin's music and his style of performance partake of the same leading characteristics—refinement rather than vigor, subtle elaboration rather than simple comprehensiveness in composition, an elegant, rapid touch rather than a firm, nervous grasp of the instrument. But his compositions and his playing appeared to be the perfection of chamber music—fit to be associated with the most refined instrumental quartets and quartet-playing—but wanting breadth and obviousness of design and executive power to be effective in a large concert hall.

Chopin's net earnings for this concert were sixty pounds.

A few days later he went to Edinburgh. During his first stay there he had met a certain Doctor Lyszczynski, a homeopath, whom he had liked tremendously. Now he went to the doctor's house for a few days of ease, and in order to have an opportunity to speak Polish. Deprived of the familiar language, Chopin was a stranger wherever he happened to be. He felt this need now more than ever before; for a whole month he had felt lost in English speech as in a wilderness.

Lyszczynski, an emigrant from Poland, was married to an amiable and musical Englishwoman who could speak French. The Doctor was most cordial to Chopin, who, whenever he came to Edinburgh, stayed with him to recuperate from his rests in lordly houses. There was a room reserved for him on the second floor, where the Doctor carried him in the evening, and where only Daniel was allowed to come in the morning, in order to arrange his master's hair. Chopin played the piano, listened to the singing of his hostess, and, feeling chilled even in the summer, warmed himself at the fireplace. He felt completely at home here; he could indulge in whims, and, in the steadily deteriorating state of his health, could seek medical help of the Doctor.

From Edinburgh he went to Johnstone Castle, which was eleven miles from Glasgow. Miss Stirling had wished him to

The Life and Death of Chopin

meet her second sister, the widowed Mrs. Houston, who occupied this beautiful and well-appointed residence. He found atrocious weather and a crowd of guests. "There are many ladies of all sorts here, aged lords in their seventies or eighties, and no young people at all, because they are out hunting." He was not enthusiastic about this company. He wrote to Grzymala:

If I were in a good mood I should describe to you one Scottish lady, a thirteenth cousin of Mary Stuart (*sic!*). Here it is nothing but cousins of great families and great names that nobody on the Continent has ever heard of. The entire conversation turns about genealogy; it's like the Gospels—this one begat that one, and then that one begat, and again that one begat, and so on for two pages down to Jesus.

The anachronistic cousins' cousins were not a pleasure, especially during rains and blizzards, when Chopin had to stay indoors for several days on end. Penned in this aristocratic stuffiness, he complained helplessly: "It is bad outside, and I am cross and sad, and people bore me with their excessive devotion. I can neither breathe nor work." Then suddenly he cried out like a prisoner in this crowded castle: "I feel alone, alone, alone, although I am surrounded . . ." and he crossed out the seven lines that followed as though unwilling to complete his painful confession.

Meanwhile, Miss Stirling busied herself with preparations for a concert in Glasgow. "They are dear here, kindhearted, they have great solicitude for me," Chopin wrote of his pupil, under a generalized designation, as he had once done in the case of George Sand. That day he had apparently forgiven his new guardian the "excessive solicitude" with which she began to bore him again on the next day.

At this time he was informed, perhaps by Lyszczynski, that Princess Czartoryska was in Edinburgh with her husband and son, and that they wished to see him. Nothing could have forced him to remain with Mrs. Houston. He took the train, put up at the Lyszczynskis', and immediately went to see his Paris friends.

He wrote to Grzymala: "Princess Marcelina is the same angel of kindness as last year. I revived somewhat under their Polish roof."

On September 27th, at half past two in the afternoon, he appeared at Merchant Hall in Glasgow before an aristocratic audience. He was assisted by a singer, Madame Adelasio de Margueritte. Muir Wood, the bookseller who had accompanied Chopin on his trip from London to Edinburgh, was in charge of the sale of tickets at one guinea each, a price without precedent in Glasgow. All of the pianist's new friends came to the concert; Lord Torphichen and Lord and Lady Murray had to travel a hundred miles. The audience also included the Czartoryskis; his meeting with them, he said, had given him "new strength for playing." Actually he felt better than usual that day; he repeated his Manchester program, and the enraptured listeners gave him an ovation. The press was very favorable, and the *Courier* discussed the concert twice. His net earnings were sixty pounds. After the concert there was a reception at Johnstone Castle; among those who attended were Lord Torphichen, Lord and Lady Murray and his friends the Czartoryskis. "You won't believe how this revived me on that day," Chopin wrote to Grzymala.

From Johnstone Castle, Chopin went to visit Lord and Lady Murray at Stachur on Loch Lyne, and from there to Keir House in Perthshire. In Keir he was greeted by Sir William Stirling-Maxwell, uncle of the "good Scottish ladies" and head of the Stirling clan. He was a cultivated gentleman, a connoisseur of Spanish painting, author of several works on aesthetics, and owner of several Murillos. Chopin, who had met him in London, spoke of him with respect.

But neither Maxwell nor even the Murillo canvases could make the world seem brighter to him or dispel the mist that enveloped everything—extending to much more than just the view from the castle's windows. On October 1st, when the fog was thicker than usual, he sat down to write a letter to Grzymala, and next to the dateline he recorded: "Sunday. No mail, no trains, no carriage (not even for a drive), nor any boat, nor even a dog to whistle to." In this long letter he told his friend of his latest journeyings, and then gave himself to these moving confidences:

If I don't write you jeremiads, it is not because you won't comfort me, for you are the only man who knows everything about me; but once I begin, there will be no end to them, and it is always the same thing. I am inaccurate in saying "the same," because with regard to the future everything goes from bad to worse with me. I feel weaker, I can't compose anything, not only because I have no desire but also because of physical obstacles, for each week I am tossed on a different tree limb. And what am I to do? Moreover, this saves me a little money for the winter. I have plenty of invitations and I cannot even go where I should like to—for instance, to the Duchess of Argyll or Lady Belhaven—because the season is too advanced for me to travel in my condition. All morning, up till two o'clock, I am fit for nothing. Then when I dress, everything bothers me, and I gasp like this until dinner, after which one must sit for two hours with the men at table, and look at them talking and listen to them drinking. Bored to death (thinking of not the same things as they think of, despite all kinds of courtesies and French remarks at that table), I go to the drawing room, where I need all my courage to revive myself somewhat, for then they are usually eager to hear me. Then my good Daniel carries me upstairs to my bedroom (which, as you know, is always on the upper floor here), undresses me, puts me down, leaves a candle, and I am allowed to breathe and dream until morning, when the same thing begins all over again. And as soon as I get accustomed to one place, I must go to some other place, for my Scottish ladies leave me no peace; either they come to fetch me or they drive me to visit their families (*nota bene*, I always insist on being personally and very much invited). They will stifle me by their kindness, and I won't stop them from doing this out of politeness.

In this condition he had no mind for anything. The day before his appearance in Edinburgh he did not know what he would play, and he did not go to inspect the hall. The concert took place in the Hopetoun Rooms, on October 4th. Chopin's recital filled the evening with the following program: *"Andante et impromptu; études; nocturne et berceuse; grande valse brillante; andante précéde d'un largo; préludes, ballade, mazurkas, et valses."*

There is a surviving legend that the prospects for the concert were none too good, and that Miss Stirling bought one hundred tickets at half a guinea each to save the situation. On the other hand, the newspapers reported that "the hall was filled," and that the audience was "select and most fashionable." The Edinburgh *Courant* classed Chopin's compositions "among the best specimens of classical excellence," and in regard to his playing, said:

Of his execution we need say nothing further than that it is the most finished we have ever heard. He has neither the ponderosity nor the digital power of a Mendelssohn, a Thalberg, or Liszt; consequently his execution would appear less effective in a large room, but as a chamber pianist he stands unrivaled.

Chopin reported to Gutmann: "I played in Edinburgh. All the distinguished people of the vicinity gathered. They say it turned out well. There was a little success and a little money."

Wholly a slave of his own and other people's amiability, he dragged himself after his ministering angels to Calder House, and from there, with the result of utter exhaustion, to Lady Belhaven's seat at Wishaw and to the Duke of Hamilton's. These trips were nothing but a crucifixion, a day-by-day ordeal amid a throng of alien persons, dull conversations, and stifling cordiality. There is not a single letter of this period in which he does not complain about his ill-health and his discouragement, and some of these letters were so "black and bad" that he tore them up. Cholera was raging on the Continent and was reported to have reached London. Chopin was alarmed for his family in Warsaw and his friends in Paris. It was autumn, invariably the worst season for him; at Hamilton Castle he was stricken with severe pains, and it took all his strength to sit through the inescapable long hours at table and in the drawing room. Finally, in a state of extreme depletion, he took leave of the Duke of Hamilton, went to Edinburgh, and found refuge at the Lyszczynskis'. He was suffering from a chill, and he was bored and disgusted with everything. He stayed in the Doctor's house for five days.

During these days, when he was at last enjoying some peace, he was clearly aware of his condition. He made his will, and referred to it in the following words: "I wrote down a kind of instruction as to what to do with my old rubbish in case I should give up the ghost somewhere." In his notebook he made a drawing of a churchyard with coffins and crosses; next to the drawing there are some musical signs.

In the course of these last wanderings Chopin succeeded in escaping from his "Scottish ladies," and this was a certain relief. Their tender tyranny and deadly solicitude had become an incubus to him. The obtuseness of Miss Stirling, who, in her attempts to help the man she venerated, was intent on doing everything that would hasten his end, seems incomprehensible. Possibly she did not fully realize the seriousness of his condition, particularly because Chopin, to every question as to how he felt, gave the familiar answer: "Couldn't be better." Yet she was aware that he had to be carried upstairs, that he was racked by increasingly severe paroxysms of coughing, and she could scarcely fail to understand the meaning of that shattered mood which made it impossible for him to muster concentration for composing.

It may be conjectured that in her pathetic, unrequited love, she was blind to everything—Chopin's character, his habits, above all his need for solitude, which was as great as his need for companionship, and finally his broken health and his mortal fatigue. In her need to possess, she clung to the idea that Chopin, now that he had left France, belonged to her; moreover, he might stay in England and need her help. Possibly Miss Stirling sought confirmation of this idea from Chopin, and Chopin no doubt avoided giving it. But it seems that in the end they had some intimate conversations. From Edinburgh, Chopin wrote to

Scottish Mists

Grzymala: "Friendship is friendship—I said so openly—but it does not give the right to anything else."

Nevertheless, the rumor went in Paris that Chopin would marry Miss Stirling. When Grzymala reported this to him, Dr. Lyszczynski's patient reacted with wistful humor:

Even if I could fall in love with someone who would also love me, as I would wish, I still would not marry, because we wouldn't have anything to eat or a place to live in. And a rich woman seeks a rich man—or, if a poor man, not an invalid but someone young and handsome. It is permissible to be poor alone, but when there are two, it is the greatest misfortune. I may die in a hospital, but I won't leave a penniless wife behind.

But the "Scottish ladies" did not lose their ardor. On October 30th Chopin wrote:

They'll be here today. They would have me stay and knock about the Scottish palaces, here and there and wherever I am invited. They are good-natured but so boring that God help me. Every day I receive letters—I don't answer any of them—and wherever I go, they follow me if they can. This may have suggested to someone the idea that I am about to marry; yet some sort of physical attraction is needed for marriage, and the one who isn't married is too much like me. How can one kiss oneself?

At the end of three months Chopin bade farewell in bitter words to Scotland and to the time he had lost:

In the meantime, what has become of my art? And where have I wasted my heart? I can scarcely recall how they sing in Poland. The world somehow passes me by. I forget, I have no strength. If I raise myself a little, I fall all the lower.

On October 31st Chopin left for London. Upon his arrival he fell ill and took to his bed. "I had a chill, with headaches, choking, and all my bad symptoms." For more than two weeks he did not leave his room. He was treated by several physicians, chiefly by Dr. Mallan, a brother-in-law of Lady Gainsborough.

The "Scottish ladies" followed him. Mrs. Erskine came to see him bearing a Bible; she read Psalms to him and tried to comfort him by saying that "the other world is better than this one."

He dreamed of returning to Paris; he was impatient "to begin to breathe better, to be able to understand people, to see friendly faces." Yet Paris had been the scene of his most devastating experience and his most painful separation. He wrote to Grzymala:

> I have never cursed anyone, but I feel so unbearably bad now that it seems to me that it would be better if I could curse Lucrezia. But there too they suffer, and they suffer all the more because they are probably aging in anger.

He urged Grzymala to find him a new apartment or else a room for Daniel near the Square d'Orléans; then, suddenly shaken in resolve, he added, "But what is the purpose of my returning? Why does not God let me die at once? Why does he kill me only gradually, making me go through these fevers of indecision?"

By November 16th he was sufficiently strengthened by Dr. Mallan's medication to be able to play at an annual ball arranged as a benefit for Polish exiles. He was persuaded to do this by Lord Dudley Stuart, by his compatriots, and by his own heart. He played several of his compositions. This was his last public appearance.

After the concert he returned to his bed. "I am all swollen from neuralgia," he wrote to Solange. He was visited by Dr. Clark, Queen Victoria's personal physician, who ordered him to leave London as soon as possible. The same advice was given by others. He decided to leave on November 23rd, a Thursday, traveling with Daniel and a Polish book dealer named Niedzwiedzki. He was to spend the night between Thursday and Friday in Boulogne, and announced that he would be in Paris on Friday at noon. "One more day here, and I'll be a madman, not a dead man. My Scottish ladies are so boring—may God save me. They have fastened themselves so tightly to me that there is no getting rid of them," he wrote to Grzymala. He asked his friend and Mademoiselle de Rozières to inspect his apartment, to get a piano from Pleyel, and to have it covered. He also asked them to notify his concierge of his coming, to order her to buy pine cones, to light the stoves, to unroll the rugs, and to hang the curtains. In conclusion he asked Grzymala to do one more thing for him:

On Friday have a bouquet of violets bought for me, so that there may be a fragrance in the drawing room. Let me at least have a little poetry in my home when I come back and go through the drawing room to the bedroom, where I will no doubt lie down for a long time.

No More Pain

Emaciated, stooped, ash-gray of countenance, his eyes bright with fever, Chopin came back to the Square d'Orléans and looked fondly about his old apartment, overjoyed to see his friends once more. It was Friday, November 24, 1848—the day on which he had said he would return. Almost immediately he had to reconcile himself to the news of the death of Dr. Molin, who had helped him to recover from his severe illness in May, 1847. "He alone knew the secret of how to treat me," Chopin said.

He tried to replace Molin with other physicians—Louis, Roth, and Simon, a noted homeopath. All of them took exorbitant fees for consultations and often came twice a day. All agreed that the Paris climate was bad for their patient and recommended rest and quiet. Chopin faithfully followed this advice, but referred to it facetiously: "Someday I'll have a rest, but without them."

His neuralgic swelling passed, and despite the winter cold he began to go out. But he recuperated very slowly, and he was impatient and full of anxiety. Early in 1849 he fell into financial difficulties. The money he had earned in England was melting away, and there could be no thought of taking pupils. To save him from worry, Franchomme undertook to handle his financial affairs and proved sufficiently skillful to conceal the actual situation from him. Other friends came to his help and in March an appeal was made to Miss Stirling, who had followed Chopin from England with her sister. What she did was in keeping with the kindness of her heart and with the eccentricity of her ways. She put twenty-five thousand francs in an envelope and asked a friend to take it to Chopin's concierge, a Madame Etienne, who was then to hand it to him. This generous gift was to be anonymous. Miss Stirling mentioned it to no one. The concierge put the envelope in a drawer and forgot about it, and its existence remained undisclosed for more than four months.

Chopin's first visits in Paris were to his friends—Grzymala, Clésinger, the Czartoryskis, Delphine Potocka. He wrote to Solange, his last link with his lost adoptive family. In his letters he touched on Nohant, but never mentioned the most significant name. The thought of George Sand aroused conflicting feelings in him. According to an account by Teofil Kwiatkowski, a Polish painter, he expected Lucrezia, as he now called her, to visit him, and gave orders to Grzymala not to admit her. But when he was no longer confined to his bed, he would run to the door each time the bell rang, pushing back his servant or his friends. With Delacroix, who frequently visited him, he spoke freely about George Sand. Delacroix prognosticated an unhappy old age for her, but Chopin disagreed with him. "Her conscience does not charge her with any of the things that her friends reproach her with," he said. "She would be affected only if she lost Maurice or if he gave himself over completely to a bad life."

The loss of George Sand, and of the sense of home and family that she had given him, was a psychic wound that never healed in him. Not even his old bond with Delphine Potocka, who now showed herself a faithful friend, had power to divert him from this feeling of void. Delphine and he often visited each other. "Yesterday I saw the charming Madame Potocka at Chopin's. I had heard her twice before. I have never met with anything more complete," Delacroix wrote in his journal in March, 1849. "I also saw Madame Kalergis. She played, but she was not very moving. However, she is truly beautiful when she raises her eyes at the piano. Then she looks like a Guido or Rubens Magdalene."

Chopin resumed his musical soirées, at which Delphine sang

arrangements for voice based on his compositions. Delacroix wrote about one such gathering: "It was marvelous. I told her what I sincerely think—that in music, and doubtless in all other arts, everything else is forgotten as soon as style, character, in brief, the serious things, appear."

With the approach of spring Chopin felt better. "The spring sun will be my best physician," he wrote to Solange. His interest in music also revived; he even attended the *première* of Meyerbeer's *Le Prophète,* which horrified him. He began to compose again, but after his two years of unproductivity he experienced even greater difficulties than before. He destroyed his drafts, one after the other, and proceeded to write new ones. He wrote into Delphine's album a sad melody to words by Zygmunt Krasinski, whose poems he now read often. Under his signature he added the words, *Nella miseria* ["In misery"]. Of his other compositions of that period only two mazurkas have survived; one is in G minor (Opus 67, No. 2), and the other, which attained only draft form, is in F minor (Opus 68, No. 4). These were his last works.

He tried to carry out his old plan of formulating his experiences as a teacher, and began to write in French a work that he referred to as his *Method of Methods.* Only fragments of this have been preserved, among them the following introductory remarks:

Words stem from sounds; sounds existed before words. The word is a certain modification of the sound. Sounds are used to create music, just as words are used to create language. Thought is expressed through sounds; an indefinite human expression is scarcely a sound. The art of manipulating sounds is music. The motion of flexing a wrist is similar to that of modulating the breath in singing.

This month of May marked the last interval of delusive hope in Chopin's illness. It seemed as though he had once again cheated death and tricked his friends, who would hear on one day that he was dying but on the next day would meet him in summer raiment on a boulevard. He went about in the colony of Polish exiles, and visited Mickiewicz, who had returned to Paris after a sojourn in

Italy. The two were no nearer to each other than before. On one occasion Chopin played in the house of Mickiewicz, who was deeply moved by his music, but scolded him as of old: "Instead of developing your gift of moving the soul, you show off in the Faubourg Saint-Germain. You could transport the masses, and you titillate the nerves of aristocrats."

In the same way Slowacki, who tried to play the Ballade in G minor, failed to appreciate Chopin at his true worth. "Have you ever," the poet wrote to his mother, "seen someone so moved by Chopin's music that on the next day he became better, nobler, more charitable—grew into a hero?"

Chopin paid him back in kind. He wrote to Delphine:

I was told that Slowacki calls me a peacock and reviles me at every opportunity. I have never spoken abusively of him, and I have always avoided him. I don't understand what this numskull wants of me. Could it be that he too is in love with you?

On the other hand, Chopin found a true devotee of his music in Cyprian Kamil Norwid, a poet and painter, who failed to gain recognition in his lifetime but later came to be ranked among the greatest Polish minds. Norwid believed that art stems from national roots and "raises the national to the universally human," and he considered Chopin a living proof of his thesis. One of Chopin's letters to Delphine Potocka refers to a discussion he had with the Marquis de Custine:

The dear man! He is interested in our national music. He knows my compositions and today he asked me to play for him the works of the greatest Polish composers. I played what I knew and could play. When I finished, he said that he could not discover in these things any indication that these were Polish works. While admitting that since he is a foreigner he may be mistaken, he insisted that these works are such that a Frenchman or an Englishman could have composed them. And he said that Polish music begins with me, and paid me other such great compliments. I contradicted him and defended those other composers. The bell rang—Norwid came in and at once asked what we were discussing. When we told him, he began to echo Custine, declaring me to be the first national composer. He feels that Polish music begins with me, that before me our music was like the dance of a lame man, etc. And they praised me thus in a duet until I fled from them to the drawing room to play, and they immediately came there too. Now I played, now we talked, and thus the night passed pleasantly. We separated only at daybreak. Norwid understands me better than Mickiewicz. While Mickiewicz urges me to write a national opera, Norwid, knowing my limitations, has never mentioned anything like that to me.

Chopin's relationship with Norwid was new; the poet had come to Paris only recently. But they became close friends very soon. "I love and greatly respect him; he is one of the greatest artists, and a man to my liking," Chopin wrote of him. Norwid made several pen portraits of the composer. Chopin sent them in a letter to Delphine, but none of them has survived.

The friendship with Norwid also had an odd interlude of consternation. Chopin wrote about it to Delphine:

You know that I am a shrewd politician and that I know how to manage people, but occasionally I too commit a blunder, for which I cannot be sorry enough later. I fell into such an unpleasant mishap with Norwid. One day long ago he came to see me and I played for him as usual. I saw that the sleeves of his shabby linen jacket were quite torn, so I told him that my concierge would mend them, and I took the jacket to Mme Etienne. Norwid sat covered with my warm dressing gown. I myself brought the jacket back from Mme Etienne, because I wanted to put some money into the pocket. Norwid did not suspect anything, put it on, and left. And now he has not come to see me for a long time. I think that I hurt his feelings with that money. He has borrowed from others, even asked his friends for money, as I know, but he never asked me for a penny, and there has never been any talk between us about money. Perhaps he wanted art to be the only bond between us. It is on the whole difficult to understand him, he is so strange, but today I realize that I should have treated him in a special way. I cannot regret this enough, and I cannot explain to him that my gesture was dictated by the heart. When I think of it, I go to pieces at once, I am inconsolable.

One day Chopin was visited by the Reverend Alexander Jelowicki, a former schoolmate whom he had not seen for a long time. The newcomer had traveled from Rome; he rang the bell at the house in the Square d'Orléans, and on seeing Frederic was amazed that life could persist in such a worn physique. "His face was cold as alabaster, white and transparent, and his eyes, for the most part veiled as with a mist, sometimes brightened with a penetrating glance. Unfailingly sweet, amiable, and bubbling with wit, and exceedingly kind, he seemed to belong only in slight degree to earth. But, alas, he was not thinking of heaven."

Chopin divined what had brought the priest to him. Madame Justyna was a pious Catholic, but her son had become indifferent to religion, and only his "exquisite decency," as Father Alexander put it, kept him from "ridiculing sacred things."

"I should not like to die without having received the sacrament, because I don't want to bring grief to my mother," Chopin said to him. "But I cannot take it, because I don't understand it in your way."

This meeting must have been painful to both. They talked about their families, about Frederic's mother, whom he had not seen for fourteen years, and about the priest's brother Edward, who had died in 1848. They wept. When the visitor rose to leave, Chopin said, "If I ever want to confess, it will surely be with you."

At the end of May, Chopin suffered a relapse. All treatments attempted were ineffective, and the spring sun did not prove as efficacious as Chopin had hoped. He even consulted some quacks, he was so anxious to recover. But nothing was of avail. To Solange, who had given birth to another girl, he wrote: "Your very unfortunate friend blesses you and blesses your child."

Cholera broke out in Paris. The heat spells began, and Chopin's friends decided to move him to the outskirts of the city, for a journey of any length was out of the question. Once again he was short of money, and he decided to sell some of his belongings.

In June he moved to an apartment at No. 74 Grande Rue Chaillot, which was then outside the city limits. He occupied the whole second floor of a small house. From his large drawing room he had a view of trees, gardens, and the city spreading out below. The rent for the season was four hundred francs; Chopin was told that it was two hundred. Princess Obreskov covered the difference.

Chopin's routine was to rise late and to be dressed by Daniel, who would then make him comfortable in a chair next to a window, where he could watch for friends coming to see him. Among his visitors were the Princess Czartoryska, the Baroness de Rothschild, the Princess Obreskov, Pleyel, and his devoted Franchomme. Delphine came from Versailles with her sister, the Princess Charles Beauvau. He was also visited by Angelica Catalani, the singer who had given him a gold watch when he was a boy in Warsaw, and one day he enjoyed a great surprise when Jenny Lind came. Chopin, who made a cult of friendship, was deeply moved by her visit. She sang to him for an entire evening.

Norwid also reappeared—the incident of the patched jacket had apparently not diminished their friendship. The poet has described the large drawing room, "where his immortal piano stood," and his account adds: "In this drawing room Chopin also dined at about five o'clock, then he walked downstairs as best he could and drove to the Bois de Boulogne; on his return he was carried upstairs, because he could not climb the steps. Several times I dined with him and accompanied him on his drives."

Chopin was now being treated by a Dr. Fraenkel, who satisfied him no more than his other physicians had. Writing to Grzymala, who had gone to the country, Chopin said of him:

There is no way of finding out from him whether I should go to some spa or to the South. He has once again taken back his infusion, and given me another medicine, and once again I don't want it—and when I ask him concerning my regimen, he says that I don't have to lead a regular life. In short, he is crazy.

The removal to Chaillot did not improve Chopin's health. "I haven't begun to play yet," he wrote. "I can't compose, and I don't know what hay I'll be eating shortly." He was depressed by reports of the ravages of the plague. Among its victims were Madame Catalani, whom he had seen only recently, and Kalkbrenner, as well as the son of Delaroche, the painter, and the Franchommes' maidservant; the son of Madame Etienne, Chopin's concierge in the Square d'Orléans, was struggling with death. Although it was said that the epidemic was on the decline, people were fleeing from the city, and sometimes Chopin sat at his window waiting all day in vain for a visitor. Norwid had disappeared again. When the "Scottish ladies" came, Chopin was alarmed. "They will stifle me with boredom," he wrote. Charles Gavard, brother of a favorite pupil, Elise Gavard, came to read Voltaire to him. Sometimes he was so exhausted that he was unable to speak and had to communicate with his visitor by means of gestures.

On the night of June 21st he had two hemorrhages. The following day he spewed blood. His legs began to swell; his heart weakened. And Doctor Fraenkel failed to appear for a week. Chopin was at the end of his strength.

Then he did something that he had restrained himself all his life from doing—he confided to his family that he was severely ill. On June 25th he wrote to Ludwika asking her to come to him with her husband and daughter, who was also named Ludwika.

My life, if you can come, do. I am weak, and no doctor will help me as much as you will. If you are short of money, borrow some; if I recover, I'll easily earn and repay it to the lender, but at present I am so out of funds that I cannot send you any. My flat here in Chaillot is large enough to accommodate you even with two children. Little Ludwika would benefit from it in every respect. Papa Kalasanty could go about all day, the farm exhibition is near by. In brief, he would have more time for himself than before, because I am weaker and I'll sit at home with Ludwika more.

My friends and well-wishers think that Ludwika's coming would be the best medicine for me, as Ludwika will surely learn from Mme Obreskov's letter. So apply for a passport. Today two persons—

one from the North and the other from the South, persons who don't know Ludwika—have said to me that it would be good not only for me but also for my sister. So, Mother Ludwika and Daughter Ludwika, bring your thimbles and knitting needles, I'll give you handkerchiefs to mark and stockings to knit, and you'll be spending a few months here in the fresh air with your brother and uncle. The trip is easier now. You won't need much baggage. Here we'll manage as inexpensively as we can. You'll find shelter and food. If Kalasanty should sometimes find it far to go from the Champs Elysées to the city, he can stay in my flat in the Square d'Orléans. The omnibuses come from the Square to the very door here.

I don't know why I have such a craving for Ludwika—it's like the craving of a pregnant woman. I guarantee that it will be good for her too. I hope that the family council will send her to me. Who knows—perhaps I'll bring her back if I recover. How we would all embrace each other then—and won't have to wait till we are wearing wigs and have lost our teeth. A wife owes obedience to her husband; thus the husband must be asked to bring his wife. So I beg him very much to do it, and if he will consider it, he surely can give no greater pleasure and benefit to her or to me, or even to the children, if he brings any (I have no doubt about the little daughter). It will mean an expense, that's true, but the money could not be better used, nor could one travel more cheaply. Once you are here, a roof will be found. Write me a word soon. . . .

The cholera is much abated; it is almost gone. Today the weather is fine. I sit in the drawing room and admire my view over all Paris —the towers, the Tuileries, the Chamber of Deputies, St.-Germain-l'Auxerrois, St.-Etienne-du-Mont, Notre Dame, the Panthéon, St.-Sulpice, Val-de-Grâce, the Invalides, through five windows, and nothing but gardens between. You'll see when you come. Now make haste without waste—take steps to get a passport and money. Write to me at once. After all, even "cypresses have their caprices"; my caprice today is to see you. Perhaps God will permit that it should go well, and if God does not permit, at least act as though He might permit. I am of good hope, for I rarely ask for much, and I would abstain even from this if I were not pressed by all those who wish me well. Bestir yourself, Mr. Kalasanty, I'll reward you with an excellent big cigar; I know someone who smokes first-class ones— *nota bene,* in the garden. I hope that my letter for Mama's name day arrived in time, and that I wasn't missing. I don't want to think about all this, because it gives me a fever; but I have no fever, thank God, which baffles and angers all run-of-the-mill doctors.

Chopin held this letter back several days, as though he had suddenly been seized by doubt as to whether he should disclose the grim truth to his family, but in the end he sent it. Then he began to wait for the coming of Ludwika. His legs were no longer swollen; he stopped spitting blood. "Only I am still weak and lazy, I can't walk, I choke," he wrote to Grzymala. The Czartoryskis sent him their old servant Matuszewska, to watch over him at night. "Jesus will take it away," she comforted Chopin, and recommended to him her own homely panacea: "Maybe a plaster of honey and flour would help."

Now there was an improvement that lasted for several days and aroused in him a sudden energy, a will to live, a desire to be saved. Solange invited him to the country, to the home of her husband's parents; she ordered his carriage to be made ready, and Chopin thought with longing of going South. The illusion was short-lived. At the beginning of July he had another hemorrhage. Because Dr. Fraenkel had ceased to come, he consulted Dr. Cruveilhier. "He prescribes almost nothing; he orders me only to rest. He says that if homeopathy did me good in the days of Dr. Molin, it was because he did not overload me with medication and left much to nature. But I see that he too thinks I am tubercular, because he has prescribed for me a coffeespoonful of something with lichen in it."

July with its heat was drawing to its end; all of Chopin's friends had left Paris, and Ludwika had not come. "I am beginning to lose hope about my sister," he wrote to Grzymala on July 28th. He now saw to his affairs himself, attended only by Matuszewska and his faithful Daniel. He was short of money, and he tried to sell his precious Bréguet watch, but even in this he had no luck. Someone again informed Miss Stirling. The "good Scottish lady" was amazed, and revealed that she had sent Chopin twenty-five thousand francs. There was general consternation, and the whole story was disclosed to Chopin. "I was completely at a loss. I did not know whether to suspect her [Miss Stirling] of suffering from hallucination, or accuse her trusted man or Madame Etienne of stealing, or consider myself an idiot or crazy—in brief, my head was bursting."

The plot of this mystery story does indeed strain credulity. It involves even a resort to the services of a telepathic medium, who was known as *Alexis le Somnambule*. Chopin described the whole affair at length to Grzymala:

This person who was entrusted with such a sum unbeknownst to him, and who did not take a receipt from Mme Etienne for the letter or packet, went to *Alexis le Somnambule*. And here the drama begins. Alexis told him that one Thursday in March (the 8th) he took very important papers to an address (Alexis wrote out my name), that this packet did not reach its destination, that he himself does not have it, that he delivered it, in a small dark room which one enters by walking down two steps, to some woman (there were two women there), that it was taken by the taller of the two, who was holding a letter that the postman had given her, and who upon taking the packet from this person told him that she would deliver it at once. However, Alexis added, she took it downstairs without even showing it to me, and so I have never seen this letter. When Alexis was asked whether he could not see what was happening to this letter, he answered that he did not see, but that if they would bring him a lock of hair or a handkerchief or a glove belonging to the person who had accepted the letter, he would tell them this. Mrs. Erskine was present at this séance with Alexis, and yesterday she came to me to tell me about it, and to ask how she might obtain something belonging to Mme Etienne. I asked Mme Etienne to come to me, by the pretext of asking her to bring me . . . handkerchiefs. When she came I pretended that Mrs. Erskine wanted a bit of my own hair for some medium who was treating sick people in St.-

No More Pain

Germain (that's where the Scottish ladies are living), and I told the concierge that if this medium, on receiving hair of Mme Etienne's, recognizes whose hair it is, I'll believe in her powers and only then will I send mine; and I added that I was sure that she would mistake the hair of a healthy person for the hair of a sick one. So Mme Etienne agreed to cut some of her hair; she wrapped it up, and Mrs. Erskine took it.

This morning the trusted agent came to me with Mrs. Erskine from Alexis. Alexis recognized the hair as that of the person who had received the packet, and said that she had put the packet, sealed, in some little piece of furniture next to her bed, that the packet was still on her premises, and that it had neither been lost, nor given away, nor unsealed. And that if this gentleman managed things right, she would give it back to him, but that he must be careful. So at noon this gentleman went from here directly to the Square d'Orléans, found Mme Etienne alone, recalled to her that in March he had given her a packet for me that, he told her, was very important. She recognized him and gave him the packet that she had received from him so many months before. It was not unsealed, and the twenty-five thousand francs were in it, intact. Mrs. Erskine unsealed it in the presence of myself and this gentleman. What do you say to this?

For some time Chopin continued to be intrigued by the strangeness of this occurrence. He wrote finis to the tale in a letter to Grzymala dated August 3rd:

As for my curious incident, there are many, many peculiar angles to it, which I cannot explain by reference to magnetism, lying, hallucination (in Miss S.), or Mme Etienne's honesty. It is even possible *que la chose a été faite après coup.* There is much to say about this; among other things, that I received another anonymous letter, which I delivered to the right person. I have not discussed any of this with Mme Etienne nor am I going to, although tomorrow a week will have passed. The packet may have been handed to her only three days in advance; since I was not at home, and since she was here, it could have been retrieved without the somnambulist just as well as with his aid. All the more so because there is a coincidence in the various conversations! Kindheartedness is there, but also an inclination to the theatrical!

At first Chopin refused to avail himself of Miss Stirling's help and wrote in this vein to Grzymala, but later he accepted part of the gift. His notebook contains the entry, "Mrs. Erskine left fifteen thousand francs."

Chaillot became animated in August. Solange with her husband and child moved to the neighborhood, and on August 8th the Jedrzejewiczs arrived with their daughter. Chopin wrote to Mademoiselle de Rozières that he was happy. This was the last time that he was to be lulled by the deception of this feeling.

Ludwika took over the housekeeping, and Frederic was surrounded by a home atmosphere. He still had enough energy to accompany his sister to his apartment in the Square d'Orléans, which he had decided to give up. Ludwika could not have any illusions about his health, and when Kalasanty departed after a few weeks to Poland, he must have said farewell to Chopin with a heavy heart.

Memories of happier times stirred again in Chopin when he received a letter from Tytus announcing that he was taking the cure at Karlsbad and was planning afterward to go to Ostende. Frederic replied to him:

My dearest, I must indeed be weak, not to be able to budge from Paris when you are coming to Ostende. But I hope that God will permit you to come near to where I am. My doctors forbid me any kind of trip. I drink Pyrenean waters in my room, but your presence would do me more good than any medicines.

Tytus took steps to obtain a passport for Paris, and Frederic set his own friends to work to help him. He wrote to Tytus about it, apologizing for his inability to hasten to him:

I had too little time to obtain permission for your coming here; since I could not go myself—I am in bed half the time—I asked an influential friend to help me. I am to hear something certain only next Saturday. I want to take the train to Valenciennes on the border in order to embrace you, but a few days ago I was unable to make the trip to Versailles to see my goddaughter, and the doctor won't let me leave Paris. They won't even let me go to a warmer place in the winter. It's my fault, for I am ill, else I would have joined you somewhere in Belgium.

Perhaps you'll succeed in getting here. I am not selfish enough to want you for myself; since I am so weak, you would have had a few hours of boredom and disappointment, mingled with a few hours of gladness and happy memories. I'd rather make the time we spend together a time of complete happiness.

Because of current unsettled political conditions in France, Tytus was not granted permission to come. Just as he had once, long ago, near Vienna, stood bereft on an empty road in the night, Frederic remained alone with his memories, his devotion, and his longing.

Through Solange or someone else, George Sand heard of Chopin's illness. Ludwika received a letter from her written at Nohant on September 1st:

I have learned that you are in Paris, which I did not know. From you I shall at last have a truthful report on Frederic. Some persons write to me that he is far more ill than usual, others that he is only weakened and suffering as I have always seen him. Please write me a line; I take the liberty of asking you for this, because one can be forgotten and deserted by one's children without ceasing to love them. Please write to me about yourself, and be assured that ever since I met you I have not lived one day without thoughts of you and cordial memories. The thought of me must have been destroyed in your heart; but it seems to me that I have not deserved everything that I have suffered.

This letter came a year or two too late. One half of its warmth, a small part of its sincerity, one sentence embodying the good will and kind intentions with which it was filled, might earlier have changed much in the life of the man for whom it was now meaningless. The letter went unanswered, and it is not known whether Chopin was told about it.

The Life and Death of Chopin

Early in September, Chopin's physicians held a consultation. Cruveilhier and Louis had invited Dr. Blache, a famous pediatrician, to confer with them. Chopin said jestingly, "He'll help me most, for there is in me something of a child."

The consultation did not result in anything new. It was established that the patient could not travel and that he must stay in Paris, and that he needed an apartment with a southern exposure. Such an apartment was found in the Place Vendôme. Chopin became animated at the thought of moving. He planned new furnishings and discussed wallpapers, and he wrote to Franchomme: "At last I'll see all of you this winter, in comfortable lodgings." The Place Vendôme became the topic of all his conversations.

In mid-September, Norwid came to see Chopin in Chaillot, and he has described his visit as follows:

One morning I dropped in to see him. The French servant said that he was asleep, so I muted my steps, left a card, and walked out. I had hardly descended a few stairs when the servant called me back, saying that upon learning who it was Chopin had asked that I come in—in brief, he had not been asleep but was not receiving anyone. So I entered the room next to the drawing room—in which Chopin slept—very thankful that he had consented to see me. I found him dressed, but reclining on his bed, with swollen legs; this could be perceived at once, although he wore stockings and shoes. The artist's sister was sitting next to him, strangely resembling him in profile. . . . He was in the shadow of the deep bed with curtains, leaning on his pillows, and wrapped in a shawl, and he was very beautiful, and as always there was something perfect, something classical, in his most casual gestures. . . . Then, in a voice broken by his coughing and choking, he began to reproach me for not having come to him for such a long time. After that he spoke jestingly and wanted to tease me about my mystical tendencies, and since it gave him pleasure, I let him do it. I talked with his sister; he had fits of coughing, and then the moment came when he had to be left alone. I said farewell to him, and he, pressing my hand, threw his hair back from his forehead, and said, "I am going . . ." and began to cough. Upon hearing this, I kissed him on the arm and, knowing that he was pleased when sharply contradicted, I said in a tone that one uses with a strong and courageous person, "You have been going in this way every year, and yet, thank God, we still see you alive." To this Chopin, finishing the sentence that was interrupted by the coughing, said, "I am saying that I am going to leave this apartment and move to the Place Vendôme."

Late in September, Chopin left Chaillot and moved to the last apartment he was to occupy, at No. 12 Place Vendôme. He reclined in his sunlit room, listening to the movers who were bringing in the furniture he had ordered. Occasionally he got up for a few hours to look over his new apartment, which was to belong to him for three weeks. Dr. Cruveilhier's treatment could not fend off the inevitable. Chopin choked in fits of coughing, gasped for breath, suffered violent rushes of blood to the head. It became evident that the end was near.

His friends never left him. Ludwika alternated with Princess Marcelina and Solange at his bedside, and Franchomme, Clésinger, Gavard, and Kwiatkowski held themselves at his disposal. Moscheles, then in Paris, wrote in his diary: "We questioned several persons, and our worst fears were confirmed. He is completely broken. His sister is at his bedside. Poor man, his days are counted. He is suffering a great deal."

On the night of October 12th it seemed that his last hour had struck. Dr. Cruveilhier sent for Father Alexander, who came at once. Chopin at first refused to see him; later, yielding to his sister's request, he held out his hand to the priest and said, "I love you, but don't say a word. Go to sleep."

On the following day, which happened to be St. Edward's Day, the priest came to see Chopin at noon and found him at breakfast. The patient's condition seemed improved; he asked Father Alexander to sit down and offered him food. "Today is my brother Edward's name day," said the priest.

Chopin sighed. He listened attentively to his visitor's words. The conversation between them was later recounted in a letter written by Father Alexander to Ksawera Grocholska. In the name of his deceased brother, he asked Chopin for a gift—for his soul. "I understand you. Take it," said Chopin.

The priest handed him a crucifix and knelt beside him. The other visitors left the room, Chopin made his confession, asked for the sacrament, and called back his friends. Princess Marcelina began to recite the litany for the dying, which the others repeated after her. Everyone knelt, Poles and Frenchmen, Matuszewska and the faithful Daniel. Chopin lay flat on his back, and tears rolled down his cheeks. He felt relieved and even asked for some music. The Princess Marcelina and Franchomme began the Sonata in G minor, but after the first few measures the music had to defer to a coughing fit.

This dying agony went on for four days. Most of the time Chopin remained conscious. When he was seized by pain, he begged for death. He wished Father Alexander to be with him and held the priest's hand and asked him to pray. At one point Chopin, who for all his fastidiousness, had resorted to crude folk idiom in his native tongue, said to his confessor and former schoolmate: "Without you, my dear, I should have died as a pig dies."

On October 15th Delphine Potocka came to the Place Vendôme. She had left Nice for Paris upon hearing that Chopin was dying. The chroniclers of her visit mention that she looked beautiful and wore white. Chopin's face brightened when he saw her, and he said, "It was to enable me to see you that God has postponed calling me to him."

As soon as she approached him he asked her to sing for him. The priest, who was praying beside Chopin's bed, supported his request. A piano was rolled in from the adjoining room. "The unhappy Countess, mastering her grief and suppressing her sobs, forced herself to sing," wrote Gavard. "As for myself, I did not hear anything. I don't know what she sang. The whole scene, its contrasts, its intense sadness—all this was more than I could stand. I recall only the moment when the patient's deadly coughing interrupted the Countess's second song."

No More Pain

According to credible witnesses, Delphine sang Stradella's "Hymn to the Virgin" and Marcello's "Psalm."

In the evening Chopin felt worse; in the night he could not speak because of sudden hoarseness, and he lost consciousness at times. On the following day he said farewell to his friends, and calmly gave his last instructions, which he had apparently decided upon a long time before. He asked Pleyel not to publish any of his remaining compositions and to destroy his manuscripts and all personal papers. He told Ludwika that he wished his heart to be taken to Warsaw. He also expressed the wish that Mozart's Requiem should be sung at his funeral Mass.

The last night came. He was seized with convulsions and was in great pain, and his arms and legs were massaged. He listened to Father Alexander's prayers, and when they ended, he said loudly, "Amen." At eleven o'clock he withdrew his hand from Dr. Cruveilhier's and would not let the physician take his pulse, saying, "It is not worth the trouble, Doctor—soon I'll rid you of me."

Then he fell asleep. He awakened after midnight. "Mother, my poor mother!" he cried, and choked with coughing.

He wanted to say something, but could not recover his voice. He was given a sheet of paper, on which he wrote with a trembling hand: "This cough may choke me. I adjure you now to have my body opened, so that I shall not be buried alive." His father had made a similar request on his deathbed.

The coughing fit lasted for a long time. When it was over, the patient's face was dark and still. The Doctor bent over him with a candle and asked him whether he was in pain. *"Plus* [No more]," he answered, in a barely perceptible voice.

Chopin died at about two o'clock in the morning of October 17, 1849. The cause of his death was given as tuberculosis of the lungs and larynx.

Requiem

R<small>EST</small> in peace, beautiful soul, noble artist! Immortality has begun for you, and you know better than we do where great thoughts and high aspirations meet again beyond the sad life of earth!"

With these words Théophile Gautier said farewell to Chopin. Chopin's life after death had begun, and throughout the last century he has indeed not been absent from this world. His art has soared above human frailty and by-passed the vicissitudes of history; and from its humble origins in "the songs on the Vistula" it has risen to the heights and its fame has circled the globe.

The ill luck that marred the earthly aspect of Chopin's existence continued to pursue him after death. Even his funeral did not proceed without obstruction. The body lay in a basement vault of the Madeleine until October 30th, when, after a last Mass, it was placed in the grave. The delay was due to Chopin's wish that Mozart's Requiem be sung at his funeral. The archbishop of Paris objected to the use of the necessary female singers, and yielded only to the request of Father Deguerry, the vicar of the Madeleine, who was an admirer of Chopin's music.

The ceremony itself was impressive. The church was draped with black. Three thousand persons were admitted by card. At noon, to the accompaniment of Chopin's Funeral March (in the orchestral arrangement by Napoléon-Henri Réber), the coffin was carried up the aisle and placed on a high catafalque. "The ceremony could not have begun in a more majestic manner, nor could there have been a nobler introduction to Mozart's masterpiece," said a Paris daily. The orchestra and chorus of the Conservatoire, conducted by Narcisse Girard, rendered the Requiem, which had not been heard in Paris since the day when the body of Napoleon had been brought back from St. Helena. The soloists were Madame Viardot-Garcia, Jeanne Castellan, Alexis Dupont, and Luigi Lablache. After the Requiem, Louis-James Lefébure-Wély, organist of the Madeleine, played Chopin's Preludes in E minor and B minor in his own transcriptions. According to the accounts published in the French and English press, the impression made by these works was tremendous, and at the close of the ceremony, when the organist played variations on Chopin themes, the audience wept.

After the Mass the coffin was taken to the Père Lachaise cemetery. The procession to the grave was headed by Prince Adam Czartoryski, as the representative of Poland, and Giacomo Meyerbeer, as the representative of the musical world. The pallbearers were Franchomme, Delacroix, Pleyel, and Alexander Czartoryski. There were no speeches at the grave. The handful of Polish earth that Chopin had preserved as a memento of his farewell evening in Warsaw was sprinkled on the coffin. Among the persons who had come to pay a last tribute to Chopin was James William Davison, the English critic who had spoken so unfavorably of the composer in his lifetime. George Sand did not attend the funeral.

Chopin's wish regarding his heart was carried out. It was taken to Warsaw and placed inside a wall of the Church of the Holy Cross, in the Krakowskie Przedmiescie, the street of his youth. But his instructions concerning his manuscripts were not obeyed. In the course of time they were published posthumously, ten of them with opus numbers and several unnumbered. His personal papers, his notebook, and various mementos were also preserved. In a drawer of his desk there was found the envelope labeled *"Moja bieda,"* in which he had tied up his letters from Maria Wodzinska and her mother and the rose from a Dresden garden.

George - Frédéric ?

The Life and Death of Chopin

In the notebook another envelope was found; it bore the inscription *"G-F,"* and it contained a lock of black hair.

However, it was not George Sand who grieved over the loss of a lover, but another woman—Jane Wilhelmina Stirling. She wore deep mourning; Jane Welsh Carlyle, who met the "good Scottish lady" in London, looking pale and dressed in crape, called her "Chopin's widow." To the end of her life she remained faithful to her unhappy love and to her idol. She lent Ludwika five thousand francs to pay for the funeral, corresponded with her concerning Chopin's unpublished manuscripts, and bought up various objects left behind by Chopin. Before the first anniversary of his death she came to Paris, and her first visit was to the Père Lachaise cemetery. On October 17, 1850, a Mass was held in the cemetery chapel, and a monument to Chopin was unveiled. It was designed by Clésinger. A committee headed by Delacroix had charged him with the work; a subscription to pay the cost of it had been initiated by Pleyel. Clésinger's sculpture, which includes a female figure with a lyre in her hand and a medallion portrait of Chopin in profile, is mediocre; it was attacked by many critics, among whom Norwid was the most outspoken. Delacroix referred to this work without enthusiasm, though in a calm tone, and Miss Stirling liked the medallion. She wrote to Ludwika that the upper part of the face reminded her of Chopin, and that the profile gave the impression that "he looked at us." Whatever mementos she had of Chopin, Miss Stirling sent to his family; she wished them to form a nucleus of a Chopin museum. She corresponded with Ludwika up to 1855, when Ludwika died leaving three sons and a daughter; her husband had died in 1853. Madame Justyna was sixty-seven when her son died; she lived until 1861.

After the death of Ludwika, the collection of Chopin mementos was kept by her younger sister, Izabela. On September 19, 1863, during the uprising against Russia, a bomb was hurled from a window of the Zamoyski palace, where the Barcinskis lived. It was aimed at General Berg, governor of Warsaw, who was riding by the palace with an escort of Cossacks. The governor and his escort did not suffer any harm; only two horses were wounded.

Requiem

But in reprisal all occupants of the house were driven out, all males were arrested, and the soldiers were allowed to plunder the palace. In the Barcinski apartment in the second story the Cossacks threw out all the Chopin mementos—many of his letters to his family and friends, his manuscripts, books, and pieces of furniture, including the Bucholz pine piano on which he had played as a student of the lyceum and the Conservatory. The soldiers made a bonfire of these trophies, and the objects that were to constitute the beginning of a Chopin museum were turned into ashes. Izabela Barcinska survived her husband by four years, dying in 1881. Their marriage was childless.

Chopin's letters to George Sand and her letters to him were also destroyed. The story of these is told in the correspondence between Alexandre Dumas fils on the one hand and his father and George Sand on the other. The first letter was written in May, 1851, from Myslowice, a border town of the Russian empire of that time, which included Poland. It was written by Alexandre Dumas fils to his father:

While you were dining with Mme Sand, dear father, I was thinking of her. Now let anyone deny the existence of affinities! Imagine, I have in my hand all of her correspondence with Chopin, covering a period of ten years. I shall let you guess whether I have copied some of those letters, far more charming than the celebrated letters of Mme Sévigné! I am bringing back a whole copybook of these letters, for unfortunately they have only been lent to me. How did it happen that in a remote corner of Silesia, at Myslowice, I should find this correspondence that flowered in the heart of the province of Berry?

The explanation is quite simple. Chopin was a Pole, as you know or don't know. Among his papers, after his death, his sister found all of these letters preserved, labeled, and wrapped up with the respect of the most devoted love. She took them with her, and on entering Poland, where the police would pitilessly have read everything she had brought, she entrusted them to one of her friends living in Myslowice. The profanation has taken place nonetheless, in that

I have looked into them, but at least it has taken place in the name of admiration rather than in the name of the police. I assure you, nothing could be sadder or more touching than these letters on which the ink has faded, and all of which were received with joy by a person who is now dead. This thing of death, at the end of these most intimate, gayest, most vivid details of life—this is an impression impossible to convey. For a while I wished that the trustee, who is my friend, should die suddenly, so that I might inherit his trust and be enabled to present it in tribute to Mme Sand, who would perhaps be quite happy to relive a little this dead past. This wretched man, my friend, is in the best of health, and since I intend to leave on the 15th, I have returned to him all these papers that he is not even curious to read. To understand this indifference it may be useful for you to know that this man is a second partner in an export firm.

On June 3rd, Alexandre Dumas fils wrote from Myslowice directly to George Sand. His excuse for an act that amounted to filching the property of other persons reads as follows:

In a few days I shall be in France and shall bring you personally, whether Mme Jedrzejewicz authorizes me or not, the letters that you wish to have. There are deeds so just that they do not require anyone's authorization. It is understood that the copy of this correspondence will be handed over to you at the same time, and that of all of these indiscretions there will remain nothing but the fortunate result that all in all they will have.

In September, 1851, the letters and copies were in the hands of George Sand, and subsequently they were destroyed. In thanking Dumas for sending her this correspondence, she wrote:

Since you have had the patience to read this collection—rather insignificant because of the many repetitions it contains—which I have just reread myself, and which seems to hold interest only for my own heart, you know now what maternal tenderness filled nine years of my life. To be sure, there is no secret in this; and I should not blush but rather be proud over having nursed and comforted, as though it had been my own child, this noble and incurable soul.

But you know now the secret side of this correspondence. It is not of very great moment, but it would be painful to me to see it commented upon and exaggerated. One says everything to one's children when they have come of age.

Thus the last material evidence of George Sand's liaison with Chopin was lost. She survived him by twenty-seven years, and throughout this time she did not cease to seek love. Since Solange never became her beloved daughter, Maurice could boast of having been George Sand's only constant passion. A painter without talent, he also tried the pen without success. He died in 1889, ten years before Solange. In the history of literature he figures mainly as the censor of his mother's letters; he deleted from the correspondence she left behind all the passages that bore witness to her love for Chopin. His meticulous labor may have been a waste of time. Edouard Ganche feels convinced that a copy of George Sand's correspondence with Chopin has survived—although thus far it has not come to the light of day.

Chopin's letters to Delphine Potocka went through curious vicissitudes. For a long time, all that was known about them was merely the fact that they existed. Ferdynand Hoesick wrote in his exhaustive monograph on the composer's life: "When they were not together, they often wrote letters to each other" (I, 479), and "They exchanged letters when she spent the winter in Nice" (II, 298).

In his preface to the first volume of his *Chopiniana* (Warsaw, 1912), Hoesick writes:

A large body of Chopin's letters to Delphine Potocka, written at various intervals between the years 1833 and 1840,[1] is said to have been preserved. But in order to obtain access to these letters, to be enabled to copy them and then to publish them, one must be luckier than the writer of these words, who made vain efforts to secure them.

In the course of time, however, Hoesick succeeded in seeing these letters, as must be inferred from an article published by

[1] Actually some of the letters date from later years, some even from 1849.

The Life and Death of Chopin

Professor Jozef Reiss, a musicologist of Cracow, in the Warsaw weekly *Nowiny Literackie* [*Literary News*] of February 8, 1948. Contrasting the tone of this correspondence with that of Mozart's "indecent" letters to Anna Maria Thekla Mozart of Augsburg, his cousin, and with the "coarse language" of Beethoven's correspondence "in a period when one of his most sublime works, the *Missa solemnis*, was maturing," Reiss observes:

Chopin's "indecencies" and intimate confidences in his letters to Delphine Potocka have a different character. Yielding to his bent for jokes and tricks, Chopin distorts her name and reads it backward as "Findelka,"[2] just as he changed his own name to "Pichon" when he wrote to his family from the country.[3] Because of the ban imposed by Delphine Potocka's family, the question of publishing Chopin's letters in their full text, without omission of the objectionable passages, has acquired an undesirably sensational character.[4] Despite this ban, I shall quote here one "intimate" passage, which was given me by Ferdynand Hoesick.

And Reiss quotes a sentence in which Chopin plays on the alliteration of a Polish bawdyism with the musical term *Des-dur* (D-flat major).

In *Rocznik muzykologiczny* (*Musical Yearbook*) for 1935, Ludwik Bronarski, a well-known Chopinologist, referring to a French edition of Chopin's letters, states that this edition "does not contain these letters [to Delphine Potocka] which are known to be in existence, though publication of them has up to now been impossible."

Public discussion of these letters began in 1945. The *Ruch muzyczny* [*Musical Movement*] of Cracow printed a report on them in its second issue of that year, and its December issue of

[2] See p. 176.
[3] See p. 45.
[4] This seems an exaggeration. The Polish press paid relatively little attention to these letters. Outside of Polish journals, there was only one article concerning the letters: this was written by Ingrid Etter and was published by the *Tribune de Genève* in its issue of February 23-24, 1946. In every instance the matter was treated with no sensationalism.

the same year contained the following item: "As we are informed by the Frederic Chopin Institute, these letters, discovered in a safe of the Commercial Bank, and somewhat singed during a fire in this bank (during the uprising of 1944), are authentic and are at present on view in the exhibition entitled 'Chopin and His Warsaw' in the National Museum."

The owner of the letters, Paulina Czernicka, who is related to the Komar family, gave a lecture about them which was broadcast by the Polish Radio. Jaroslaw Iwaszkiewicz, a well-known Polish writer, also lectured on them on the Polish Radio, and his lecture was later printed in *Radio i świat* [*Radio and the World*]. In *Nauka i sztuka* [*Science and Art*], of May and June, 1946, Paulina Czernicka published an article entitled "Chopin and the Poets," in which she quoted eleven fragments of previously unknown letters from Chopin to Delphine Potocka. This article was accompanied by a photostatic reproduction of one of the fragments. *Kuźnica* [*Smithy*] of September 15, 1947, published fourteen fragments of these letters; of these, nine had already been quoted by Paulina Czernicka, and five were new. Two new works on Chopin published in Poland in 1949, by K. Stromenger and Z. Jachimecki, contain a number of quotations from these letters. A larger selection, edited by B. E. Sydow, is planned for publication by the Frederic Chopin Institute in Warsaw.

The language of these letters is characteristically simple, direct, sometimes blunt, and abounds in idioms and colloquialisms that are found in other letters written by Chopin (for instance, *czemciś, iść w tory, pójdzie do czubków, paniebracić się*, etc.). A play on words involving *Des-dur* occurs also in another letter. Writing to Tytus Woyciechowski on December 12, 1831, Chopin refers ironically to the remarks of a critic on his Variations, Opus 2, in these words: "He comments on the fifth measure of the adagio by saying that Don Juan kisses Zerlina in *Des-dur*. Yesterday Plater asked me where she has that *Des-dur*." It is not known whether the fact that the so-called "Minute Waltz" (Opus 64, No. 1), dedicated to Delphine Potocka, is written in D-flat major (i.e., in *Des-dur*) is merely a coincidence.

The Life and Death of Chopin

Obviously the clarification of all the content and associations of these letters will require considerable time and labor. Since they have been lost to sight for a hundred years, many allusions in them have become obscure. This writer presents at their face value the fragments to which he has had access and which can be related to specific periods of Chopin's life. The passages quoted in this book include both material published in Poland and material that has had no previous publication.

In addition to Chopin's letters, Delphine preserved printed copies of his compositions annotated in his own hand. She offered these to Karol Mikuli, who had been a pupil of Chopin, and who, as Director of the Lwow Musical Society, was preparing an edition of Chopin's collected works. She also made available the compositions that Chopin had written into her album.

Delphine's subsequent life was marked chiefly by her liaison with the painter Paul Delaroche. She died April 2, 1877.

Chopin suffered in order to create and he enriched the world by something that had not existed before him. In his work he knew only one standard—the unremitting quest of perfection; and thanks to this discipline, the legacy he had left to music contains fewer imperfect works than that of any other great composer. His art opened new horizons not only in relation to the music of his homeland, to which he was faithful from his first childish polonaise to the last mazurka he wrote with enfeebled hand, but also in relation to the music of the world. His boldness in breaking obsolete rules, his refusal to compromise with current taste, his rediscovery of the soul of melody in the piano, and his beneficent influence on his contemporaries and on posterity, assure him a place among the greatest contributors to music. He knew the wisdom of Goethe's saying, *In der Beschränkung zeigt sich der Meister* ["Self-limitation reveals the master"]; he stood firm in his own truth and never betrayed it. This inward morality is reflected in the purity of his art.

Out of the mischances of his life, his music has survived like a treasure smuggled across the frontiers of human limitation—

past the barriers of despairing love, anguishing illness, and all the crippling frustrations of human existence. If art is an expression of man's longing for eternity, Chopin invites us to share in this sublime aspiration. This is the mission of the greatest spirits.

SOURCES

ASKENAZY, SZYMON: *Książę Józef Poniatowski* [*Prince Jozef Ponia-towski*]. Poznan, 1913.

BAINVILLE, JACQUES: *Histoire de France* [*History of France*]. Paris.

BALZAC, HONORÉ: *Lettres à l'étrangère* [*Letters to a Foreign Lady*]. Paris, 1899-1906.

BANDROWSKI, KADEN JULJUSZ: *Życie Chopina* [*Life of Chopin*]. Warsaw, 1938.

BAUDELAIRE, CHARLES: *L'art romantique* [*Romantic Art*]. Paris, 1925.
Œuvres posthumes et correspondances inédites [*Posthumous Works and Unpublished Letters*]. Paris, 1887.

BENNET, JOSEPH: *Frederic Chopin*. London.

BIDOU, HENRI: *Chopin*. Paris, 1926.

BINENTAL, LÉOPOLD: *Chopin*. Warsaw, 1930.

BRONARSKI, LUDWIK: *Etudes sur Chopin* [*Studies on Chopin*]. Lausanne, 1944, 1946 (2 vol.).
Chopin et l'Italie [*Chopin and Italy*]. Lausanne, 1947.

BROWN, IRVING H.: "George Sand and Her Son, Maurice." In *Romantic Review*, July-Sept., 1933.

CHARPENTIER, JOHN: *George Sand*. Paris, 1946.

CHOPIN, FRYDERYK: *Listy, zebral i przygotowal do druku Dr. H. Opieński* [*Letters, collected and edited by Dr. H. Opienski*]. Warsaw, 1937.

CZERNICKA, PAULINA: *Chopin i poeci* ["*Chopin and the Poets*"]. In *Nauka i sztuka*, May-June, 1946.

DELACROIX, EUGÈNE: *Correspondance générale* [*General correspondence*]. Paris, 1936-1938.

Journal. Paris, 1932.

DOUMIC, RENÉ: *George Sand.* Paris, 1909.

FERNET, ANDRÉ: *George Sand.* Montreal.

FERRÁ Y PERELLO, BARTHOLOMÉ: *Chopin und George Sand in der Cartuja in Valldemosa* [*Chopin and George Sand in the Monastery of Valdemosa*]. Palma de Mallorca, 1934.

FINCK, HENRY T.: *Chopin and Other Musical Essays.* New York, 1897.

FISHER, H. A. L.: *A History of Europe.* Boston and New York, 1936.

GANCHE, EDOUARD: *Frédéric Chopin, sa vie et ses œuvres* [*Frederic Chopin, His Life and Works*]. Paris, 1936.

Dans le souvenir de Frédéric Chopin [*Recollections of Chopin*]. Paris, 1925.

Souffrances de Frédéric Chopin [*The Illnesses of Frederic Chopin*]. Paris, 1935.

Voyages avec Frédéric Chopin [*Journeys with Frederic Chopin*]. Paris, 1934.

GIDE, ANDRÉ: *Notes sur Chopin* [*Notes on Chopin*]. Paris, 1948.

Grove's Dictionary of Music and Musicians. New York, 1938.

GUÉRARD, ALBERT: *France: A Short History.* New York, 1946.

HALECKI, OSKAR: *A History of Poland.* New York, 1943.

HEDLEY, ARTHUR: *Chopin.* London, 1947.

HEINE, HEINRICH: *Briefe* [*Letters*]. Hamburg, 1865-1866.

Lutèce: Lettres sur la vie politique, artistique et sociale de la France [*Lutetia: Letters on the Political, Artistic, and Social Life of France*]. Paris, 1855.

HEYLLI, GEORGE D': "*Lettres inédites de George Sand*" ["*Unpublished Letters of George Sand*"]. In *Revue des Revues,* 1899.

HOESICK, FERDYNAND: *Chopin, życie i twórczość* [*Chopin, Life and Work*]. Lwów, 1932.

Chopiniana. Warsaw, 1912.

Warszawa [*Warsaw*]. Poznan-Warsaw, 1920.

HOWE, JEANNE MARIE: *George Sand, the Search for Love.* Garden City, 1927.

HUNEKER, JAMES GIBBONS: *Chopin, the Man and His Music.* New York, 1900.

IWASZKIEWICZ, JAROSLAW: *Fryderyk Chopin.* Lwów, 1938.

JACHIMECKI, ZDZISLAW: *Fryderyk Chopin, rys życia i twórczości*

Sources

[*Frederic Chopin, Outline of His Life and Work*]. Cracow, 1927. New Edition, Warsaw, 1949.

JAMES, HENRY: *French Poets and Novelists*. London, 1908.

JONSON, G. C. ASHTON: *A Handbook to Chopin's Works*. New York, 1905.

KARASOWSKI, MORITZ: *Life and Letters of Chopin*. London, 1879.

KARÉNINE, VLADIMIR: *George Sand, sa vie et ses œuvres* [*George Sand, Her Life and Works*]. Paris, 1899-1926.

KARLOWICZ, MIECZYSLAW: *Pamiątki po Chopinie*. [*Mementoes of Chopin*]. Warsaw, 1904.

KLECZYNSKI, JEAN: *Chopin's Greater Works*. London, New York.

KRASIŃSKI, ZYGMUNT: *Listy do Delfiny Potockiej 1839-1845* [*Letters to Delphine Potocka*]. 2 vol. Poznan, 1930-1935.

KRIDL, MANFRED: *Literatura Polska* [*Polish Literature*]. New York, 1945.

LAMARTINE, ALPHONSE DE: *History of the French Revolution of 1848*. Boston, 1866.

LEICHTENTRITT, HUGO: *Friedrich Chopin*. Berlin, 1920.

LENZ, WILHELM VON: *Die grossen Pianofortevirtuosen unserer Zeit* [*The Great Pianofortists of Our Time*]. Berlin, 1872.

LISZT, FRANZ: *Chopin*. Paris, 1941.

Correspondance de Liszt et de la Comtesse d'Agoult. Paris, 1933.

MAUROIS, ANDRÉ: *Frédéric Chopin*. New York, 1942.

MURDOCH, WILLIAM: *Chopin, His Life*. New York, 1935.

NIECKS, FREDERICK: *The Life of Chopin*. London, 1890.

NIEMCEWICZ, JULIAN URSYN: *Pamiętniki* [*Memoirs*]. Poznan, 1876-1877.

NORWID, CYPRJAN: *Czarne i biale kwiaty* [*Black and White Flowers*]. Lwów, 1910.

NOWACZYŃSKI, ADOLF: *Mlodość Chopina* [*The Youth of Chopin*]. Warsaw, 1948.

OPIEŃSKI, HENRYK: *Chopin*. Lwów.

PADEREWSKI, IGNACY JAN: *O Szopenie* [*On Chopin*]. Lwów, 1910.

Pamięci Cyprjana Norwida [*In Memory of Cyprjan Norwid*]. Warsaw, 1946.

PORTE, JOHN F.: *Chopin the Composer and His Music*. New York, 1935.

POURTALÈS, GUY DE: *Chopin ou le Poète* [*Chopin, or the Poet*]. Paris, 1927.

Życie Liszta [*Life of Liszt*]. Warsaw, 1948.

The Life and Death of Chopin

PRZYBYSZEWSKI, STANISLAW: *Chopin und Nietzsche*. Berlin, 1892. *Szopen a naród* [*Chopin and the Nation*]. Cracow, 1910.

REVUE MUSICALE. Special number devoted to Chopin. Paris, December 1931. Articles by the Comtesse de Noailles, Paderewski, André Gide, Alfred Cortot, Karol Szymanowski, Stanislas Niewiadomski, M. Glinski, Cyprian Norwid, Edouard Ganche, Ernest Schelling, Henryk Opieński, Louis Aguettant, Bronislawa Wojcik-Keuprulian, Georges Migot, Wanda Landowska, Yvonne Lefébure, Stéphanie Lobaczewska, Léopold Binental, Henry Prunières, and Frédéric Goldbeck.

ROCHEBLAVE, SAMUEL: *George Sand et sa fille* [*G. S. and Her Daughter*]. Paris, 1905.

SAND, GEORGE: *Correspondance*. Paris, 1882-1884. *Histoire de ma vie* [*History of My Life*]. Paris, 1928. *Un hiver en Majorque* [*A Winter in Majorca*]. Paris, 1869. *Lucrezia Floriani*. Paris, 1888.

SCHERMERHORN, ELISABETH: *The Seven Strings of the Lyre*. Boston, 1927.

SCHUMANN, ROBERT: *Gesammelte Schriften über Musik und Musiker* [*Collected Writings on Music and Musicians*]. Leipzig.

ŚLIWIŃSKI, ARTUR: *Powstanie listopadowe* [*The November Uprising*]. London, 1946.

SOBIESKI, WACLAW: *Historja Polski* [*History of Poland*]. London, 1941.

STROMENGER, KAROL: *Fryderyk Chopin*. Warsaw, 1949.

ŚWIDERSKA, ALINA: *Zygmunt* [*Sigismund*, biographical novel about Z. Krasinski]. Warsaw, 1939.

SZOPEN, monografja zbiorowa pod redakcją Mateusza Glińskiego [Chopin, symposium edited by Mateusz Glinski]. Warsaw, 1932.

SZULC, M. A.: *Fryderyk Chopin*. Poznan, 1873.

SZYMANOWSKI, KAROL: *Fryderyk Chopin*. Warsaw, 1925.

TRETIAK, JÓZEF: *Slowo o Chopinie* [*Discourse on Chopin*]. Lwów, 1877.

VUILLERMOZ, EMILE: *La vie amoureuse de Chopin* [*Chopin's Love Life*]. Paris, 1927.

WASYLEWSKI, STANISLAW: *O miłości romantycznej* [*On Romantic Love*]. Poznan, 1928.

WEINSTOCK, HERBERT: *Chopin, The Man and His Music*. New York, 1949.

Sources

WINWAR, FRANCES: *The Life of the Heart*, New York, 1945.

WODZINSKI, COUNT: *Les trois romans de Frédéric Chopin* [*The Three Romances of Frederic Chopin*]. Paris, 1886.

WOJCIK-KEUPRULIAN, B.: *Melodyka Chopina* [*Chopin's Melodies*]. Lwów, 1930.

Z nieznanych listów Chopina do Delfiny Potockiej [*Chopin's Unpublished Letters to Delphine Potocka*]. In *Kuźnica*, Sept. 15, 1947.

ZALESKI, ZYGMUNT L.: *La Patrie Musicale de Chopin* [*Chopin's Musical Fatherland*]. Paris, 1917.

INDEX

Index

Index

Index

Index